★

THE EAST IS BLACK

THE EAST IS BLACK

Cold War China in the Black Radical Imagination

ROBESON TAJ FRAZIER

Duke University Press

DURHAM AND LONDON

2015

Printed in the United States of America on acid-free paper ∞

Designed by Kristina Kachele Design, llc

Typeset in Quadraat OT with Rockwell display by Copperline

Library of Congress Cataloging-in-Publication Data
Frazier, Robeson Taj, 1981–
The East is black : cold war China in the black radical
imagination / Robeson Taj Frazier.
·   pages cm
Includes bibliographical references and index.
ISBN 978-0-8223-5768-1 (hardcover : alk. paper)
ISBN 978-0-8223-5786-5 (pbk.)
ISBN 978-0-8223-7609-5 (e-book)
1. African American political activists. 2. African Americans—Relations
with Chinese. 3. Civil rights movement—History—20th century.
4. China—Politics and government—1949–1976. I. Title.
E185.615.F728 2015
320.95109'04—dc23 2014023500

Cover art: Detail of "Dadao Mei di! Dadao Su xiu!"
(Down with American imperialists and Russian revisionists!), 1967.
Courtesy of the University of Westminister.

To Ebony, Seu, and my parents.

IN MEMORY OF
Julian W. Pyles
Doris Brooks Cheatem
Shawishi Monroe
And my grandparents, Pearline, Huelett, De Lois & Jay.

Contents

Abbreviations

CCP	Chinese Communist Party
CCRG	Central Cultural Revolution Group
CPSU	Communist Party of the Soviet Union
CPUSA	Communist Party of the United States of America
FNLA	Frente Nacional de Libertação de Angola; National Front for the Liberation of Angola
GLF	Great Leap Forward
GMD	Guomindang (China's Nationalist Party)
GPCR	Great Proletarian Cultural Revolution
MPLA	Movemento Popular de Libertação de Angola; Popular Movement for the Liberation of Angola
NAACP	National Association for the Advancement of Colored People
PIC	Peace Information Center
PLA	People's Liberation Army
PRC	People's Republic of China
UN	United Nations
UNITA	União Nacional para a Independência Total de Angola; National Union for the Total Independence of Angola
USCPFA	U.S.-China People's Friendship Association
USSR	Union of Soviet Socialist Republics

Acknowledgments

As a preteen and adolescent, I spent portions of my summers and holidays helping my father rummage through and catalogue his deceased clients' belongings. An attorney who handles estates, wills, and probate, he is frequently left with the task of organizing and obtaining an accurate value assessment of his clients' assets. Years ago, this often meant using my slim and tall frame to squeeze through doorway openings crammed partially shut by boxes, climb through windows, or crawl through the dark passageways of attics, garages, and basements. Nine times out of ten the client was a hoarder, one of those people who you might see on television who has accumulated a treasure trove of random artifacts and goodies. I laugh now recalling my shock when on one occasion I found three extremely old pistols. The next day one of my father's colleagues confirmed that they were pre–Civil War weapons and were worth a serious chunk of change.

Leafing through someone else's belongings, usually in dingy, badly lit, dust-filled, cramped spaces—"the dungeons and tombs of the dead" is how I described them to my friends—gave me an intimate introduction to the archive as both immaterial and material. In these people's records, books, photographs, art, newspaper clippings, magazines, letters of correspondence, diaries, coins, plates, and other weird and interesting items were some aspects of the lives they lived, the communities and individuals with whom they identified and loved, and meanings through which they came to make sense of their existence and the periods through which they lived and struggled. Amid the age, decay, and chaos of their homes and the articles they valued, I was interacting with the past, present, and future—all at once. Coincidentally, around this same time of my life, my mother enrolled me in a Mandarin Chinese–language class.

This book in its embryonic form and, moreover, my passion for writing, research, and teaching are influenced by many people. For one, this book is a product of instruction by numerous educators and mentors: Julian Pyles,

Yen-Lung Liu, Willy MacMullen, Robert Allen, Vèvè Clark, Ula Taylor, Charles Henry, Leigh Raiford, Percy Hintzen, Waldo Martin, Ramón Grosfoguel, Victoria Bonnell, Evelyn Nakano Glenn, Peter Monroe, Quamè Love, Lindsey Herbert, Glenn Robertson, Manning Marable, Barbara Savage, Susan Peterson-Pace, Max-Henri Covil, Oni Faida Lampley, James Spady, Herman Beavers, Farah Griffin, Guthrie Ramsey, Robert Engs, Robert Vitalis, Anthony Monteiro, Chad and Madeleine Williams, Valerie Swain-Cade McCoullum, Patricia Ravenell, and the staff and leadership of the Greater Harlem Chamber of Commerce. I must add that Gerald Horne and Robin D. G. Kelley's insight, scholarship, and generosity have been integral to this work. At different moments, they have challenged and nuanced this book's claims and broadened my understanding of diasporic black radicalism; the relationship between history, politics, and culture; and the shifting dynamics of global capitalism. Other scholars have provided fantastic support, guidance, and feedback, in particular Carol Anderson, Sherle Boone, Thomas Borstelmann, Herb Boyd, Rod Bush, John Jackson, Minkah Makalani, Erik McDuffie, and David Perlmutter.

My editor Courtney Berger has been a lifesaver. Besides identifying readers whose reviews were substantially helpful in clarifying my ideas and expanding several running threads, she went far beyond the call of duty in enhancing the manuscript's revision. Additional gratitude must go to Erin Hanas, Danielle Szulczewski, and the rest of the Duke University Press staff for finalizing this work's transition from disparate text and images to coherent product.

I want to especially thank my colleagues Josh Kun and Sarah Banet-Weiser, two brilliant people whose ever-constant generosity, support, and friendship have been instrumental in this book's evolution and completion. I also wish to express my gratefulness to my other Annenberg School colleagues, particularly Sandra Ball-Rokeach, Alison Trope, Chris Smith, Tom Hollihan, Jonathan Aronson, Yu Hong, Lian Jian, Robert Scheer, Michael Cody, Nick Cull, Andrea Hollingshead, Henry Jenkins, Dorine Lawrence-Hughes, Félix Gutiérrez, Allyson Hill, and JaBari Brown. I must especially thank Lori Kido-Lopez, Su Liu, and Lin Zhang for their phenomenal research support, and Dean Ernest Wilson, Vice Dean Larry Gross, Imre Meszaros, Peggy McLaughlin, Christine Lloreda, Billie Shotlow, and Carol Kretzer for their institutional support and for facilitating a generative teaching and research environment for the book's completion. Exchanges with other University of Southern California affiliates were also vital, especially discussions with Shana Redmond, Lanita Jacobs, Kara Keeling, Francille Wilson, Dayna Chatman, Inna Arzumanova-Bell, Sophia Azeb, Maytha Alhassen, Joshua Goldstein, Stan Rosen, Ange-Marie Hancock, Jack Halberstam, Dorrine Kondo, and Neetu Khanna.

Work of this nature is nothing without the assistance and time of institutions and people committed to advancing scholarship and research. A huge debt is owed first to those people who allowed me to interview them and examine their families' archives: Lincoln and Miranda Bergman, John and Mabel Williams, Sidney Rittenberg, Carlos Moore, and Grace Lee Boggs. I must also thank Lincoln Cushing, Deborah Rudolph, and the C. V. Starr East Asian Library at the University of California, Berkeley; Karen Jania and the staff at University of Michigan's Bentley Historical Library; Claude Marks and the Freedom Archives; Harriet Evans, Emily Williams, and the University of Westminster's China Poster Collection; the Center for the Study of Political Graphics; and staffs at the Schomburg Research Center, Wayne State University's Walter Reuther Library, Beijing's National Library, the University of Hong Kong Library, New York University's Tamiment Library, and the National Archives. This book was also aided by fellowship support from the Mellon Mays Program, the Woodrow Wilson National Fellowship Foundation, and the University of Southern California's Advancing the Humanities Initiative.

Sidebars, solidarity, and laughter with amazing compadres over the course of the last decade have helped temper my anxieties about this study and life in general. Thus major big-ups to close friends, colleagues, and family members, old and new, who have been generous with positive energy and encouragement—you all know who you are. Special thanks to those of you who have watched my back (even when I didn't deserve it!): Paul Dunoguez, Samir Meghelli, Petra Rivera-Rideau, Erinn Ransom-Ofori, Debon Lewis, Rashad Frazier, Rahsaan Gandy, Larraine Daniel, Ra-Jah Kelly, Shakira Daugherty, Ron Frazier, Nikki and Matt Bradley, Adé Williams, Carl Chisolm, Wayman Newton, Weldon McMillan, Jason Wiley, Andrew Crabbe, Kelechi Nwanyanwu, Paul Williams, George Suttles, Larry Braithwaite, Tamika Guishard, Shaun Depina, Eyram Simpri, Jeff St. Andrews, Nicole Andrewin, Nisha Deshmukh, Jessica Koslow, Lia Bascom, T.L. Smith, Wendell Hudson, Malik McClean and Adria DeWette. And a big shout-out to all of my family—my in-laws, aunts, uncles, godparents, cousins, nieces, nephews, surrogate parents, fraternity brothers, and amazing friends, all of whose love, prayers, bigheartedness, and encouragement ignite me every day. You keep me humble and ardent, always appreciative of the blessings and lessons that God brings forth. I extend my deepest gratitude and love.

To my parents: your guidance, encouragement, love, and incredible parenting have helped nurture this book, the overall trajectory of my intellectual and creative pursuits, my care for the power of education and knowledge of self and the necessity of social justice, and the importance of acknowledging and striving for àshe in all things I do. I would never be on this journey if not for your hard work, passion, sacrifice, and prayers. Dad, from an early age you instilled in me the value of service, doing the right thing, and developing a strong sense of purpose. Mama B, you have supplied me with faith—that is, to know the power of God and our ancestors and to locate this energy and life-force in fellowship with those around me and in my love, work, and treatment of others. And Ma, you have given me the power and passion to imagine—to believe in my ability to express and manifest the creative thoughts, images, sounds, and sensations that oscillate and reverberate in my mind, body, and soul.

To my lovebug, Seu Romare, your kicks were the best clock for completing this book that Daddy could ask for. You now have my *full* attention. And to Ebony Melissa, my companion and 瓢虫: your patience, reassurance, vivacity, and joie de vivre envelope these pages and just make life splendid.

Introduction

> I've learned that my people are not the only ones oppressed. That
> it is the same for Jews or Chinese as for Negroes. . . . I found that
> where forces have been the same, whether people weave, build,
> pick cotton, or dig in the mines, they understand each other
> in the common language of work, suffering and protest.
> — PAUL ROBESON

"Qilai! Buyuan zuo nuli de renmen!" (Arise! All who refuse to be slaves!), Paul Robeson sang on a moderately cool evening in 1940. Moments earlier, before an audience of seven thousand people, under the twilight of the Harlem sky, the baritone soloist walked downstage at the Lewisohn Stadium for his final song. This concert, like most others, had revealed the diversity of the thespian-activist's musical catalogue. The set included "Ol' Man River," the landmark tune about dockworkers made famous in the play and film *Showboat*; "I Dreamed I Saw Joe Hill Last Night," an ode to the early twentieth-century Swedish American labor activist and miner; and the classic African American spiritual "Go Down Moses" (commonly referred to as "Let My People Go").[1] But to close the performance, Robeson opted to sing a new piece, albeit a song that had been sung over the course of the previous decade by troops in defiance of Japanese occupation. "I want to sing a song for the heroic Chinese people in battle," he explained.[2]

Instructing the audience to "qilai!" (rise up), Robeson launched into "March of the Volunteers" ("Yiyongjun jinxingqu"), China's anthem of resistance against Japanese and Western domination, a song later adopted as the Chinese national anthem:

> Arise!
> All who refuse to be slaves!
> Let our flesh and blood forge into our new Great Wall!

The Chinese people face their greatest peril,
Every person is forced to expel his very last cry.
Arise!
Arise!
Arise!
Our million hearts beating as one,
Brave the enemy's fire,
March on!
Brave the enemy's fire,
March on!
March on!
March on![3]

In time this song became part of Robeson's musical set, the singer prefacing it with criticism of the role that U.S. tax dollars and private interests played in sheltering the repressive leadership of the Chinese Nationalist Party, a staunch U.S. ally. On other occasions, he specifically directed the song's message toward African American listeners, emphasizing the song's antislavery theme. "It stands, I was told, for a spirit of fighting against mighty power," Robeson once remarked.[4] "March of the Volunteers" ultimately crystallized his multiple avenues of support for Chinese self-determination. Throughout the 1940s Robeson raised funds for China's war campaign against Japanese occupation, served on behalf of United China Relief initiatives, and acted as an honorary director of the Chinese Defense League.[5] This work led him to endorse the Chinese Communist Party (CCP) and its middle-aged chairman, Mao Zedong, a revolutionary who called for the creation of new socialist society based around the will, determination, and creativity of Chinese peasants and the rural poor.

Robeson was not alone in advocating for China's autonomy. His support tied into a wave of expressions of African American radical solidarity with China. Quite a few blacks likened Japan's invasion of Nanjing in 1937 to Italy's invasion of Ethiopia in 1935, denouncing the encroachment of Chinese sovereignty. Just two hundred miles east of Nanjing, collaboration between the American trumpeter Buck Clayton and the composer Li Jinhui in the Shanghai music scene led to fusions of jazz and Chinese folk music. Across the waters, as the poet Langston Hughes urged China to "break the chains of the East," Robeson's "March of the Volunteers" collaborator Liu Liangmo used his *Pittsburgh Courier* column to gain support for the repeal of the Chinese Exclusion Act, a U.S. bill that restricted Chinese immigration and excluded Chinese residents from citizenship.[6]

Particularly noteworthy though are the different geographical locations, political contexts, and cultural ends from which Robeson's rendition of "March of the Volunteers" took life. It was broadcast through radio around the world when he sang it in Moscow in 1949 to commemorate the establishment of the People's Republic of China (PRC), a country finally free from imperialism and capitalist domination. And in the 1950s the song's message was felt within the travails of the Korean War, where loudspeakers in prison camps transmitted Robeson's voice to Chinese soldiers and African American prisoners, some of whom used it to articulate racial and political connections across enemy lines.

Comparing the communicative power of musical performance to that of language, Robeson divulged: "Folk music is as much a creation of a mass of people as language. Both are derived from social groups which had to communicate with each other and within each other."[7] Here he theorized the spaces of communication and collective struggle people built with other groups through song. Thus, as with most folk songs, "March of the Volunteers" embodied narratives of human struggle that extended beyond the external borders of national territories, confronting structures of injustice and difference near and far. Made into a sonic symbol of radical internationalism and a transracial signifier of the bonds described by the artist-activist in the epigraph above, Robeson's version of "March of the Volunteers" formed a connecting link between China's national struggle, black collective resistance against racial oppression, and a world movement against imperialism, white supremacy, and Western elite dominance.

★

MEDIA AND IMAGINING

The socialist thinkers and human-rights activists W. E. B. Du Bois and Shirley Graham Du Bois, the foreign correspondent William Worthy, the Marxist feminist Vicki Garvin, the militant freedom fighters Mabel and Robert Williams, and several black war veterans built upon Robeson's metaphor of shared struggle. From China and elsewhere, they imagined both themselves and Asian revolutionary movements with broad language and metaphors that reshaped the differences (geographical, historical, political, and racial) distinguishing China and other Communist Asian nations' struggles against imperialism from that of black Americans' struggles against social and economic injustice. These black radical travelers also drew attention to the entanglement of racial discrimination, capitalism, and U.S. empire by producing media that communicated "an alternative vision to hegemonic policies, priorities, and perspectives." Through travel and the production of literature, newspapers, newsletters, pamphlets, radio, film documentary, and critical pedagogy, these radicals "express[ed] opposition vertically from subordinate quarters directly at the power structure" and worked to "build support, solidarity, and networking laterally against . . . the very survival of the power structure."[8]

This book offers a study of the political and cultural traffic fashioned by these people and the Chinese government between the years of 1949 and 1976. For one, I seek to explain how these radical internationalists deployed and grappled with media, travel, and travel narrative in their interactions in China and in their formulations of transnational politics. I argue that within their leftist radicalism, travels to China, and cultural representations of these experiences was a passionate commitment to interrogating and reframing dominant Cold War mappings of race, foreign policy, and world relations. Their media and travels additionally offer a valuable, although unquestionably bounded, porthole to the productive and controversial processes and acts of cultural creation that facilitated such connections. I maintain that unpacking both the fruitfulness and inconsistencies of this history of political solidarity and transnational media can help broaden understandings of U.S. and Chinese Cold War political cultures and the diverse cultural productions and representations that animated these cultures.[9]

By and large, the Cold War refers to the complex transformation of the international system primarily, but not solely, by the United States and the Soviet Union during the period of 1945–91. But the Cold War furthermore speaks to the immense productions of force, violence, ideology, and discourse through which consensus and ideas about modernity, national security, citizenship, and world relations were manufactured, circulated, reshaped, and rejected in different national, social, and geographical contexts. In the United States in particular, liberal democracy, discourses of "American exceptionalism," and anticommunism promoted the image of "a new national and international 'freedom loving' subject": U.S. nationals and foreigners whose freedom and self-determination could only be protected by containing and defeating communism's expansion.[10] Conflating communism with totalitarianism, representatives of government, business, media, and numerous civic and popular institutions deployed these discourses to interpellate Americans and non-Americans with a potent teleological construction of global affairs. The sum of these discourses was a national and supranational ideology of globality, a regime of power that the magazine publisher Henry Luce laid out in his famous 1941 article, "The American Century." Distinguishing the post–World War II global order from the world system of imperialism that preceded it, Luce justified America's transimperial project to reorganize world trade along the same lines as the United States' existing economic system. Protection of free will and liberty within the marketplace and the voting bloc required expanding America's political and economic model to the *grand area*—territory consisting of the Western Hemisphere, the remainder of British Commonwealth and its dissolving empire, the Dutch East Indies, China, Japan, and various African territories. "Tyrannies may require a large amount of living space," Luce asserted, "but Freedom requires and will require far greater living space than Tyranny."[11] His statement about the decentered and deterritorial aspirations undergirding the ideology of freedom and global capitalism of the United States amounted to the relaxation and outright removal of barriers separating national and international capital and the expansion of the U.S. military's power to penetrate the farthest corners of the world as global cop and enforcer. The postwar advance and secularization of U.S. global power therefore represented the reconstitution of an ongoing, long historical process inaugurated centuries earlier, a new stage in the capitalist world system's corporate and epistemological imposition of Western domination on other ways of life, thinking, and existence.

Composed of activists and thinkers of diverse ideological leanings, "the long movement" of African American struggle directly engaged this emerging global order, giving great effort to confront the limits of the welfare state, liberal democracy, racial discrimination, and the inequality and conditions engendered by capitalism.[12] The leftist and black-nationalist internationalists of this contingent represented one of the most dynamic U.S.-based forces against the systemic violence and exploitation generated by domestic racial oppression, global white supremacy, Western imperialism, and the expansion of global capitalism, militarism, and corporate injustice by the United States and its allies. Opposed to U.S. imperialism abroad and capitalism and antiblack racism at home, black leftist radicals such as Worthy, Garvin, the Du Boises, and the Williamses made it known that the social and economic treatment of black Americans and racial minorities in the United States amplified the inadequacies of the country's paradigm of international relations and world community. These radicals additionally challenged the primacy of liberal democracy and free-trade capitalism as the dominant ideology and model of modernity and sociopolitical economic development around which to organize U.S. life and the postwar international order. While many of their domestic liberal counterparts identified the fight against racism, social injustice, and economic exploitation as primarily a national issue that could be resolved through desegregation, legislative changes, fair employment statutes, and greater and gradual inclusion and access to the public and popular realms, radical internationalists called attention to the struggle's global dimensions and broader circumstances. They argued that the subjugation U.S. racial minorities endured was contiguous to the hardship, repression, and abuse felt by nonwhite populations on the world scale; these complexes in their totality served the interests of capital accumulation, privatization, male supremacy, and a white-dominated power structure, that is, a system of racial capitalism.[13] Cognizant of the transnational and global basis of racial capitalism's expansion, these activists-intellectuals resolved that combatting this system required not just political action at the local and national levels but additionally transnational and international assemblages capable of opposing and ending this injustice.

The Chinese people were one of numerous populations to which these black activists sought political ties. For some of them, China became what the leftist historian Max Elbaum has described as a "location-turned-emblem" that took on vibrant anticapitalist and antiracist meanings.[14] Among other reasons, black leftist radicals perceived the CCP's elimination of foreign occupation and exploitation and its rhetorical commitment to peasant radicalism and social uplift as one of several viable globalist Cold War alternatives to a world fueled by capitalism and military expansion.[15] Furthermore, these radicals understood that the growth of communism in China and other Asian territories posed a risk to America's access to new foreign markets, cheap raw materials and foreign labor, and foreign-located industries and sites to put Americans to work. China's socialist experiment and its brand of Third World Marxism, therefore, offered them one, though not the only, utopic model of economic democracy, mass political participation, and antiracist global modernity.

Simultaneously, the Chinese government worked to explicitly align itself and its anti-Western rhetoric with that of other exploited nonwhite populations. They centered China as the leader of an anti-imperialist world struggle against capitalism, U.S. empire, and white supremacy. And in this narrative, representations of black struggle, particularly that being waged by African Americans, were of serious importance. The Chinese government produced propaganda that unambiguously denounced U.S. racism and militarism and articulated China's support for black social movements. Moreover, in these portrayals, African American antiracist struggle was identified in anticolonial Marxist terms. It was depicted as an example of a larger decolonial wave that was subverting Euro-American dominance and instituting a new world order (see figure I.1). What's more, China's leaders recognized several Civil Rights and Black Power Movement activists and critics of U.S. foreign policy as *waiguo pengyou* (friends of China). Through political outreach and hosted stays in China, the Chinese leaders worked to proselytize and inculcate these select visitors with China's road to socialism and global revolution.

The formations through which African Americans and the Chinese government constructed such ideas, images, and emblems of transnational political community demonstrate the crucial work of *radical imagining* in engender-

FIGURE I.1: "Wan'e de zhimin zhuyi, diguo zhuyi zhidu shi suizhe nuyi he fan-mai heiren er xingsheng qilai de, ta ye bijiang suizhe heise renzhong de chedi jiefang er gaozhong" (The evil system of colonialism and imperialism arose and throve with the enslavement of blacks and the trade of blacks, and it will surely come to its end with the complete emancipation of the black people), Mao Zedong, 1968. Courtesy of Ann Tompkins (Tang Fandi) and Lincoln Cushing Chinese Poster Collection, C. V. Starr East Asian Library, University of California, Berkeley. Also published in Tompkins and Cushing, *Chinese Posters*. Digital image courtesy of Lincoln Cushing/Docs Populi.

ing and nurturing practices of liberation and radical democracy in the face of global injustice and inequality. The imagination describes the interaction and transformation of hearts, minds, and souls into beings, subjects, and collectivities. It speaks to a person's expressive and inventive capacity to render abstract visions, intentions, and drives into material processes, lifelike renderings, and socially grounded outcomes. Imagining here is thus displayed as a process of ideology that marshals and deploys cognitive faculties, consciousness, and social life for the process of contesting the worlds we inhabit and making and shaping them anew.[16]

It is with this definition that I begin to interrogate the functions of travel, political communication, cultural representation, and traditional media (print culture, radio, film, political cartoons, graphic iconography, and teaching pedagogy) in black radicals' and the Chinese government's constructions of "China," "Chinese communism," "black liberation," "racial solidarity," and "Third World internationalism."[17] Of chief concern is how these constructs were employed dialogically as sites of struggle and contestation against the dominant U.S. and Soviet frameworks of race, international relations, and Cold War geopolitics.

To consider this question involves engaging in comparative analysis and at-tending to the unique cultural systems and political processes that shaped and resulted from these African American and Chinese interactions and cultural productions. This means unpacking the ideologies (the concepts and material practices through which people represent, interpret, and make sense of social existence) and discourses (the signifying systems through which ideologies and subjectivities are learned, given meaning, and deployed) that animated black radicals' and the Chinese government's articulations and representa-tions. What then becomes more apparent are the diverse content, symbols, and practices—what the historian Akira Iriye has termed "the '*imagined*' nature of a given reality"—that black radicals and the PRC made use of to define and por-tray African American–Chinese connections, as well as how these depictions of internationalism were circulated and consumed by different publics.[18]

The empowering images and narratives of resistance fashioned by this group of radical travelers grew from rigorous, didactic unpacking of media's function as a site of power and knowledge production within racial capitalism. Black radicals grasped that media was a key mode of cultural representation through which U.S. racial and economic violence and ideologies of white superiority were legitimated. Media therefore was identified as an unavoidable site of an-tiracist struggle; it was a requisite for contesting oppression and reshaping the image of black people and other nonwhite populations throughout the world. Moreover, in these radicals' media, blackness was distinguished as a fluctu-ating node, or what the intellectual Stuart Hall has described as a "floating signifier," through which to comprehend the connections between U.S. rac-ism and Euro-American militarism and imperialism abroad.[19] The scholar Jane Rhodes explains: "Blackness is not a fixed racial category, but part of a rather fluid and malleable set of representations that change meaning dependent on time, place, and context. . . . [It is] a floating signifier that is under contesta-tion by media producers, media subjects, and media audiences."[20] Along these lines, the Chinese government and the activists and thinkers detailed in this book produced representations of race and blackness that were African Amer-ican and Chinese in tone, but nonetheless international and transnational in scope and cross-cultural in outreach and communication. In addition, these representations coalesced around arguments regarding the global parameters of capitalism and white supremacy, and new time-space-place mobilizations of group identity and human connectedness that linked peoples across bor-ders of region, country, nation, language, and race.

The critical interrogation of mass media by this book's protagonists resem-bled that of the Frankfurt School scholar Walter Benjamin, who supplied a ma-terialist and noninstrumentalist approach. Benjamin viewed media's form and content as not disconnected from power and domination but rather as integral to their making and legitimization—that is, as a significant activity of living and means through which reality is manipulated and regulated. Political ideology and identity, he insisted, were therefore communicated in and with media rather than simply through it. It was consequently the responsibility of "the author as producer" to challenge such systems of subjugation and exploitation, her or his duty being "not to report but to struggle; not to play the spectator but to intervene actively," which thus required culturally "re-functioning" mass communication and artistic production toward "a revolutionary useful value."[21]

It was with this purpose that Garvin, Worthy, the Du Boises, the Williamses, and other black thinkers and media practitioners used media as a transnational political practice to impact people's political consciousness. For these black radicals, media and technologies of representation were not simply descriptive; they were also inscriptive, capable of helping reshape human experience toward new modalities of perception and knowing. Media "signal[s] new subjectivities," the media scholar Lisa Gitelman explains, effectively working to interrupt, "ratify, stretch, or commodify contemporary parameters of identity" and "new sense[s] of public existence." The scholar Rubén Gallo agrees, noting that "technological media are not mere tools at the service of representation; on the contrary, they shape, define and determine the possibilities of representation."[22]

Exploring the media of black radical travelers therefore illuminates how these people both made use of and were impacted by media, exercises that aided them in ephemerally refunctioning the dominant racial and ideological mappings of the Cold War. They perceived the Cold War and Third World struggle as more than just ongoing geopolitical conflicts between various state powers and national liberation movements. The Cold War and Third World struggle were also discursive spaces represented and portrayed through visual, aural, and textual forms for different audiences. Media and cultural representation by the likes of Western governments and the Western press thus were essential in influencing American and non-American understandings of global affairs, primary agents in "organiz[ing] and reorganiz[ing] popular perceptions of difference within a global economic order."[23] But through media and travel, black radicals also absorbed that Cold War cultural representation and production were vibrating with decolonial possibilities. The medium, these people maintained, could therefore have central influence in creating a message. Consequently for the people detailed in this book, one begat the other—media practices within acts of travel to China and political displacement became sources for the production of new kinds of power, knowledge, and political subjectivity and thus part of a praxis of producing transnational publics rooted in a collective, transcultural consciousness. With this black radicals were afforded productive and challenging situations for contesting U.S. hegemony. Furthermore, they were able to rethink the frameworks and categories used to define the scope of their subject positions and that of different communities of color worldwide.[24]

Still, while my original definition of imagining conveys the fertile inventiveness and creativity that animated these travelers' constructions of racial connection, what this definition does not highlight are the limitations, contradictions, and ambivalences that encompassed these radicals' politics of media, travel, and cultural representation. Considering how racial connection and racial difference were made and traveled across cultural lines through these people's circuits of media and political activity thus also requires distinguishing how the imagined content of their articulations coincided and failed to measure up with national and geopolitical realities abroad. This means interrogating the dissonance of imagining—namely the divergences between how cultural identification and relation were seen in the mind's eye and how they manifested in the lived relations of these black travelers in China. It is to consider the problematic subjective and structural processes and social negotiations through which these people and the PRC fashioned radical political identities and sentimentalist investments.

So, for instance, one thing that must be taken into account is how claims and practices of political coalition and solidarity, whether conservative or progressive, are often organized around an imagined inclusiveness and wholeness—black Americans, for instance, as constituents of a global anticolonial majority, as members of a Third World whole. But such coherence and wholeness is chimerical. It is a product of what the cultural critic Rey Chow summarizes as "the process of loss, substitution, and identification that is at play in the formation of a subject" and the "dismemberment brought about by the imperialistic violence of Westernization" on subjugated peoples. The Chinese government's and U.S. black radicals' constructions of racial connection and global struggle thus produced "a fetishizing imagining of a 'China' that never [was]"—political renderings whose musings, rhetoric, and iconography of cultural union frequently contrasted with the disorganized, unstable, and unequal features of these relations.[25] In the process, both U.S. black radicals and the Chinese government and people relied, at times, on reductive and essentialist depictions of Asian Communism and black-radical internationalism, images of racial internationalism and global Third World solidarity that reinscribed problematic, narrow understandings of transnational political connections and Chinese and African American life.

Such can be discerned, for example, by revisiting how the depictions of China propagated by both the Chinese state and the radicals examined in this book revolved around dichotomizing China and the United States, and likewise their purported analogs of East and West. While this was intended to boost China's image among international parties, a looming question is to what domestic ends did such constructions serve? The comparative literature scholar Xiaomei Chen maintains that these dialectical imaginings—China and the East as the leader of world proletarian revolution and the United States and the West as the former's imagined Other—embodied "both a discourse of oppression and a discourse of liberation" that essentialized the West "as means for supporting a nationalism that suppresses its own people."[26] Chen explains that by constructing Chinese communism as global capitalism's antithesis, Chinese communists, particularly Mao's radical-leftist following in government, instilled socialist ideological control over Chinese publics and people who struggled against the CCP and Mao's rural revolutionary approach. Thus, in a similar vein as the rigid binary of East-West depicted by the United States and its allies, the ideology of Eastern liberation articulated by Mao, the CCP, and other China supporters did not represent an empirical reality but rather embodied a discourse as a means of power. Through it, the Chinese government and society disciplined and domesticated Chinese citizens with the ideological hegemony of the party-state and Mao's philosophical dominance. One component of this project was exploiting and rescripting the racial dynamics of the United States and foreigners' racial imaginaries of China. Race consequently became a primary lens through which China differentiated its model of global power from that of the United States and the Soviet Union, influenced oppressed populations of color, and increased the aura and power of Chinese communism on Chinese citizens.

Black-radical travelers participated in this Chinese project of international influence and domestic hegemony. Their voices, bodies, and reification of the East and West helped China's influence grow both at home and abroad, effectively increasing the ideological power of the CCP as a central agent in the making of a progressive global future. But simultaneously black radicals' inclusion and contributions to this narrative helped conceal the Chinese government's repressive domestic practices and policies and the PRC's efforts to build nationalist support among Chinese citizens by any means. "Mao fully understood that only when China's superior moral position in the world had been recognized by other peoples would the consolidation of his continuous revolution's momentum at home be assured," the historian Chen Jian asserts.[27]

Alongside consideration of these contradictions, this book also genders black radicalism. I unpack the influence of attitudes and structures of gender on both Chinese and black radical constructions of racial internationalism and anticapitalist struggle. For example, the Chinese government and radicals such as W. E. B. Du Bois and Robert F. Williams circulated gendered constructions and metaphors of racial solidarity, interstate conflict, defense of the nation, socialism, national liberation, and Third World struggle. In these radicals' articulations, the race, the Third World, and radical Afro-Asian partnership were often depicted through language, imagery, and symbols that privileged male intellectual production and agency over that of women, and through metaphors of interracial romance and racial kinship that were skewed in favor of reproductive heteronormativity—the heteronormative male was thus frequently treated as the anchor and stimulus of international revolutionary struggle.[28] This was also the case even when women were featured in black-radical and Chinese renderings of revolutionary internationalism and Afro-Asian solidarity. In many of these representations and articulations, female agency and femininity conformed to male standards; subversive women were dominantly framed in hegemonic masculine and heteronormative terms.

The East Is Black therefore deems it imperative to interrogate the different mechanisms and manipulations of gender through which black leftist travelers to China and the Chinese government demarcated the transnational and international realms as "a space of men desiring."[29] Throughout the twentieth century, various tropes of African American political agency—the black sovereign, the charismatic race leader, the laborer at sea, the black worker, the soldier, the Pullman porter, the musician and visionary artist, the militant insurrectionist, the martyr—have been invoked as masculine. This was also the trend among some black travelers to China. Various people mobilized the aforementioned tropes and other signifiers, often negating the plurality of African American and Chinese women's radical thinking and internationalist investments. However, these male-heavy renderings were not the only images and discourses articulated and shared by this group. The black feminist socialists Shirley Graham Du Bois and Vicki Garvin prioritized female revolutionary internationalism on its own terms and interrogated the relationship between racism, capitalism, and patriarchy. Of particular interest is how these two women mobilized depictions of political transgression that challenged both liberal and Marxist-Leninist gender conventions and that did not betray a parochial U.S.-centric feminist narrative.

★

CHINA AND BLACK-RADICAL HISTORIOGRAPHY

The East Is Black is in conversation with several bodies of literature, most centrally scholarship on twentieth-century black internationalism, African American radical media, and Chinese political communication with foreign groups.[30]

The past two decades have witnessed a growing wave of studies that examine African American contributions to U.S. foreign affairs, as well as works that frame the U.S. Black Freedom Movement from an international perspective. This scholarship has challenged international relations' general shortsightedness concerning the global implications of race-related issues and struggles.[31] Simultaneously, historians have highlighted the international and diasporic labor of black Marxist-Leninists and socialist-oriented nationalists during the Cold War. These scholars' intellectual work has been invaluable and insightful, particularly in light of the fact that mainstream U.S. accounts of both the Cold War and black struggles for freedom continue to ignore leftist and militant histories, as well as the depths of black intellectual outreach and participation in political and cultural movements outside U.S. borders.[32] The correspondence, words, and images fashioned by and between African American radicals and China have suffered a similar fate. Minus the attention supplied by a few historians and political scientists, the variant of Third World Marxist-Leninism and socialism advocated by black-radical travelers to China has been cast aside to the dustbin of history.

My consideration of this underexplored subject is indebted to Shelley Streeby's and Cynthia Young's recent intellectual contributions. Streeby supplies a dynamic model of transnational radical cultural history where visual analysis and critique take center stage. Filled with political cartoons, linocut prints, portraits, newspaper clippings, photographs, and more, her book *Radical Sensations: World Movements, Violence, and Visual Culture* (2013) details the new forms of media and visual culture cultivated by North American–based radical world movements during the late nineteenth and early twentieth centuries. Young's *Soul Power: Culture, Power, and the Making of a U.S. Third World Left* (2006), likewise, gives attention to a diverse range of radical cultural production. She argues that for the generation of U.S. leftists and nationalists whose radical consciousness came of age during the 1960s and 1970s, practices of media and travel engendered a "time-space compression that helped bridge geographic, ideological, and experiential gaps between U.S. minorities and Third World majorities" and which "in a very real sense, shrank the distance between national contexts and the people in them."[33] Building on Young's and Streeby's scholarship, I posit black radicals' media, visual culture, travels, political communication, and periods of residence in China as sources to unpack these people's and the Chinese state's attempts to translate their respective struggles to one another and, moreover, build a world movement capable of shortening the distance between political realities in China, the United States, and elsewhere. At its best, this political and cultural labor produced a radical crossroads where public diplomacy (what is often referred to now as "soft power"), anti-imperialist militancy, advances in media technology, boundary crossing, and Third World leftist politics and identity intersected, albeit unevenly and at times in a volatile manner. But it was in these encounters that the people examined in this book expanded on their visions of radical democracy and contested the ideological dominance of liberal bourgeois conceptions of democracy, the latter of which has little trouble defining democracy alongside free-market capitalism and white supremacy.

The East Is Black is also influenced by and pulls from historiography invested in challenging previous scholarship's masculinist framing of Cold War black-radical intellectualism. The male-dominant arch of scholarship on twentieth-century black radicalism and, furthermore, the masculinist logics embedded in twentieth-century black radical and internationalist thought and cultural production often goes without mention.[34] Critical of both tendencies, black feminist scholars have highlighted how black women remain at the margins of both historiography and critical theory on African American radicalism, an erasure that mirrors that of Third World women activists within many Cold War historiographies. Black feminist scholarship has thus pushed for more nuanced and critical awareness of the complex contours of gender in discourses and practices of black radicalism and internationalism.[35]

I am motivated by a similar impulse; therefore a fundamental premise of this book is the productive and problematic gendered terms and representations through which black radicals and the Chinese government constructed discourses and strategies of black-Chinese solidarity. As with master U.S. nationalist narratives that allocate private life to the feminine and the different spheres of public life (which include international relations and interstate politics) to the masculine, W. E. B. Du Bois's, Robert and Mabel Williams's, and William Worthy's narratives of black radical internationalist resistance fell prey to identifying anti-imperialist struggle as a space primarily composed of men.[36] Although they never said this explicitly, their media and writings reveal that they often assumed direct associations between radical internationalism, anti-imperialist struggle, and masculinity. In contrast, Shirley Graham Du Bois and Vicki Garvin actively sought to present a more multifaceted and gender-balanced depiction of black internationalism and Chinese communism—their arguments in line with the PRC's "Women Hold up Half the Sky" edict that people could not upend imperialism without also ending the exploitation and oppression of women. Examining these black travelers' gendered renderings of black-Chinese solidarity and political communication, and, furthermore, the distinct ways gender and sexuality structured the Chinese government's and people's conduct toward these black visitors, can broaden understandings of the varying specifics of identity, subjectivity, and location—nation, race, class, and gender—raised by these people within the context of China's political outreach to foreign publics. *The East Is Black* thus takes very seriously scholar M. Bahati Kuumba's assertion that "social movements are also sites for 'gendering consciousness,'" where radical thinking and social resistance "foster awareness of gender roles and relations even when the target and ultimate objectives of the movement have nothing to do with gender equity."[37]

Exploring this history moreover entails thinking across disciplinary boundaries, which has thus far been a productive, though nonetheless extremely flawed, enterprise and challenge within East Asian studies, international relations, political science, and African American studies.[38] For example, a fundamental shortcoming of the first three fields has been the marginalization of decolonization as a constitutive feature of Cold War Chinese political communication. In addition, by frequently privileging states and interstate activities as the primary units of analysis in considering Chinese foreign affairs, international relations and political science scholarship have given insufficient consideration to the cultural and social dimensions of Cold War Chinese politics. East Asian studies scholarship in contrast, especially works published in the last two decades, has tended to this gap. Various works have explored different facets of Cold War Chinese political culture, supplying intriguing information regarding the importance of propaganda posters, radical literature and pamphlets, education, art, opera, music, sports, advancements in scientific technology, and outreach to foreigners in broadening the CCP's base and securing Mao's cult of personality. But like international relations and political science, much of this scholarship has said little about China's outreach to African American publics or about how ideologies of race and racial internationalism took shape within China's Cold War foreign policy.[39] Among African American studies scholarship, on the other hand, several works have interrogated black engagement of China and Chinese Communism. This scholarship has helped counter the problematic nation-state parameters (rather than diasporic parameters) through which African American political culture is conventionally framed. However these works heed little attention to the explosive and intriguing dynamics of Chinese political culture and communication with foreign populations. In a nutshell, after poring over these works, what readers are left with is primarily a U.S.-centered narrative, where Chinese life and politics are difficult to locate, as are black experiences traveling and living in China.[40]

Despite these shortcomings in scholarship, there are exceptions that should be mentioned. The political scientist Anne-Marie Brady, for instance, has supplied a fascinating analysis of China's policies toward Western foreigners and these foreigners' experiences navigating China's treacherous political waters. Her fellow political scientist Vera Fennell and the historians Yunxiang Gao and

Matthew D. Johnson have also called attention to their fields' deafness to China's relations with black Americans and to issues of race and racial internationalism within Chinese history and China's Cold War foreign policy. Along similar lines, the scholars Jamie Monson's and G. Thomas Burgess's works on China's relations with Tanzania and Zanzibar offer intriguing portals into how China negotiated issues of racial and cultural difference in its aid projects in Africa, as well as how African radical nationalists and communists refashioned Maoism and Chinese history to suit futurist discourses framed around nation building, Afro-Asian partnership, and provincializing the West. Furthermore, the historian Judy Tzu-Chun Wu has recently explored the Cold War international journeys of numerous Americans to Vietnam, examining the radical connections and collaborations forged between these travelers and several Asian thinkers and organizations. Wu's framing of these relations as embodying a particular form of "radical orientalism" ties into the images of political solidarity forged by the Chinese government and the people considered in this book. In a similar fashion, both groups' representations relied on empowering and romanticized depictions of anti-imperialism, images and discourses that at times rein-scribed problematic, essentialist depictions of Asians and African Americans.[41]

Ultimately, like these latter works, *The East Is Black* attempts to wed histories and political cultures that are too frequently assumed to be separate and unrelated. African American and Chinese history, media studies, visual analysis, cultural theory, diaspora theory, and gender theory therefore aid me in capturing the richness of black travels and representations of Chinese communism and anti-imperialist internationalism. But my assessment also does not shy away from the incongruities, conflicts, and violence that mired these relations and depictions of solidarity. This book consequently underscores both the ambivalence and fecundity of black-radical travelers' acts of global race making. In so doing, rather than reproducing an uncritical celebration of the imagination as solely a transgressive political practice, my analysis calls for "the imagination to be tough enough to test its own limits," specifically those instances when imagining has "provide[d] alibis for new civilizing missions, [and] mak[ing] us mischoose our allies."[42] It is with consideration of these issues that I situate black radical media and travel representations of China as facilitating particular imaginings of collective identity and solidarity (Afro-Asian, antiwar, nonalignment, Third World guerrilla, and Third World feminist, for instance). These were formations that unlocked new points of identification and alternative arrangements of time, space, place, and race. To put it plainly, they resulted in the construction of a China of black radical imagining—a rendering of China, Asian Communism, and racial internationalism, albeit problematic, that was suited toward galvanizing both black American and Chinese publics within specific black radical and Chinese understandings of anti-imperialist, multiracial, transnational community.

Through this history of negotiations and ambivalence, contestation and contradiction, this book finds its name, the title an appropriation of the extravagant Chinese opera and song "Dongfang Hong" ("The East Is Red"). The song for a brief period of the 1960s replaced "March of the Volunteers" as China's national anthem. It was a consequence of the Great Proletarian Cultural Revolution (GPCR), an immense social struggle that upended Chinese life yet secured Mao's power and doctrinarism over the CCP. Lyrically, "The East Is Red" equated China to the rising sun, whose brightness above the horizon denoted Mao and the party's rise to power and importance in restructuring the world political landscape. Today, though, "The East Is Red" is a reminder of the harsh violence and injustice constitutive of Cold War Chinese life, a society where both the government's and other institutions' revolutionary rhetoric and ideology often masked reactionary positions and wide domestic political divides.

Similarly, this book's title signifies not just the achievements of political coalition but also the inconsistencies and failings of these relations—the disjunctive and ambivalent contours of transnational radical imaginings. The idiom *dongfang hei* (the east is black) then both foregrounds and disassembles some of the articulations and representations that resulted from African American radicals' encounters and media representations of China. Beyond conveying how these activist-intellectuals situated China within their media significations or how the PRC publicly supported blacks' struggles, the idiom gestures toward the ambiguities and incongruity that inhabited these claims, how geopolitical and national realities clashed with the rhetoric and discourses of international coalition. Within these signs and articulations were patchy asymmetries, misperceptions, missteps, and points of miscommunication. Ultimately, what is revealed is that racial internationalism and the political imaginaries through which such formations are produced have their limits; national and cultural differences and the subject positions of radical internationalism's shapers frequently demonstrate the ideology's unevenness and inevitable points of friction.

In the end, I posit travel narratives and media representations of China, Asian communism, and African American–Chinese solidarity as significant, though misleading and erratic, practices of Cold War black radical imagining. Such can be discerned by examining the image with the caption "Dadao Mei di! Dadao Su xiu!" (Down with American imperialists and Russian revisionists! [1967]; see figure I.2). The men's red armbands signify the Red Guard, the GPCR's violent youth forces, whose lawlessness brought devastation to Chinese life. In addition, both men clasp copies of *Mao zhuxi yulu* (*Quotations*

FIGURE I.2: "Dadao Mei di! Dadao Su xiu!" (Down with American imperialists and Russian revisionists!), 1967. Courtesy of the University of Westminster.

from Chairman Mao Zedong [1964]), what came to be known globally as "the little red book." Underlying this image of international solidarity was the lionization of Mao and his communist model, a depiction that veiled the disastrous policies of an extremely repressive totalitarian government and its guerrilla-philosopher leader, a man who evolved into both an international icon and a calculating demagogue. Such contradictions were part and parcel of China's rhetoric of Asian-African internationalism. China's universalist framing of world proletarian revolution negated the differences of colonial history and internal conflict (racial, ethnic, and class-based dynamics unique to each specific location) that distinguished third-world countries from one another, as well as the different postwar conditions and national realities to which these countries' populations were compelled to contend. And just as China's claims and representations of international solidarity were limited and problematic, black radicals' articulations could also be extremely narrow. Reliant upon U.S.-based definitions of blackness and versed in neither Mandarin language nor the different ways arguments about race and perceptions of blackness operated in the Chinese context, they found themselves lost in transit, translation, and selective perceptions, periodically romanticizing developments in China and elsewhere. In addition, the uniqueness of their experiences did not override the reality of their displacement. U.S.-state repression and surveillance and the superintendence, control, and censorship instituted by their Chinese host placed these radicals and their media under close watch and regulation.

Still, the cultural productions that black radicals and the Chinese government created highlight "the significance of interconnectedness as a political and aesthetic impulse" within both Cold War Chinese and African American political cultures.[43] I should point out that the connections forged between these groups were not historically inevitable. They were rather the product of intellectual and material labor by the likes of the people examined in this book, as well as by numerous others whose contributions go unmentioned. And yet what becomes more apparent are the dynamic ways engagement with China, and inversely contact with U.S. black radicalism, provided productive, though ephemeral, alternatives to the global trajectory posited within the U.S. project of incorporation, expansion, and empire. Racial and political formation and subjectivity were ultimately expressed through media and travel to local and global audiences, blackness being translated as a cultural metaphor and category capable of embedding Chinese communism and radical internationalism with antiracist, antisexist, and antibourgeois meanings.

The book is divided into two main chronological parts, each of which consists of two chapters that highlight different travelers' encounters and representations of China. Each part begins with a concise overview of Chinese history and diplomatic policy during a particular decade. My intention is to provide readers with some background and intellectual context to comprehend the history and analysis shared in the part's corresponding chapters.

The book's first part, "The 1950s: Losing China, Winning China," opens by briefly discussing how the CCP came to power, what it meant in relation to U.S. foreign policy and the repression and containment of left-leaning American internationalism, and what the immediate aftermath of victory meant for African American leftists more specifically. Chapter 1, "Ruminations on Eastern Passage," then tracks the movements and writings of the intellectual sage W. E. B. Du Bois and the activist and cultural producer Shirley Graham Du Bois. Censured, assailed, and isolated from mainstream U.S. intellectual and political forums, the Du Boises' 1959 journey to China (a trip that Du Bois described as "the most fascinating eight weeks of travel and sight-seeing, [he had] ever experienced,") offered the couple instructive lessons about the challenges facing decolonial movements and newly independent Third World governments.[44] The chapter begins by pointing to the selective perceptions and differences between Du Bois's and Graham Du Bois's literary and media accounts of this visit, particularly regarding the gender politics of their evaluations of China. I also consider how the Du Boises' representations of this travel brings into light both the achievements and contradictions of China's postrevolutionary phase, particularly the government's attempts to conceal foreign visitors from the impact of the state's political repression and economic mismanagement on Chinese life. The chapter then closes by putting some of the missteps of the Du Boises' journey in conversation with sections from the *Worlds of Color*, one of W. E. B. Du Bois's final works. In this historical novel, Du Bois theorized international travel and the political imagination as potentially radical and liberating, though limited, modes of perception and community formation. Ultimately, Du Bois's model offers a productive starting point to unpack the politics of travel, media, and radical imagining cultivated by the other black travelers to China considered in this book.

Chapter 2, "A Passport Ain't Worth a Cent," builds on this thread by following along the trail of the intrepid foreign news correspondent William Worthy, the first American journalist to report and broadcast from China since the establishment of the PRC. The chapter begins by examining how Worthy challenged and recast representations of black prisoners of war and Chinese communism during the 1950s. Reporting on the politicization of several American prisoners of war in North Korea, he explored how black opposition to the war and to global white supremacy took shape in the Chinese-run prison camps, particularly within the uneven interactions between African American prisoners and their Chinese captors. I then consider how this renegade journalist built on such news coverage and on the topic of black-Asian cultural contact when reporting from other locations. Intrigued by connections between U.S. black political struggle and Asian anti-imperialist movements, Worthy's radical journalistic practice took him to Vietnam and later China, where he risked his credibility and passport to inform the world about what he learned.

The book's second part, "The 1960s: The East Is Red and Black," opens by briefly contextualizing how China's ideological and geopolitical bout with the Soviet Union impacted its foreign-policy outreach to anticolonial and antiracist movements. This part foregrounds the influence of both the Sino-Soviet rift and the decadelong GPCR on China's efforts to increase the international aura of Chinese communism and establish symbolic connections to the evolving U.S. Black Power and Liberation Movement. Chapter 3, "Soul Brothers and Soul Sisters of the East," then tunes in to the radio transmissions, print iconography, political cartoons, and travel documentary of the freedom fighters Mabel and Robert Williams. From Havana first and later Beijing, the Williamses produced media that linked political developments in China and Vietnam with the necessity of cultivating a grassroots black liberation movement trained in guerrilla warfare and connected to revolutionary struggles elsewhere. Although engaging with emergent discourses and representations of Third World anticolonial revolution, the Williamses' articulations relied on gender-specific constructions of radical internationalism. I explore these issues, as well as how the couple's media framed African Americans and Chinese as soul sisters and brothers in arms against U.S. empire. Lastly, I mull over how the shifting international context of the Cold War impacted the Williamses' political consciousness and their altering relationships to various political regimes.

Chapter 4, "Maoism and the Sinification of Black Political Struggle," visits the Shanghai classroom of the veteran black feminist leftist Vicki Garvin. Of interest are the ways Garvin used Mao Zedong's writings to reinterpret and translate the history of African American liberation to Chinese English-language students. As an instructor entering Chinese higher education, Garvin was offered a hands-on view of the immense national and international effort to dogmatize Mao's thoughts and the social and political struggles that ultimately produced China's Cultural Revolution. Her seminar lectures, syllabi, class activities, pedagogy, and use of Chinese writings provide an intriguing entry point to these shifts in Chinese education and moreover Chinese domestic political life. They also serve as interesting examples of cross-cultural fusion, with Mao Zedong Thought and polemical writings being employed by Garvin to teach histories of black resistance and the divisions existent within African American political culture.

In addition, while chapters 3 and 4 demonstrate how particular non-American locations—Cuba and Ghana—served as central sites to introduce black-radical travelers to Chinese Communism, these chapters also reveal the complexity and contradictions of expatriate life in China. The Williamses and Garvin provide important portals to consider China's racial claims toward black Americans during the 1960s, as well as black expatriates' experiences living in China. Given political refuge by the Chinese state, these people's expressions of international racial coalition with China were deeply structured by the unequal power relations existent between them and their hosts and also by the geopolitical divides of the Cold War. They had little choice but to propagate representations that affirmed the superiority of Chinese Communism and that paid insufficient heed to the contradictions of Chinese society and Chinese Communist ideology. When China's internal political upheavals came crashing down around them, Garvin and the Williamses were compelled to reassess the difference between the rhetoric and reality of Chinese social revolution.

Then, in "The 1970s: Rapprochement and the Decline of China's World Revolution," the book closes by summarizing how a handful of people evaluated President Richard Nixon's now-infamous 1972 trip to China and China's evolving engagement with Africa during this decade. To the extent that Nixon's visit signified the prospect of China's shift toward capitalism, it was China's actions in Africa that unambiguously demonstrated its decline as a leader of Third World struggle and the end of its racial claims toward groups of African descent.

FIGURE P1.1: From left to right, Shirley Graham Du Bois, W. E. B. Du Bois, Deng Xiaoping, Zhou Enlai, and Mao Zedong viewing the Anniversary Parade from the balcony of the Forbidden City, Beijing, October 1, 1962. W. E. B. Du Bois Papers, Special Collections and University Archives, University of Massachusetts Amherst Libraries.

PART I

THE 1950s
Losing China, Winning China

What kind of spirit is this that makes a foreigner selflessly
adopt the cause of the Chinese people's liberation as
his own? It is the spirit of internationalism.
—MAO ZEDONG

The decimation of Hiroshima and Nagasaki by the Allied forces'
atomic bombs and Japan's subsequent surrender, what effectively
brought World War II's Pacific Front to its end, did not produce immediate calm or peace within Asia Pacific. If anything, several of the
region's ongoing national and anticolonial conflicts persisted, entering a new age of geopolitical struggle. China was no different.

American government officials had their own plans for China's
function within the postwar global order. President Harry Truman's
administration (1945–53) envisioned China serving as a centerpiece in
repelling Soviet and Asian communism and in further opening East
Asia to Western capital. Prior to World War II and throughout the
war, the U.S. government had established close relations with China's leading political party, the Nationalist Party, better known as the
Guomindang (GMD). It was this force that the United States armed
and aided in eliminating Japanese occupation of China. Moreover, the
United States favored the GMD over its rivals, the Chinese Communist
Party (CCP), as the collective that should take control of China's government at the war's end. At the Yalta Conference of February 1945,
the meeting where the governments of the war's chief victors—the
United States, the Soviet Union, and Great Britain—deliberated over
the postwar organization of Europe, Joseph Stalin promised support
for a GMD government in exchange for Moscow's reacquisition of all

lands lost to Japan in the 1904–5 Russo-Japanese War, territories that included Manchuria. But several months afterward, the Soviets reneged on the agreement, viewing potential American intervention in China as endangering Soviet influence and power in northeast Asia. The Soviets would come to perceive the CCP as a useful ally, though not an equal partner, in its globalist agenda of spreading communism and weakening American hegemony.

The CCP was established in July of 1921, the outcome of a decades-long radicalization of numerous sectors of Chinese society frustrated with foreign dominance of Chinese life, the Versailles treaty's failed promises of self-determination for colonized peoples, and the exploitative rule of Chinese warlords and landholders. Composed at its founding of no more than fifty-seven members, the CCP set about increasing its membership, organizing workers' unions, advocating in support of women's rights and peasant access to literacy and education, and opposing local warlords' and landlords' exploitation and domination. But it was the influence of the Communist Party of the Soviet Union's (CPSU) Comintern International, the organization responsible for establishing affiliate Communist parties in foreign countries and producing a global communist movement that prompted the CCP to establish a united front with the much larger GMD in 1922.

However, from the onset, what the alliance could not overcome were the differences between both parties on the economic and social changes required to transform China into a modern power.[1] The GMD's objective was to position China as a major global competitor within capitalism; it had no qualms about maintaining the class divides and inequalities already existent within Chinese society. The CCP, in contrast, aimed to challenge capitalism's dominance in China and throughout the world. Their vision of China's future was thus foregrounded on eradicating the power of private property, inheritance, class distinctions, and exploitation of lower classes from Chinese life. The CCP's leaders maintained that because China was primarily an agrarian society partially colonized by foreign powers and native industrialists and landlords, it was integral for a Chinese revolutionary movement to depose the country of capitalist relations of all forms, native or foreign. Creating a national system committed to redistributing property and power along level classless lines and led by a party that prioritized the rights of the most downtrodden sectors would be the subsequent task. Ultimately, the GMD'S and the CCP's antithetical blueprints for Chinese modernity led the GMD to betray the alliance. In 1927 it waged a campaign of terror, murdering more than five thousand CCP members, union organizers, and peasant leaders. With only of a fraction of its party and base of support left, the CCP fled from urban areas.[2]

It was among these survivors that the party's particular philosophy of Marxism-Leninism took shape. Firstly, they criticized China's violent treatment of women, and thus actively endorsed female literacy and women's right to equal employment, education, and free choice in marriage, void of parental arrangements. Furthermore, they paid close attention to the everyday lives and struggles of peasants and the rural poor, and over time came to perceive the primary role these groups would play in inducing a powerful grassroots revolution. The CCP maintained that Chinese citizens should no longer see themselves as sitting within the waiting room of political modernity, biding their time to one day participate in world affairs as a sovereign body. Instead, China's masses should self-identify as on the front lines of constructing a socialist movement and national Marxist revolution unique to China. The CCP's assertion that this revolution could occur in a dominantly agrarian society made up mostly of impoverished peasants went against Marxist theory's tenet that such political movements could only develop among working-class populations led by a centralized party of activists in a largely industrial society. Nonetheless, it was this agrarian-centered philosophy that the party inculcated its members and peasants with. The party's radicalization of its followers was only heightened following the Long March (*changzheng*, 1934–35), the CCP's tumultuous journey to the northwest province of Shaanxi and their establishment of a base of operations in Yan'an. Fleeing from the GMD, more than eighty thousand CCP troops and thirty-five women embarked on a six-thousand-mile westward odyssey. Led by the CCP member Mao Zedong, the survivors rebuilt the party in Yan'an through outreach to millions of poor farmers, village dwellers, and rural and urban vagabonds. From this base they established rural militias and armed volunteers throughout the country, the People's Liberation Army (PLA) gradually growing into a force capable of overwhelming the GMD.

The CCP and GMD suspended their conflict in 1937 to mobilize a unified, all-out offensive against Japanese imperialism. But in June 1946 full-scale civil war again broke out between the CCP and GMD. Defying their Soviet allies' advice to establish a coalition government with the GMD, the CCP military raged for three years against a GMD military armed with superior American weapons. Controlling more-favorable strategic positions, and better capturing the minds and hearts of Chinese people of different class backgrounds, the CCP compelled GMD forces to retreat southward into Taiwan, an island off the coast of the mainland. Driven into refuge, the latter's rout was solidified by the CCP's declaration of victory and subsequent establishment of the PRC in October 1949.

Having unseated the opposition, the CCP focused its attention on the dual tasks of achieving national unification and eliminating foreign encroachment and influence from Chinese life. No longer just an advocate for peasants and workers, but now the central force mandated to organize and regulate social life, the CCP, to some degree, abandoned some of its more radical leftist and populist propositions of engendering a worker- and peasant-led anticapitalist social movement fueled by massive agrarian reforms and democratic transformation of industrial workplaces. The CCP instead embarked on several moderate economic and social projects that endorsed the state and economy's interest over that of the populations who helped bring the CCP into power. For example, despite the CCP's anticapitalist rhetoric, China would remain, to some degree, beholden to private capital over the course of the 1950s, where bureaucratic hegemony was given greater priority than proletarian revolution and workers' rights. This was one of several pragmatic decisions by the CCP that in retrospect convey the inherent difficulty in building an independent workers' state amid global capitalism.[3] At any rate, under the principle of *qian dasao fangzi zhaodai xin keren* (cleaning the house before entertaining new guests), the party-state did reduce foreign influence and privilege in China. Foreign property and enterprises were purchased or confiscated, Christian missions and Western-funded schools were shut down, and many foreign news agencies, journalists, and expatriates were forced to leave the country. Concurrently, the government dedicated resources toward nationalizing business and modernizing the nation.

Truman's administration and U.S. ruling elites were frustrated by the CCP's victory. They feared that a communist government in China could impede the progress of expanding America's share of world trade and its quest to institute a new capitalist economic order in the Asia Pacific region. Consequently, in the aftermath of the PRC's founding, a popular anticommunist discourse about China took shape in the United States, what came to be known as the country's "loss of China" to communism. This discourse portrayed China as an "enemy of freedom" and as the "cat's paw" of the Soviet regime, communist ideologues whose policies were directed by officials several thousand miles away in Moscow. But future developments drastically transformed these American perceptions. China's ability to withstand U.S. forces during the Korean War and, later, its development of a nuclear arsenal and support for communist revolutions and national liberation struggles elsewhere persuaded U.S. officials to no longer underestimate the CCP. Gone was the image of China as mere Soviet pawn; more and more Americans began to view China as a sleeping giant in pursuit of immense power. Other events solidified the negative tone of U.S.-China relations, particularly the Formosa Strait Crisis of 1954–55 and 1958. China's artillery shelling of Quemoy and Matsu, groups of islands controlled by the newly reformed GMD government in Taiwan, for instance, almost brought the United States and China to the brink of nuclear war.

The U.S. government took steps to curb the CCP's influence and access to the international world. First, travel to China on a U.S. passport was outlawed, and business relations with Chinese enterprises were frowned upon. Secondly, the U.S. government and its European and Japanese allies placed an embargo on trade to China, preventing Chinese people's access to certain foreign-produced commodities. In addition, the U.S. government monitored and constrained other Asian countries' and overseas Chinese communities' trade and political contact with China. Relentless pressure on Asian governments was central to America's mission of isolating China. Japan, South Korea, South Vietnam, for example, became home to major U.S. military installations and served as vital sites for U.S. influence and domination of Asian trading patterns. America's line of defense against China also took shape through constant efforts to prevent China a seat in the United Nations, a strategy that was effective until 1971. Simultaneously, a network of GMD officials and businesspersons, right-wing U.S. politicians, hired American agents, and American businesses made it their priority to influence the U.S. president, Congress, and American public to regard communism's rising influence in Asia as a force that would bring doom to freedom and Western democracy if not checked.

But outside of foreign policy, one of the greatest forces in America's anti-China ideological campaign was media and propaganda. News reports, films, and cultural criticism about China frequently mirrored

U.S. foreign policy.[4] By regularly casting China through provocative terminology ("Communist China," "Red China," "the Chinese menace," and so on), the United States and its enemies were represented as embodying two antithetical geocultural realities. Pro-GMD newspapers and periodicals (*Young China*, the *Chinese Nationalist Daily*, and the *China Monthly: The Truth about China*), top American newspapers and magazines (*American Mercury, Colliers, Human Events, Life,* the *New Leader, Reader's Digest, Saturday Evening Post,* and *U.S. News & World Report*), and organizations (the American China Policy Association, the China Emergency Committee, and the Committee to Defend America by Aiding Anti-Communist China) played a major role in creating this anti-China climate.[5] Their one-sided depictions of China (news coverage that the Chinese history expert John King Fairbank lambasted as, at best, "elementary news reporting"), of course, did not represent the totality of U.S. media and literature produced about the region.[6] But the U.S. State Department's ban on travel to China was effective in preventing on-the-ground, critical coverage of Chinese affairs by American reporters and cultural producers. The department's policies thus forced news consumers to rely on reports generated either by foreign journalists and non-American "China watchers" free to travel to China or by U.S. reporters stationed in Hong Kong. One writer likened these Hong Kong–based reporters to "an absurdity comparable to reporting United States affairs from an observation post in Tijuana, Mexico."[7]

Its isolation within the international arena, however, did not stifle the Chinese government's ability to generate mass support nationally. With its increasing domestic influence came the cultivation of a unique Chinese leftist ideology, one that the PRC would later export and which ultimately called into question Soviet hegemony over the international communist movement and the Soviets' self-identification as the leader of proletarian world revolution. The death of Stalin in 1953, and the subsequent rise of what the CCP's radical wings deemed to be a moderately political Soviet regime led by Nikita Khrushchev, convinced Mao and the Politburo Standing Committee, China's most powerful decision-making body, to gradually dissolve its policy of replicating Soviet economic policies and to drift away from the Sino-Soviet alliance. Despite China's "lean-to-one-side policy" (*yibiandao zhengce*) of favoring the Soviets over the United States, China's leaders fashioned their own model of Marxist-Leninist proletariat revolution. Their model was explicitly antiracist and was framed as more favorable to the economic and social challenges faced by social movements in Asia, Africa, the Caribbean, and Latin America. In so doing, the Chinese government depicted itself as a racial ally in solidarity and struggle and as an anti-imperialist counterweight to the West.

How did China work to nurture both Afro-Asian and Third World solidarity? One of the first key sites where China articulated its position was at the Bandung Asian-African Conference of 1955.[8] At this meeting, which attracted representatives from twenty-nine Asian and African governments, the Chinese delegation articulated China's commitment to supporting Asian and African independence and development free from foreign influence and dominance. Delegates were therefore encouraged to "seek common ground" with China "rather than emphasize [their] differences." In attendance were representatives from six African countries—Egypt, Ethiopia, Liberia, Libya, Sudan, and soon-to-be independent Ghana—as well as representatives from various African liberation movements who were attending as observers. To these attendees, the Chinese delegation leader Premier Zhou Enlai maintained that with China African nation-states could serve as the counterforce to the U.S. and Soviet Union power blocs. He also persuaded those delegates who were aligned with the United States to not fall victim to America's anti-China stance. "We have no bamboo curtain, but some people are spreading a smokescreen between us," Zhou stated. "Let us, the Asian and African countries, be united."[9]

Zhou's outreach to these groups, however, was no mere discursive strategy. In time, the PRC extended financial, technical, and military aid to several of these states and national liberation groups. Egypt was the first African country to accept this support. Its diplomatic recognition of China in 1955 and opening of a Chinese embassy one year later launched the PRC's evolving relations and activity in the continent. China's agreement to purchase Egyptian cotton, and later its denunciation of Israel and Allied Western forces' invasion of Egypt after the Egyptian president Gamal Abdel Nasser nationalized the Suez Canal in 1956, also helped strengthen Sino-Egyptian relations. The embassy in Cairo thereafter became one of several important ambassadorial spaces where the PRC extended itself to visiting African delegations and diplomats. For instance, in this embassy a key alliance was forged with Algeria's National Liberation Front, the leading revolutionary force in opposition to France's colonization and occupation of Algeria.

Ultimately, China's policies regarding Africa were three pronged: to increase China's sphere of influence among Africans, to sway African states away from the influence of the United States and later the Soviet Union, and to supplant Taiwan as the sole internationally recognized government of China. By the next decade China worked to meet these objectives by offering African countries aid and support through multiple channels—military assistance, technical and financial support, infrastructure development, and official pronouncements of support. Chinese leadership and participation in organizations such as the Afro-Asian People's Solidarity Organization, the All-China Afro-Asian Solidarity Committee, the Chinese-African People's Friendship Association, the Permanent Bureau of Afro-Asian Writers, and the Afro-Asian Journalists Association also helped to facilitate these cultural and political connections.[10]

China's project to align itself more closely with anticolonial and anti-imperialist movements worldwide was also shaped within Chinese diplomatic affairs, what is referred to as *waijiao shiwu*, or *waishi* for short.[11] Of high priority was influencing foreign views of China by building close diplomatic relations with foreign governments, thinkers, and activists. As Mao relays in the epigraph, the idea was that it was the foreign voices, rather than China, who could best transmit the aura of Chinese communism and revolutionary internationalism throughout the world. Peace activists and socialists were subsequently invited to visit China for extended tours and to observe China's road to socialist modernization. A few foreigners were also offered opportunities to contribute to the Chinese Communist Revolution as university teachers, broadcasters, doctors, translators, language polishers, and technicians. Included in China's outreach to foreigners were a small number of African Americans. Interested in seeing Chinese sovereignty and communist development with their own eyes, black travelers defied the U.S. State Department's ban on travel to China, decisions that rattled the U.S. government and that led to serious political controversy stateside. In the aftermath several of these Americans even opted for political refuge in China to escape the intellectual and physical repression of U.S. racism and anticommunism.

Black radical interest in China developed amid scathing political attacks on the U.S. Left and the Civil Rights Movement's more militant and socialist wings. With the rise of the Soviet Union as the central superpower opponent of the United States, a flexible anticommunist ideology was propagated by U.S. political officials and numerous non-state institutions. America and the Western world's defense, it was argued, required "containing" the forward expansion of Soviet communism and its satellites in Eastern Europe and Asia. Communism, these Americans explained, worked both externally and internally, through propaganda and ideological workers. Consequently, it was of dire importance to police and weed out communism's supporters and ideologues in the United States. Via nongovernment cultural agencies, mass-media institutions, and a newly formed government bureaucracy devoted to surveillance, intelligence, national defense, and cultural warfare, a political culture of extreme intellectual and societal repression—that is, a *containment culture*—was instituted.[12]

No one articulated the purpose for containment more explicitly than the State Department adviser and containment witch doctor George Kennan. In a 1946 telegram, he pointed to the necessity of defeating communism both outside and inside the United States: "Much depends on health and vigor of our society. World communism is like malignant parasite which feeds only on diseased tissue. This is the point at which domestic and foreign policies meet. Every courageous and incisive measure to solve internal problems of our own society, to improve self-confidence, morale and community spirit of our own people, is a diplomatic victory over Moscow."[13] At the hands of the Truman administration's loyalty programs, Senator Joseph McCarthy and the House Un-American Activities Committee's communist witch hunts, and surveillance, spying, and invasion of privacy by the J. Edgar Hoover–led FBI, critics of U.S. foreign policy were targeted and framed as national pariahs, the domestic "parasites" to which Kennan had cautioned. "The real object was to prevent American citizens of any sort from daring to think or talk against the determination of big business to reduce Asia to colonial subserviency to American industry; to reweld the chains of Africa; to consolidate United States control of the Caribbean and South America; and above all to crush socialism in the Soviet Union and China," W. E. B. Du Bois explained.[14]

U.S. containment also had a particular racial edge. The Achilles' heel of the U.S. Cold War strategy of global power was Jim Crow segregation and antiblack violence in the United States. In short, the country's racial reality burst and hindered U.S. credibility abroad; it was the loose thread in the American government's and private interests' endeavors to globalize the world along the path of free trade, deterritorialization, and U.S. militarization. What's more, the rise of anticolonial, socialist fervor in Asia, Africa, the Caribbean, and Latin America magnified the incongruity of the U.S. rhetoric of spreading democracy and capitalism into new territorial hot spots. In short, U.S. racial oppression provided foreign countries with easy ammunition to criticize U.S. postwar foreign-policy ideology. To combat these attacks, elements of the U.S. government and larger political-cultural establishment promoted the country's racial reform and advancement. The United States was portrayed as the leading agent in bringing forth a globalism never seen before, one respectful of cultural and racial difference that viewed foreign countries as partners, rather than subjects, in strengthening world affairs and communication. U.S. national culture was, moreover, situated as embodying the multicultural, democratic archetype that industrial and financial capital and U.S. superintendence could help replicate elsewhere. In this global public-relations campaign, race therefore took on great geopolitical and ideological significance. "A contest over the meaning of race, the shapes of racial solidarities, and the character and allegiances of new Asian and African states began with the Cold War itself," the historian Penny Von Eschen notes.[15]

Over the course of the 1950s, the U.S. ruling class was thus compelled, at a snail's pace, to accept the gradual assimilation and integration of blacks and other racial minorities into American national life through legal desegregation and voting protections.[16] But crucial issues such as wealth distribution, black control of black community resources, police harassment, and disparities in health, education, and housing were left off the table. From this perspective, at its most basic level, black political struggle represented a national challenge that could be fixed by racial liberalism—namely, denunciation of America's racial past and the slow reform of Jim Crow de facto and de jure segregation. But the idea of black Americans, and moreover oppressed U.S. workers and racial minorities, as members of a global majority made the U.S. global model of market-oriented economic and political development extremely vulnerable. This would then mean that U.S. racism and class exploitation were manifestations of a larger, worldwide problem.

Powerful U.S. institutions employed containment culture and anti-communism to suppress the radical domestic and globalist demands made by unions, civil rights activists, and black war veterans, among other constituencies, and the links forged by black American leftists, nationalists, and peace activists with anticapitalist movements elsewhere.[17] Moreover, by publically accusing numerous Americans of disloyalty and circulating discourses about potential foreign threats operating under the cover of black political activism, the U.S. government forced black Americans of different political stripes to choose sides. The historian Thomas Borsetlmann explains: "The onset of the Cold War . . . forced them [African Americans] to choose between retaining an internationalist perspective . . . or adopting a more nationalistic, anti-Communist stand that supported U.S. foreign policy while pursuing racial equality more narrowly at home. . . . [This] implicitly raised the question of whether African Americans identified themselves primarily in racial or national terms. Did they represent a potential fifth column of the world's nonwhite majority within American walls, or were they loyal American nationalists?"[18]

Ultimately, America's anticommunist crusade influenced many African Americans' perceptions of China, as well as of communist Vietnam and communist North Korea. A 1969 poll that examined black viewpoints on U.S. foreign policy between the years of 1937 and 1967 revealed that the majority of people believed that Americans "could not, in the long run, 'live peacefully,' with Communist China."[19] Periodic depictions of black Americans as cultural workers against Asian communist influence and infiltration facilitated these negative outlooks about China. Images of loyal and patriotic black war veterans, U.S. racial integration, and the ethnic diversity of the American population, for instance, helped spark greater black consent to the U.S. anticommunist crusade of demonizing China. In addition, racist depictions of Chinese communism buttressed some black Americans' imaginaries of Asian communism. China, North Korea, and Vietnam were often framed as made up of "yellow bastards," "gooks," and "apes," representations that revived discourses of "Yellow Peril" and Asians as an invading force endangering U.S. cultural values and national security.[20] Even President Dwight Eisenhower chimed in, commenting that the worst mistake the U.S. government had made was "bow[ing] before the triumph in China of Communists." "We are always wrong when we believe that Orientals think logically as we do," he insisted.[21] Such representations of Asian communism tied into a long-standing white U.S. tendency to differentiate Asians into camps of "good Asians" and "bad Asians," a historical racial calculus that has shifted depending on the particular political circumstances and domestic and geopolitical conflicts of the time period.[22] Thus, with the onset of the Cold War, the image of Japan as America's top threat in East Asia was replaced with that of China and other communist Asian countries, territories that prior to World War II were depicted in U.S. culture through the "good Asian" trope. Simultaneously, throughout the Cold War several of America's Asian allies (Japan, Taiwan, South Korea, South Vietnam, and the Philippines, for example) were portrayed as models of freedom and democracy that contrasted with the totalitarianism of Asian communism.

Such portrayals clearly informed many African Americans' attitudes about China. Yet it is also important to note that a solid number of blacks, despite their anticommunist stance, still favored that China remain free of foreign imperialism and influence.[23] Others acknowledged that America's anticommunist policies served the strategic interests of the U.S. state and powerful elites, and thus worked to mute black Americans' relations to world anticolonial and anti-imperialist movements. In openly reaching out to China, these critics of U.S. foreign policy called for their fellow citizens to seek out alternative models of economic and political activity than that posited by U.S. global power. China's road to socialism, they insisted, embodied one template to consider, not as an archetype to be replicated in the United States but rather as offering instructive principles and praxis for the making of a U.S. revolutionary movement.

The small number of black militants and leftists who traveled to China gained greater awareness about China's postrevolutionary phase. Most chiefly, they took seriously the government and people's mission to carve out a socialist system and revolutionary culture unique and pertinent to China's national culture and historical struggles and which prioritized the contributions and agency of the working class and rural poor. Moreover, by advancing the idea that progressive political transformation required constant assessment and radical reshaping of the central institutions of social and economic life (what Mao and the CCP often described as *changqi douzheng*, or protracted struggle), and supporting foreign liberation and communist struggles, China supplied an alternative example of political modernity and world relations than that promoted by the United States and its allies.

Such an image, for instance, is conveyed in the CCP propaganda poster with the caption "Quan shijie renmin fandui Mei diguo zhuyi de douzheng bi sheng!" (The fight against U.S. imperialism by people of the whole world will succeed! [1965] see figure P1.2). The image

全世界人民反对美帝国主义的斗争必胜！

FIGURE P1.2: "Quan shijie renmin fandui Mei diguo zhuyi de douzheng bi sheng" (The fight against U.S. imperialism by people of the whole world will succeed!), 1965. Courtesy of Ann Tompkins (Tang Fandi) and Lincoln Cushing Chinese Poster Collection, C. V. Starr East Asian Library, University of California, Berkeley. Also published in Tompkins and Cushing, *Chinese Posters*. Digital image courtesy Lincoln Cushing/Docs Populi.

displays a multiracial and multinational grouping who in partnership and solidarity represent the world's majority, a force capable of remaking the world. And emblazoned behind this mass of revolutionaries are the red colors of the Chinese national flag and the international communist movement, what signifies China's leadership of such a global anticapitalist force. Through similar representations and efforts to establish political communication between China and black America, several black travelers and the Chinese government identified China's model of domestic uplift and international socialist struggle as the corollary of the radically shifting, decolonizing, Third World landscape—a global movement that was resulting and making more evident the crisis of Euro-American imperialism and global white supremacy.

One of the first visitors to articulate this view and soak in the changes brought about by China's shift in power was Eslanda Goode Robeson—world activist, anthropologist, journalist, and spouse of Paul Robeson. Traveling to Beijing in late December 1949, just two months after the establishment of the PRC, she attended the Asian Women's Federation meeting. Journeying later to Shanghai, Nanjing, and Tianjin, she marveled at China's social transformation and the importance of women's contributions to these changes. It was these images that stuck out in her mind after she returned to the United States. In newspapers and in speeches thereafter, she tirelessly advocated for the Chinese Communist Revolution, pointing out to black Americans the racial dynamics of a socialist revolution on the other side of the world. She assured them that if they saw what she saw, they too would comprehend the significance of China's overthrow of white supremacy. Robeson insisted, "Every Negro . . . who has not been allowed to enter the public libraries, parks, theatres, stores; every Negro who has been denied proper respect, human dignity and human rights—All these Negroes will be able to understand and fully appreciate what is happening in the Chinese People's Republic."[24]

Other black Americans echoed Robeson's assertion. Langston Hughes's poem "Consider Me" (1951), for instance, emphasized such connections, encouraging blacks to consider the structural and ideological links that tied populations in Beijing to black communities of the U.S. North and South:

> Black,
> Caught in a crack
> That splits the world in two
> From China
> By way of Arkansas
> To Lenox Avenue.[25]

It was this kind of thinking that led some black radicals to identify in the Chinese Communist Revolution a movement of which other blacks required greater awareness and understanding. The defeat of the GMD and the onset of a Chinese government and society that prioritized social struggle and the uplift of workers and the poor had to be shared and learned from, most centrally by people attempting to galvanize similar developments elsewhere. Through travel narratives and media, these black travelers' impressions and imaginings took on greater meaning.

1

RUMINATIONS ON EASTERN PASSAGE

The traveler must take with him much knowledge or he will
never see what is before his eyes, or hear with his ears. . . . Of
China what little he knew was mostly distortion. Through that
false fog he saw little even when he stood with open eyes.
—W. E. B. DU BOIS, *Worlds of Color*

China changes before one's eyes. It is the "Land of Tomorrow."
—SHIRLEY GRAHAM DU BOIS

Xiyou ji (Journey to the West), Wu Ch'êng-ên's sixteenth-century tale, is a parable about the travels and travails of Sun Wukong (the Monkey King)."[1] Born from stone, the Monkey King's supernatural powers continuously develop during his travels and study of Taoism. As his abilities multiply, he is summoned inside the gates of heaven to receive his place as one of the deities. Once inside, however, he is insulted when the Jade Emperor assigns him a lowly position in the celestial kingdom. Angry and in defiance, he breaks into the garden owned by Xiwangwu, the "Queen Mother of the West," and steals her prized peaches of immortality. War commences between him and heaven's army, and in the end it is the Monkey King who is victorious. But his feat is short-lived. The Buddha visiting from the West intercedes. Sun Wukong is quickly subdued and imprisoned for five centuries. He is only released in exchange for his pledge to protect a Buddhist monk on his pilgrimage.

After winning the Chinese Communist Revolution, Chinese communists appropriated the Monkey King parable to describe their elimination of foreign rule in China. Mao Zedong remarked, "We have been like the 'Monkey King Upsetting Heaven' in the old play. We have thrown away the Heavenly Rule Book. Remember this. Never take a Heavenly Rule Book too seriously. One must always go by one's own revolutionary rules."[2] Across the Pacific, W. E. B. Du Bois was listening. For him, the Monkey King's tale of struggle and resurrection symbolized both China's rise to independence and how the Chinese Communist Party's (CCP) victory signified a shift in the imperial crucible faced by people of color worldwide.[3] During a visit to China in 1959, Du Bois wrote that he could "never forget the assault of the Monkey King on the hosts of Heaven, facing God and the angels," or the ways "the Monkey King fool[ed] the hosts of Heaven and overthr[ew] the angels."[4] For Du Bois, China was doing more than just defying the imperialist and globalist aims of the United States and Europe. China's commitment to regenerating domestic economic and social growth was producing new relationships between individuals and the larger society. This was evidence to Du Bois that China was cultivating "a nation where human nature was so abreast of scientific knowledge; where daily life of everyday people was so outstripping mechanical power and love of life so triumphing over human greed." Just as the Monkey King was released to help guide the monk westward, the lessons of the Chinese government and public in its postrevolutionary period directed Du Bois eastward. "I have never seen a nation which so amazed me and touched me as China in 1959," Du Bois related.[5]

The activist Shirley Graham Du Bois, his travel partner and spouse, was also fascinated with all she came in contact with while in China, noting how the Peking Opera's *The Monkey King* "foretold the upsurge and rebellion of the people long before it took place."[6] But she also described her journey with her husband in different terms and inscribed it with different meanings than he did. Acknowledging that she knew little about China before arriving in Beijing, Graham Du Bois was taken aback with the hospitality with which she and Du Bois were treated, the scale of China's multiple development initiatives, and Chinese citizens' incessant affirmations of the Chinese Communist Revolution and the CCP's role in building a new China. She also met numerous women who were playing prominent roles in China's social transformation, features of the trip that influenced her evolving feminist outlook.[7] Summing up the visit she recounted: "We have seen how the Chinese people literally move mountains, level valleys and change the course of rivers."[8] It was these experiences, she explained in an editorial for the *Pittsburgh Courier*, that led her to believe that China's development represented the future of the Third World, or, as she termed it, "The Land of Tomorrow."[9]

Assessing intellectual work on W. E. B. Du Bois, scholars Kate Baldwin, Gerald Horne, Brent Hayes Edwards, and others have noted that scholarship, with some exceptions, has generally avoided critical engagement of Du Bois's final years. This was a tumultuous period in his life, an era when his socialist and communist leanings were met with intense government scrutiny and suppression. Eric Porter has recently challenged this negation, examining what

FIGURE 1.1: The Du Boises on stairs of a guest house in Changtu, April 1959. W. E. B. Du Bois Papers, Special Collections and University Archives, University of Massachusetts Amherst Libraries.

he describes as "the early late period" of Du Bois's life, specifically the years of 1940–52. But despite the soundness of Porter's assessment, he too disregards Du Bois's last decade alive and his affiliations with the Soviet and Chinese governments during this period. Porter rules these features of the elder sage's closing years as "significantly less nuanced," failing to "respond more directly to a specific set of social and historical phenomena."[10]

My appraisal of the short-lived relations Du Bois cultivated with the CCP contrasts with Porter's evaluation and, moreover, with the dominant scholarly tendency of overlooking and downplaying Du Bois's shift to communism.[11] In particular, I find Du Bois and Graham Du Bois's two-month journey through China in 1959 complex and captivating. I argue that it offers a productive preface to consider China's Cold War political outreach to U.S. black radicals and the different tropes, analogies, and designs through which black-radical travelers came to represent the Chinese Communist Revolution.

Ultimately, travel to China widened Du Bois's and Graham Du Bois's perceptions of the process of galvanizing less-developed, formerly colonized nations toward economic sufficiency and social values of selflessness, sacrifice, and collective toil. In writings and journalistic accounts, the couple waxed lyrical about the political energy permeating Chinese society, frequently emphasizing their faith in the possibilities of an Asian-African tactical alliance. In effect, these portrayals situated China as a leading figure in an international decolonial collective, a body composed primarily of African nations to which China's influence would spread. But this was not the only political imaginary through which the couple identified China's political importance. The Du Boises asserted that the Chinese Communist Revolution was an extension of a long history of anticapitalist and antiracist struggles, movements that in their totality composed a distinct transnational collective capable of confronting the U.S. Cold War model of global relations and political modernity.

Of significant note though is that the couple, in some measure, defended their endorsement of China through claims of evenhanded perception. They argued that they were supplying Americans with a more straightforward, on-the-ground evaluation of Chinese life than that which was transmitted in U.S. media and government reports. But in the process, the Du Boises never openly weighed in on the regulated nature of their visit. They neither dissected how their Chinese hosts labored to facilitate and influence the couple's perceptions of China nor whether or not their encounters and impressions were a viable reflection of the quotidian realities and treatment experienced by Chinese citizens.

This chapter revisits this episode. It mulls over the Du Boises' representations of their travel to China in print media and literature by focusing on several things: how their travel and reflections helped to propagate China's achievements; how these writings and media offer a window to China's methods and strategies of impacting foreign visitors' viewpoints; and the notable differences between Du Bois's and Graham Du Bois's depictions of China, particularly regarding gender and sexuality. Bearing in mind the limitations and misunderstandings of the Du Boises' encounters in China and their portrayals of this visit, the chapter then closes by briefly thinking through Du Bois's socialist-realist novel *Worlds of Color*, a work he completed just prior to the trip. Certain sections of the novel help tease out some of the gaps of radical imagining—

that is, the negotiations and ambivalence, contestations and contradictions—demonstrated by black radical travelers in their endeavors to represent and inscribe China with particular racial meanings. In the novel, encounters in China display how the prohibitive state regulations of the host country and the subject position of the traveler can work to organize and restrict the traveler's perceptions abroad. Among other lessons, what is conveyed is the difficulty in not collapsing the self and the Other in imagining and cultivating transnational racial solidarity.

★

JOURNEY TO THE EAST

The couple's trip to China came at the culmination of Du Bois's near decade-long fight for his passport. In 1951 the U.S. State Department seized his passport after the federal government indicted him as a foreign agent of the Soviet Union. These accusations stemmed from his public support for several communist governments and his political work in two lobbyist organizations, the anti-imperialist Council on African Affairs and the short-lived antinuclear Peace Information Center (PIC). Branded as Soviet affiliates by the U.S. right wing, these organizations and Du Bois fell victim to the McCarran Internal Security Act (1950), a bill that required persons suspected of engaging in subversive or communist activities to register with government. Amid allegations that the PIC's leadership in facilitating the Stockholm Appeal's antinuclear campaign was in fact a front for the Soviet regime, Du Bois and four other PIC officials were charged and forced to stand trial.[12] The charges came just two years after Du Bois was sacked from his position in the National Association for the Advancement of Colored People (NAACP), an organization he helped to found. Summing up this political backlash, Du Bois solemnly remarked: "I found myself being punished before I was tried."[13]

Although Du Bois would be acquitted of these charges in 1951, it took almost a decade for the Supreme Court to reverse the State Department's seizure of his passport. Prevented from international travel, he found himself with little to no savings and income, marginalized from employment, and abandoned by various wings of the mainstream black political and intellectual establishments. It was this last fact, the failure of black liberals and the black intelligentsia to publically support Du Bois's freedom of speech and political ideology, that left him most dispirited. While he attributed some people's abandonment of his cause to the fear instigated by anticommunist intimidation and coercion, he also felt that access to wealth, status, and gradual racial inclusion was inducing old allies and educated blacks to shrink from the tasks and responsibilities of social leadership. Rather than establish "a new cultural unity, capable of absorbing socialism, tolerance, and democracy," this group was being freed "to ape the worst of American and Anglo-Saxon chauvinism" and "become American in their acceptance of exploitation as defensible."[14]

Yet facing these challenges supplied Du Bois with a reinvigorated cultural and political perspective. He commented that he no longer felt encumbered by his own reductive reading of racial struggle. His political isolation, and furthermore his introduction to nonblack radicals and members of the Communist Party of the United States of America (CPUSA) by the likes of Graham Du Bois, freed him from what he described as "that racial provincialism which [he] always recognized." He felt poised to make "new friends and liv[e] in a wider world than ever before—a world with no color line."[15] He insisted that it was this world, the space of radical democracy and ensuring the ability of the poor and oppressed to develop their societies and cultures on their own terms, void of Western interference and influence, that more black Americans, in their demands for civil and human rights, needed to consider. "American Negroes have now entered the current of world affairs. . . . Their inner struggle parallels the struggle of the modern world," Du Bois explained in 1953. "This is the new problem which faces the American Negro,—the problem which many colored and colonial peoples have already faced."[16] Du Bois pointed out that the "problem"—the direction in which U.S. black political struggle must proceed—was not a quandary exceptional to black Americans. Instead, it was part of a world-historical struggle. Liberal proposals of U.S. racial integration and world community, he argued, were attempting to wrestle workers and global colonized populations' anticolonial efforts away from alignment with a global anticapitalist movement. Du Bois, however, countered that what people required was worldwide socialism, a global system with "workers as the chief citizens of the state" and that restructured commerce and industry away from private interests and toward public welfare, wealth redistribution, collective ownership, and public sustainability.[17] Consequently, over the course of the decade Du Bois would become more adamant in his endorsement of socialism and, later, communist ideology. Growing relations with the CPUSA, moreover, led him to join the party in 1961, two years before his death.

Graham Du Bois, an author and playwright, also endured serious setbacks as a result of McCarthyism's political attacks on the U.S. Left. As a closeted communist, her political alignment and work in the world peace movement and with radical organizations, including the CPUSA, led the State Department to seize her passport, leaving her unable to travel abroad for work, political outreach, and leisure. Thereafter, she dedicated most of her time to helping lead the charge for Du Bois's legal defense, playing a central role in the national committee that solicited and raised money for him and his PIC codefendants. While traveling across the country, she spoke in support of Du Bois's freedom of speech and travel, her own income and national book sales suffering as a result of being linked with Du Bois and communist ideology. She did not let this suppression halt her leftist radicalism though. She continued to serve as a contributing editor for the left-wing journal *Masses & Mainstream* and as a member of several black arts initiatives. She additionally authored several biographies and journalistic accounts while building close relations with various diplomats and UN political dignitaries.[18]

In comparison to earlier decades though, Graham Du Bois's political life during this period was somewhat insipid. Prior to marrying Du Bois in February 1951, she had achieved major accomplishments as a highly acclaimed artist and writer, composing musical scores, musicals, plays, dramatic works for radio, and numerous biographies. Moreover, most of this was done as a single mother, raising two sons amid severe racial oppression, indignity, and modest means. "She was a twenty-five hour-a-day worker," her son David Graham Du Bois divulged.[19] Beyond her creative work, she was extremely active politically. During the 1940s, Graham Du Bois contributed to radical leftist political groups, including CPUSA, Sojourners for Truth and Justice, the Council on African Affairs, and the Civil Rights Congress. But after marrying the senior Du Bois, a substantial amount of her time was devoted to aiding him with his declining health and struggling to meticulously organize the couple's political and intellectual activities, financial matters, and household. The historian Gerald Horne notes about Graham Du Bois: "The years she was married to Du Bois, 1951 to 1963, were in many ways the least interesting and least productive of her long life, in part because of the subordinate role she felt obligated to adopt."[20]

It was in this context that the Du Boises' journey to China came to fruition. In June 1958, amid growing public defense of the couple's right to travel free from government or ideological restraint, the Supreme Court handed down a decision that the State Department was not mandated the authority to deny passports based on citizens' political beliefs or refusal to publically divulge their political beliefs. The decision's result was that the couple's unwillingness to sign a political affidavit explicitly stating their political stance did not mean they could be refused a passport. With their passports reissued and having received invitations to visit several countries, the Du Bois wasted no time in leaving the United States, embarking on a one-year journey that took them to Western and Eastern Europe, the Soviet Union, and China. "I felt like a released prisoner," Du Bois wrote.[21] The opportunity to travel to China came as the couple was wrapping up their London stay. In September Guo Moruo, a statesman and prolific writer, and Soon Ching-ling, a government official and the widow of the Chinese revolutionary Sun Yat-sen, cabled the Du Boises with an official invitation from the Chinese national affiliate of the World Peace Council.

Graham Du Bois had never traveled to China. Furthermore, what little she knew of the country was either stereotypical, coming from experiences "in Chinese restaurants or laundries," or from books "written by Westerners or by Chinese who had defected to the West."[22] But her son, David Graham Du Bois, a World War II veteran and activist in the making who went on to become the editor-in-chief of the Black Panther Party's weekly newspaper, had journeyed there in 1950. Attending a conference in Prague that convened student-activists from all over the world, the younger Graham Du Bois was one of two delegates from the Young Progressives of America invited by the Chinese delegation to travel to China at the conference's end. On a train filled with student-leaders from all over the world, he traveled through north and south China for three months, stopping in cities and rural areas to visit factories, schools, and collective farms. At each stop he was enamored by the sheer scale of Chinese people's eagerness to build a "new China": "To see the enthusiasm and the absolute, very highly demonstrated delight of particularly young people at the emergence of the People's Republic of China; you could never question the fact that this was a major change in the life of these young people, and a major change in the life of China. And it was clearly demonstrated by the enormity of the reaction on the part of everywhere we went. . . . Everywhere we went we were overwhelmed with the new China." Having joined the CPUSA just two years prior, he acknowledged that seeing this energy and its impact on the country enabled him to strategize about how communism and "all [he] had learned would be applied in America."[23]

His stepfather too had traveled to China, but decades earlier, in the winter of 1936. Du Bois found the country's citizens ravaged by Japanese occupation and Western exploitation. The racial, ethnic, and class hierarchy that governed Chinese life called to mind his lifelong experiences with U.S. racism. Shanghai, for instance, China's most economically developed city, seemed "both modern and colonial." While foreign governments and corporations reaped immense economic and cultural benefits from the city, making it a cosmopolitan attraction for world travelers, foreign residents, and foreign businesspersons, Chinese residents, most especially the poor, remained at the bottom of the pecking order. "It looked quite like Mississippi," Du Bois reported.[24] Despite defending Japanese imperialism in China as the lesser of two evils (Western imperialism representing the more dominant evil) throughout the

1930s, by the 1940s he had changed his mind. Furthermore, after Japan's defeat in World War II and its being forced to surrender its power in China, Du Bois also denounced the prospect of China being led by a Nationalist Party (GMD) government. GMD, he insisted, was merely a surrogate for the anticommunist, antiworker, exploitative stance of the United States. Calling out the GMD's leadership's repressive, antipopulist tactics, Du Bois wrote: "Chiang Kai-Shek is fighting farmers and laborers in China by calling them communist."[25]

Therefore, it was with enormous glee that Du Bois viewed the GMD's defeat and the establishment of a communist-led China in 1949. Identifying this moment as signaling a larger shift in refiguring America's postwar global order, Du Bois emphasized that waves of revolution were surging throughout Asia. He wrote, "This is a morning when the sunlight is streaming from the East, and I mean the East: China and India and Indonesia."[26] Du Bois furthermore rejected anticommunist denunciations of China, defending Chinese communists' endeavor to build a socialist model unique to the nation's history and culture. In a newspaper column, he implored Americans to support China's right to self-determination, sovereignty, and a government responsive to the needs of its people. He asserted, "It is time that Public Opinion . . . refuse to be stampeded by the silly yell of 'Communist' and try to give the great and long suffering Chinese people a chance to have real voice in their own government."[27] He added that it was this fact, the potential worldwide influence of China's socialist ambitions, that was most politically applicable to U.S. black social struggle and that the U.S. government feared. "White America fears that the example of the Soviet Union and China may tempt the Negroes of America to see the salvation in socialism rather than in the free enterprise of capitalism," he maintained.[28] Du Bois thus concluded that Americans should not underestimate China's revolutionary appeal. Reasoning that the U.S. public had grown too accustomed "to sneering at Asia and insulting her and stealing from her," he cautioned that "[China's] possibilities are enormous. As China grows in power [so will] her influence."[29] It was consequently with these thoughts that Du Bois eagerly anticipated travel to China. "I wanted to re-visit China because it is a land of colored people," he later explained.[30]

Arriving in Beijing by plane on February 14, the Du Boises were aware that by entering China they were violating the State Department's ban on U.S. citizens' travel to China, a law that the department maintained was in place to protect U.S. travelers. Du Bois sarcastically mocked this contention, seeing it as flimsy justification. "Certainly the United States could give me no less protection in China than it could in Mississippi," he joked.[31] Protection was the last thing the pair would require while abroad. Over the course of two months, they were treated as honorary guests of state. They traveled several thousand miles, visiting Shanghai, Chengdu, Hankou, Wuhan, Guangzhou, Chongqing, Nanjing, and Kunming, and were received by Chinese leaders, including Mao Zedong, Zhou Enlai, and Chen Yi, and spent quality time with various members of China's Western expatriate community.

During their stay, the Du Boises took note of the immense development of Chinese industry that had taken place from 1953 to 1957, products of China's First Five-Year Plan, a program modeled after the Soviet Union's mode of economic development. The focus on industrializing and modernizing what many considered a backward economy through investments in heavy industry, and later collective and cooperative farming, demonstrated to Du Bois the economic and social possibilities that could arise when mobilizing the peasantry toward socialism. But what was most remarkable to the Du Boises was the scale and speed of these developments. Throughout the couple's visit they watched the laying of concrete for roads and railways for trains and cable cars, and the construction of factories, buildings, sewer lines, and irrigation pathways.

Years earlier, Du Bois had maintained that the Chinese Communist Revolution represented an important shift in global capitalism. It symbolized "more than freedom for a colony," he remarked. "It marks a new aspect of colonialism." The main fear the United States had of China, he explained, was that Chinese economic growth would overtake U.S. domination of industrial production and world exports. Whereas the colonial nations of the era of old imperialism were unable to produce goods dependent on high-skilled production, China's robust labor force and determination to modernize the nation in a short period of time would enable it to produce goods for export at a far lower cost than other countries. Its production would then become unmatched, where it would be in all countries' best economic interest to purchase Chinese goods. But by replacing U.S. production and capital's monopoly, Chinese manufacturing would force U.S. businesses to lose profit and possibly deindustrialize, a fate the U.S. government and Western capital were working to prevent. Du Bois, moreover, reasoned that what America feared most was the CCP preventing U.S. control of Chinese and East Asian markets; economic access to China was thus essential to preserving America's place as the top economic and geopolitical power. "This new Chinese market could easily be the economic salvation of the western world," he wrote. "It could make it possible for America to be prosperous, with high wages and government subsidized social progress, without depending upon high taxation and growing expenditures for war and war materials."[32]

Du Bois believed that China's rejection of U.S. domination and its projects

FIGURE 1.2: Du Bois with Ghanaian embassy officials, the novelist Mao Dun (third from right), and several Chinese hosts, ca. 1959. W. E. B. Du Bois Papers, Special Collections and University Archives, University of Massachusetts Amherst Libraries.

to induce China's economic advancement could aid decolonial efforts in Africa. As populations vying for independence or in the early stages of self-rule, these groups were facing economic challenges similar to that of China, most especially the difficulty in becoming economically competitive and technically skilled. Du Bois ruled that what Africans lacked in education, technology, and capital could be attained via close relations with China. In a speech to thousands at Peking University, which was also broadcast internationally, Du Bois advised African countries to build close relations with China. "No nation better than China can offer this," he remarked. "China is flesh of your flesh, blood of your blood. China is colored and knows to what a colored skin in this modern world subjects its owner." Sidestepping European and U.S. investment and structuring African economic and social modernization around aid and assistance from the Soviet Union and China could provide Africans with a far more advantageous road to become self-sufficient and preserve their economic and political sovereignty. "Turn from the West," Du Bois closed, "and face the rising sun."[33]

Du Bois's recommendation to build Chinese-African "friendship and sympathy" echoed Mao Zedong's and the Chinese government's foreign policy of establishing youyi (friendship) with African movements.[34] Mao asserted that generating the communist transformation of China required the country to embark on a different sociopolitical and economic journey than that specified within classical Marxism and by the Soviet leadership. Mao believed that China could bypass the period of bourgeois capitalism that Karl Marx and Vladimir Lenin argued was the precedent to socialism. Instead, China would embark first on a new democratic revolution (xin minzhu zhuyi geming). This would begin with a nationalist, patriotic, and united front that would eliminate imperialism and foreign influence from China. This multiclass force would then spur a movement whereby revolutionary parties fostered a coalition between classes as a means to withstand bourgeois democracy's tendencies of divide and rule. By "unit[ing] with the forces of the Left, win[ning] over the middle, and isolat[ing] the rightists," China would then focus on the task of building socialism.[35] Furthermore, through rapid economic modernization and collectivization, particularly of agriculture and light industry, the sectors of labor worked by peasants and the most downtrodden economic classes, China would bypass bourgeois capitalism. These ideas contradicted Marxism-Leninism's tenet that only by experiencing an industrial revolution and the capitalist mode of production and class relations could the oppressed masses forge a revolutionary socialist movement. But as the historian Arif Dirlik notes, Mao's development model and process of socialist revolution was distinctly suited to the underdeveloped context of the Third World. By "recast[ing] Marxism in a global perspective," Mao and the CCP offered similar rural-based developing countries, especially rising African nation-states, with a development model and ideology of Third World Marxism that contrasted with the modernization models put forth in Soviet-centralized socialism and Western capitalism.[36]

To some degree, Du Bois's remarks were a reiteration of his rejection of the classical Marxist-Leninist definition of "the proletariat." From World War I onward he had called attention to the role of colonial labor, imperial conquest, racial formation, and racial citizenship in capitalism's expansion, noting the entanglement of race and racism with class exploitation and class warfare. He thus ruled that many Marxists' identification of the Western industrial (white) working class as the world-historical, anticapitalist subjects of modernity ignored the resistance and radicalism vibrating among "the dark workers of Asia, Africa, the islands of the sea, and South and Central America." Challenging dominant Marxist thinking, Du Bois maintained that it was these nonwhite groups who truly constituted capitalism's greatest opposing force. "It is the rise of these peoples that is the rise of the world," he wrote.[37] In the period leading up to his travel to China, Du Bois reaffirmed this stance. In various statements and writings, he identified rising decolonial and antiracist resistance in Africa, the Americas, and the Caribbean alongside the Bolshevik and Chinese Revolutions. "The struggle of this part of the world," he insisted, "is more than the last battle of the West. It is the third battle of the Rising East. The first was the Russian Revolution. The second was the revolution of China to free yellow labor. The third coming revolution, in black Africa, is to free black labor, and thus to complete Negro emancipation in the United States."[38] Through this genealogy, Du Bois encouraged people of Asian and African descent "to close ranks against" European and U.S. imperialism and cultivate "Pan-Colored" proletariat partnership.[39] "The East" in his proposal thus did not denote a formation uncomplicatedly oppositional to, or representing the direct antipode of, the West. Instead it was a metaphor and comparative example that helped describe the struggle against U.S. globalism and global white supremacy by a world proletariat movement led by the "darker races of the world"—a collective body that came to represent what one scholar has called Du Bois's historical materialist "global model of race."[40]

Still, one drawback of Du Bois's proposal for Chinese-African friendship was that it perpetuated a paternalist framing of Sino-African relations: Africans as under Chinese tutelage. In short, Du Bois's encouragement of Africans to learn from China was an early version of a discourse that became far more prominent during the 1960s and 1970s, when China was frequently depicted as a "shepherd of a flock of African parties."[41] In such claims, African countries and populations were never positioned as having something to offer China in terms of knowledge production, cultural exchange, and geopolitical strategizing. Instead they were positioned merely as the recipients.

Furthermore, Du Bois's celebration of the Chinese economy did not match up evenly with the reality of economic and social upheaval internal to China. The image of China's economy that he and Shirley Graham Du Bois were supplied contrasted with the real economic troubles and social hardship that the country was beginning to experience. Throughout the couple's stay in China they were frequently inundated with *da yue jin*, the Great Leap Forward (GLF), a state-sponsored project that came to describe the first three years of China's Second Five-Year Plan (1958–62). The GLF was an attempt to increase the speed of China's modernization through a model of economic development and political radicalization specific to the Chinese context, one shifting away from the moderately paced road to socialism laid out in the Soviet-influenced policies of China's First Five-Year Plan. Organized around the elimination of private property and the addition of collective ownership of land and machinery, the GLF fused hundreds of thousands of farms into massive, autonomous rural *renmin gongshe* (people's communes) and *nongye hezou she* (agricultural cooperatives) manned by peasants, city workers, intellectuals, and bureaucrats. Mao insisted that such collective labor in agriculture and light industry would enable China to "leap" to socialist modernity.

This, however, was not the case. The GLF ultimately resulted in calamity, mired in food shortages, mismanagement, unproductive labor, corrupted leadership, and imbalanced and exaggerated production expectations. By the early 1960s, the GLF had a dreadful impact on Chinese life, resulting in a famine that led to what some scholars have estimated at anywhere between twenty and forty million deaths.[42] Some of this was a consequence of Mao's directives. Throughout his leadership, he was extremely critical of the growth of an imperial bureaucratic elite and intellectual class not engaged with the everyday struggles of the rural and working-class masses. One consistent strain in his thought was that the rise of an independent China had brought forth new contradictions, the most important of which concerned the state's relationship to civil society. He argued that China's postrevolutionary period had produced a class of bureaucrats reliant upon political graft and disconnected from the project of building socialism and the everyday lives and difficulties of Chinese peasants.

The GLF was built out of Mao's demand that China rapidly transition toward socialism. Mao argued that implementing such a system required both swift economic development and decisive radicalization of consciousness. The GLF was thus one of several state-established national campaigns aimed at reinvigorating the leftist radicalism of the Chinese Communist Revolution and purging the CCP and the nation of conservative elements. Its precursor was the *baihua yundong* (Hundred Flowers Campaign). Spanning from 1956 to 1957, this initiative encouraged nonparty intellectuals to freely express their dissent and criticisms of the government and "let one hundred flowers bloom, let one hundred schools of thought contend."[43] Members of the intelligentsia, a class spurned by both the CCP and Mao, heeded Mao's call for open ideological criticism of the state. In official newspapers, pamphlets, and wall posters, as well as in numerous public meetings, they condemned CCP officials for being corrupted by material advantages and privileges. The intelligentsia asserted that there was an extreme gulf between the party and nonparty professionals and that the former's authoritarianism and centralization of power repressed the pursuit of building a classless society. Mao's outlook in favor of criticism, however, changed drastically once the intelligentsia's denunciations were redirected toward him, various intellectuals calling into question Mao's leadership. Thereafter, Mao remobilized the Hundred Flowers Campaign as an "antirightist" purge of those intellectual dissidents who criticized the government. The regime's critics were no longer identified as agents for transformation and revolution. They were instead perceived as having betrayed the Chinese Communist Revolution's mission by challenging the CCP. Forced to renounce their criticisms and sent to the countryside to labor alongside the peasantry, these people became pawns in Mao's dictums of constant revolution and protracted struggle.

The CCP's control of foreign visits and censorship of viewpoints in opposition to the party's main line prevented many visitors and expatriate residents from learning about this, never mind the GLF's severity. Furthermore, those foreigners with knowledge of the social upheaval's impact, particularly foreign residents of China, added to the culture of disinformation by denying Western media reports of famine in China.[44] Yet it is baffling that as the Du Boises championed the strides being made by the Chinese government, frequently employing GLF terminology, the Chinese public at large was beginning to contend with the real social and economic costs of the GLF. Moreover, Chinese victims of the CCP's antirightist campaign were simultaneously experiencing a containment culture analogous to, if not more severe than, that to which the Du Boises were subjugated in the United States.

★

GENDERED BORDERS AND THE POLITICS OF SEEING

In different mediums, the Du Boises documented their visit to China. Graham Du Bois summed up the trip in several journalistic accounts for the *Pittsburgh Courier* and later in a postmortem biography on Du Bois, whereas Du Bois detailed the trip in his final autobiography. Regarding style and genre, their writings took very different approaches. Graham Du Bois's writings slid between participant ethnography and diary entry, paying close attention to details and commenting often in poetic terms about the sights, sounds, tastes, and smells that surrounded her. Du Bois's account, on the other hand, was more moralist soliloquy. What it lacked in description and detail it made up for in grandiose story line—his multiple visits to China and the CCP's rise to power depicted in epic, *Iliad*-like fashion.

At certain points Du Bois and Graham Du Bois pinpointed similar encounters as novel—witnessing Guangzhou's immeasurable production and export of retail goods, visiting a commune in Chengdu where sixty thousand people labored for the collective good, and meeting members of the Yi minority group in Sichuan province. In addition, they both championed the government's efforts to incorporate into national life China's ethnic minorities (*shaoshu minzu*), fifty-six ethnic groups who for centuries were not universally accepted as ethnically Chinese, a contrast to the dominant Han ethnic group. Both of the Du Boises also noted perceiving a lack of unemployment throughout the country; everyone they encountered appeared "to be at work."[45] Little sights of an informal economy led them to believe that through infusion of formal employment and national pride, the poor were being incorporated into the project of nation building. "There were no signs of want," Graham Du Bois wrote, "no beggars, no gaunt, hollow-eyed children on the streets, no frail young girls who had to sell their bodies to exist."[46] And the couple was continually astonished by everyday people's excitement about China's social and economic transformation. For the couple, the fact that it was these Chinese people—what Du Bois described as "the laboring people, the people who in most lands are the doormats on which the reigning thieves and murdering rulers walk"—who were rebuilding the country was of supreme magnitude. "We saw the planning of a nation and a system of work rising over the entrails of dead empire," Du Bois explained.[47]

But by and large, what distinguished the couple's accounts was how they represented China through gender. Although Du Bois praised the ways the Chinese Communist Revolution was emancipating women from patriarchal rule and oppression, his writings about Chinese communism primarily relied on masculine metaphors and examples. His account began by figuratively distinguishing China of past times to that of his 1959 visit. Reflecting on his travel to China in 1936, he described Shanghai as the "epitome of the racial strife, the economic struggle, the human paradox of modern life. Here was the greatest city of the most populous nation on earth, with the large part of it owned, governed and policed by foreign nations." But according to Du Bois, the China of 1959 was a transformed country, "a miracle land," arming Chinese people with hope and a sustainable system of work and living through rapid advancements in industry, health care, and education. Du Bois further added that this evolution of Chinese life was the result of the Long March leadership of Mao Zedong, Zhou Enlai, Zhu De, and others. For Du Bois, the Long March's culture of peasant radicalism embodied the CCP's rise and served as a metaphor for the historical progress of the nation-state. He wrote, "This monster is a nation with a dark-tinted billion born at the beginning of time, and facing its end. This struggle from starved degradation and murder and suffering to the triumph of that Long March to world leadership. Oh beautiful, patient, self-sacrificing China, despised and unforgettable, victorious and forgiving, crucified and risen from the dead."[48] Du Bois's depiction, however, was pervaded with masculine rhetoric. By frequently establishing the Long March and the Chinese Communist Revolution as movements led and fought for by men, he gendered China's transformation as a male-induced achievement. Such constructions persisted; he described China as an "amorphous mass of men . . . [with] impenetrable will to survive," and Chinese children visiting Tiananmen Square, according to Du Bois, were informed: "Your *fathers* are building new palaces for you."[49] Through this language, Du Bois portrayed China mainly through tropes and attributes of manhood.[50]

By the conclusion of Du Bois's account, Eastern communism was pitted against Western capitalism, a Manichean struggle between good and evil. But in this section, his depiction of China remained explicitly embedded with ideas and arguments about sexuality. Western imperialism was identified as a sexually pathological male culture, incapacitated by lust and exploitation. It was composed of "grafters, whoremongers and gamblers," people with a preponderance to "skimp and save, cheat and steal, gamble and arm for murder." Chinese communism, on the other hand, was framed as sexually composed, its desire restrained in the interest of the people, of the collective good. Whereas "the people" and the "Chinese worker" were presented as synecdoche for the nation-state, it was Chinese women who stood in for the restrained sexuality of the nation. Du Bois remarked, "The women of China are becoming free. They wear pants so that they can walk, climb and dig; and climb and dig they do. They are not dressed simply for sex indulgence or beauty parades."[51] Despite Du Bois's suggestion that Chinese women's physical labor and the covering of their bodies with clothing was producing less sexual objectification and exploitation of women in daily life, he perpetuated a patriarchal reading of women in the aforementioned schema. In his statement, women were framed as people whose clothing, or lack thereof, helped yield in both Western and Eastern contexts either the nation's (i.e., male's) sexual deviancy or its restraint of sexual desire. In the end, control over women's bodies and attire was subtly linked to the progress or failure of the nation-state.

That Du Bois harnessed mild masculine rhetoric and ideology in his representation of Chinese communism does not efface his condemnation of women's oppression and his support for feminist causes throughout his life. But as various black feminist intellectuals have noted about the trajectory of Du Bois's thought and writing, what Du Bois's commentary does relay is the prominent role masculinism played within his political arguments and theoretical models of race and radical internationalism.[52] Du Bois's representation of Chinese communism was thus gender specific, denoting male activity, male knowledge, and a geopolitics as a site of male struggle. While this comes through via his language, it was also expressed through his failure to imagine and represent Chinese women as leaders and equal participants in China's revolution and reconstruction. In his account, Chinese women were barely implicated in the country's development; they only had agency in relation to the changed sexual mores of the country, and even in his description this is not of their own individual merit and collective doing but rather the proletarian culture instituted by the CCP. Chinese women were thus made to remain outside of Chinese history and Chinese communism. Having barely made mention of them throughout the bulk of his account, they were only included in his final paragraph, portrayed as mothers, workers, and professionals gaining greater access to employment and government leadership—but always on male terms and male standards. Nowhere were they represented through their words, their own definitions of communism, their own agency in uplifting China from imperialism and capitalist exploitation.

In contrast, Graham Du Bois's various accounts reflected her feminist sensibility. In her writings women were prominently featured, their voices, agency, and history, to some extent, made audible. In one of her accounts, the first person readers were introduced to was the minister of public health, Li Dequan, also chairperson of the Red Cross Society and the first woman to become a full minister in the newly established government. Li was a champion of women's and children's rights, establishing more than fifteen primary schools that offered free admission to women and girls from poor families and to the children of peasants. As a leader of several women's organizations and organizations committed to protecting children's welfare, she actively challenged conservative Chinese perspectives about women's rights, maintaining that the struggle to upend patriarchy had to be perceived as a crucial feature of all national liberation movements.[53] From Li, Graham Du Bois learned about China's health clinics and the role of doctors in educating Chinese publics about family planning and birth control. Graham Du Bois was also impressed with the minister of justice, Shi Liang, the second woman to be selected as a full minister in the PRC government. One of the first women to be admitted to the Shanghai bar and to practice law, Liang primarily specialized in marriage cases and representing political prisoners. It was her commitment to justice that drew her into the wings of the CCP, where she ultimately became a leader in the All China Women's Federation and later the head of the PRC's legal-affairs and judicial branch.[54]

Graham Du Bois also highlighted the elderly women inside the Forbidden City in Beijing. Their physical bodies and movements immediately struck her. These women were victims of the mutilating practice of *chanzu*, China's custom of tightly binding young girls' feet to prevent growth. They "hobbled around the courtyards," Graham Du Bois remarked, "hobbled because their feet had been bound and, after years of torture, were permanently crippled." For Graham Du Bois, these women's bodies displayed the physical and psychological violence Chinese women experienced at the hands of patriarchy. Here, Graham Du Bois implicated Chinese society in these patriarchal conditions. Chinese women's treatment was not just a product of imperialism; it was also the result of China's own oppressive gender relations and inhumane treatment of women. Graham Du Bois could not help but watch though as these women moved at a snail's pace, "peer[ing] at the wonders of ancient China which had been denied them" by class and gender oppression. Despite physical disability and trauma, these women still demonstrated a compelling resolve, traveling to Beijing to obtain a glimpse of China's social transformation. "These old women wanted to see for themselves," Graham Du Bois noted.[55]

Meeting women who worked in various branches of government, labor, and education convinced Graham Du Bois that China was on a rapid pace toward the elimination of gender oppression and toward the social sufficiency of all citizens. She concluded, "Chinese women today are, in my opinion, more the equal of men than in any country I know. . . . In China this equality is neither a courteous gesture nor an issue to be debated. Chinese women are sharing on every level in building New China."[56] Graham Du Bois's celebration of these changes did not prevent her from acknowledging the reality that the majority of Chinese women, and moreover Chinese people in general, were still living in abject poverty. Traveling from Wuhan to Chongqing by boat along the Yangtze River, the families and workers she saw living and laboring in the countryside were a reminder of the long road China had ahead of it in modernizing the country and improving the material conditions of these people's lives. Describing the journey, she wrote: "We were meeting crowded junks, sampans and sailboats. . . . Along a footpath walked peasants carrying baskets hanging from poles from their shoulders. . . . Evidently it was an arduous task. Here was old China again."[57]

Still, observing these people's destitute lives did not dissuade Graham Du Bois from being hopeful about China's future. China's potential was best demonstrated to her by the self-sacrificing commitment and service of the Du Boises' interpreter, a female teacher and translator named Bei Guangli.[58] Near the end of the couple's journey, Bei informed them that after completing her duties as their interpreter, she wanted to participate in the erection of the People's Hall of Congress in Beijing, which at that time was in early stages of construction. Bei explained, "It doesn't matter what job they give me. I want to be able to tell my children that I myself, with my own hands, helped put up our Hall of Congress. . . . I'll have special reason to be proud." Shocked to hear the ambitions conveyed by this slight woman, "with her dainty hands and feet," Graham Du Bois concluded that Bei's political consciousness was emblematic of the country. "Bei Guangli is China," she reckoned.[59] Like Du Bois, Graham Du Bois exoticized aspects of these encounters, likening Du Bois's nurse to a Chinese doll and the countryside landscape to silk-screen art prints. But through Graham Du Bois's explicit and detailed attention to women's experiences and female voices, China was characterized as a country of profound female political agency and sacrifice, a model that should be implemented in the United States.

FIGURE 1.3: Graham Du Bois talking with children at a workers' community center in Kunming, in the Yunnan province, 1959. W. E. B. Du Bois Papers, Special Collections and University Archives, University of Massachusetts Amherst Libraries.

It should be pointed out that, retrospectively, what is also conveyed in Graham Du Bois's and Du Bois's accounts are some of the tactics through which the Chinese government staged and showcased China's uplift for foreign eyes and how such activities worked to engender positive impressions from foreign visitors. For instance, the Du Boises' travels were chaperoned by Tang Mingzhao, head of the Chinese People's Committee for Defending World Peace (*Zhongguo renmin baowei shijie heping dahui*; commonly referred to as the China Peace Committee), and director of the Department for Liaison with English Speaking Countries.[60] Four others joined him in supervising the Du Boises' visit: Ding Xilin and Zhu Boshen, two leading officials of the Chinese People's Association for Cultural Relations/Friendship with Foreign Countries (*Zhongguo renmin duiwai wenhua xiehui*); the interpreter Bei Guangli; and Wang Huifang, a nurse assigned to aid Du Bois and monitor his health.[61] The goal of this group was to provide the Du Boises with an exceptionally idealized depiction of Chinese life and politics. Thus, every moment of the couple's tours was scripted and preplanned. Led around and trailed at all times by government-assigned guides and handlers, guests of state like the Du Boises were generally only allowed to engage with people, institutions, and societal realities preapproved by the government, of course with some exceptions (Graham Du Bois's consideration of the impact of *chanzu* on Chinese women, for instance, being one example). Nonetheless, foreign visitors like the Du Boises were offered few, if any, opportunities for informal contact and chance conversations.

This careful orchestration of foreign guests' movements and encounters was a chief tactic of Chinese foreign policy.[62] The Chinese government frequently invited and hosted foreign activists and intellectuals who were critical of the United States and who appeared to be receptive to China. They believed that if these travelers had positive hands-on experiences in China, they would return to their homelands lauding the PRC and advocating on its behalf through media, public speaking, and criticism of U.S. policy. "Visitors were selected for their credibility and their favorable attitude toward Beijing," the political scientist Ann-Marie Brady explains. "A visit to see new China was not meant to be an exchange of ideas: the visitors' role was to learn and admire, and if possible write favorable reports which could be used in China and the West."[63] These tours and the various rallies, day trips, and public demonstrations that foreign visitors were taken to were carefully planned spectacles designed to engender positive impressions. With itineraries preapproved by government officials, foreign travel groups' days were jam-packed with events and visits that were performative in nature. Attending rallies and visiting communes, factories, schools, and large-scale infrastructure projects conveyed that China was experiencing modernization and demonstrated the aura of Chinese communism. By simulating experiences that felt distinctive, unforced, intimate, and enriching, the tours ultimately shielded foreigners from aspects of Chinese life that contradicted the government's position. Such practices of "selective exposure and display" manipulated "the mystique of personal experience and the belief in the superiority of being-on-the-spot."[64]

These ritualized demonstrations for foreign activists and intellectuals also took on central importance in the CCP's project of unifying the nation and indoctrinating Chinese citizens with the revolutionary ideas and leadership of Chairman Mao and the party. Depicting China as the exceptional leader of a world struggle enabled the Chinese government to instill in the Chinese masses the need to play their part as workers in constructing a new China and be representatives of the nation in their daily labor and in their encounters with foreigners. The historian Chen Jian explains, "A revolutionary foreign policy helped to make Mao's various state and societal transformation projects powerful *unifying* and *national* themes supplanting many local, regional, or factional concerns."[65]

Linking China to foreign movements and hosting foreign visitors thus helped mobilize Chinese citizens around the CCP's platform, everyday Chinese citizens being positioned as having an important role to play in China's diplomatic outreach to foreign publics and expanding the country's influence abroad.[66] And the Du Boises' accounts offer an intriguing portal to this spectacle of nation making—various Chinese people tasked with representing and performing the nation for foreign eyes and ears. Through labor, politeness, affirmation of the CCP's central line, and patriotism, people such as Bei Guangli stood in for the nation, supplying the Du Boises with a rewarding, though uncomplicated, image of nationalism and communist success.

Whether or not the Du Boises deeply questioned these features of their travel is unknown. Graham Du Bois implied some skepticism. Referring to the couple's team of chaperones, she described each of them using a particular title or signifier of their purported duties, titles that the couple most likely didn't come up with on their own but that were relayed to them by Chinese officials or by Bei Guangli, their interpreter. According to Graham Du Bois, Tang Mingzhao was the "manager," whereas the others were "advisors" and "special attendants."[67] She used quotes around each of these titles, which might be construed as betraying certain suspicions she held of her chaperones' true duties. But other than this example, conflicts and contradictions internal to China were, to a large extent, unexplored by the Du Boises in their writings, and, moreover, were relentlessly misrepresented to the couple throughout their visit.

The most blatant example of such misrepresentation was Chinese explanations regarding the Tibet rebellion, a popular revolt that erupted during the second month of the Du Boises' visit. Anti-Chinese and anticommunist sentiment became violent in Lhasa, Tibet's capital, in March 1959, after nearly a decade of strained relations between the PRC and Tibet. From 1911, the year of China's successful republican revolution and elimination of the Chinese monarchial system, until the CCP's 1949 defeat of the GMD, Tibet had operated as a de facto independent polity. However, with the establishment of PRC, the CCP rejected Tibet's claims of being an independent nation-state and countered that Tibet remained a part of China. Ultimately, in the view of the CCP, Tibet's location made it a geographical buffer between India, Nepal, and Bhutan; Tibet was consequently perceived as just as valuable as, if not more than, Taiwan in protecting China from foreign incursion. In October 1950, People's Liberation Army (PLA) troops attacked Tibet, first seizing Chamdo/Qamdo (officially Chengguan). Incapable of repelling the PLA, Tibet's feudal theocratic government had little choice but to concede, agreeing to Chengguan's status as Chinese territory. However, CCP and PLA presence in Tibet over the course of the 1950s and rising inflation and food costs were met with fury by Tibetans, numbers of whom formed the Four Rivers and Six Ranges guerrilla group, a CIA-trained force that initiated an armed rebellion against Chinese rule.[68] Come 1959, this Tibetan anger erupted after rumor spread that the CCP had concocted a plan to kidnap and arrest the Dalai Lama, Tibet's paramount spiritual leader and de facto head of state. Tibetans demonstrated and attacked PLA soldiers, Tibetans of Han ethnicity, and Tibetans who sided with the PRC government.[69]

To the Du Boises, this armed resistance was portrayed as a minor conflict motivated by and generally composed of upper-class, landholding Tibetan elites. This claim deliberately disregarded the revolt's multiclass composition and the reality that it represented a popular Tibetan rejection of the PRC's claims to Tibet. But by framing the rebellion as being waged by reactionary elites frustrated with the CCP's efforts to create an equitable socialist society, the Chinese government appeared justified in its speedy suppression of the rebellion. In any case, the complexity of the rebellion was not relayed to the Du Boises. Graham Du Bois referenced the rebellion, yet refrained from taking a position on it. Du Bois on other hand defended China's claims over Tibet, insisting that "Tibet has belonged to China for centuries."[70] That the couple lacked an understanding of the ethnic divides and disputes that fueled Tibetan rejection of Chinese rule and Tibetan demands for independence is evident. For the Tibetan rebels, China represented an alien force that was encroaching on Tibetan self-determination and sovereignty. The couple's unawareness of the anticolonial features of Tibetans' struggles was thus a product of their own ignorance and, moreover, indication of their handlers' success in presenting a heroic depiction of China.

After returning to the United States, Du Bois wrote that "China is no utopia" and conceded that he "did not see everything" and "may have been in part deceived." But he also defended his perceptions as based on on-the-ground experiences. He additionally pointed out that his encounters challenged the anti-China reporting of Western reporters who had never even visited the country. "The truth is there," he claimed. "*I saw it*."[71] Graham Du Bois defended her account of the couple's visit with similar language. She asserted, "I shall not here attempt to pass judgment but only record something of *what we saw*."[72] The couple's descriptions of their travel were thus presented, in some measure, as eyewitness accounts, reports suffuse with claims about sight and objectivity. In effect, the Du Boises singled out their eyes, and, correspondingly, their writings, as direct, untampered-with portals to what they encountered and experienced abroad.

Numerous scholars have unraveled the power of discourses of objectivity and sight in intellectual production and cultural representation. At the heart of these scholars' critiques is deconstruction of the notion of cultural representation as a mirror, replica, and "re-presentation" of what a person sees or experiences. The act of representation, it has been argued, is no mere indicator of objective truth. Mary Louise Pratt, for example, considers these issues within Western travel writing and travel narratives. Pratt asserts that these genres of literary representation were an essential element of European continental and national identities, simultaneously informing European understandings of both Europe and non-Europeans and legitimizing Western ways of knowing and organizing the world. Through tropes of discovery and vision, European travel writers framed their depictions of "the foreign" as heroic, observant, and objective—merely conveying an unbiased and trouble-free account of the geographical spaces and peoples that the writer and traveler witnessed and encountered abroad. The travel writer's *politics of seeing* was thus organized around demonstrating the "cultural authority to represent, to depict, or recreate what he sees." Pratt continues, "The act of discovery itself . . . consisted of what in European culture counts as a purely passive experience—that of seeing." But Pratt maintains that such cultural representations and politics of seeing are not passive and evidence of empirical truth, but rather always constructed, always tied to efforts to control the definition of both Europe and non-European worlds. Imperial practices of representing "the foreign" were therefore dependent on "the relation of mastery predicated between the seer and the seen," where the travel narrator (the seer) was singled out as "both the viewer to judge and appreciate it [the seen], and the verbal painter who produces it for others." Imperial travel writing (and later Western journalism and other genres of media and representation) ideologically relied on legitimizing the idea that the seer "sees all there is."[73] Nonetheless, as Pratt points out, such inscription of the foreign rests on unequal power dynamics between reporter and reported, narrator and narrated, and seer and seen; Franny Nudelman similarly explains, "to judge, compare, report back . . . belie an imperialist's sense of superiority."[74]

While the Du Boises' representation of China did not hint of such blatant imperialist objectivism, I do think it important to trouble the couple's accounts, specifically regarding their defense of what they "saw." For the couple, lauding China in journalistic and biographical writings provided a mode to mediate between their perceptions of China and their valuation of what these perceptions might mean to others. It was a modality of their radical imaginaries, a practice in the Du Boises' efforts to create transnational political connections between black Americans and China. But the couple's representations were steeped in a credulous "politics of seeing," one that gave little attention to questioning, identifying, and reconciling the inconsistencies of PRC-sponsored visits by foreigners.

★

THE COLOR OF ASIA

The misunderstandings, misperceptions, and contradictions of international travel were not subjects foreign to Du Bois. Considering how imperial governments employed diplomatic visits and tourism as modes to mask their nations' true realities of domination and exploitation, he once pointed out: "Empires do not want nosy busybodies snooping into their territories and business. Visitors to colonies are, to be sure, allowed and even encouraged; but their tours are arranged, officials guide them in space and in thought, and they usually see what the colonial powers want them to see and little more."[75] Du Bois's point, of the different techniques and narratives that states employ to shape foreign visitors' perceptions, offers a more nuanced consideration of the politics of international travel during the Cold War than that which he and Graham Du Bois tendered after their travel to China.

Likewise, in the historical novel *Worlds of Color*, a book that Du Bois completed just prior to leaving for China, he fruitfully mulled over this same dilemma. In a chapter titled "The Color of Asia," in particular, Du Bois attended to the prohibitive features, limited politics of seeing, and tendency to collapse self and Other that sometimes constitute international travel experiences and efforts to imagine and represent transnational coalition. Published by the Marxist-Leninist journal *Masses & Mainstream* in 1961, *Worlds of Color*, what one scholar describes as Du Bois's "low-budget mass-media broadcast," was the closing text of the *Black Flame Trilogy*, a three-volume narrative centered on the life of a Southern educator, Manuel Mansart.[76] The trilogy surveys Mansart's evolution from racial compromiser and integrationist to political dissident and global citizen of color. Sprinkled throughout these texts are historical events and symbolic moments from Du Bois's life, elements that give the novel some verisimilitude.[77] Past experiences and writings are curated into three historical novels that seem to be concerned with figuratively revisiting symbolic themes and contradictions from the U.S. social struggle, as well as from Du Bois's own history of political activism and intellectualism.

Worlds of Color covers the final twenty years of Mansart's life (1936–56), examining Mansart; Jean Du Bignon, his confidante and future spouse; and other characters' journeys toward a leftist political disposition. Mansart begins the novel as a sixty-year-old college president, well respected among his peers, and aided in thought, work, and life by Du Bignon, his personal secretary. Following the suggestion of colleagues, he takes a sabbatical and embarks on a trip around the world, hoping to broaden his narrow understanding of labor exploitation, colonialism, and global politics. Du Bignon later makes her own journey to several non-U.S. locations and experiences a growth in her political perspective. The novel then follows as the two of them, along with Mansart's adult children, develop global awareness and an anticapitalist stance amid the ideological shortcomings of the black American antiracist movement and the political repression and containment ethos of Cold War U.S. liberalism.

Mansart's Wanderjahr leads him on a journey through Europe, the Soviet Union, Japan, and China. At the heart of this plotline is his ideological evolution toward a global understanding of the "Negro Problem." The author explains that for Mansart, "the 'color line' was principally a matter of admission to street cars, trains, schools, and restaurants. Of an equality higher and broader than this, involving economic equality, he had not given much thought."[78] However, traveling abroad reveals his narrow understanding of racial inequality: "All the old certainties were gone—all that neat little world. . . . What now was this thing called the 'Negro Problem' at which all his life he had been working?" (1). Clued into his simplification of the global depths of racial and class oppression, Mansart has no choice but to consider the connections between U.S. racism and the injustice experienced by groups outside the United States and the shortcomings of antiracist politics centered merely around racial integration. Du Bois writes, "[Mansart] began to have a conception of the world as one unified dwelling place. He was escaping from his racial provincialism. He began to think of himself as part of humanity and not simply as an American Negro over against the white world" (53).[79]

Building on a similar dialectic as that conveyed in Du Bois's 1925 essay of the same name, *Worlds of Color* frames travel as a praxis that facilitates heightened, critical consciousness.[80] Travel is represented as ideological and political, never neutral. It is depicted as always entrenched in viewing the world from positions of power and standpoints of dominance, exploitation, inequality, and resistance. Travel is also portrayed as a methodology for interrogating the structural forces and relations of power that organize different places and which shape travelers' particular preconceptions, perceptions, and assessments of these places. But travel is also depicted as capable of challenging the demand for national allegiance and instead inducing the birth of new cultural subjectivities and alternative forms of citizenship and community. "Travel becomes the other of [U.S.] expansionism," Kate Baldwin explains about both Du Bois's writings and political practice. As a mode of movement and trope for critical politics, Du Bois's concept of travel therefore encourages theorization and identification "across specific national borders as [means for] internationalist counters to Americanization."[81]

Alongside the conceptual importance of travel, the metaphor of color helps to differentiate and connect the distinct realities of racial and economic oppression that Mansart and Du Bignon encounter while abroad. The novel's first five chapters are titled "The American Negro's World," "The Color of England," "The Color of Europe," "The Color of Asia," and "Color in the West Indies." Within this chapter-by-chapter structure is a formation of the global landscape of empire, a shaping of the world and the relations forged by capitalist accumulation and white supremacy.

But even more important is that through this narrative arc, Du Bois tenders what James Clifford has identified as the "possibility of 'travelling East'": an alternative "root and route" of consciousness and subjectivity than that which characterizes dominant Western discourses of political modernity.[82] Worlds of Color thus commences with each of the protagonists yearning to redefine their cultural citizenship, politics, and relationship to the world in terms and practices neither constricted nor bound by Western elitism, the reign of the marketplace, and white supremacy. Over the course of the novel, Mansart, Du Bignon, and other characters embark on their own personal long march, journeys metaphorically akin to that treaded by the CCP. As these characters become more radicalized in their political thought and criticisms of Euro-American imperialism, militarism, labor exploitation, and racial injustice, these same people also endure turmoil, harassment, and hardship. In the end they are not triumphant or revered within their society. These people are rather increasingly regulated, marginalized, and isolated by U.S. containment culture. Traveling east consequently embodies these characters' byways toward rethinking what it means to be black, American, and global citizens of a leftist ideological bent, as well as the struggles these people face due to their unwillingness to abide by America's racial, economic, and political status quo.[83]

Throughout Mansart's international travel, each sojourn offers conflicting ideas and points of self-reflection, China most strikingly. There, he is astonished with the magnitude of Chinese people's historical struggle, which in his view easily displaces that of the Western world. This realization compels him to rethink "where the population of the world really centers." After admitting that "never before has a land so affected" him, he concludes: "China is inconceivable. . . . China . . . is incomprehensible." In this place he has "missed the whole meaning of a people." "Any attempt to explain the world without giving China a place of extraordinary prominence, is futile," he remarks. "Perhaps the riddle of the universe will be settled in China" (39).

At certain points, Mansart's descriptions replicate Western representations of China, particularly Europe's inscription of Asia as feminine. The cultural theorist Edward Said has detailed how Asia was represented in the European modern imagination as its contrasting image and spatiotemporal and ontological Other. Racist and demeaning images of Asia were frequently rendered through "metaphors of depth, secrecy, and sexual promise" that rationalized Europe's domination of Asia through the narrative of sexual encounter—the masculine West possessing the feminine East. "The Orient was routinely described as feminine, its riches as fertile, its main symbols the sensual woman, the harem and the despotic—but curiously attractive—ruler," Said wrote.[84] Mansart, to a lesser degree, frames China through such metaphors. The country is "pregnant with history," he states after arriving in Beijing, going on to describe China at later points through similar coded language (39).

But what also becomes clear is that the representation of China in this section of the novel is not aimed at supplanting Europe's demeaning representation of China with a more optimistic depiction, or with a narrative where China is easily integrated into black American internationalist understandings. It's rather the opposite. China helps bring into focus and trouble the standpoint and frameworks through which Mansart perceives and deciphers African American–Chinese cultural exchange and solidarity.

For one, Mansart's tentativeness in inscribing China with particular meanings—"China is inconceivable. . . . China . . . is incomprehensible"—enables him to aesthetically disarticulate imperialist travel narratives of discovery and objectivity, as well as the libidinal discourse of mastery and possession expressed in Said's formulation of Orientalism. In Mansart's commentary, China is depicted as incapable of being entirely grasped, comprehended, or inscribed. The epigraph by Du Bois articulates Mansart's view. He relates that "what little" Mansart knows about China is "mostly distortion," and admits that even "through that false fog" of Orientalist discourses Mansart sees "little even when he stood with open eyes" (42). Yet it is Mansart's willingness to face his own blurred and impaired view and his acknowledgment of his short-sightedness that enable Mansart to take on what Édouard Glissant describes as a *relational identity*: an identity "linked not to a creation of the world but to the conscious and contradictory experience of contacts among cultures." Mansart's voyage demonstrates that to represent what travelers see, as well as what they didn't see and in fact *how* they see—through what dispositions—was always a selective, contradictory, and prohibitive enterprise. He consequently identifies China and other locations, in Glissant word's, "as a place where one gives-on-and-with rather than grasps."[85]

These themes pervade Mansart's train ride through northern China.[86] As he travels in a U.S.-made Pullman railroad car from Moscow into Manchuria, Mansart's memories of labor, race relations, and technology are countered by newfangled encounters with Asia. On the train he is reminded of black porters who serve and cater to whites inside railroad cars in the United States. Mansart at that moment realizes that the train he is riding in is not segregated by race. He subsequently feels aware of "a new world," one where "color was nothing unusual" (39). His romanticism ties into the broader culture of mid-twentieth century Western reflections about train travel in communist China. Discussing Western travelers' descriptions of visits to China, the political scientist Paul Hollander notes that "the fascination with trains was especially noticeable among American travelers." For these travelers China's steam locomotives represented the introduction of modernity to a humble population not yet corrupted by the greed and selfishness of Western life. Chinese trains, Hollander concludes, were therefore viewed with "an almost pre-industrial nostalgia."[87] Be that as it may, Western evaluations of Chinese trains reinforced a Euro-American model of socioeconomic development, the notion being that the influx of Western technology and knowledge was modernizing Chinese people away from their pastoral history and toward economic and social progress.

Mansart, in contrast, does not value the train within the framework of Western development. It is not perceived as a mechanical device that will haul Chinese people into the future. Instead, the lure of the train resides in its subversion of racial hierarchy. In this confined physical space Mansart experiences egalitarianism nonexistent within his homeland, an encouraging treatment of racial difference that has not yet been made manifest within the United States. Cultural theorist Paul Gilroy has briefly pointed to "the chronotope of the train" in Du Bois's writings, explaining how it works as a figurative site for "the exploration of new territories and the cultural differences that exist between and within groups called races."[88] Mansart's experience definitely corresponds with this explanation, the train portrayed as taking on a racial hue and as a point for contemplation and cultural awareness. How Mansart experiences the train then inverts, while not transcending, the fetishism of the train exhibited by Hollander's subjects. While Hollander asserts that foreigners perceive the train—that is, Western culture—as transporting China toward modernity, Mansart suggests that it is China that should be transporting the West.

This moment, however, illuminates the misperceptions and selective perceptions that encompass experiences of travel. Mansart's racial imaginary of the train ignores the presence of Japanese empire. While he champions the train as a space of racial egalitarianism, outside the train's windows sits Manchuria, a region of China incapacitated by Japanese imperialism and subject to a racial, class, and gender hierarchy that adversely impacts Chinese people.[89] In addition, Mansart seems to overstate the tolerance of the train environment. He, for example, says nothing about the other forms of segregation that were practiced and mapped onto Chinese passenger locomotives, such as how people's class background impacted what seats they could purchase and who they could interact with; class distinction could be discerned within the train's specific classes of seats: hard seat (*yingzuo*) versus soft seat (*ruanzuo*), hard sleeper (*yingwo*) versus soft sleeper (*ruanwo*). This is one instance in the novel where Eastern passage signifies the contradictions and misunderstandings of international travel and transnational affiliation.

Such symbolism continues in Manchuria. When Mansart's train enters a war-zone territory, the passengers are instructed to pull down the curtains on their windows or face punishment. Mansart complies with the order and for a period of time is prevented from viewing the terrain. It is odd that Mansart neither reflects nor says a great deal about this directive, his acquiescence, or his inability to view outside the train. "I wanted to look out," he remarks, however he tersely confirms: "I did not look out" (39). Here, Du Bois's aesthetic use of the train again contrasts with the descriptions of trains supplied by other Western travelers of that time. Hollander asserts that for many Western intellectuals, another novelty of Chinese trains were the windows, which offered travelers a view to observe China's agrarian countryside. "The poetic qualities of the countryside were especially hard to resist," he explains, where trains became means to witness the countryside's serenity and the evolution of "mellow landscapes, gentle people."[90] Du Bois's depiction of the train window undermines this structure. The window is depicted not as a site for seeing and gaining open access to truth or unmediated images of Chinese life but rather as a site of power and regulation. The window insulates and prohibits travelers from contact and perception of images and realities that might reveal inconsistency and flaw. The closing of the window curtains and Mansart's compliance in not looking encapsulate the ungraspable, regulated, and complicit features of many travel encounters.

Besides emphasizing the different techniques of state coercion and regulation present within his travel, this train scene showcases how Mansart's desire to locate racial connections makes him, at times, oblivious to cultural difference and to his own reductive tendencies. These themes resonate later in Shanghai, when Mansart witnesses a racist act against a group of Chinese children. Angry and astonished, Mansart challenges a group of Chinese businessmen and intellectuals to justify how such practices can occur without any recourse in a nation where Chinese outnumber foreigners. He alleges, "The whites here treat the Chinese just as we Negroes are treated in the Southern United States. . . . The white foreigners rule your city, force your children into separate schools and in general act as though they owned China and the Chinese. Why do you permit this?" The Chinese intellectuals provide clarity to his question. They respond that improving China's education system and abolishing racial and class discrimination cannot occur without first eliminating the influence and power of foreign capital. One man explains, "The chief difficulty is industrial. . . . That is a start. But of course only a beginning, so long as industry is monopolized by outsiders. They own the factories and ships" (41).

This discussion ultimately demonstrates to Mansart "how abysmally ignorant he was of China and her history" (40). But while this scene again reveals Mansart's (and Du Bois's) idealized figuration of China as a woman, it also offers a subtle lesson. Here, Mansart ashamedly becomes conscious of how he is transferring "the Negro Problem"—a narrative that he himself repudiates for its lack of nuance and compassion and its essentialist features—into the Chinese context. Du Bois writes of Mansart: "When he asked why they submitted to the West, there was a sensible pause. . . . Mansart remembered how often he had sat in similar quandary when well-meaning strangers had stripped his soul bare in public and blandly asked him why and how and what" (40). This comment brings to a mind the opening lines of *The Souls of Black Folk*, where Du Bois asserts: "Between me and the other world there is ever an unasked question. . . . How does it feel to be a problem? I answer seldom a word."[91] In both of these statements, Du Bois dismisses conventional discourses of the "Negro Problem" as reductive. Therefore, to juxtapose Mansart's narrow understanding of China's struggles to these statements, what becomes clear is that Mansart's conversation with the Chinese intellectuals offers him a situation to become aware of and acknowledge his own reductionism, his own collapse into essentialism and Orientalism. By framing China's struggle simply through the U.S. narrative of civil rights and racial discrimination, Mansart downplays the complexity of China's political struggles and projects a limited understanding of imperialism and racial capitalism. The East may be black, but not through the paradigm that Mansart proposes.

In these encounters and exchanges, China is displayed as an object of Mansart's desire, his wish for transnational affiliation and mutuality. But Mansart's construction of internationalism is hindered by his reliance on a U.S. racial narrative—U.S. racial oppression and segregation remain at the center of his global imaginary. Chinese anti-imperialism consequently remains misconstrued and misperceived within his U.S.-centric scope, bound by the conceptual parameters of U.S. racial history. The two scenes—Mansart on the train and Mansart speaking with the intellectuals—thus work in tandem to demonstrate some of the ineluctable challenges of foreign travel and articulating transnational and transracial connection. In these sections, the inconsistencies of Mansart's (and potentially Du Bois's own) inscription of Chinese political struggle are subtly made evident. In so doing, Du Bois conveys the downside in flattening out the plurality of Euro-American imperialism and white supremacy—the drawbacks when it is constantly framed in unifying language, rather than as forces that operate unevenly in diverse contexts and disparate historical moments. Mansart therefore exhibits black-radical internationalism and Afro-Asian solidarity as, respectively, an ideology and political formation with serious limitations, whose potential can always be shortened by prohibitive strategies, coercion, and illusions, as well as by the national, racial, class, and gender subject positions and worldviews of its agents—traits that also undermined the Du Boises' evaluations of Chinese Communism during their 1959 trip.

Yet readers of *Worlds of Color* also obtain an example of how unpacking a national discourse within an international context and taking account of one's subject position (the processes, structures, and ideologies that have produced them as subjects) can illuminate important lessons about global hierarchies of power and multiaxial relations of inequality and domination. Mansart becomes self-aware of the poverty of his radical imagination. He discovers that compressing Chinese and African American political struggle into a unitary and identical historical narrative fails to consider and address the specificity of both black and Chinese people's lives and struggles. While the two histories should not be perceived as untouched and disconnected from other political movements and histories, it is nonetheless essential to pay close attention to their differences. In recognizing the error in his ways, Mansart is able to forgo what the feminist intellectual Chandra Talpade Mohanty describes as a "politics of transcendence"—that is, a universalist imaginary of anti-imperialist resistance. Instead, he opts for a "politics of engagement," one interested in building relations through acknowledgment of the boundaries and differences that both connect and distinguish struggles and people from one another.[92] Here, Mansart discovers that similar to the U.S. black struggle, the complexity and texture of Chinese subjugation and anti-imperialist activism cannot be absolutely summed up or translated, especially not in the simple terms and national discourses with which he understands U.S. social conflict and Euro-American empire. Consequently, in this moment Mansart enacts a *symbolic identification* with the Chinese intellectuals with whom he speaks, what Slavoj Žižek defines as when "we identify ourselves with the other precisely at a point at which he is inimitable, at the point which eludes resemblance."[93] From this standpoint, it is only when China and the imperial challenges and diverse oppressions that the country endures evade easy representation and imagining that Mansart identifies with the Chinese intellectuals in a meaningful way.[94]

Worlds of Color consequently oscillates around a desire for union with the world and Afro-Asian solidarity, albeit on very different terms than Mansart's original aspirations. Toward the end of the novel, in a heated discussion, Mansart explains that when abroad he became more conscious of his national and racial subject position and the underlying frameworks that constitute it. This recognition enabled him to better identify how such ideology structured and occluded his comprehension of the complexity of non-American racialized subjects' struggles. "Not since I girdled the globe, not since I conceived of One World instead of increasing congeries of new peoples and nations, infinitely dividing and subdividing until nationalism becomes a virulent cancer that threatens to kill humanity," he explains, did "I realize that unity in variety is the true end of this world and also I can see that the world is ripe or ripening for such union" (210). "Unity in variety," Mansart's schematic formation of cross-cultural coalition, seems to infer a transhistorical model of cultural pluralism. But by the novel's endpoint the phrase embodies a network of interacting communities and peoples who are tied by difference and struggle against racial capitalism rather than by sameness and liberalism.[95]

It is safe to assume that Du Bois's travel to China in 1959 provided him with similar visions, and hope that China's anti-imperialist project might dynamically shape the global landscape. China offered him a stirring example to prophesize the socialist transformation of the world and blacks' radicalization in opposition to Cold War liberalism and U.S. globalism. The Du Boises returned to China in 1962 and again marveled about the developments altering the country. Graham Du Bois often remarked that her husband was reborn during these trips, his conviction in the possibilities of radical democracy reinvigorated. "Du Bois found truth in the People's Republic of China," she stated. "The light came out of the red sun rising in the east, and he saw that the world and all its abundance not only belongs to the people, but that the people shall claim and hold it for their own. Here in China was the proof!"[96]

Graham Du Bois also found truth in this country of near 700 million people. She went on to cultivate her own ties with the Chinese government and its project of global revolution throughout the 1960s and 1970s. Still, her and Du Bois's reflections and representations of their travel to China offer instructive entry to some of the challenges incurred by black radical travelers attempting to carve out racial solidarity and representations of China that countered its dominant portrayal in Western media and U.S. popular culture. Similar limitations were present in the articulations and representations of others who traveled and lived in China—they too influenced and at times blinded by their adamant rejection of America foreign policy and their positive impressions of Chinese communism and Third World internationalism. Like Du Bois, their criticisms of U.S. empire and fascination with decolonial, anti-imperialist movements were also laced with ideologies of gender and desires for Asian-African solidarity.

Even so, these issues don't outweigh the symbolic identifications that the Du Boises' journey to China stimulated. Days after Du Bois's death in August of 1963, Mao cabled his condolences. "Du Bois [is] a great man of our time," Mao remarked. "His deeds of heroic struggle for the liberation of the Negroes and the whole of mankind, his outstanding achievements in academic fields and his sincere friendship toward the Chinese people will forever remain in the memory of the Chinese people." Until Du Bois's dying day, a slender volume of Mao's poems remained at his bedside, a gift given by the chairman after their discussions in 1959. In the volume, one of Du Bois's favorite works bespoke a vision of Eastern passage and protracted struggle:

> Soon the dawn will break in the east,
> But do not say we are marching early.
> Though we've travelled all over these green hills we are not old yet,
> And the landscape here is beyond compare.
> Straight from the walls of Huichang lofty peaks,
> Range after range extend to the eastern ocean.
> Our soldiers, pointing, gaze south towards Kwangtung,
> So green, so luxuriant in the distance.[97]

FIGURE 1.4: Du Bois and Mao in a garden, Lake Country, central China, April 1959. W. E. B. Du Bois Papers, Special Collections and University Archives, University of Massachusetts Amherst Libraries.

2

A PASSPORT AIN'T WORTH A CENT

One wonders anew about the roots of our China policy. Is it possible
that this policy stems in part from a sense of outrage that hitherto passive
nation of "little yellow men" should stand up to the West and insist on full
respect? . . . America, the leader of the West, still expects "Uncle Tom"
reactions and hat-in-hand servility from Nehru, Mao Tse-Tung and the rest
of the world of color. . . . [But] there is a world of meaning in a 1948 speech
by Mao Zedong [where he stated] . . . : "We have stood up. We have lifted
our heads. . . . We will no longer be the laundrymen of the world."
—WILLIAM WORTHY

Every other race has the right to go wherever its members want.
The white man has gone all over the world and done exactly what he
wanted for his own benefit. Don't I have the right to do the same thing?
I wanted to get an education, and I knew I wasn't going to get it here.
I wanted to have a good job, and I wasn't going to get it here.
So I chose to go to China to improve my life.
—CLARENCE ADAMS

As the Du Boises' 1959 visit to China came to its end, they in all probability pon-
dered over whether or not the U.S. State Department would seize their passports again. Travel to China went against the department's mandate. As early
as 1952, the department had bracketed communist nations, including China,
North Korea, and several Eastern European countries, as invalid for travel by
U.S. citizens and journalists. This decree built upon a number of legislative
bills targeting communist activities. Section 6 of the Subversive Activities Control Act, for example, made it unlawful for any suspected member of a communist organization to obtain a passport. Such policies were necessary, the American government claimed, because they prevented Communist Party members
and U.S. subversives from engaging in international activities that would "be
prejudicial to the interests of the United States" and "the orderly conduct of
foreign relations."[1] By means of this act and other pieces of legislation, the

FIGURE 2.1: William Worthy displays the passport he refused to give to the State Department (one month later the department denied his application for passport renewal). February 10, 1957. Courtesy of United Press International.

State Department restricted the international travel of numerous Americans, including Paul Robeson, the civil rights activist Charlotta Bass, the Communist Party of the United States of America leader William Patterson, the painter Rockwell Kent, the novelist Howard Fast, the American Civil Liberties Union (ACLU) director Corliss Lamont, the congressman Leo Isacson, the chemist Linus Pauling, the interfaith leader Reverend J. Henry Carpenter, and the playwright Arthur Miller.[2] Similar policies were also deployed to prevent foreigners from traveling into the United States, as well as to deport leftists of non-U.S. origin, such as the Trinidadian Marxists Claudia Jones and C. L. R. James.

In any case, the journalist William Worthy was paying close attention to the Du Boises' unauthorized journey.[3] Reporting on the Du Boises' return leg to the United States, Worthy relayed that despite hearing rumors that the couple would be arrested and their passports lifted, "not a single question was asked when Dr. and Mrs. W.E.B. Du Bois arrived here last week."[4] Nonetheless, how the government would respond to the Du Boises' daring violation of the State Department's ban was of deep concern to Worthy. In the spring of 1957, the State Department had refused to renew his passport, the result of his illicit travel to China just several months earlier.

In January of 1957, the *Baltimore Afro-American*, the country's largest-circulation black newspaper, gestured readers to "Follow William Worthy into Red China." On the newspaper's cover an arrow directed a path of giant footprints toward a territory labeled "Red China." Underneath was a caption: "In Your Afro-American—Mr. Worthy is first again to give us a series of articles you won't be able to read in any other American newspaper. Read his interviews with GI's who refused to return home after the Korean War; what they are doing, how they live." Reporting from Beijing, Worthy offered newspaper readers a snapshot of the lives of several black servicemen and former prisoners of war (POWs) who had opted for life in communist China rather than return to Jim Crow America. In Worthy's news coverage, perspectives such as that articulated in the epigraph by the then-China resident and former POW Clarence Adams were given equal footing with the anti-China stance circulated by the U.S. government's various talking heads. Furthermore, besides giving soldiers like Adams an opportunity to defend their decisions, Worthy also dedicated serious time to analyzing Chinese communism alongside Euro-American imperialism and Jim Crow racism, the last two of which he described as the twin expressions of U.S. globalism. Worthy argued that white supremacy was not unique to U.S. history but was rather a structural feature of world affairs. He explained that Chinese communism was therefore not simply an ideology that stood in opposition to capitalism and liberalism; Chinese communism was also a historical response to the imperialist, bourgeois-centered, and white supremacist logics that embedded Western domination of the world. It was this reality, he conveyed, that his visit to China and other Asian countries confirmed: "It is not enough to look at communist China and merely see an ever more regimented society that frankly labels us Americans as Enemy No. 1. . . . We must recall the humiliations of the 'Chinese not allowed' signs which one short decade ago the now expelled missionaries failed to raise their voices against. Given the white man's pride of race, the foreign troops on Chinese soil and the arrogance of carving out foreign 'concessions' a Chinese revolution was inevitable."[5]

Worthy's journey and news coverage from China, however, were of grave concern for the U.S. State Department. Behind closed doors, officials lamented over if the trip might supply the Chinese government with an opportunity to refashion its international image among nonwhite populations. But bigger than this, the department was infuriated by Worthy's public display of dissent. Worthy was the first American foreign correspondent to report from China since the victory of the Chinese Communist Party (CCP) in 1949, and his travel was a blatant violation of the department's ban on American travel to China.

Over the course of the 1950s, Worthy recognized that one of the most essential aspects of the U.S.'s Cold War culture of containment was its domination and regulation of meaning and mobility. Anticommunism worked to subjugate and domesticate American minds through particular arguments about race, citizenship, and U.S. interventions in foreign countries, as well as through the repression of outlooks that did not correspond with the dominant U.S. political orthodoxy. This suppression of antiracist leftist dissent was one factor among many that drove Worthy and other radical critics to formulate alternative politics and ideologies of opposition that transcended national barriers, often in the most surprising of places.

In sum, Worthy employed journalism and foreign correspondence as a transnational political practice. Believing in the power of public opinion and the necessity of a well-informed citizenry for the struggle for peace and social justice, he committed himself to producing journalism that situated global events within the local and national understandings of Americans and that linked the U.S. black freedom struggle to foreign anti-imperialist movements. Amid allegations of brainwashing and U.S. POWs in North Korea collaborating with Chinese Communists, Worthy interviewed black war veterans and former POWs. In these discussions, the veterans detailed their efforts to survive captivity in the prison camps and their interactions with Chinese soldiers and prison-camp authorities, as well as these authorities' efforts to promote racial exchange and solidarity with them. Messages of black and Chinese populations as mutual subjects of white supremacy, the veterans explained, were a prominent feature of the camp's culture. While these interviews ruptured dominant U.S. portrayals of the war and U.S. military service, they also helped stimulate Worthy's attention to Asian anticapitalist movements.

Consequently, over the course of the decade, Worthy ventured to report from Vietnam and China, predominantly interested in the antiracist and anti-imperialist features of these struggles. Throughout his travel, he made connections between the aforementioned radical struggles and the militancy vibrating among working-class black populations. But Worthy's efforts also drew the wrath of the U.S. State Department, which perceived Worthy's renegade style of journalism as a threat to U.S. foreign interests. This ultimately came to a head with a struggle over Worthy's passport and his right to travel and produce journalism free from government dictates of where he could and could not report from. For many people, Worthy offered a more nuanced evaluation of Asian communism while also challenging the travel and journalism mandates of the U.S. government. But his interest in the global dimensions of antiracist struggle did not preclude him from acknowledging the limitations of discourses and practices of transnational racial solidarity, most chiefly the drawbacks of framing Asian opposition to U.S. globalism through an uncomplicated U.S. racial narrative.

Worthy was a member of a spirited, august family. His grandmother, Bathsheba Worthy, was arrested in 1915 for picketing the Boston premier of *Birth of a Nation*, D. W. Griffith's racist silent film and America's first blockbuster movie. Mabel Posey Worthy, Worthy's mother, was a Florence, Alabama, native who became the first black female employee in Boston's postal service. She was also the founder and president of the Massachusetts Colored Women's Democratic Club and a dedicated member and leader within Boston's branch of the NAACP. Worthy's father, William Worthy Sr., was reared in Forsyth, Georgia. After graduating from Lincoln University, Worthy Sr. received his medical degree from Boston's College of Physicians and Surgeons in 1908. However, he was compelled to return to Macon, Georgia, to complete his physician's residency requirement because prior to 1931, black physicians were not permitted to serve their internships in Boston hospitals. Returning to Boston with his family one year later, Worthy Sr. became a prominent physician in the city. Furthermore, as a trustee at the historic Charles Street African Methodist Episcopal Church and leader of the Massachusetts Medical Society, the South End Medical Club, and the National Medical Association, Worthy played a prevalent role in the movement to integrate Boston City Hospital and Boston's nursing core.[6] In time, his and Mabel's offspring would join the ranks of the path breakers, following in their family's footsteps as professional pioneers and critics of U.S. racial injustice and discrimination.

Born in 1921, William Worthy Jr., the only son, was radicalized as a student at Bates College during the onset of World War II. There he became a pacifist and avid critic of U.S. military intervention abroad. He soon joined the ACLU, where he campaigned for the Socialist Party of America presidential candidate Norman Thomas and refused to enlist in World War II, claiming conscientious-objector status. After completing undergraduate studies, Worthy studied adult education at the University of Oslo and worked for a short time as the public relations assistant to A. Philip Randolph, president of the Brotherhood of Sleeping Car Porters, the largest African American–led workers' union. Worthy also participated in the Journey of Reconciliation, a 1947 initiative sponsored by the Fellowship of Reconciliation and the Congress of Racial Equality after the Supreme Court's 1946 decision to outlaw segregation in interstate transportation. Alongside a group of seven black men and eight white men, Worthy rode Greyhound and Trailways buses and trains throughout states in the upper South over the course of two weeks. Their intention was to see that the Court's decision was upheld in practice and to contest the larger de facto customs and practices of Jim Crow racial discrimination.[7] This political activity was one factor among many that led Worthy to pursue employment as a journalist and foreign correspondent. Eventually, he landed work, first with the *Baltimore Afro-American* and later with CBS.

One of Worthy's first assignments was to cover the Korean War. The war's origins can be traced to the thirty-eighth parallel, a border that divided the Korean peninsula that was established by the Soviet Union and the United States at the conclusion of World War II. North Korea's communist government rejected this carving up of Korea, deeming the parallel an arbitrary boundary that prevented Korea's unification and aided and abetted the presence of the U.S. military to ensure the propping up of a right-wing government in South Korea. After obtaining endorsements from the leadership of the Soviet Union and China, the North Korean leader Kim Il-sung authorized 135,000 members of the Korean People's Army to invade South Korea and seize the capital city of Seoul in late June 1950. Viewing these actions as a direct encroachment on the territorial sovereignty of a U.S. ally and on the parameter of U.S. power in East Asia, President Harry S. Truman's administration obtained UN approval to establish a multistate military force to retake Seoul and repel the Korean People's Army. Over the next three months, the two sides fought intensely. The Western forces went on to drop enormous quantities of napalm over the peninsula, actions that brought horrific and uneven results. Things took a more serious turn for the worse when UN Command troops entered North Korea and after Truman dispatched the U.S. Navy's Seventh Fleet into the Taiwan Strait to curb the possibility of a Chinese invasion of Taiwan.

China did not take the threat of UN troops and a U.S.-backed Korean regime across its border lightly. Consequently, in the early months of the conflict, Mao Zedong's government determined that it would have to aid North Korea in some fashion. A communist victory, the CCP determined, would drastically alter the landscape of power in East Asia in favor of China. But there were other reasons motivating China's support for North Korea. Considering that the People's Republic of China (PRC) was only a mere eight months old, Mao and the CCP leadership recognized that the war would enable them to build on the momentum of the Chinese Communist Revolution by rallying and unifying Chinese citizenry under the banner of Chinese revolutionary nationalism and internationalism. War against a common enemy could be a powerful force in domesticating the public with the CCP's ideological might, as well as in increasing the CCP's following. Furthermore, it would enable the CCP to accelerate China's influence abroad as a viable counter to Western power.[8] Gambling on the notion that the UN forces would not expand the war into China, on October 8, 1950, the Chinese government authorized its People's Liberation Army

(PLA) to enter into the war and assist the Korean People's Army in repelling UN forces. Underestimated by UN military forces and armed with Soviet hardware, the Chinese and North Korean forces launched a stunning counteroffensive that drove the UN forces southward. Within months, the UN forces effectively responded with their own counteroffensive. Thereafter, for the most part, neither side obtained the definitive upper hand. The fighting continued for two more years, finally coming to an inconclusive end on July 27, 1953, with both sides agreeing to a cease-fire and signing an armistice.[9]

Prior to the war, increases in national-defense spending, personnel shortages, and Truman's July 26, 1948, issuance of Executive Order 9981, which formalized equal treatment and opportunity in the armed services and the protection of employees from discrimination, altered the U.S. armed forces' racial makeup. Truman's order came on the cusp of widespread criticisms and mobilization by the likes of organizations such as the Committee against Jim Crow in Military Service and Training, which threatened the U.S. military with a campaign of mass draft evasions by blacks if the military did not enact a substantive legislative commitment to the elimination of de jure racial discrimination. Worried about how the Soviet Union and its allies would exploit this issue and how it might also impact the pending presidential election, Truman relented.[10] But while Truman's order provided what some believed to be a potential doorway to blacks' inclusion into U.S. cultural citizenship and the expansion of the law to include protections against racial injustice, it, as one historian notes, "did not explicitly call for the military's desegregation."[11] Still, the promise of steady income, GI benefits, and upward mobility as a career military person convinced greater numbers of blacks and Latinos, particularly poor and underemployed persons, to enlist. And in effect, the military grew overnight. As a result of Executive Order 9981, the rapid increase in the military's annual budget, and the 1948 Selective Service Act, which mandated that young men between the ages of eighteen and twenty-six register for the draft, the military's size doubled between the years of 1950 and 1953. During the months after the elimination of recruiting quotas, for instance, African American recruits grew from 8.2 percent to 25 percent of all army enlistments. In 1951 alone the number of African American soldiers reached 27,000, which represented around 13.5 percent of U.S. armed forces in Korea.[12]

As the first war fought by a desegregated U.S. military composed of white, black, Latino, and Asian troops fighting alongside South Korean troops, and as an international conflict where defending an ally meant drawing the United States back into East Asia barely five years after the completion of World War II, the racial implications of the Korean War were significant.[13] Still, African Americans' perspectives on the war ranged. Some civil rights leaders viewed

Truman's legislative act and black participation in the war with high optimism and desire. Early on, the labor organizer A. Phillip Randolph, the NAACP head Walter White, the NAACP board of directors, and several black-oriented media entities voiced support for U.S. involvement in the war. The general sentiment was that North Korea and China represented expansionist, aggressive regimes that threatened the possibility of democracy in Asia Pacific, and that military desegregation and black contributions to the war would provoke more rapid elimination of U.S. racism's structural impediments. But other black people came out against the war, most notably Shirley Graham Du Bois, W. E. B. Du Bois, Charlotta Bass, Paul and Eslanda Robeson, the feminist and NAACP founding member Mary Church Terrell, and the painter Aaron Douglas. They argued that the clash in Korea represented a civil conflict that should be fought and determined by Korean peoples, not by U.S.-led intervention. They also emphasized the war's racial overtones, pointing out that it would be mainly poor black Americans and Koreans who would lose their lives. "Our own American boys, those sons and husbands of ours now fighting in Korea, are murdering and making human torches of the woman and little helpless Korean children by dropping jelly fire bombs on them. We must and can stop this terrible war," Graham Du Bois insisted.[14] Along similar lines, Paul Robeson asserted that the U.S. military's "armed adventure in Korea" represented not simply a conflict over the unification of North and South Korea, or pitting capitalism versus communism, but a struggle over U.S. domination of the world. China and North Korea's rejection of U.S. hegemony was therefore a "war of color," he and others maintained, an anti-imperialist struggle against global white supremacy that had to be identified alongside other movements worldwide.[15]

For twenty-eight months, Worthy traveled throughout Asia reporting on the war, his news commentary often articulating a similar political line as that of Graham Du Bois, Robeson, and other antiwar activists. In Rangoon, the capital of Myanmar (Burma), Worthy attended the Asian Socialist Congress, and in New Delhi he participated in a seminar on Gandhi's philosophy. In these forums, Worthy gained insight into Asian anticolonial nationalism. He learned that Asian movements were waging wars for the "revolutionary lifting of living standards and for an immediate attainment of genuine human dignity."[16] Numerous Asians Worthy met along these travels furthermore informed him that they viewed African Americans as a colonized population who should be warring against Euro-American domination of the world. "America is the most hated nation in the world today," Worthy admitted. "I was made to feel welcome solely because I was not white."[17] Ultimately, Worthy concluded that such proclamations of Asian nationalism, anti-imperialism, and opposition to white supremacy were evidence that America's "Asian policies are wrong from A to Z." For him, these encounters abroad, and even more broadly, North Korea's and China's efforts to repel U.S. hegemony in East Asia, were "the unmistakable signs that the worm has begun to turn in Asia, racially speaking."[18]

Worthy was also present at the war's armistice signing and exchange of POWs at Panmunjom, and later at the Freedom Village in Munsan-ni, South Korea, where he covered the repatriation of U.S. prisoners. In these environments he discerned that a substantial number of the prisoners did not want to discuss the war; those who did often framed it through the common argument of "fighting against communism." Such explanations also took shape in reporters' coverage of the troops. Some of Worthy's *Baltimore Afro-American* colleagues, for instance, lauded black POWs for their courage, undying defense of U.S. democracy, and knack for killing Chinese communists.[19] Worthy criticized these accounts. Besides perpetuating demeaning representations of Asians, such stories merely echoed America's dominant anticommunist political line. Many American newspaper readers thus did not end up with a more comprehensive account of the war, but instead stories that affirmed the U.S. government's anticommunist position. Worthy noted that some journalists were even "tempted to put words in the mouths of returning POWs," their news stories and interviews reliant mainly on "individuals who stand ready to say what others wish to hear." Worthy quipped, "The one theme song which nearly every anxious white American wishes to hear again from . . . each and every colored American is that 'I'm not taken in by all that Red propaganda. I'm loyal!'" Worthy, however, maintained that what was left out of this reporting and rarely stated by many of these black POWs was the reality that North Korea's confrontation with UN forces represented more than a struggle over communism. It was an Asian rejection of white supremacy and Western imperialism. Worthy consequently asserted that U.S. news media and the black political establishment's reluctance to "raise the roof about white supremacy and [the] imperialistic premises" of U.S. foreign policies displayed how "narrowly defined" and "internationally myopic" was the state of American political affairs. "Caving in on external foreign policy matters involving race and color and imperialism," he insisted, played a crucial role in perpetuating black Americans' "domestic slavery." "It seems to me, now on my way home after seven months in Asia, that colored Americans like most of their white brothers, are incredibly out of touch with political realities out here," Worthy concluded.[20]

Worthy returned to the United States in September of 1953. Back stateside, he reassessed the dominant news media's coverage of the war and found that aspects of the reporting conflicted with his encounters abroad. Analyzing the *New York Times*, Worthy determined that the newspaper was cheating readers of a balanced view. Worthy's experiences abroad led him to view the U.S.-backed

Republic of Korean Army as "a hard-bitten, graft-ridden military dictatorship, propped up with U.S. dollars and arms," yet the New York Times portrayed the army as Korea's most progressive military force. The New York Times and other news media additionally refrained from discussing the real disagreements fueling the conflict. Rarely stated was the fact that the differences distinguishing the North and South Korean governments were not over the "choice between totalitarian communism and democratic liberty but rather between communism in the north and fascism in the south." By framing the war through the standard Cold War narrative of communism versus democracy, news media presented ideology in place of empirical evidence, a slant that helped to generate a U.S. public composed of "newspaper fooled folks" who were "being taken for one gigantic counter-revolutionary ride by the righteous smokescreens emanating from Washington's propaganda mills." Worthy additionally concluded that such distortion by U.S. media contributed to America's low standing among some Asian populations. This is a "perfect example of why colored peoples of Asia [are] increasingly distrustful of the flamboyantly advertised 'ideals' of white America," he maintained.[21]

One subject that Worthy was drawn to and skeptical of were news reports of misconduct by U.S. POWs held in Chinese-run prison camps in North Korea. It was argued that some of these troops, a considerable number of whom were black, had collaborated with the enemy after undergoing Chinese practices of political education and physical and psychological indoctrination—what the American media, government, and public sensationalized as China's successful tactics of "communist brainwashing." Moreover, while it was alleged that the POWs had worked against their comrades while in the camps, the larger fear among some Americans was that these former POWs were establishing communist cells in the United States, all under the guise of the global peace movement and antiwar activism.

Although scholarship generally confirms that both North Korean and Chinese troops used excessive violence in their torture tactics against prisoners, many works also relay that the Chinese-run prison camps were not nearly as brutal as those of North Korea and the UN prisoner camps on Koje-do Island. For instance, of the three to four thousand U.S. prisoners who died in captivity, an overwhelming majority died during the war's first nine months, specifically during the long marches to North Korean prison camps located in the northern part of the country. Starvation, mistreatment, disease, exposure, bad weather conditions, and killings at the hands of North Korean and Chinese troops were the cause of most of these deaths. But when Chinese officials took over many of the camps in 1951, much of the systematic killing of U.S. prisoners was reported to have ceased. Nonetheless, Chinese soldiers did take violent liberties, beating and executing prisoners at whim to instill discipline and compliance.[22]

The Chinese-run prisons' main practices of punishment were interrogation and extreme forms of physical and psychological breakdown. Prisoners were forced to undergo a two-phase process that began with extreme manual labor, minimal food, lack of medical treatment, and sleep deprivation, tactics aimed at weakening prisoners' morale and resistance to foreign ideology. During the second stage, prisoners were given more rations of food, better means to maintain hygiene, and improved living conditions and clothes. They were also required to attend *laogai dui*—reeducation lectures and indoctrination sessions organized around self-criticism, thought reform, and criticizing U.S. society and foreign policy. Twice a day, prisoners convened for lectures on a hill or in particular cabins. There, Chinese camp instructors and translators sermonized about capitalism's collapse, the contradictions and failings of liberal democracy, and the impact of U.S. imperialism abroad. The camp instructors also drilled the prisoners with lessons on Marxist-Leninist philosophy, Chinese history, and communist critique of global affairs.[23] However, when the camp authorities and instructors determined that the communist slant of the lectures was "untenable and unacceptable to the prisoners," the instructors, following the advice of Premier Zhou Enlai, shifted the lectures' focus. They began to devote the majority of the time to condemning the Korean War and U.S. race relations, as well as encouraging prisoners to author and sign peace petitions calling for the UN to end the armed conflict.[24]

A small segment of the prisoners were receptive to the ideas and arguments shared in the political-education classes. Within this group, a few were drawn to communist ideology. But even more of them agreed with the instructors' criticisms of U.S. racial oppression and proposals for global peace. Taking aim at both the Korean War and Western intervention in other foreign contexts, this population of prisoners went on to organize and sign peace petitions while in the camp. They also aired and publicized their grievances against U.S. foreign and domestic policy on Chinese international radio broadcasts. Identified by the prison authorities as "progressives," these prisoners were frequently contrasted against those prisoners who adamantly rejected the lectures' proposals, the latter group classified as "reactionaries." Being tagged as a "progressive," however, did not mean being an informant or "rat," the latter used to describe those prisoners who regardless of ideological stance provided information to officials in exchange for favorable treatment.[25] Nonetheless, at the war's end the progressives were viewed with great suspicion by the U.S. military and American public, perceived by many people as "brainwashed" stooges of Chinese communism.

The CIA operative Edward Hunter introduced the term "brainwashing" to the U.S. public in a series of 1950 articles for the *Miami Daily News* and *New Leader* magazine. Brainwashing, also popularly referred to as "menticide," was a literal translation of the Chinese colloquialism *xinao*, "to wash a person's brain."[26] Hunter asserted that in the prison camps U.S. POWs endured a variety of technological and psychological torture methods, practices that transformed them into spies, informants, and collaborators. Comparing these indoctrination techniques to "medical treatment" and "witchcraft," Hunter alleged: "War has changed its form. The Communists have discovered that a man killed by a bullet is useless. . . . The objective of communist warfare is to capture intact the minds of the people and their possessions, so they can be put to use." He subsequently asserted that this hidden manipulation of minds compelled everyday Americans to be on guard. Walking among them were war returnees who in secret were working on behalf of Chinese communism. "For the first time in history, Americans . . . swallowed the enemy's propaganda line," he insisted. "The United States is [now] the main battlefield in this Red War."[27]

Hunter's allegations were part of a larger cultural trend in the United States, what one scholar describes as the rise of a new "type of propaganda by Americans, about Americans, directed to Americans."[28] While the number of troops investigated on charges of collaborating with the enemy was substantial (565 of the total 4,428), only a few were found guilty. Still, U.S. media and popular culture became transfixed with the narrative of American servicepersons' declining loyalty and the Chinese government's epic powers of mental manipulation.[29] The writer Eugene Kinkhead, for instance, alleged that more than one-third of the POWs had succumbed to collaborating with the enemy. American paranoia about these accusations was further increased after the U.S. military psychiatrist Colonel William E. Mayer claimed that the POWs' transgressions raised "serious questions about the American character."[30]

Brainwashing discourses operated dualistically, mobilizing a nationwide backlash against U.S. POWs and Chinese communism. Coming off the cusp of World War II, North Koreans and Chinese now replaced Japan as the "bad Asians" and "gooks" within U.S. discourses about East Asia.[31] But popular U.S. representations of brainwashing offered a different twist to this racist epithet. Brainwashing was depicted as a "distinctly 'Oriental' practice," where Chinese communism was singled out as embodying a potentially graver national-security threat than Soviet communism.[32] China was consequently represented as composed of menacing scientists and Soviet devotees who were turning U.S. POWs into androids for international communism.[33] Numerous Americans believed that China had mastered "the art of mass manipulation"—that is, the "capacity to gnaw from within or to encircle from without."[34]

But African American prisoners were also singled out in these representations. Throughout the war black soldiers were periodically accused of exhibiting poor combat performance. The most notorious cases were allegations
that black soldiers were prone to fleeing from the site of battle and were secretly "fragging" (killing) superior white officers. Furthermore, the court-
martial trials of sixty infantrymen from the all-black 24th Infantry Regiment
and conviction of thirty-two of them for issues related to conduct increased
the criticisms of black troops.[35] After the war, similar charges of misconduct
were made; however, these alleged that black POWs were easy targets for their
captors' criticisms of U.S. life. In the prison camps, indoctrination lectures
were frequently spent examining the segregation and oppression of racial and
ethnic minorities in the United States. Several journalists argued that Chinese
troops' concentration on lynching, unfair labor practices, low-quality housing
and living conditions, and blacks' second-class citizenship created dissention
and divides between the prisoners along racial lines and generated an unfavor-
able view of U.S. life among the black prisoners. White prisoners echoed the
journalists' claims; nearly one-quarter of the white POWs who returned to the
U.S. indicated that those POWs who were members of racial minority groups
were the primary recipients of Chinese propaganda.[36]

Stories of preferential treatment for black prisoners were further heightened
by news that three black prisoners, Corporal Clarence Adams, Corporal William C. White, and Private LaRance V. Sullivan, had chosen residence in China
over repatriation back to the United States. At the war's end, Truman's administration cultivated a policy of repatriation particular to the war, one that took
a different approach than the 1949 Geneva Convention's *Joint Pledge on POW's
Rights*, which mandated the comprehensive exchange of all POWs.[37] At the end
of the Korean War, prisoners from both sides were given the option of either
returning to their homelands or obtaining political refuge in the homeland of
the opposition. The 47,000 Chinese and North Korean prisoners who opted for
life in the United States helped reinforce ideas of U.S. democracy and capitalism as the sole progressive alternative to communism. But America's pristine
image was cracked when twenty-three U.S. soldiers refused repatriation; two
men later changed their minds (the twenty-one would be joined by one Briton
and 367 South Koreans).[38]

The twenty-one nonrepatriates rationalized their decisions as political acts
for peace. They were not renouncing their citizenship but taking a collective
stand "for peace and freedom, not only for ourselves but for the American people and people of the world." "We are Americans. We love our country and our
people," they maintained.[39] Before this decision and, moreover, prior to the
war, White, Adams, and Sullivan had little to no formal experience or affilia-

tion with U.S. political affairs. White grew up in rural Plumerville, Arkansas, and had enlisted two months prior to his eighteenth birthday and high school graduation. Sullivan had been raised in Santa Barbara, California, his childhood and adolescence mired by poverty, abuse, and an unstable household. He joined the army just after completing high school. Adams, a Memphis, Tennessee, native, enlisted in 1947 at the age of eighteen in order to avoid police charges for stabbing a person and attacking a white man who had solicited Adams and his friends to help him locate a prostitute. In any case, the three young men's lack of much formal education and political involvement left many Americans wondering how these soldiers could make such a decision to remain in Asia.[40]

The idea that U.S. troops would prefer life in China left a heavy stain on the cloak of liberal democracy and generated widespread attention and debate. Politicians, psychiatrists, military officials, and journalists all chimed in to offer observations about the soldiers' decisions. Some suggested that it was a consequence of the prisoners' low IQ scores, lack of formal education, and naïveté. Others, however, offered more-extreme criticisms, lambasting the prisoners as bought off by "Communist offers of girls, wealth, and power" and accusing them of being turncoats, drug abusers, sociopaths, sexual deviants, homosexuals, and war criminals. As one senator put it, the prisoners' conduct left them stateless, soldiers "without a country."[41] White, Sullivan, and Adams were periodically singled out in these denunciations. The NAACP executive secretary Walter White, for example, wrote a letter to the trio encouraging them to reconsider their decision.[42] But a small number of media outlets went further, alleging that the three troops represented a more general crisis of communist sympathies among black Americans. Black war veterans, one journalist stated, were now workers in "a global brainwashing assembly line which began in a North Korean POW camp."[43]

Such characterizations, though, were not the norm. A variety of military psychologists and academics maintained that the three black troops were exceptions to the rule and that the majority of black POWs, like their white comrades, held up well during captivity.[44] Along similar lines, Edward Hunter championed black POWs as compatriots who proved that China "failed miserably in their efforts to . . . win the minds of the non-white peoples of the world." Yet Hunter's assertions were coated in racist assessments of black humanity and black music. He described black prisoners' resistance to brainwashing as the product of black people's primitive disposition, elements of which were best embodied in African American music. "The colored man was stripped down to his naked character. . . . This quality is exemplified in Negro songs generally. They are without bitterness and without hate," he wrote. "The Negro had resources for survival to which he turned when most desperate. These were usually simple in nature."[45]

These narratives of black heroics and black war returnees as a barometer for patriotism and ideal U.S. citizenship, nonetheless, helped stigmatize the black troops who relocated to China, as well as black veterans who were critical of the war and U.S. racial injustice. Those soldiers who did not fit into this idyllic image were identified as exhibiting a frailty of nationality, loyalty, morality, and psychological stability. "Returning prisoners of war became victims of America's crisis of confidence," the historian Charles S. Young explains. "Their performance was exhibit A that the individual citizen was becoming weak and vulnerable."[46] Brainwashing and collaboration were thus framed not simply as a form of subliminal psychological conditioning and mind control but additionally as constituting a sign of the declining character of the U.S. fighting man and "a failed generation of American young men"—that is, a sign of flawed and failed masculinity.[47] But even more, stories of black prisoners' heroics and loyalty were useful in policing black ideological perspectives not in line with the pro-war, pro-capitalist political orthodoxy dominant in American life. And by emphasizing the image of Asian communism as the evil Other, blacks were coaxed to follow the example of heroic black prisoners and reject racial solidarity with Asian communists. As several scholars note, while the Korean War "revealed anew abundant white American prejudices against both Asians and blacks," brainwashing constituted a Cold War "black-Asian racial calculus," where "loving blacks (or at least seeming to) was an important credential in the Cold War business of vilifying 'Orientals.'"[48]

Worthy sought to unpack and nuance this milieu. Were black POWs defenders against Asian communism or its collaborators? And to what extent did the prison camps' authorities and black prisoners actually construct racial mutuality and meaning inside the camps? Hoping to gain insight into these issues, Worthy set out on a two-thousand-mile trip to uncover the experiences of black troops who had been held captive in North Korean and Chinese prison camps, a group that he described as the "colored veterans of a novel experience in a novel war."[49]

A good portion of the returnees Worthy spoke with had been confined to Camp 5, the largest compound of the permanent prison camps in North Korea. Located on a peninsula outside the town of Pyoktong, along the Yalu River separating North Korea and Manchuria, the camp housed approximately three-quarters of U.S. prisoners and was manned by two hundred Chinese soldiers. Food there was extremely scarce and inadequate, the camp's occupants forced to maintain a diet of mainly hard corn, rice, and beans.[50] While all of Worthy's interviewees confirmed the mistreatment and dreadful conditions they endured there, a few noted that their North Korean and Chinese captors shared similar living conditions, also having to contend with malnutrition, cold climate, and sickness. Speaking about the compulsory indoctrination lectures and group study sessions that they were required to attend, the soldiers stated that certain themes were continuously emphasized throughout the lectures, particularly the failures of liberal democracy and capitalism. Corporal Harrison West and Sergeants Tommie Hampton and William Coz, for example, maintained that the Chinese lecturers attempted to garner influence among black and Puerto Rican prisoners by giving close attention to the deplorable living conditions endured by many African American and Puerto Rican communities in the United States. The soldiers also claimed that while these lectures at times stirred up racial antagonisms among the prisoners, these lectures demonstrated the Chinese authorities' intent to make an impression on both black POWs and, potentially, their home-communities back in the United States. Sergeant Edward Hewlett agreed, arguing: "The Chinese held that a cause will not die, that even one prisoner converted to 'the truth' would have an influence back in his home community."[51]

The veterans also informed Worthy that media played a prominent role in the propaganda used toward black POWs. They were specifically targeted through films about lynching, job discrimination, and black disfranchisement, as well as through music. For instance, the camps' public-address system played Russian and English versions of Paul Robeson's renditions of "Ol' Man River" and "March of the Volunteers." Thereafter, Chinese troops expressed to black prisoners their admiration for Robeson. "They held him up as a great man," Major John Harlan of West Virginia remarked.[52] Yet, the Chinese troops also remarked that they deemed Robeson's political views as "progressive but freelance," that is in need of closer engagement with the daily realities of political movements outside of the U.S. Calling into question the American government's confiscation of Robeson's passport and efforts to prevent him from traveling and performing abroad, the Chinese troops reasoned, "If he [Robeson] were permitted to travel abroad, he would be able to see more and develop his ideas."[53] In all probability, Chinese authorities used discussions about Robeson and the playing of his music for two objectives. First, it may have been used to create dissention and divisions among prisoners, where it was hoped that playing it might make white prisoners believe that black prisoners were being given special treatment and convince some black prisoners to look more favorably at the Chinese government. If this was the intention, then it worked as governmentality—that is, as a mode of governing and producing different types of prisoners within camp. But it was also used for public diplomacy—namely, as a strategy to call attention to U.S. racial injustice and Western imperialism and to improve China's image as a critic of these structures of oppression. One Chinese general and leader of the military's wartime political department explained: "Our psychological warfare did not work well, being largely handicapped by language barriers . . . [but] we were fighting not only a military but also a political battle," one where influencing U.S. soldiers and international opinion were of high significance.[54] The prison authorities' frequent lauding of Robeson however produced mixed results among black POWs. "The official hero worship of the man as singer, "progressive" and "leader of your people" grew hard for the POWs to take," Worthy asserted. "The daily renditions of 'Ol' Man River' over the brassy public–address systems dampened all thrill of a glorious voice and became an integral part of a bottomless prison ennui." But some of Worthy's interviewees also disclosed that the constant playing of the song was a reminder of the paradoxes of American democracy. While Robeson was being attacked in his homeland for his political views, U.S. enemies halfway around the world celebrated Robeson's music and activism. "To most of the colored GIs who came home, Robeson is not the political ogre or ostracized reject wishfully portrayed by U.S. publicists abroad," Worthy concluded.[55]

The customs and rituals of the black church provided another unique site for cultural exchange between black prisoners and their captors.[56] Former POWs Roosevelt Williams and Alonzo S. Johnson relayed to Worthy that black religious practices had altered the social and cultural relations of the prison camp. After convincing the Chinese troops to provide facilities for worship services, Williams, nicknamed "Rev'" by other prisoners, along with Johnson ran the camp's worship services. Together, they also established a church board, singing quartets, a camp band, and a choir. They held monthly communion and performed baptisms, practices that reshaped the racial dynamics between some prisoners. Johnson explained, "When religious freedom in the camp was finally won, it produced a side effect. Though the Chinese had segregated us by race in living quarters, Rev' preached consistently to unsegregated congregations—an opportunity not available to him back in Chicago." In time, the Chinese troops recognized the implications of the church's interracial congregation and sent a photographer into the worship services to take "propaganda shots of the men praying." The purpose of this propaganda, Johnson pointed out, was to "tell the outside world of their [China's racial] 'tolerance.'" Nonetheless, what was truly exceptional to Johnson and Williams was that several Chinese guards were drawn to the church services. These people subsequently asked Johnson to teach them the Lord's Prayer and a number of hymns. Johnson was impressed by this outreach and quietly gave the guards credit for attempting to understand the subtle resistive features of black Christian traditions. Such lessons and exchanges however led the camp's authorities to ban several spirituals sung in the prison church services and censor sermons that they felt might clash with the CCP's doctrine. "The Chinese caught on to what American slave-owners seldom realized," Worthy ruled. "A group reduced to weakness can camouflage protest and hatch the spirit of rebellion in song and humor."[57]

Although emphasizing that such genuine exchanges between prisoners and prison guards were rare, several of former POWs did disclose to Worthy that what connected them to their captors was their mutual experiences with global white supremacy. Even in the camps they felt the weight of America's racial hierarchy. The soldiers explained to Worthy that numerous prisoners persisted in expressing racist outlooks about various nonwhite populations, quite a few of them referring to the Chinese as "those yellow, slant-eyed so-and-sos."[58] Some white prisoners even organized white-supremacist sects, one group identifying themselves as the Ku Klux Klan. In private discussions, several Chinese lecturers and camp officials admitted to black prisoners that these activities and perspectives were microexamples of U.S. empire. Johnson, for instance, explained that the lecturers assured him that "colored people were just like them [Chinese people]," and that "the white man didn't like them either because their skins were yellow."[59] Major John Harlan had similar experiences; Chinese officials often asserted to him: "There is no reason for you defend America. You are a black man and black men are under lynch law in America."[60]

The prison authorities' proclamations of racial egalitarianism, however, contrasted with dominant Chinese ideologies and constructions of race. Modern notions of Chineseness were grounded in claims about China as a "powerful yellow race" (qiangda de huang zhong ren) and arguments of yellow superiority, where belonging and citizenship were framed in biological language and ideas about blood, lineage, and descent. While Europe only began to describe China, and in fact all of Asia, as "yellow" at the end of the seventeenth century, the color yellow (huang) had been significant to both racial and national consciousness in China since antiquity, coming to be associated with China's ancient imperial elite, most notably the Chinese emperor Huangdi.[61] The emperor is identified as the paramount racial and ethnic antecedent of the Han people (Hanzu), the majority ethnic group in China, which thus means that being Han takes on specific racial meanings in relation to China's fifty-five other ethnic groups. The scholar Frank Dikötter, for instance, notes that it is Chinese custom to associate Han ethnic identity with race, where the Chinese term zu, meaning "group," shifted from referring to lineage and common-descent group to signifying race, ethnicity, and nationality. Furthermore, in the early twentieth century, an amalgamation of government, science, and popular culture helped this discourse congeal. State discourses of yellow superiority mixed with folk arguments that based identity on patrilineal descent. Chinese anthropologists and scientists' promotion of racial purity, eugenics, polygenesis, and arguments about Chinese people's biological and mental superiority further aided this racial project, where for many people being Chinese was guaranteed by skin color, blood, and ancestral lineage.[62]

Arguments about dark-skinned people and groups of African descent as culturally deficient and inferior contributed to buttressing this China-specific racial ideology. Chinese conceptions of black people can be traced back to the fourth century, where the term *kunlun* denoted enslaved non-Chinese with darker skin, particularly Africans and Southeast Asians (the term derives from the Kunlun mountains in northern Tibet). Because the Chinese viewed these populations as being of lower cultural rank, *kunlun*, came to signify derogatory meanings of backwardness and Otherness; Africans, in particular, were perceived as culturally savage, lacking history, and racially inferior.[63] Centuries later they would be depicted in Chinese educational institutions as descendants of gorillas and chimpanzees and frequently described as the "black slave race" (*heinu zhongzu*) and "black devils" (*heigui*).[64]

Both Worthy and his interviewees were unaware of this history. Nonetheless, most of the former POWs admitted to Worthy that they didn't find the prison authorities' claims of racial mutuality compelling. But some confessed that they also could not deny the truths of the prison camp's criticisms of U.S. race relations. "At the heart of many of the men's confidential comments was the recurrent theme that a good bit of the wearisome Communist propaganda in the camps was true when it dealt with the American race problem," Worthy wrote. In singling out America's "piecemeal, stop-and-go progress toward racial equality," the Chinese were therefore persuading black prisoners to have "no patience with the calculus of normal social change" and the West's "privilege of 'gradually' changing their ways."[65] Several former POWs additionally acknowledged that while their experiences in the camp had not transformed them into socialists, they did perceive themselves as pacifists and advocates for world peace. They moreover rejected the idea that this concession meant that they had been brainwashed.[66] Johnson divulged that he retained "a warm place in his heart for the Chinese in the camp," and Williams acknowledged: "I have nothing against the Chinese, man to man. We were born in America, we're used to America, we know American ways. If someone else is born in China, he knows Chinese ways, and he thinks those ways are right. He, like us, has a right to be patriotic."[67]

The admissions of Worthy's interviewees were seconded decades later by Clarence Adams, one of the three black POWs to refuse repatriation and spend several years as a resident of China. During his second tour of duty, Adams began to have serious doubts about the war. "What were we fighting for? To be oppressed? To be segregated?" he wrote in his autobiography. "Some of us also began to understand that the North Koreans had not done anything to us, so why were we trying to kill each other?" Captured by Chinese troops and imprisoned in Camp 5, Adams initially regarded the propaganda lectures as having little value. But his opinion began to change when he learned the backgrounds of the instructors, a few of whom happened to be writers, educators, and editors, a professional sector of society that Adams had little prior contact with in the United States. From their lectures, Adams developed what he believed to be a better understanding of world economic development and history, and as a result he found himself more critical of social and economic inequality: "The more I thought about my life, the more I felt I had been used, cheated, and betrayed. . . . I had great difficulty in seeing what democracy and freedom had done for me." He asserted, "The more I thought about all this, the more I believed there was some truth in what the Chinese were telling us. Critics in America later called this brainwashing, but how can it be brainwashing if someone is telling you something you already know is true?"[68]

Adams's evolving radical stance was given additional life through *Toward Truth and Peace*, the camp's POW-produced newspaper. Adams became a leading contributor to the publication, to the point that even his Chinese captors took notice of his budding understanding of historical materialism and world affairs. In the aftermath, he was frequently selected by prison officials to give lectures to other prisoners about race relations, imperialism, and the importance of world peace.[69] These ideas were also made audible on Radio Peking, where Adams and other prisoners petitioned the United Nations to end the war. On air they described the war as consumed with "senseless killing" and representing a great "injustice in human society." "I realize that I am one individual, expressing my democratic values, but they are in accord with the millions of people of the world over," Adams insisted. "Thousands of men are on the battlefront, they are being deprived of their right to live a long and happy life." Alongside several other prisoners, Adams called for the American public to question the reasons for the United States' intervention in Korea: "Why were we sent five thousand miles away from home to be captured and spend twenty-nine months as POWs? When we could have been home, living our life, as a useful American citizen. Was our country being threatened? I don't live in Korea."[70]

In later years Adams described the camp as a space where he experienced serious political and intellectual growth. He explained that it was in this environment that he first derived "a sense of mission [he] had never felt before." He said, "It was like being a part of something much greater than my own life." There, he was able to better understand the necessity of fighting for peace and

FIGURE 2.2: Corporal Clarence Adams (center), who defected to China following the Korean War, 1954. Courtesy of United Press International.

equality on a worldwide scale. "I never became a Communist or a Chinese citizen," Adams remarked. "I was looking for something much more fundamental. I wanted to be treated as a human being, and I wanted the opportunity to live a better life. Although our Chinese captors never became close to any prisoners, they at least treated black and white prisoners with equal dignity—or indifference. Thus, for the first time in my life, I felt I was being treated as an equal rather than as an outcast."[71] Adams consequently was adamant that his connections to other human beings, most especially to non-U.S. publics, would not be surrendered to the ideological constraints of U.S. nationalism. "Brainwashed? The Chinese *unbrainwashed* me," he asserted. "The Negro had his mind brainwashed long before the Korea War. If he stayed in his place he was a good nigger."[72]

In Worthy's interviews, many soldiers were critical of Adams's decision to relocate to China. They believed he and the other nonrepatriates' actions was a consequence of being poorly educated and easily impressionable. Yet, several admitted that Adams's commitment to fighting racial injustice and willingness to risk his citizenship for the opportunity to live and make a life abroad also reflected a bit of courage. Describing him as "dumb guy with a lot of guts," they pointed out that before he left for China he encouraged many of them to not sit idly once they returned to the United States but instead "fight for the rights of colored peoples, that we should join Paul Robeson and fight for peace."[73]

As Adams's summation highlights, in the prison camp was a collision of national and international discourses regarding race and democracy. While the Chinese used criticisms of U.S. racial oppression as means to create dissension among prisoners and to challenge idyllic portrayals of U.S. life and American democracy, they to no surprise evaded discussing the history of racial formations and racism in China. Their attempt to fashion racial coalition with black and brown prisoners illuminates the asymmetry of their internationalist discourse. Furthermore, as some black prisoners fought to survive the camp's conditions and the oppressive treatment of their captors, they became extremely critical of racial and class oppression inside and outside the United States. They determined that service to the military did not mean they must adhere to the dictates of U.S. nationalism and continue to participate in America's carnage on oppressed populations worldwide. What is also remarkable is that practices involving sound, movement, the body, and the spirit provided members of these two groups with some of their most compassionate, though ephemeral, interactions.

It is an overstatement to suggest that these experiences and opinions were widespread among black prisoners. The brutality of the war and the extremely violent and inhumane treatment and conditions of the prison marches and later the prison camps led to, according to official military and news media reports, the death of 2,701 of 7,140 troops (38 percent) held in captivity; other scholars suggest that these official statistics should be raised to as high as 58 percent.[74] And Worthy did not hesitate to broach this topic. In numerous articles, he detailed his interviewees' explanations of the various methods of torture and mistreatment that they were forced to endure, as well as the psychological trauma they experienced and brought home with them.

But Worthy's interviews with these former prisoners also conveyed a more subtle, yet pivotal, truth. "In more ways than one, the United States lost the war in Korea, make no mistake about it," Worthy wrote.[75] For him, this was made evident by the fact that in the midst of war and imprisonment, numbers of black soldiers were politically transformed, their consciousness becoming more critical and dejected by the U.S. government's actions at home and abroad. "The people in power in the USA know what's happening in the world," one former POW informed Worthy. "They're not interested in helping me." The war and prison camps had thus directed troops such as this young man to connect the devastating reverberations of U.S. armed warfare with the quotidian inequality and injustice felt by blacks at home. "[The black soldier] is doing his thinking with a new set of ABCs," Worthy remarked after completing the interviews.[76] Although he reasoned that the number of troops who held such outlooks might be "numerically small," Worthy reminded newspaper readers that greater public awareness of this sentiment could be extremely "politically embarrassing" for the United States. But such was the point. If Americans were ever going to wake up to the ties bridging Jim Crow racism to imperialist plunder elsewhere, who better to hear from than the country's "Korean War veterans who have learned a great deal in Asia about racial equality and white pretentiousness and who will become embittered if they must return to the same old pattern of segregation."[77]

★

JIM CROW TRAVEL, WHETHER HOME OR ABROAD

Worthy's charges that U.S. news media played a facilitative role in solidifying America's culture of opposition to communist-leaning Asian movements intensified after his travel to Vietnam in 1953. He was sent to Saigon to cover the First Indochina War, an eight-year conflict that escalated from low-scale guerrilla attacks against French occupation to a full-scale war pitting the U.S.-backed French military against the Ho Chi Minh–led Việt Minh Army. It took little time for Worthy to discern that America's economic and military investment in this conflict represented what he described as a "potential colonial prelude to a World War III of color." But more importantly, covering the war from Saigon led Worthy to discern that the U.S. media was misinforming Americans about the war, particularly regarding the large amount of territory that the Việt Minh Army controlled and how wide its support and influence was among Vietnamese people. While the U.S. media portrayed France's Vietnamese allies in a positive light, the Việt Minh were ubiquitously depicted as Soviet surrogates antithetical to the future of democracy and freedom in East Asia. And by framing the war as a struggle pitting Western democracy against Eastern Communism and the Việt Minh as radical extremists and Moscow proxies, some U.S. media entities blatantly disregarded that this was not just a war over communism, but instead a struggle over Vietnam's independence from foreign rule and that the majority of the Việt Minh were not simply communists but revolutionary nationalist freedom fighters. These American portrayals of Vietnamese communism, Worthy noted, were thus extremely similar to American reporting on the North Korean government during the Korean War:

These facts about the war (and there are many more . . .) expose the terrible power of the daily press to lead readers to conclusions about Asian events which not only Asians but also Westerners on the spot know only too well to be false. This, then, shows Negroes that many of their "domestic friends" . . . are desperately backing atomic foreign policies which have as their sole aim the maintenance of their unduly high American standard of living—even if every last starving Asian and African has to die in our wars fighting for it. What a pity.[78]

Worthy's final point, of the need for greater African American critical thinking and awareness of the nationalist impetus of Asian socialist and anti-imperialist movements, crystallized after the Montgomery Bus Boycott. He was sent to Alabama in March 1956, and Worthy's reports gave close attention to the boycott's working-class rank and file. "The key to understanding Montgomery," he wrote, was grasping the "spontaneous movement" and "militant tone" of the boycott's foot soldiers: laborers, porters, cooks, poolroom boys, taxi drivers, educators, and church members. Worthy added that these groups' commitment to civil disobedience and resisting Montgomery's vicious and racist structure at all costs represented a sentiment felt by other oppressed populations. "The dictionary always defines a word in terms of other words. A writer, it now seems in retrospect, must define Montgomery for readers in terms of the surrounding region," he stated. But in his opinion, "the surrounding region" was not the U.S. South. Instead, Montgomery's black community evoked memories of Asia: "I can't help but think of some of the underdeveloped and newly free countries I have visited in Asia. . . . I've seen enough of determined Asian peoples—both those free and those still struggling against colonial rulers—to know."[79]

Perhaps the boycott's challenge to racial-segregation laws regarding public travel and transportation influenced Worthy to consider how the State Department's regulatory policies regarding international travel were similarly unjust. And perhaps the demand for self-determination and collective energy to which Worthy referenced provoked him to take an ultimate risk. He never directly said so. But in December 1956, as the boycott came to its end with the U.S. Supreme Court ruling against Montgomery's bus-segregation laws, Worthy was secretly finalizing his plans to violate the State Department's ban on travel to China.

Months earlier relations between the United States and China took a severe hit when the U.S. secretary of state, John Foster Dulles, flatly refused China's offer to admit eighteen U.S. newsmen and radio commentators to report from China's interior (rather than from Hong Kong) for a period of thirty days. In the aftermath, a number of U.S. journalists and news companies mulled over disregarding Dulles's directive and furtively traveling to China. Concerned over whether or not the reporters might take this risk, the State Department devoted the autumn months to persuading news entities, including CBS, NBC, the Associated Press, and the *New York Post*, against such unauthorized travel. A State Department official commented, "The present flurry may be only a tempest in the teapot which will, like those in the past, die out. But it is certainly logical to assume that the Chinese Communists will sooner or later open their door to U.S. correspondents, and that the desire of the correspondents to pry the door open will also increase."[80]

On fellowship at Harvard as a Nieman Fellow, Worthy was intrigued by China's offer.[81] He had already petitioned to travel to China in 1953 during his whirlwind tour around East Asia, but was turned down by Hong Kong's consulate general. Two years later he requested again but was denied by the U.S. State Department.[82] The third time was the charm. On December 12, 1956, he received a cablegram from Zhu Le, the secretary of the Information Department of the Chinese Foreign Ministry. Zhu informed Worthy that the Chinese government had granted him a one-month visa that he could collect in Sumchon, China. On Sunday, December 23, Worthy traveled to Hong Kong. And there, in Lo Wu, along the border separating Hong Kong from Shenzhen, Worthy entered Mainland China, traveling thereafter by train to Guangzhou, where he met with the Chinese Intourists travel agency to organize his accommodations and the rest of his journey.[83] He then embarked on a nine-hour flight from Guangzhou to Beijing. After nearly two days of travel, he celebrated his arrival in China by enjoying a Christmas Day feast of *Beijing kaoya* (Beijing roast duck). Days later, the *Look* magazine journalist Edmund Stevens and the photographer Philip Harrington followed Worthy's lead, the pair traveling to China from the Soviet Union.[84]

The State Department immediately went into spin control. It claimed that while the reporters' travel jeopardized U.S. foreign policy, the lack of a U.S. embassy in China left the journalists susceptible to Chinese intimidation and imprisonment.[85] Behind closed doors though, the department debated over what methods might be best to coerce the journalists to leave China as soon as possible. The department contemplated freezing the newsmen's bank accounts, employing the regulations of the Office of Foreign Assets Control to rule them as "designated nationals," whereby the journalists would be prohibited from doing any future business with U.S. companies, and federally charging them under the provisions of Trading with the Enemy Act. Ralph N. Clough, the director of the State Department's Office of Chinese Affairs, for one, spoke to the importance of formulating an aggressive disciplinary response. "It is obvious that we are now faced with a test case of our policy aimed at preventing Americans from traveling to Communist China," he wrote in a brief. "If no punitive action is taken against Worthy, the ban on travel to the China mainland will collapse rapidly, as he will be followed by a stream of other correspondents and probably also by missionaries, scholars, and others. . . . It is essential to take action against Worthy which will deter others from following his example."[86] Following Clough's directive, the department took quick action. On December 28, it revoked the journalists' passports on the basis that they had "fallen in with Communist purposes."[87]

Worthy was not intimidated by these actions. For forty-one days he endured China's winter cold, traveling to Nanjing, Shanghai, and Beijing and broadcasting reports that were directly beamed to San Francisco. At the official residence of Premier Zhou Enlai, Worthy spoke with the official and his aide, Pu Shan. Besides discussing what Zhou identified as the hypocrisies of U.S. foreign policy, particularly its closed-door stance toward China, Zhou criticized the U.S. government's revocation of Worthy's, Stevens's, and Harrington's passports: "The fact that the United States government revoked the passports of the three American journalists in China shows that the United States government hasn't taken into account the desire of the American people to improve relations between China and the United States and to have contacts with the American people." Zhou commented, "On China's part, we are willing to meet this desire."[88]

News of this conversation with Zhou frustrated State Department officials. One unnamed official speculated that Zhou would exploit the interview along similar lines as the Chinese delegation's actions at the Bandung Conference, where the delegation successfully articulated a vision of nonalignment and Third World peaceful coexistence. The official remarked that Worthy's interview supplied Zhou with another opportunity to distinguish China's position from that of the Soviet Union and strengthen China's alliances with other Asian nation-states. "[Zhou] conducted himself as the representative of a conventional power, rather than as an emissary of Communism. . . . [He] will strengthen the trends in Asian thinking set in motion during the Bandung conference," the official explained. "This is because Asians . . . strongly tend to believe that Communist China is unlike the USSR—basically Asian, nationalistic, not subordinate to Russia, and more moderate."[89]

After completing the interview with Zhou, Worthy documented the activities of China's street committees (jiedao banshichu), local organizations that administered programs concerning economic affairs, charity, and public health. From interviews, he discerned that the committees were producing "a quiet liberalization movement."[90] Worthy commented, "The Chinese had virtually wiped out contagious diseases. There were no people starving in China and no trucks going around picking up bodies of people who had died the night before."[91] But he also deduced that government manipulation and coercion compelled the committees to patrol and keep tabs on societal members' thoughts and deeds, identifying individuals who criticized or disagreed with the government's mandate. Fear of the committees and government thus meant that few people were willing to speak honestly with Worthy about these institutions. "[People] say what is safe to say," he wrote. "I don't know whether they believe it or not."[92]

Worthy personally sensed the extremity of the Chinese government's totalitarianism when he was given thirty minutes to interview Reverend Paul J. Mackensen Jr., one of ten U.S. missionaries imprisoned in Shanghai.[93] Describing this meeting as "one of the most moving and tragic experiences" he had ever had, Worthy found Mackensen's treatment appalling and unjust.[94] Yet he felt strongly that he could not separate Mackensen's predicament from the larger context of Western imperialism. Western religious practices in China resembled U.S. racial customs—missionaries had "carried their home-pattern abroad" and "transfer[red] their 'American Color Line' abroad to other people." Worthy therefore conceded that the jailing of the missionaries, although inhumane, was a terrible consequence of decades of Euro-American empire-building. "In the course of human affairs, it is inevitable that a day of retribution comes. It is the great American tragedy and will remain so until we do something about our color consciousness. The missionaries were . . . just as bewildered as the Alabama whites in the Montgomery Bus Boycott," he wrote.[95] Worthy added that the residue of Western imperialism and foreign occupation could also be perceived within Chinese government policy. In attempting to rapidly develop the nation so that it could be sustainable and independent, and so that it could compete economically, technologically, and militarily, China's leadership had spared no costs. This included ignoring the human rights of its citizenry and curbing their ability to police the state's expanding power: "Authoritarian temptations to cut corners and suppress freedom would face any government that tackled the problems of meeting the needs of a population that increases by one million mouths each month."[96]

The contradictions of Chinese communism materialized even further for Worthy after his interview with twenty-five-year-old Corporal William C. White, one of the three African American POWs who declined repatriation at the war's end. By the point of Worthy's travel to China, White was a student of law at the People's University in Beijing, one of the few remaining U.S. non-repatriates still living in China. Over the course of the decade, the contingent of war prisoners who had opted for life in China had decreased substantially. By 1958, the total number was reduced to nine, the majority having returned to the United States to face dishonorable discharges, imprisonment, and media scrutiny. All three of the black soldiers—White, Clarence Adams, and

FIGURE 2.3: Worthy stands in front of the prison in Shanghai where he interviewed Reverend Paul Mackensen, February 1, 1957. Courtesy of AP Photo.

LaRance Sullivan—had stayed on. After completing their preliminary studies at People's University, Adams had been sent south to study Chinese contemporary literature and history at Wuhan University, whereas Sullivan had been sent to work as a lathe operator in a Hankou auto plant. But Sullivan's time in the plant was short-lived.[97] He joined the exodus of nonrepatriates and returned to the United States in the spring of 1958. Homesickness, not communism, he insisted, was the cause.[98]

Over the course of two hours, White defended his decision to relocate to China. "To confuse the American people, the United States Government said we were brainwashed," he said. "If brainwashed is wanting peace, equality, and an end to all unjust and fascist systems then I've been brainwashed." White furthermore maintained that it was his reluctance to face U.S. racial discrimination that prompted his choice. The freedoms and support of Chinese society, he remarked, contrasted sharply with Jim Crow antiblack violence and discrimination. "The only ways for us colored people to have equality is to have a system like this Chinese system," White asserted. Worthy, however, questioned the sincerity of White's claims. White's statements lacked "original thought and analysis," Worthy later wrote, and appeared to be "mechanical playbacks of lectures and indoctrination, spoken in practically neutral tones as if from memory." For instance, White condemned capitalism yet offered no consideration of China's socioeconomic structure or awareness of the government's repressive tactics toward Chinese citizens. Similarly, he denounced U.S. racial discrimination but had little knowledge about the treatment and conditions experienced by China's ethnic minorities. Of White's romanticization of Chinese life and mimicry of communist ideology, Worthy remarked: "It is easy to detect in his rote answers the impact of the pre-law Party-line courses that he recently completed."[99]

To a large extent, White's uncomplicated evaluation of Chinese communism seemed to be a product of his dependence on assessing China through the prism of U.S. race relations. Worthy acknowledged the seductiveness of this standpoint: "Colored Americans, wherever they may be, view events in terms of color. This I know from self-examination of my own mental workings." He admitted, "Colored visitors from the States find themselves peering at institutions and social relations in a one-track effort to determine whether life there would mean an end to the haunting self-consciousness of dark pigmentation." This "one-track" evaluation, however, prevented some African Americans from making sense of the conditions and realities impacting groups elsewhere. White, for example, conveyed this in his inability to effectively comprehend social inequality and government repression in China. To evaluate China's conditions on the basis of U.S. racial segregation was a drastic oversimplification. Worthy quipped, "Were freedom from color discrimination the only consideration in the pursuit of human happiness[,] China of 1957 could be a Mecca for half the population of Mississippi and all the residents of Harlem." Nonetheless, Worthy admitted that while it was imperative to "fit the anti-Western communist pattern of this country [China] into the broader Afro-Asian revolt against white supremacy," it was also crucial not to ignore societal injustice and the government's dictatorial rule of law.[100]

One important topic that Worthy did not probe White about was the differences between White's treatment in China and that experienced by African exchange students. As part of its trade and diplomatic relations with various

African countries, the Chinese government in 1958 began offering scholarships to African students, the first wave admitted to Beijing's Institute of Foreign Languages and Beijing Medical College. Once in China, most of these students found life difficult. They complained of frequent political indoctrination, food shortages, censored mail, and surveillance. While they admitted that the privileges they were afforded made their lives comparably better than that of their Chinese classmates and Chinese citizens in general, they also relayed experiencing recurrent racial discrimination, a reality that contrasted with Mao's and the CCP's constant claim that racism was a Western disease that had not taken hold among Chinese people. One of these African students even authored a book detailing this mistreatment, noting how much of it was bred by Chinese frustration with poverty and government mismanagement and negligence.[101] Several students were physically accosted and attacked, the most violent example being in 1962 at the Beijing Peace Hotel when three Zanzibari expatriates were beaten by a mob.[102]

Some of this discrimination was the result of African men's fraternization with Chinese women, their interracial relationships and friendships viewed as taboo by some Chinese citizens. While African-Chinese romantic relationships were condemned and obstructed (some Chinese women were sent away to communes and prisons for engaging in such affairs), other foreigners, particularly Western expatriates, were permitted to date Chinese women. This included the African Americans nonrepatriates White and Adams; both men went on to marry Chinese women and father mixed-race children. While these two men also experienced some backlash as a result of their relationships, their social lives and romantic partnerships nonetheless were not policed in the same fashion as that of African male students.[103]

In any case, the racism exhibited against African students led many of them to request to return home. The Chinese government initially refused these appeals out of fear that news of the students' treatment would diminish China's credibility abroad. The intensity of the students' demands for repatriation, however, led the students to stage hunger strikes and public demonstrations. Fearful over these protests receiving world attention, the Chinese government by 1963 approved the expulsion of almost one hundred African students.[104] Ultimately, these students' experiences reveal additional inconsistencies in White's positive portrayal of black student life in China and in the Chinese government's depiction of China as a racial safe haven. In addition, what is evident is that ideas and practices concerning race and blackness structured black American exiles' and African students' expatriate experiences in China very differently.

Be that as it may, six weeks of travel made quite an impression on Worthy. Much of this was due to the assistance of the twenty-two year-old Yan Shao

Hua, an Intourist representative; Madame Gong Peng, the head of the Foreign Ministry's Information Department and the English secretary to Zhou Enlai; and Zhen Hui and Si Yun, two members of the liaison section for foreign journalists. Although they were unable to secure Worthy an interview with Mao, their persistence and ingenuity led to his dialogues with Zhou, Mackensen, and White. These were not "the conventional press interviews," Worthy admitted. "A decision was obviously made on a high level to 'reward,' with bonuses as it were, the three newsmen who defied the State Department ban on travel." But what also concerned Worthy were the requests that were vetoed and the high level of state regulation that he encountered. He was not allowed to visit any homes or trade-union meetings, and he was prevented from meeting with Chinese journalists and intellectuals. "The Chinese have their country now so rigged that only authorized news gets out," he commented.[105] Worthy still reasoned that having permanent U.S. press coverage in China would broaden Americans' exposure to Chinese life and politics. No longer reliant solely on secondhand reports, permanent correspondents could develop relationships with government insiders and follow up on leads, personally obtaining information and producing coverage that would help the United States "revolutionize its thinking about the Chinese government."[106]

Worthy left China in early February.[107] When his passport expired one month later, the State Department seized the opportunity, denying his application for passport renewal. This decision contrasted with the department's willingness to reinstate the *Look* magazine journalists Harrington's and Stevens's passports. Citing provisions of section 51.136 of Title 22 of the Code of Federal Passport Regulations, the department ruled that Worthy's travel was "contrary to known and existing United States foreign policy and was otherwise prejudicial to the interests of the United States." The department added that curbing his right to travel was necessary since he displayed an unwillingness to "abide by [the] geographical limitations . . . which may be placed in the passport."[108]

What followed was a two-year appeal by Worthy's ACLU legal team before the State Department's Passport Appeals Board. Worthy's attorneys argued that because the secretary of state was not sanctioned with the statutory power to designate "restricted geographical areas," "the question of 'defying' or 'complying' with State Department regulations was never raised" when Worthy first planned the trip.[109] The lawyers additionally asserted that the U.S. Constitution protected Worthy's right to an unrestricted passport. The State Department's actions therefore made Worthy "a prisoner in his own country."[110] Framing Worthy as a World War II draft dodger and antigovernment troublemaker, the State Department denied claims that its insistence on not renewing Worthy's passport was an example of government regulation of the press.[111] Leaning toward the State Department's argument, the Appeal Board ruled that Worthy's passport could only be renewed if he pledged to abide by the State Department's restrictions during his future travels. Worthy refused to make such a pledge, arguing that he could not "abide by what he consider[ed] an unconstitutional condition."[112] His appeal was consequently denied.

Worthy's attorneys next appealed the case at the federal level, but the court upheld the original ruling. The court explained in *Worthy v. Herter*, "The right here involved is not a right to think or speak; it is a right to be physically present in a certain place. Freedom of press bears restrictions. . . . Merely because a newsman has a right to travel does not mean he can go anywhere he wishes." The court added that the restriction of Worthy's travel rights was not motivated by disagreement with his political beliefs or his polemical writings.[113] It rather was a consequence of Worthy's presence in particular "trouble spots," travel that ultimately "impede[d] the execution of American foreign policy." The court concluded, "The authority to determine what would and what would not better our foreign relations is not vested in individual citizens, even though they be newsmen. . . . To order the Secretary of State to do something, because we believe it would be better for our foreign relations than his plan, would be a gross usurpation of Executive powers."[114] In 1959, the Supreme Court affirmed the federal court's ruling by opting to deny Worthy's case a review.

Among the journalists and politicians in the mainstream who defended Worthy's travel to China, there were two main strains of argument. Some read the case as being primarily about the rights of the news media. The attack on Worthy, these journalists insisted, was an attack on the First Amendment, preventing media institutions' access to freedom of speech and freedom to cover stories void of government regulation and manipulation.[115] Other journalists and political officials maintained that the State Department's actions impeded on Worthy's constitutional rights to mobility and free thought and worked against the promotion of unrestricted access to information by U.S. citizens.[116] Nonetheless, while Worthy received serious grassroots support, mainstream news institutions were reluctant to outwardly endorse his appeal. In addition, a host of people came out against Worthy. The white-supremacist Ku Klux Klan even weighed in, suggesting that Worthy relocate to the USSR and take advantage of the travel privileges granted to citizens there.[117] In the end, Worthy and his leftist supporters took both the U.S. press and the larger U.S. public's failure to support him as a sign of the power of the antiradical political attacks that were pervading U.S. life.[118]

Nonetheless, Worthy's reports on the interactions between black POWs and Chinese prison-camp instructors, and later his violation of the State Department's ban on travel to China, challenged dominant U.S. depictions of the

FIGURE 2.4: The Chicago Committee to Defend William Worthy, January 15, 1963. Courtesy of Sun-Times Media.

Korean War and Chinese Communism. To impede his knack at locating connections between the U.S. government's treatment of populations of color at home and abroad, and to silence his efforts to supply a more complex and factual portrayal of Asian revolutions, the U.S. government revoked his passport. This political attack on Worthy was not unique. Throughout the Cold War, passport regulation was a central instrument of U.S. power that prevented both freedom of travel and thought and that worked "to link individuals to foreign policy and . . . classify travelers as safe or dangerous, desirable or undesirable."[119] But restricting Worthy's ability to travel and report from abroad also aided the government in maintaining, what Worthy described as, the role "of the press in carrying out the foreign policy of the United States government." By limiting both who could travel abroad and what information could be reported, the U.S. government planted "seeds of control" in the news media and American minds.[120]

Be that as it may, confiscation of his passport did not stop Worthy from producing high-quality foreign correspondence. In late 1957, months after the State Department Passport Appeals Board's decision, Worthy secretly traveled to Cuba. He entered and exited the country only with an affidavit of identity, and this was the first of several trips he made there over four years. During this period, he reported on the revolutionary struggles being waged in Cuba, devoting great attention to the 1959 defeat of the U.S.-supported Fulgencio Batista regime by the 26th of July Movement led by Fidel Castro. Worthy's articles rejected the Eisenhower and Kennedy administrations' foreign policy on Cuba. The U.S. government, Worthy explained, was dismayed that a former slave colony and one-crop West Indian economy was challenging the U.S. dominance of Latin America: "The economic and political colonialism of the West has always had its color rationale. . . . [To the] equally twisted U.S. backers[,] the contagious racial equality in revolutionary Cuba looks dangerously like an incoming tide of black supremacy." Worthy concluded that Cuba's aversion to "play the familiar role of a Latin Uncle Tom" was therefore preventing the United States from putting "Afro-Cubans back into their Jim Crow 'place.'"[121]

And so it was that on October 10, 1961, Worthy's passport woes met another roadblock. Returning by plane to Miami International Airport after eleven weeks in Cuba, Worthy was stopped by an Immigration and Naturalization Service officer after he failed to produce a passport. Carrying only his birth certificate as proof of citizenship, Worthy was charged for traveling without a passport and for violating the government's ban on travel to Cuba. Six months later he was federally indicted under the Immigration and Nationality Act of 1952 (also known as the McCarran-Walter Act), a provision that although originally created to restrict immigration into the United States was used to bar suspected U.S. subversives from reentering U.S. borders after traveling abroad. One year later Worthy was found guilty and sentenced to three months in prison and nine months on probation. The secretary of state, Dean Rusk, endorsed the ruling, arguing that "unrestricted travel by U.S. citizens to or in Cuba . . . would be inimical to the national interest." The Florida district court, moreover, defended its ruling on the basis that Worthy's actions disregarded a presidential mandate and thus served to potentially weaken the president's power. The "determination of a state of emergency, including a ban on travel to Cuba," the court stated, "was a Presidential power 'not subject to judicial inquiry.'"[122] Worthy's legal team spent the next two years appealing the district court's decision. They were ultimately successful. In February 1964 a federal appeals court overturned the conviction, ruling that it was unconstitutional for the government to create a crime out of an U.S. citizen's return to the United States without a passport. Thereafter, Worthy continued to report from overseas, traveling without a passport to North Vietnam, Indonesia, and Cambodia until he was finally issued a new passport in 1968.

The case surrounding Worthy's travel to Cuba brought direct attention to the history of U.S. imperialism in Cuba and to Cuba's growing significance as a hub for radical internationalism. As a member of Fair Play for Cuba Committee, an organization dedicated to increasing awareness about Cuba, Worthy was featured in *Yanki (Yanqui), No!*, a documentary produced for television that examined the reasons for Cuba's opposition to U.S. policy; Worthy also appeared in *The Truth about Cuba*, a film made during his seven-week visit to Cuba. In addition, he helped author "Cuba: A Declaration of Conscience by Afro-Americans," a document signed by a legion of black-radical activists that called for collective black American support for Cuba. "Afro-Americans, don't be fooled—the enemies of the Cubans are our enemies, the Jim Crow bosses of this land where we are still denied our rights. The Cubans are our friends, the enemies of our enemies," the document read.[123]

Over the course of the 1960s, one name on the document loomed large in terms of U.S.-Cuba relations and African American–Chinese cultural exchange: the NAACP leader Robert Franklin Williams. As the next chapter conveys, by the end of the 1960s, Williams and his wife, Mabel, presided over a transnational and radical media apparatus and network that operated out of Havana and later Beijing. It is no wonder then that when the Williams family fled their home in Monroe, North Carolina, after Robert Williams was falsely accused of kidnapping in 1961, Worthy was one of the first people to report the family's whereabouts. In a cable to the *New York Gazette*, Worthy relayed: "Robert F. Williams is safe in Cuba. I know because I ran into him today (Thursday) as he was leaving the Ministry of Foreign Affairs."[124]

Three years later Worthy, by then a leader and organizer of the Freedom Now Party, an independent political party whose objective was to get black candidates elected to public office, authored an exposé for *Esquire* where he again referenced Robert Williams. In the article Worthy recalled a 1961 demonstration outside the UN building where a black contingent of protestors denounced the federal government's failure to protect black citizens from racial violence. There, among the picket lines, Worthy noticed something unusual. Alongside signs demanding justice for black victims of racial oppression were posters hailing "the anti-colonial leadership of Mao Zedong in China." At that time Worthy was extremely skeptical of this revelation of black identification with China. "In 1961 no once anticipated a Peking rendezvous," he maintained. A mere three years had brought a whirlwind of difference to the look and feel of black American struggle though, aspects that could be discerned in the budding relationship between Williams and the People's Republic of China. It seemed that political exile had transformed the NAACP organizer into a "Red Chinese American Negro," an image that more and more young black radicals were viewing as the new "archetype of . . . a black revolutionary."[125]

Nonetheless, for Worthy, freedom of travel and access and participation within an open and ethical media environment were human rights necessary for the defense of democracy and lessening the economic and social divides structured by imperialism and white supremacy. "[We must] dispel the superficial notion that the right to travel is nothing more than the right to go away on a pleasant vacation," he insisted. The U.S. government's repressive policies against him and other radical travelers worked to "disarm the people and the press" by hindering their ability to depict, view, and understand world relations from a critical and well-informed perspective. "Until the nationalism and the quasi-official party line disappear from the daily output of the mass media, the American people will remain out of touch with the realities of life in Africa, Asia, and Latin America," Worthy concluded. "Travel control is thought control and intellectual control."[126]

In the "Ballad of William Worthy," the folk singer Phil Ochs paid tribute to the fearless newsman:

> So, come all you good travelers and fellow-travelers, too
> Yes, and travel all around the world, see every country through
> I'd surely like to come along and see what may be new
> But my passport's disappearing as I sing these words to you
> William Worthy isn't worthy to enter our door . . .
> Went down to Cuba, he's not American any more.
> But somehow it is strange to hear the State Department say,
> "You are living in the free world, in the free world you must stay."

Ochs's lyrics offered a melodic rejoinder to the contradictions of America's Cold War arguments about travel, communication, and freedom. The esteemed poet Langston Hughes expressed an even shrewder viewpoint, albeit through his narrative news columns about the fictional everyday-man Jesse B. "Simple" Semple. At the funeral of a man named Rocky, Simple and other community members eulogized the deceased by sharing stories about the man. As the group lamented over Rocky's passing, an attendee pointed out that Rocky spent his last hours in a dreamlike state reminiscing about his travels, and that one of these journeys had been to China. Slipping in and out consciousness, Rocky offered an earful about his life, one statement of which stands out, although it's a bit unclear whether Rocky was referring to a future visit to China or forecasting his own impending death. "Where I am going, I will not need a cent," Rocky said. "Neither will I need a passport."[127]

FIGURE P2.1: "Jianjue zhichi Meiguo heiren fandui zhongzuqishi de zhengyi douzheng!"
(Resolutely support the just struggle of black Americans against racism!), 1963.
Courtesy of the Collection of Pierre-Loïc Lavigne.

PART II

THE 1960s
The East Is Red and Black

An extremely powerful revolutionary force is latent in the more than twenty million Black Americans. . . . The world revolution has entered a great new era. The struggle of the Black people in the United States for emancipation is a component part of the general struggle of all the people of the world against U.S. imperialism, a component part of the contemporary world revolution.
—MAO ZEDONG

In a 1967 article for *Esquire* magazine, William Worthy examined the internationalist practices of several emerging black-radical individuals and organizations. These people were screening documentary films detailing the plight of various Third World liberation movements, broadcasting statements to U.S. troops stationed in Vietnam, and traveling with small delegations to war-torn areas to network with guerrilla rebels and witness the atrocities of war firsthand. Worthy's interviewees explained that through this work they hoped to encourage African Americans to be more "aware of the global character of the fight against black men" and to view black struggle as "not just an American but an international development." Listing a number of foreign popular struggles to which black leftists, cultural nationalists, and militants looked with envy while also forging substantive connections, Worthy pointed out that "the black panther of Stokely Carmichael" was now working in tandem with "the dragon of China." "The American Negro is dead," Worthy surmised, "and risen as a black man of the world, soul brother to non-whites everywhere."[1] Throughout the 1960s, a central factor that helped engender black radical interest in Chinese communism was the Chinese government's willingness, at least rhetorically, to privilege both class rule and white supremacy as phenomena of capitalism. The historians Betsy Esch and Robin D. G. Kelley point out that China, through its rhetoric on anti-imperialism, racial struggle, and international solidarity, "offered black radicals a 'colored,' or Third World, Marxist model that enabled them to challenge a white and Western vision of class struggle."[2] This was not privileged information. Over the course of the decade, growing numbers of activists and thinkers, while perhaps distancing themselves from Soviet communism, still acknowledged the three features of Mao Zedong's particular ideology of Third World Marxism. "The expression 'anti-white' could summarize all the 'antis'—anti-capitalism, anti-colonialism, anti-imperialism—which Mao Zedong has always advocated fervently," one reporter contended.[3]

Mao first framed China's doctrine of internationalism through his theory of intermediate zones (*zhongjian didai*). Conceived in the late 1940s, Mao maintained that China and other oppressed non-Western countries embodied the intermediate zones between the United States and the Soviet Union. He explained that in the struggle between these two governments, the United States and its allies would work to dominate and control the intermediate zones in order to weaken and defeat the Soviets. It was thus necessary for the countries of the intermediate zone to unite and aid one another in decolonization, national liberation, and anti-imperialist struggle, regardless of whether or not these revolutions were led by communists or radical nationalists. Through this idea Mao situated the concept of "proletarian world revolution" within an explicitly decolonial, antiracist, and anti-imperialist hue that went beyond its common Soviet-centered meaning of global class struggle.[4]

By the 1960s though, China's internationalism became explicitly anti-Soviet, a strategic attempt to counter the ideological supremacy of the Soviet Union among movements worldwide. What began as a 1950s disagreement between Chinese and Soviet leadership over the Stalinist socioeconomic development model transformed into a major geopolitical and ideological dispute. The post-Stalin Soviet regime's criticisms of Stalin's period in power, as well as China's abandonment of the Soviet model of economic development, were early indications of an increasing ideological divide between the two governments. The Soviets were also critical of China's economic policies during the Great Leap Forward. They perceived Mao's dictum that China could leap ahead of Marxist and capitalist development models as a flawed socioeconomic analysis. But it was the Soviets'

1956 policy of détente and peaceful coexistence with the United States and later its discussions with several Western governments about instituting a nuclear weapons test ban that drew the ire of the People's Republic of China (PRC). Some Chinese officials read Moscow's conciliatory tone toward the Western bloc and its proposals of peaceful relations with capitalism and nonviolent transition to socialism as acts of capitulation. It was proof, China's leadership maintained, that the Soviets were abandoning the international communist movement. Incensed by these charges and the increasingly negative tone of Sino-Soviet relations, the Soviets first cancelled their aid to Chinese nuclear weapons programs in 1959, an act that slowed down China's effort to develop its first nuclear warhead. The Soviets then followed up this action, some months later, by recalling all 1,390 Soviet scientists, technical experts, and engineers stationed in China. By the early 1960s the Sino-Soviet alliance and collaborative attempt to build a world revolution was no more.[5]

This political context influenced Mao and the Chinese Communist Party (CCP) to be more adamant in their articulation of China's ties to foreign revolutionary movements, particularly the one being waged by African Americans. Twice over the course of the 1960s, Mao authored major public statements where he endorsed the social movement being waged by blacks in the United States; portions of the second speech, for instance, introduce this section. Although most likely genuine in his support for African American liberation, Mao's speeches were a tactical maneuver, part of a series of strategic gestures that publically shed China of its Soviet shell and more firmly situated Chinese communism alongside anticolonial and antiracist struggle. Endeavoring to cultivate its own socialist-oriented Third World camp, the PRC depicted the USSR as an outsider to the African, Asian, and Latin American political contexts. At Asian-African forums in Moshi, Tanganyika (what became Tanzania), and in Jakarta, Indonesia, for example, Chinese delegations argued that Soviet representatives should be excluded from the proceedings. The USSR was not an Asian or African power, Chinese delegates argued, but a white power with imperial ambitions to dominate Afro-Asia.[6] The Chinese government also accused the Communist Party of the Soviet Union (CPSU) and Communist Party of the United States of America of failing to give full support to the black American struggle, reasoning that Soviet peaceful coexistence with U.S. imperialism led these communist parties to endorse nonviolent civil disobedience over armed self-defense as the central strategy of African American activism. Chinese officials maintained that such policies helped to suppress black militancy and encouraged blacks "to pin their hopes on the kindness of the United States rulers."[7] In response, Soviet leadership denounced these portrayals, asserting that China's claims were "dangerous and intolerable."[8] The Soviets argued that China was fanning the flames of racism, replacing the "Marxist-Leninist principle of the unification of the proletariat of the world and the oppressed peoples with that erroneous and reactionary thesis which wants to unite the peoples on the principles of skin color, races, and continents."[9]

Besides friction with the Soviets, other geopolitical rivalries compelled China to rearticulate its ties to the Third World. News of the grievances of African students studying in China (detailed in chapter 2) and, moreover, China's border clashes with India in 1959 and 1962 fueled China's efforts to strengthen its ideological foothold among foreign leftists. The 1962 war with India, for instance, a brief conflict over territory along the Himalayan border that separated the two countries, severely impacted China's political capital and its Bandung Conference articulations about Asian-African support. That China had initiated an offensive against a fellow Asian power far outweighed the fact that the conflict ended after only one month with a cease-fire.

Zhou Enlai's eleven-country visit to Africa from December 1963 to February 1964 was one key space where China attempted to reaffirm its commitment to Asian-African solidarity. Unconditional, interest-free loans with easy repayment schedules and top-quality equipment and experts for infrastructure development, Zhou asserted, could help protect Third World countries from Western or Soviet influence and dependency. He stressed, "It is not our intention to make them dependent on us. We believe that newly independent countries can build themselves up by relying primarily on their own efforts. The independent development of their national economies will enable them to free themselves from the control of capitalism, both old and new, and thus weaken imperialism."[10] This articulation corresponded with Mao's August 1963 statement regarding African anticolonial movements' struggles for national liberation. "The people who have triumphed in their own revolution should help those still struggling for liberation," he remarked. "This is our internationalist duty."[11]

In the 1970s, Mao's intermediate-zone theory was reconceived via his redefinition of the widely popular concept of "the Third World." The demographer Alfred Sauvy's idea of *tiers monde* (third world), first theorized in 1952, postulated that the decolonial fervor emerging among populations and governments in Africa, Asia, and Latin America after World War II paralleled the centuries-earlier resistance of the French Revolution's third estate.[12] Activists worldwide later adopted Sauvy's term to distinguish the United States and its allies (the First World) from the Soviets and Eastern Europe (the Second World) and from Asian, African, and Latin American countries (the Third World).[13] Through Mao's "three worlds theory" (*san ge shijie de lilun*), China again reworked the framework, this time by distinguishing its foreign-policy ideology from that of the U.S. and Soviet governments. In China's rendering, the Soviet Union was positioned alongside the United States as an imperialist power and primary antagonist of global revolution. The Second World, however, was then composed of the First World's allies in Europe, whereas the Third World continued to be made up of Africa, Asia, and Latin America. Mao and the CCP consequently articulated that it was the task of the Third World to combat the hegemonism (*baquan zhuyi*) of both the United States and the USSR, the latter nation by then identified as representing a "revisionist" (*xiuzheng zhuyi*) form of Marxism-Leninism.[14] Anticolonialists and anti-imperialists worldwide were to *fan xiu, fan di* (oppose revisionism, oppose imperialism) and perceive their struggles for self-determination as constituting *san dou yi duo* (three struggles, one increase), meaning a triad global movement against imperialism, revisionism, and reactionary tendencies.[15]

Black radical travelers' positive portrayals of Chinese communism aided the PRC in facilitating this image of China as a leading Third World force. In these people's writings and their media, China was depicted as on the front lines of confronting global white supremacy and U.S.-Soviet hegemony. A crucial time for these portrayals of China was during the Great Proletarian Cultural Revolution (GPCR; *wuchan jieji wenhua dageming*), a tumultuous period (1966–76) of social unrest and turmoil that rocked Chinese life, politics, and economic growth.[16] The revolution was a consequence of numerous factors, most chiefly the rise of a new dominant class composed of peasant revolutionaries and dispossessed propertied classes, and brewing political divisions among China's leadership. As detailed in chapter 1, the Great Leap Forward, Mao's ambitious five-year plan to modernize China and set in motion the rapid socialist reorganization of the country, was a disaster. In its aftermath, Mao was compelled to relinquish some of his power. Although he was able to retain his position as party chairman, it was demanded that he step down as head of state. Thereafter, while the CCP leaders Liu Shaoqi, Deng Xiaoping, Lin Biao, and Zhou Enlai gained greater decision-making power, China's leading government body, the Politburo, redirected China's economy away from Mao's commune and agricultural collective-driven policies and toward the reinstatement of free markets and private ownership. Simultaneously, a new generation of communist elites was coming to the fore, numbers of whom were children of CCP members and the old educated elites whose economic and cultural capital had been redistributed after the PRC's founding. It was this generation that was being trained for the task of leading the future state bureaucracy.

Viewing these shifts as undercutting China's transformation into a classless society, Mao, his political allies, and cadres loyal to him waged a campaign to purge all party veterans, local officials, and communist elites who were not aligned with his more radical communist view. This endeavor to dismiss and disgrace Mao's opposition and secure his leadership over the party metamorphosed into a chaotic attempt to liquidate the CCP and old and new communist elites. A decade of epic power struggles and social discord thus followed, the central issue of contention being the future of Chinese political, social, and economic development. Framed around Mao's "mass line" philosophy (qunzhong luxian), Chinese citizens were persuaded to fight against sijiu, meaning "the four olds"—old ideas, old culture, old customs, and old habits. They were also told to pao da siling bu (bombard the headquarters)—that is, to challenge elitism, bureaucratism, and revisionism in all institutions; to seize these institutions; and to repurpose them toward the interests of the downtrodden, cong qunzhong, xiang qunzhong (from the masses, to the masses). In sum, Mao's followers were to eliminate counterrevolutionary activities and redistribute power toward the ideals of communism. Some of this resulted in the advancement of education and public health in the countryside. But despite these feats at various local levels, the national movement to secure Mao's hegemony had calamitous effects. While the GPCR usurped power and decision-making abilities away from elites and moved them into the hands of workers and rural-based populations, a culture of lawlessness came to dominate everyday life.

The Central Cultural Revolution Group (CCRG), a newly created government entity that replaced the CCP's Propaganda Department, instigated much of this action. Functioning as the central articulator of Mao's fanatical dictums, the CCRG identified numerous officials and bureaucrats as capitalist roadsters whose "revisionist black" (i.e, counter-revolutionary) ideologies clashed with Mao's philosophy. Declaring that these people's power had to be overrun, the CCRG called on students, workers, and peasants to suppress the corruption of a growing class of Chinese capitalist bureaucrats who were supplanting the Chinese Communist Revolution. China, it was argued, was in need of a new vanguard to help invigorate a new revolution and class struggle.

This call to action led to the formation of the Red Guards (hong weibing), bands of students, young adults, and youths who took it upon themselves to bring Mao and the CCRG's decree to life. Tasking themselves with the responsibility of cleaning the ranks of the CCP and Chinese society, the Red Guards traveled from all parts of the country into Chinese cities and rural communities, congregating in urban universities, secondary schools, and workplaces. In these spaces they called for China's reconstruction. Collectively, they produced millions of dazibao (big character posters) that condemned government and institutional bureaucracy, as well as instituted public hearings where people accused of betraying the Chinese Communist Revolution stood trial and were forced to engage in self-criticism of their "reactionary" and "revisionist" political perspectives. Persecuted individuals also endured other forms harassment and punishment, including public humiliations, the disgracing and dividing of families, physical abuse and torture, sexual abuse and rape, murder, and induced suicide. Mao's government faction, moreover, abetted such activity by sending targeted individuals and families to prisons or countryside communes. And such attacks reached the furthest depths of China's political machine. By the revolution's end, many key party members were sacked from power and either imprisoned or dead, the three most widely known victims being the military leader and Mao heir, Lin Biao; the head of state, Liu Shaoqi; and the official Deng Xiaoping.[17]

During the years leading up to the GPCR and the first few years that followed its commencement, it was difficult for foreigners traveling and living in China to not get pulled into the revolution's widespread enthusiasm and the growing notoriety of Mao's Marxist philosophy. One of these travelers was the Communist journalist and organizer Claudia Jones. Born in Trinidad, Jones had made the United States her home for thirty years, until she was deported in 1955 for her affiliation with the Communist Party. Given political exile in London, she thereafter became a prominent leader among the city's African Caribbean community and campaigned against racial discrimination in housing, education, and employment while also editing the anti-imperialist and antiracist newspaper the *West Indian Gazette and Afro-Asian Caribbean News*. Months before her death in December 1964, Jones traveled to China as an honored guest of state. Throughout her visit she was extremely impressed with the socialist culture being developed by everyday Chinese people: "The great achievements in Socialist Construction in New China . . . permeates every aspect of its society." She commented, "A new morality pervades this ancient land which less than fifteen years ago was engaged in a bitter, protracted anti-imperialist armed struggle to free itself from the ravages of feudalism, semi-colonialism, bureaucratic capitalism and imperialism." In a poem she authored after the trip, Jones concluded that "the dream" of socialism was "unfold[ing]" in China, she too giving central credit to Mao's political thought in helping China forge its revolutionary path.[18]

As translators, educators, language polishers, and media producers in China, other black radicals were of a similar mind as Jones. There they joined a community of Western expatriates that included the Marxist-Leninist journalist Anna Louise Strong, the China insider Sidney Rittenberg, the New Zealand writer Rewi Alley, the former U.S. government official Frank Coe, the Afro-Brit and World Peace Committee member John Horness, the Korean War prisoners Clarence Adams and William White, and many others. Alongside these China residents, African American expatriates and visitors championed Mao's ideas, the Chinese state's achievements, and the GPCR's revolutionary ideology. Navigating the shadowy terrain of Chinese diplomacy and warfare, they thus functioned as unofficial government surrogates, endeavoring to link the social momentum of China's internal struggles to that emerging among U.S. activists. But in helping to expand the CCP's influence outside of China's borders, these radical travelers often minimized the damage caused by Mao's policies and the GPCR's chaotic social environment. Chinese citizens critical of the CCP, or who simply were identified as opponents of Mao's supreme doctrine, as well as various nonwhite populations and governments (India, Taiwan, Tibet, and by the 1970s, Vietnam), found themselves in conflict with the Chinese state, developments that ultimately displayed defects in the CCP's rhetoric of racial internationalism and global proletarian world revolution.

3

SOUL BROTHERS AND SOUL SISTERS OF THE EAST

Your country is so broad so vast,
Yet it does not allow your footprints.
Beautiful is your native town,
But there you may not dwell.
What crime have you committed?
Only that your skin is black . . .
They tried to put the sun in jail.
You found refuge in Cuba, but your heart
Was with your nineteen million brothers . . .
Robert Williams,
I see you standing before a map of your land, thinking:
We must have a people's America . . .
Robert Williams,
Look around at the whole world.
On the banks of the Yangtze where the sun is rising,
You have six hundred and fifty million brothers in arms.
— ZUO ZHONGLING, "TO ROBERT WILLIAMS"

We were able to survive, having built networks of people who had really
the true interests of the people at heart—all over the world. And I think
there still is that element of people who are out there working and
that we all constitute a real power but we don't know it.
— MABEL WILLIAMS

In his poem "An Ocean's Roar of Peace" (1962), the African American militant Robert Franklin Williams encouraged oppressed populations to become "one great voice," their unified "roar" powerful enough to usurp forces of oppression and reshape world affairs.[1] Two years later, the Chinese poet Zuo Zhongling built on Williams's narrative of transnational affiliation. In Zuo's poem the sun functioned as a metaphor for both Williams and China, simultaneously referring to the U.S. government's aversion to engaging China on the world stage and its efforts to imprison Williams for a crime he did not commit.[2] Williams was also treated as a synecdoche for the African American public, particularly black men; Zuo urged the latter to expand their viewpoints beyond the "map of [their] land" to "the whole world." African Americans were not a national minority of nineteen million, Zuo pointed out, but rather constituents of a global majority that included their "six hundred and fifty million brothers" in China.

Such messages resonated with Robert and Mabel Williams, his spouse and intellectual partner. As political refugees, the duo produced dynamic propaganda that emphasized the political connections shared by African Americans and the outside world.[3] Through the *Crusader* newsletter; *Radio Free Dixie*, a self-produced radio show; *Robert Williams in China*, a documentary produced in conjunction with the Chinese government; polemical pamphlets; and political cartoons, the radical couple fed a generation of freedom fighters hungry for militant modes of political activism and seeking stronger connections to revolutionary movements outside the United States. "[Life in] the international scene . . . showed that we were not isolated from struggles of the Third World," Mabel Williams explained. "We thus took it upon ourselves to build a grassroots underground media network that became worldwide."[4]

In the Williamses' media, African Americans and the Third World were identified as *soul brothers and sisters*, an everyday slang term and idiom of endearment commonly used among blacks Americans in the heyday of 1960s black cultural nationalism. This populist sensibility vibrated throughout the Williamses' media, where the couple emphasized social and cultural literacy over dense rhetoric and high-culture sensibilities. Like the communist propaganda art of that time, the images and symbols showcased in the Williamses' media "were part of everyday discourse; as a particular molding of cultural and political forms, they could potentially appeal to a vast and relatively uneducated public in perhaps more powerful ways than the staid narratives contained, for example, in official documents, newspaper editorials, and the like."[5] But even more, the Williamses' various forms of media functioned as strategies of self-defense and transnational resistance against the systematic violence of Jim Crow racial tyranny and U.S. imperialism.[6]

It is worthwhile to explore the Williamses' representations of black solidarity with China. Additionally, the aesthetics of race and internationalism fashioned in their media should be put in conversation with their expatriate travels and Chinese communist propaganda art of the period.[7] But also pertinent are the gender politics that came to shape the Williamses' and the Chinese government's portrayals of black-Chinese connection. Despite the strengths of this iconography, the Williamses' representations, as with the propaganda

FIGURE 3.1: Robert and Mabel Williams are greeted by their hosts. Robert F. Williams Archive, HS 1104, Courtesy of Bentley Historical Library, University of Michigan.

of proletarian world struggle that adorned Chinese Communist Party (CCP) posters and popular imagery, frequently relied on problematic, gender-specific conceptions. Time and again it was the primarily the "soul brothers" of black struggle who took precedence.

★

TRANSNATIONAL PROPAGANDA MACHINE

On the evening of August 28, 1961, the Williams family went underground. Robert Williams and four others (Mae Mallory, Harold Reape, Richard Crowder, and John Lowry) stood accused of kidnapping. These charges were the result of trumped-up allegations by the Monroe, North Carolina, police that this group had kidnapped a white couple who had driven into the Williamses' neighborhood. Pursued by the state police, Robert and Mabel Williams and their two sons, Bobby and John, were secretly driven north during the wee hours of the night. Assisted by a network of civil rights activists and socialists, the family over the following days evaded authorities before making their way into Canada. Once across the border, though, the family learned that fleeing Monroe meant that Robert was also charged with unlawful interstate flight and that the FBI and Royal Canadian Mounted Police had consequently joined in on the hunt for him.

Born and reared in Monroe, a small cotton and textile town southeast of Charlotte, Mabel and Robert Williams grew up experiencing the love and supportive bonds of black community. However, while Monroe's black residents worked extremely hard to carve out spaces of collective support, kinship, and fellowship, assaults on black life were a daily fact. It was a town where racial tyranny and the lawless antiblack violence reigned, where it was commonplace for the Ku Klux Klan and other white supremacists to rally in motorcades of as many as fifteen thousand people around the town's center, led by the police chief of all people.[8]

As a young man, Robert Williams joined the wave of blacks who opted for voluntary exile and what they believed would be better living conditions and work opportunities in northern states. Those dreams were short-lived. As a seventeen-year-old assembly worker in Ford Motor Company's defense plant in Detroit, Williams got bogged down in one of the most devastating race riots in U.S. history. After the smoke cleared, this 1943 clash between black and white residents, the police, and federal troops claimed thirty-eight lives and destroyed property valued at two million dollars.[9] Williams's rejection of white supremacy soon caught the eye of the FBI. By the time he was twenty-one the bureau began building what developed into a budding dossier on the young insurgent.[10] A short time later, Williams left Detroit, going to work briefly in California before being drafted into the army in 1944. Military service however offered him no respite from the racial intolerance and injustice he had endured in Monroe. Consequently, by 1945 Williams's militant and defiant antiracist tone led his military superiors to end his tenure in the armed services. Hit with an undesirable discharge, Williams returned to Monroe in November 1946.

It was back in his hometown that he met sixteen-year-old Mabel Ola Robinson, six years his junior. The sister-in-law of one of Williams's close friends, Robinson had, to some degree, experienced a very different upbringing from Williams, at least in terms of the political perspectives vocalized within their households. Several of Williams's elder family members adamantly rejected Monroe's racial status quo; in contrast, Robinson's family was more moderate in publicizing their views, the family fearful of the consequences of outwardly bucking white supremacy. "Most of the people that I knew were accepting the system as it existed and, as my stepfather used to say, 'staying out of the way of white folks and staying in our place,'" Mabel Williams explained. "You see, I grew up in a time when segregation was accepted by my family and it was just the norm. . . . My parents, they were trying to keep us from getting killed in the segregated South and trying to get us to get our education to get out of there to live a better life somewhere else. . . . They wanted to get us out of the South, because they figured we had no hope for the future."[11]

In no short time, Williams and Robinson were smitten with one another, and by the midpoint of 1947 the young couple was married. At the onset of their marriage, she had little knowledge about political struggle. But her political consciousness was raised in the first years of their partnership, one central site being as an organizer for several social-work programs affiliated with Monroe's Catholic Church. There, she ran a daycare center for working mothers, managed a "clothes closet" that provided poor people with free clothing, and petitioned the town's government for the placement of streetlights, paved streets, and sidewalks in black neighborhoods. It was in the couple's search for employment and efforts to financially support their family, though, that the economic inequalities and class features of Jim Crow racism hit home. Mabel Williams found work mainly in segregated menial jobs, toiling as a hotel maid, a hospital worker, and a poultry processor in a turkey plant. Robert Williams, on the other hand, like many other young black men of that time, could not find local long-term employment and was thus compelled frequently to travel out of state for work. Back in Detroit, for instance, he worked in an aircraft factory and was a member of the United Automobile Workers of America and the Congress of Industrial Organizations, unions that brought together black and white workers. Mabel Williams resolved that the lack of quality employment for black men, the migrant nature of the jobs they could find, and some black women's status as the family breadwinner were leading factors in many black families' dissolution. "I always wondered why my husband could not get a job and keep a job, but I could get jobs, small jobs but jobs nonetheless. I recognize today that that too was a part of the system to divide black men from black women. Black women were given a better opportunity to make a living than black men," Mabel Williams stated. "The young black men didn't really have a chance to get a job that was meaningful enough to support their families. It was a very difficult time that put pressure on marriages and families."[12]

Nearly a decade into their marriage, the Williamses resettled in Monroe. It was in this context that the couple emerged as important voices in the national struggle against Jim Crow racism. In 1955, Robert Williams was elected president of the NAACP's Union County chapter, a collective that was then composed mainly of Monroe and the surrounding areas' black middle class. Aiming to increase the chapter's membership and ties to other demographics, the couple devoted energy to drawing more working-class community members into the chapter. With this critical mass, the chapter then focused its attention on challenging Monroe's segregation laws, particularly restrictions against black use of various public facilities. National awareness about the chapter began to grow as a result of the chapter's rush to defend and build support for two black preteen boys from the area who were imprisoned for kissing a young white girl.[13]

But what the Union County chapter ultimately came to be known for was its reputation as an armed defender of the county's black communities. With a substantial number of former servicemen, workers, and displaced farmers in its membership, the chapter began patrolling black neighborhoods to ward off violence by the police and bands of white supremacists. The severity of these attacks and the North Carolina judicial system's failure to protect the lives of black citizens ultimately prompted Robert Williams to condemn the U.S. South's culture of antiblack violence: "The Negro in the South cannot expect justice in the courts. He must convict his attackers on the spot. He must meet violence with violence, lynching with lynching."[14] His statement broke with the NAACP's national policy of nonviolence, but many black Southerners received his message favorably. Although the Union County chapter's explicit armed self-defense stance did not represent a general trend among other NAACP chapters, throughout the region male and female NAACP members and nonmembers were arming themselves and their households, prepared to defend their communities against attacks from racist militias such as the Ku Klux Klan.[15] The news media, nonetheless, had a field day with Robert Williams's statement, singling out the Union County chapter along with Malcolm X and the Nation of Islam as the faces of African American militancy. These news reports gave little attention to the fact that self-defense represented a more widespread black sensibility than the mere two organizations to which reporters supplied credit. Still, the media fiasco that resulted prompted the NAACP's national leadership to denounce Williams's comments, remove him from his post as chapter president, and suspend him from the national organization for six months.[16]

It was during this time that Robert and Mabel Williams determined that they needed an independent media platform to counteract this barrage of negative coverage and highlight the severity of Southern racial oppression.[17] The Williamses felt that many black newspapers were moving away from the black media's historical legacy as "defenders of the human rights of Afro-Americans and oppressed peoples throughout the world." Instead, the black media was perpetuating the misleading bourgeois images of U.S. life supplied by mainstream U.S. media, functioning as nothing more than "a black echo of the sinister master voice of brainwash."[18] Furthermore, mainstream black media failed to connect U.S. black resistance to anticolonial and anti-imperialist efforts abroad. "They were not talking about the struggles of our people, or the struggles going on among African people," Mabel Williams explained. "We couldn't get that type of information in the South. We [therefore] had to talk about international affairs because it was not being done."[19] The Williamses consequently determined that they must cultivate independent media geared toward radical black perspectives—what the couple came to colloquially refer to as their "personal propaganda machine." With this platform, they could enlist African Americans as vital participants in a global struggle against white supremacy and increase non-American awareness of the harsh realities and brutality of U.S. race relations. "[The] purpose was to throw some light on the problems of [black] people in the States, also to try to inspire [black] people and to inspire them to resist oppression and injustice," Robert Williams maintained. "The idea was to create a link and also to reach [the] people."[20]

The first medium of this propaganda machine was the *Crusader Weekly Newsletter*. First published and distributed on July 26, 1959, the newsletter took its name from the 1920s publication of the African Blood Brotherhood, a Harlem-based black-radical organization. From its inception, the *Crusader* framed blacks' struggles in the South with an internationalist hue, situating U.S. black political struggle against antiblack racism alongside atrocities and oppressive systems in other countries. Echoing a viewpoint that Malcolm X would articulate years later to the United Nations, the *Crusader* encouraged readers to perceive attacks on African Americans as human rights violations. "Wherever there is oppression in the world today, it is the concern of the entire race," the Williamses wrote. "My cause is the same as the Asians against the imperialist. It is the same as the African against the white savage. It is the same as Cuba against the white supremacist imperialist."[21] An early issue of the newsletter, for instance, explained that a progressive radical practice and internationalist outlook went hand in hand. A revolutionary should "so completely identif[y] with mankind," the editorial maintained, that he or she be "impatient with talk of the 'closing of frontiers'" and rather envision "every man [as] a piece of the continent."[22] Cartoons also helped make this point. One image portrayed everyday life in "Dixie," the U.S. South, as analogous to an Eastern European concentration camp. In the image, an elderly white man with a shotgun stood on guard behind the camp's fence deriding the black prisoners. In his comments the elderly guard referenced the 1956 Hungarian Revolution, a spontaneous nationwide uprising that pinned Hungary's people against the Hungarian government's Soviet-imposed policies. Referring to the failure of this mass revolt, the old guard snidely remarked: "Yall can't do lak dem Hungarians and git away wit it!" In another similar cartoon, Nazi Germany was depicted with the caption "Dixie-ism Spreads Abroad."[23]

An international development that drew a great deal of the newsletter's coverage was the 1959 Cuban Revolution. When a band of leftist revolutionaries and rural nationalist guerrillas overthrew the U.S.-backed government of the Cuban president Fulgencio Batista, Cuba, according to the Williamses, became the "source of hope for all oppressed people throughout the world."[24] This was not hyperbole. The toppling of Batista's government by the 26th of July Movement, a force led by Fidel Castro and the military theorist Ernesto "Che" Guevara, spelled out the end of U.S. private interests' semioccupation of Cuba. By the tail end of the 1950s, U.S. companies dominated almost every aspect of the Caribbean island's economy, owning and controlling nearly all mines, oil and mineral extractions, cattle production, sugar plantations, and casinos. Simultaneously, average Cubans found themselves and their country's economic interests curbed by Western exploitation of Cuba's natural and productive resources. Forced to flee to the Dominican Republic and later given political asylum in Portugal, Bastista watched from afar as Cuba transformed from U.S. capital's pawn into an example for radical movements worldwide.

From the point of its establishment, Cuba's new government instigated a gross campaign to rid the nation of corruption, poverty, social inequality, and the influence of foreign capital. Adopting Marxism-Leninism as the nation-state's guiding ideology, Castro's government over time became more greatly influenced by the Cuban Communist Party and the Soviet Union. Still, Castro's regime did not allow close relations with the Soviets to set the course for Cuba's policies. While the government nationalized industry and introduced free health care and education, it also prioritized aiding revolutionary socialist movements in other countries and condemning the oppression of racial groups worldwide, particularly that of U.S. racial discrimination. Identifying Cuban society as an example of racial advancement in-progress, the Cuban government initiated the national abolition of racial codes that privileged white Cubans.[25]

These policies drew the ire of U.S. politicians and businesspeople. Within months the United States broke diplomatic ties with Cuba and prohibited exports to the country. And by the time that President John F. Kennedy entered the White House, one thing that aligned his administration (1961–63) with that of the Eisenhower administration (1953–61) and CIA was its intent on deposing Castro and instituting a regime that was friendlier to U.S. interests.[26]

Cuba's rejection of U.S. dominance and its commitment to engendering self-determination and redistribution of wealth captured U.S. black radicals' imaginations.[27] Media, moreover, played a central role in facilitating these connections. The advertising firm of Rowe-Louis-Fischer-Lockhart, co-owned by the former U.S. boxing champion Joe Louis, was hired by the Cuban Tourist

FIGURE 3.2: Williams (left), Fidel Castro (fourth from left), and others attend a dinner. Robert F. Williams Archive, HS 1089. Courtesy of Bentley Historical Library, University of Michigan.

Bureau to popularize Castro's government among African Americans.[28] Thereafter, black trade magazines and periodicals featured advertisements detailing Cuban racial equality. In these images and captions, African Americans were informed that Cuba lacked segregation and that Afro-Cubans were no longer second-class citizens but rather participating equally alongside Cubans of European and Asian descent in reshaping Cuban life.

Interested in seeing these developments with his own eyes, Robert Williams traveled to Cuba in June 1960. In his travel group were the CBS correspondent Richard Gibson and John Singleton, two members of the Fair Play for Cuba Committee (FPCC), a pro-Cuba U.S. organization that brought greater public awareness to Cuba's process of social and economic development.[29] There the trio met with Prime Minister Castro (see figure 3.2). Castro and Williams immediately took a liking to one another, with both men admiring the other's intellectual prowess, bravado, and righteous belief in his respective cause. Upon Castro's recommendation, Williams was interviewed on Cuban television and radio and was invited to coedit a special issue of the Cuban magazine *Lunes de Revolución*, which featured works by black American writers.[30] "I wish every American Negro could visit Cuba and see what it really means to be treated like a first-class citizen," Williams commented after departing the island.[31] He returned one month later with Mabel Williams and a group of prominent African American activists and artists.[32] Thereafter the Williamses' fascination with

Cuba did not subside. When Castro traveled to New York to speak at the United Nations in September 1960, the Williamses were among a select group allowed private time with the leader in his Harlem accommodations.

Over the subsequent year, Robert Williams toured with the FPCC, visiting black communities across the country to speak in support of Cuba's sovereignty.[33] Cuba, he argued, deserved a chance at true independence and self-determination, one void of U.S. intervention, occupation, militarism, or economic dominance. Accused by liberal and conservative pundits of being a puppet for Cuban and Soviet communism, Williams maintained that while he was extremely skeptical of the Communist Party's arguments about the revolutionary potential of white workers, he did believe that international communism was helping to highlight the glaring contradictions of U.S. liberal democracy and racial liberalism. "Communism is not lynching black people! Communism offers equality," he asserted. "Afro-Americans who constantly listen to news reports about the integration struggle in the USA know that U.S. officials are more concerned about Russia's criticism than they are about the Negro's dislike for Jim Crow." Furthermore, after the failed April 1961 Bay of Pigs invasion and attempt to overthrow the Cuban government by a paramilitary band of Cuban dissidents trained and funded by the CIA, Williams angrily insisted that black Americans view the attack on Cuban sovereignty as an attack on one of their own. "The enemies of the Cuban Revolution are the enemies of U.S. blacks," he declared.[34] Within the next four months the Cubans would convey a similar standpoint when they came to the Williams family's aid.

On August 27, 1961, Robert Williams and several other Union County NAACP members defended a group of Freedom Riders being attacked by the Monroe police and a contingent of racist whites.[35] Fearful of reprisals from the police, state troopers, and racist militias, residents from the Williamses' neighborhood patrolled the community to prevent further attacks. In the midst of these activities, they stopped a car driven by Charles and Mabel Stegall, a white couple whose vehicle resembled that used the day before in a white-supremacist rally. Determining that the crowd's anger and the Stegalls' unabashed racist demeanor was putting the couple in danger of assault or worse, Robert and Mabel Williams deemed it best to temporarily house the Stegalls in their home until things calmed down. Fearful for their safety, the Stegalls accepted the Williamses' offer; they remained in the family's home for several hours until they were escorted outside the neighborhood. But soon after, the Williamses received a phone call from the Monroe police chief who stated that they had received word that Robert Williams had kidnapped the Stegalls and that, consequently, by nightfall Robert would be lynched. This death threat, anxieties about another violent confrontation between police and Monroe black residents, and the police department's trumped-up charges of kidnapping prompted the Williamses to flee the town in the middle of the night.[36]

On the lam, the family traveled north, evading U.S. authorities and slipping into Canada. However, news that they would not find long-term safety in Canada forced them to resolve that there might be only one place where the family would be safe and could remain together—Havana. Although the Williamses' close relations with the Cuban government was a key factor in considering Cuba as a potential site of refuge, what was also significant was that Cuba lacked an extradition treaty with the United States, a fact that ultimately led the country to become a hub for U.S. political refugees throughout the 1960s. "I could think of no other place in the Western Hemisphere other than Cuba where a Negro would be treated as a human being," Robert Williams wrote. "I came to Cuba because I had no alternative."[37]

The family secretly traveled to Havana; Robert journeyed alone and Mabel, Bobby, and John Williams arrived several months afterward. They were housed in several apartments and hotels until issued a private residence. In addition, their living costs were covered by a small monthly stipend provided by the Cuban Institute for Friendship with Foreigners, supporters' donations, and money Robert earned as a writer for the Cuban magazine *Bohemia*. Additional income was generated from sales of *Negroes with Guns* (1962), a book composed of press clippings and speeches by Robert Williams that he completed while in Cuba.

The Williamses' arrival coincided with that of contingents of diplomats, liberation groups, and student groups from Africa, Latin America, and the United States. Among these populations the Williams family was exposed to a wide array of radical political outlooks. Over drinks, food, and cigarettes, hardline communists, socialist intellectuals, aspiring national liberation movement leaders, guerillas in training, and artists discussed world affairs and anti-imperialist struggle. Conversations with FPCC traveling groups also enabled the Williamses to pass along some lessons to visiting young black American militants.[38] To these visitors, the Williamses rationalized that the family's political labor from Cuba would have no impact unless it was helping to galvanize subversive thinking and action among younger generations inside the United States. "To continue the fight from without it must be constantly attacked by our people from within," Mabel Williams explained to them.[39]

With assistance from Cuba's National Institute for Agrarian Reform and use of the institute's print shop, the *Crusader*'s circulation increased from two thousand copies per issue to fifteen thousand. This operation offered the Williamses a far more robust media platform and transnational network. "When first printing *The Crusader*, we focused on local people to get them to understand what was going on. In the process we began exchanging with other left wing and black media and began to get wider distribution," Mabel Williams explained. "By the time we got to Cuba we had a national and international following," she claimed.[40] Produced as a small pamphlet on a higher-quality stock, the newsletter entered the United States through a circuitous route, shipped and carried across U.S. borders, sometimes through Mexico and more often through Canada.[41] The newsletter also obtained foreign distribution through several embassies in Cuba that imported it into their home countries.

The newsletter was enhanced by the artwork of the Chinese Canadian cartoonist Anne B. Lim. Organized around satirical political commentary and jargon, caricatures, and iconography of self-determination and global coalition, Lim's drawings aesthetically inverted the global politics of power in favor of populations of color. These images were also successful in conveying political ideas of global struggle to a broader audience, particularly to black readers who lacked extensive formal education. "We had readers who were illiterate or semi-literate. If the publication was only text, this would marginalize and exclude many potential readers. So we decided to include comics," Mabel Williams stated. "It was a fun thing to do. . . . A lot of people couldn't read, but they could understand the subtlety of the cartoon."[42]

Through this imagery, the *Crusader* cultivated a visual lexicon of Jim Crow racism and white supremacy as global phenomena. One cover adjoined Western imperialism and U.S. racism. It depicted two crows labeled "Jim Crow racism" and "Jim Crow imperialism." Perched on the same branch, the two birds denoted that Jim Crow racism and U.S. foreign policy were "birds of the same feather" and "limbs of the same tree branch." In another cartoon, a dismayed white man stood fearful to move, surrounded by TNT cartons marked "black Ghetto," "Student Revolt," "Violence & Police Brutality," "Mass Unemployment," "Vietnam," and "the Middle East" (see figure 3.3). The image suggested that a revolutionary explosion was imminent in the United States—that various domestic and international conflicts were on the verge of sparking a U.S. social revolution.[43] Other cartoons depicted the police dog as emblematic of state coercion and antiblack violence. In one image the police dog was a sign of physical attacks on black American bodies, and in another it signified military bombings on Third World groups. Moreover, the dogs were always portrayed with white men, a visual assertion that white masculinity was buttressed by racial violence.

The second arm of the Williamses' propaganda machine was broadcast journalism. With Castro's permission, they produced and hosted an international radio show—*Radio Free Dixie*. They had been interested in operating a radio show long before they arrived in Cuba. In Monroe, they were regular listeners

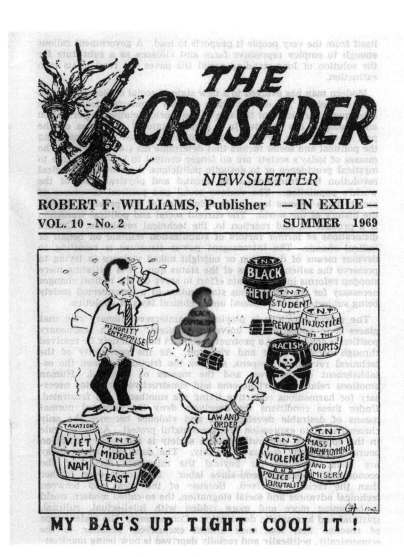

FIGURE 3.3: *Crusader* 10, no. 2 (Summer 1969). Robert F. Williams Archive, HS 11748. Courtesy of Bentley Historical Library, University of Michigan.

of Radio Moscow, Radio Free Europe, and *The Voice of America*; however, they were often disappointed by these stations' slim coverage of the American Civil Rights Movement and decolonization movements outside the United States. According to Mabel Williams, these programs disregarded the "persecution of black leaders and black people in general," yet constantly highlighted "the advances of democracy and middle class wealth." *Radio Free Dixie* was therefore envisioned as a means to provide black Americans with another "pulpit from which to preach and bring attention."[44] "This will be the first completely free radio voice that black people have had to air their case against brutal racial oppression," Robert Williams insisted. "When I am on Radio Free Dixie, I am agitating for my people."[45]

Robert Williams and the Cuban personality Jo Salas hosted *Radio Free Dixie*; Mabel Williams contributed cultural affairs reports; the Afro-Cuban activist Carlos Moore supplied international news coverage. And in between reports, the show played the hottest jazz, blues, rock and roll, and soul music. This music was a central node of the Williamses' political approach. Three nights a week at midnight, the music of Nina Simone, Paul Robeson, Max Roach, John Lee Hooker, and Lead Belly transported listeners to the oral culture and sonic experiences of black America. "John Brown's Body" opened each show. The song's somber melody brought to mind not only the racial tribulations of slavery and the militancy of the abolitionist hero and martyr John Brown but also the everyday sacrifices being made on the front lines of the Black Freedom Movement and other international struggles. By the show's midpoint though, the pianist Erroll Garner's "The Way Back Blues" denoted political refugees' experiences of exile and longings to return home. Similarly, Art Tatum's "Aunt Hagar's Blues," Thelonius Monk's "Bolivar Blues" and "Fivespot Blues," the Trinidadian Winifred Atwell's "Vine Street Boogie" and "Yancey Special," Pete Johnson's "Central Avenue Drag," and Duke Ellington's "C Jam Blues" constituted a contact zone for African American–Cuban encounters and translations of freedom. In short, through these songs music was conceived as a constitutive medium of blacks' worldview, black existence, and the transformation of their condition. "The blare of the juke box," Robert Williams wrote, "the funky, bluesy music lingers far back in your subconscious mind. Somehow its always there, when you're relaxed enough to hear it. It's the soul of black folks. It's the timer that puts the rhythm in our lives, the soul in our dark bodies."[46]

Alongside their work on *Radio Free Dixie*, the Williamses spent time networking with foreign governments and movements critical of U.S. globalism. In 1962, Robert and Mabel Williams initiated a letter-writing campaign to foreign leaders, including Mao Zedong, the Chinese chairman; Ahmed Sukarno, the Indonesian president; Kwame Nkrumah, the Ghanaian president; Norodom Sihanouk, the Cambodian king; and U Thant, the Burmese diplomat and UN secretary-general. Robert Williams stated that by publically condemning U.S. racial practices and taking a united position against "the terror and oppression of Afro-Americans," these leaders could help "halt [the] Ku Klux Klan government persecution" of black freedom fighters.[47]

What prompted the couple to reach out to Mao is unknown. Prior to their relocation to Cuba, they had used the *Crusader* as a vehicle to demand that the United Nations end China's isolation "from the mainstream of international life" and include China's delegates in the UN General Assembly. Referencing France's colonial and military activities in Southeast Asia, the Williamses poked holes in U.S. claims that China's exclusion from the United Nations was based on the aggressive foreign policy of the People's Republic of China (PRC) and inhumane treatment of its citizenry: "What's the difference between a Chinese murderer and a French one?" The Williamses concluded that U.S. efforts to marginalize China were mainly provoked by China's unwillingness to heel to America's agenda in East Asia. "The Chinese Red Army is the only fight America didn't get . . . to dictate," the couple remarked.[48] In addition, there were similarities between Robert Williams's ideas about armed self-defense and Mao's argument that "political power grows out of a barrel of a gun."[49] While Williams spoke to the importance of exploited peoples being able to defend themselves from state violence, Mao identified seizure of the instruments of force and violence and rule over the military as a requisite for any successful program of overthrowing state power. Both men also pointed to the importance of galvanizing the most exploited and dominated groups.

The Williamses' advocacy for China's inclusion in the UN and the parallels of Mao's and Robert Williams' political thinking must have been providence for what was to come. On August 8, 1963, three weeks before the March on Washington for Jobs and Freedom, Mao publically acknowledged the two letters that the couple had previously written to him. In a speech to a visiting African delegation representing various nationalist organizations and guerrilla movements, he declared China's support for the U.S. black liberation movement.[50]

★

THUNDER IN THE EAST

One of his first statements to be publicized internationally in almost six years, Mao's proclamation positioned U.S. liberal democracy and capitalism as the paramount agents of both U.S. racial oppression and worldwide imperialism. He asserted, "The fascist atrocities of the U.S. imperialists against the Negro people has exposed the true nature of the so-called American democracy and freedom and revealed the inner link between the reactionary policies pursued by the U.S. government at home and its policies of aggression abroad." Still, Mao relayed that the explosion of demonstrations and resistance among black Americans displayed the inevitability of defeat for the U.S. liberal democracy. "The American Negroes will be victorious in their just struggle," he insisted, reminding blacks that the size of their mass far outnumbered that of white Americans and Europeans. "We," Mao said of the world's nonwhite populations, "are in the majority and they," referring to whites and the U.S. power structure, "are in the minority."[51] The message was broadcast on Radio Beijing and circulated throughout the world in pamphlets published in multiple languages. What's more, on the day of the March on Washington for Jobs and Freedom, a documentary film about antiblack demonstrations and U.S. racial violence was shown in theaters throughout Beijing.[52]

The Chinese government also issued a propaganda poster that celebrated U.S. black militancy, the first of a series of images to commemorate the U.S. Black Freedom Struggle (see figure 3.4). With the caption "Jianjue zhichi Meiguo heirende zhengyi douzheng!" (Resolutely support the just struggle of Black Americans!) at the top and bottom of the poster, the image's right corner includes one section of Mao's statement in support of civil rights. It reads: "The evil system of colonialism, imperialism grew on along with the enslavement of the Negroes and the trade in Negroes. It will surely come to its end with the thorough emancipation of the black people." The poster also displays two black men leading an insurrection of black men, the first leader defending himself by tightly gripping the wrist of a white hand that attempts to strike him with a baton, while the other leader stands with hand raised high, leading the charge. In the distance of this black rebellion sits the U.S. Capitol, which relayed that U.S. race relations were either going to be transformed through radical legislative action or through the revolutionary dissolution of the institutions that permitted such injustice.

Various elements of the poster aesthetically conveyed key points from Mao's speech. Above the two rebellion leaders are signs written in multiple languages calling for opposition to imperialism and racial discrimination. This denoted the internationalist ethos of Mao's statement, where he called upon "people of all colors throughout the world to oppose the racial discrimination practiced by U.S. imperialism." The poster also frames black resistance in masculinist terms, the agitators dominantly male bodied. Of additional note is that these insurrectionists carry pitchforks and other farming tools rather than guns. Black struggle was thus represented as having not yet reached the point of firearm use, but nonetheless armed and no longer nonviolent. Rather than suggesting that black self-defense was a new development in African American political activity, the poster depicted it as a continuation of a long history of black resistance. For instance, throughout Mao's statement, he positioned black Americans as an enslaved population, working in what he described as "the most backbreaking and most despised jobs," and whose resistance was "unarmed, bare-handed." Black political struggle was thus, to some degree, likened to slave resistance of previous centuries, the poster's depiction freezing black Americans in time.

The poster is one example of a growing line of CCP-produced art, imagery

FIGURE 3.4: "Jianjue zhichi Meiguo heirende zhengyi douzheng!" (Resolutely support the just struggle of black Americans!), 1963. Courtesy of Stefan R. Landsberger Collection, International Institute of Social History (Amsterdam).

intended to export Chinese communism's merits to foreign populations and Chinese publics. Within CCP policy, art became a central mode of educating Chinese citizens with the ideology of classless society and the dominance of the party-state. A decade earlier Mao had charged artists and writers to produce art that would help construct a new socialist nation. Such art should be centered on uplifting China's most marginalized populations and transforming Chinese citizens' consciousness toward the work of communism. "Revolutionary culture is a powerful revolutionary weapon of the broad masses of the people," Mao stated. "It prepares the ground ideologically before the revolution comes and is an important, indeed essential, fighting front in the general revolutionary front during the revolution." Mao later maintained that alongside China's military what the country required was a "cultural army," a creative force able "to ensure that literature and art fit well into the whole revolutionary machine as a component part, that they operate as powerful weapons for uniting and educating the people and for attacking and destroying the enemy." Condemning the idea of art for art's sake, Mao echoed Lenin's assertion that art should serve "the broadest section of people."[53]

Socialist realism, the Soviet Union's preferred style of art, was subsequently introduced into China and eventually decreed as the country's official art style. Socialist realism, a rejection of Western styles that glorified the aristocracy, lionized the working masses and the teleology of communism's advancement. Such depictions best came to life in *xuanchuan hua* (state-sponsored propaganda pictures or posters).[54] Generally inexpensive, mass circulated, posted on public walls, and sold in stores, these posters supplied Chinese viewers with a visual means to learn communist ideals. Modern print technology aided in this task; the CCP was able to print and issue these posters in large quantities for mass consumption. Considering that the rate of illiteracy in China was just over 57 percent by the early 1960s, these propaganda posters played a central function in transmitting Chinese communist principles to Chinese publics in what appeared to be an uncomplicated, easily graspable way.[55]

The CCP's iconography of black American struggle was therefore intended not just for black viewers and foreign audiences but also for Chinese publics. The poster framed black Americans as oppressed and enslaved rural laborers and unemployed people—namely as elements of the global rural poor. This image tied into the CCP's Third World Marxist line, specifically into Mao's theory of world revolution (*shijie geming*), where he privileged the countryside as the seedbed of revolution. For Mao and other Chinese officials, the category of "the countryside" represented both Chinese peasants, who were identified as principal agents of change in China, and the Third World, a force that Mao argued would inevitably crush the city-like dominance of Euro-American capitalism and imperialism. The iconography in the poster therefore offers Chinese publics an accessible encoding of black Americans' political plight. Blacks are depicted as the U.S. equivalent to the revolutionary class that, according to the CCP, was transforming Chinese life and that ultimately would defeat global capitalism. The figures in the image thus denote a metaphorical transfer of embodiment between black Americans, China, and the world revolution—the Capitol in the distance of the image symbolizes the West, the heavenly red hue signifies communism and the East's rising wind, and the black rebels indicate both Chinese peasants and the crushing force of a world proletariat movement. The poster, in sum, functioned within a broad ideological framework organized around substantiating a discursive link between Chinese communism, black struggle, and world revolution, with China subtly depicted as a model for U.S. black liberation and global revolutionary struggle.

For the CCP, this was an important statement to make. China's endorsement of the Civil Rights Movement and proposals of racial, anticapitalist internationalism were, to some degree, instigated by China's developing rift with the Soviet Union. Positioning Chinese communism as an ally of U.S. racial struggle aided in emphasizing two political lines that became more prominent over the course of the 1960s—that Soviet communism was disconnected from the realities of the Third World and that the Soviets were a racist, white imperialist power. In addition, the poster and statement supporting the U.S. black struggle may have been mobilized to curb the news of the mistreatment experienced by African students at Chinese universities and the mass expulsions of almost one hundred African students one year prior (detailed in chapter 2). It is most likely not a coincidence that Mao first read the statement in support of black Americans in front of a group of African dignitaries visiting China on a diplomatic visit. Whatever the case may be, asserting solidarity with black resistance served multiple strategic purposes: it worked to stigmatize Soviet communism, strengthen the aura of Chinese communism, and reemphasize China's opposition to white supremacy and imperialism. In short, it was a political project with wide ambitions.

After the issuance of Mao's statement, a rally was held in Beijing, where more than ten thousand Chinese and a contingent of Western expatriates echoed the call.[56] The Williamses were ecstatic to learn of these gestures of support. The couple immediately cabled the Chinese government to express their gratitude.[57] Mao and the Chinese people's actions, the Williamses ruled, had "elevate[d] [black] people's struggles to the fold of world revolution."[58] Back in the United States, however, China's show of solidarity received mixed reactions. After publishing sections of Mao's statement on the front page, the New York Times described Mao's call for support as "the beginning of the Chinese worldwide racial campaign in favor of colored people."[59] Much of mainstream U.S. media seconded this claim, arguing that the statement was a strategic attempt to engender violent mayhem in the United States. While one reporter framed Mao's decree as "a barely disguised appeal to racist revolution," another maintained that "Mao's call for racial warfare" was "aggressively promoting a program of subversion within our borders."[60] China was subsequently accused of infiltrating U.S. student organizations, labor unions, and Chinese American civic organizations.

African American leaders' responses to Mao's statement were anything but homogenous. On the international radio show *Voice of America*, the Congress of Racial Equality member Marvin Rich repudiated the gesture.[61] Roy Wilkins, the NAACP executive secretary, responded in a similar manner; he argued that China's treatment of its own people warranted criticisms analogous to that which Mao made of the United States: "We await the opportunity to send our felicitations to Chinese citizens gathered in a huge demonstration in your nation's capital to protest living conditions under your government and welcomed there by your heads of state."[62] An editorialist for the *New York Amsterdam News*, on the other hand, contended that China was "play[ing] off the susceptibilities of blacks." "To kindle, or sustain or direct racial animosities all over the world," the journalist reasoned, "is the golden opportunity not to be missed."[63] However, the black nationalist and evolving internationalist Malcolm X was of a different mindset. Malcolm X acknowledged that for black Americans, China's open support for black struggle communicated an important message: "We are not alone."[64] The historian and writer Joel A. Rogers offered a more nuanced assessment. The U.S.-Soviet détente and brewing tensions between China and the Soviet Union, he explained, were the real factors provoking Mao's proclamation. To China's fortune, the intensification of blacks' campaigns was occurring simultaneously with the advancement of the U.S.-Soviet rapprochement: "China is now claiming that she is the logical champion of the darker races; that she is colored; and the Russians are white. Chinese are discriminated against in Western lands because of race; the Russians aren't." Rogers concluded, "The result as I see it is that the darker peoples . . . will lean more and more to the Chinese. . . . This present racial explosion in the United States is far more important in international politics than we dream of."[65]

Amid debates over the legitimacy of China's claims of racial coalition, the Williamses were invited by the China Peace Committee to participate in Beijing's fourteenth annual National Day celebrations. Accepting the invitation, Robert and Mabel Williams traveled to China in late September 1963. "The people of the whole country welcome you," Guo Moruo, the chairman of the China Peace Committee, informed them at their arrival. "The name Robert Williams is even known to Chinese children."[66] Such honorary treatment continued throughout the Williamses' stay where, by its end, the couple was exuberant in their celebration of Chinese life and politics. "More of our Freedom Fighters should visit our Chinese brothers and sisters," the Williamses stated in a *Crusader* special edition dedicated to their China travels. "To see China is to see the hope of all of the oppressed and dehumanized."[67] Included in the special edition were Mao's statement in support of black struggle in its entirety, a speech by the Chinese head of state Liu Shaoqi that bespoke China's ties to Third World anti-imperialist movements, a press release announcing China's successful test explosion of an atom bomb, and Zuo Zhongling's "To Robert Williams" poem.[68] The Williamses also authored an article that detailed China's efforts to eradicate the discrimination and inequality experienced by the country's fifty-three ethnic minority groups. The Williamses argued that the Chinese government's "special attention" to these ethnic groups was a model that the U.S. government should implement in its treatment of U.S. racial minorities. "Justice for minorities, long denied equality," the couple explained, "requires more than just equal rights. It requires special privileges to help prepare minorities for fair and equal competition."[69]

The newsletter also featured letters of support from Chinese citizens. Fu Ru Tie, a Chinese engineer at the North China Design Institute, stated that he had experienced Jim Crow racism firsthand when visiting the United States. Racism, he explained, was therefore "one of the cruelest depressions from the capitalistic class." But Fu added that the racism he experienced while in the United States was a reminder of the racial ties shared between black Americans and Chinese people. To black Americans Fu asserted, "650 million Chinese people and their great leader Chairman Mao will give you full support whenever you need." A group of students from Senshi province's Northwestern Industrial College seconded this support, writing: "You can hear our voices. The Ocean cannot separate us."[70] Overwhelmed by these messages, the Williamses beckoned their U.S. supporters to recognize the Chinese as their racial siblings in struggle. "The East is Red," the couple declared, "650 million soul brothers cable support!"[71]

Political cartoons in the *Crusader* helped to visually portray these connections. For example, one image depicted black men as Afro-Asian defenders against atomic warfare. In the cartoon, American cultural icon Uncle Sam is shown carrying two nuclear bombs toward a territory marked "Afro-Asian Countries." But as Uncle Sam advances, a black man holding a pistol obstructs Uncle Sam's path. "Going somewhere, Bub?" the black man asks. The cartoon was also accompanied by an article in which Robert and Mabel Williams reemphasized the cartoon's main argument. Violent military campaigns against foreign peoples, the Williamses asserted, must be viewed in relation to racial violence inflicted on African American communities. Likening napalm bombings on North Vietnam to the bombing attack on the Sixteenth Street Baptist

Church in Birmingham, Alabama, the Williamses asserted: "[The U.S. military] is turning villages and towns of children into smoldering tombs of death. He darkens the sky with wings of war and rains fire and brimstone. . . . He bombs little girls while they are praying in Sunday school for brotherhood and human rights." The article closed by returning to the metaphor of the police dog, the aesthetic representation of U.S. violence. "The wolf [now] growls at China," the Williamses maintained. The couple thus pressed the U.S. public to reject the anti-China discourse prominent within U.S. culture. "From here on in it will behoove the American people to do their own thinking," the Williamses remarked.[72]

The cover of another issue of the *Crusader* similarly caricatured U.S. racism as a white man who can no longer turn his back to the Third World (see figure 3.5). He holds a leash connected to a police dog named "Violence" and stands next to two campfires labeled "Hatred" and "KKK Racism." Facing him is a small black man labeled "U.S. Negroes" who points to the white man's rear. Towering over the white man is a group of four people of different nationalities and races identified as the "Non-Anglo-Saxon World," scale being deployed to signify the Third World as a global majority. Seeing that this group's physical size dwarfs that of the white man, the black man comically mocks the white man. "You a majority Charlie?" the black man quips. "Just look behind you!"[73] This image of internationalism was extremely similar to a Chinese propaganda poster with the caption "Mei diguo zhuyi zai quan shijie renmin de chong-chong baowei zhi zhong" (U.S. imperialism is surrounded by the people of the world). Created by Lu Shaoquan, the poster personifies President Lyndon B. Johnson as the United States. Johnson's hand clutches an atomic bomb, but surrounding him is a larger multinational and multiracial force of men whose bayonets, guns, and spears force Johnson to retreat and be swept into the sea.

In these representations, the Cold War is symbolized by the image of an atomic bomb. The cultural historians Alan Nadel and William Chaloupka have examined the atomic bomb as a fundamental symbol of U.S. Cold War culture. They argue that atomic weapons were frequently framed as indicative of the threat of communism and foreign encroachment. Such discourse, according to Nadel, relied "on narratives of Other and Same that construct a site of simultaneous threat and negotiation, with the origin of threat always indeterminable, impossible to pin down as definitive product of either inside or the outside." These narratives bifurcated the world into U.S. allies and U.S. threats, where the atomic bomb was made to represent both the threat of communist internationalism and a national weapon that could defend the nation-state from a chaotic international world.[74] In contrast, the Williamses' political cartoons and the Chinese state's propaganda art visually reversed this

MONTHLY NEWSLETTER

ROBERT F. WILLIAMS, Publisher —IN EXILE—

VOL. 5 — No. 2   **FEBRUARY 1964**

REVOLUTION WITHOUT VIOLENCE?

WE ARE an oppressed and dehumanized people, who have been long suffering and much too patient and tolerant of our status in America. We have begged and prayed for justice to no avail. Are we to forever remain aloof to the

FIGURE 3.5: *Crusader* 5, no. 2 (February 1964). Robert F. Williams Archive, HS 11747. Courtesy of Bentley Historical Library, University of Michigan.

logic. The atomic bomb was instead depicted as signifying U.S. hegemony and mayhem on exploited groups. Furthermore, "the non-Anglo-Saxon world" was represented as the only force capable of defending the world from atomic warfare.

What's also important to note is that in the representations and rhetoric of the *Crusader* the Williamses frequently positioned the guerrilla warfare of Cuban, Chinese, and Vietnamese peasants as a model for U.S. black militancy. For instance, amid the Williamses' exchanges with China and Cuba, the *Cru-*

sader's insignia went from depicting a Christian soldier on horse, à la the military campaigns of the medieval Crusades, to showcasing the torch of liberty interwoven with a machine gun. In addition, in several articles the Williamses encouraged black Americans to take on a "new concept of revolution" and become urban guerrillas. Blacks were to engage in massive violence, destruction of property, social disorganization, and sabotage of businesses, transportation, and communication lines. This would be implemented through a "Do-It-Yourself-Kit" of modernistic, high-technology weaponry, and a "poor-man's arsenal" of everyday, low-cost weapons and homemade devices. "[The] simple flame of a match" inside air-conditioning systems, the Williamses explained, could produce explosions of immense proportion.[75] Continuous anarchy and combat in cities would therefore bring the reality of war to America's doorstep, a manifestation that could convince the U.S. government and ruling class to redistribute wealth and power and radically restructure American life—what the Williamses described as the "peopleization" of America's poor communities.[76] The Williamses' point was that by destroying and commandeering consumer goods, technologies of state, and corporate property, poor Americans would be enabled to denounce their subhuman conditions of living and begin reclaiming their lives. In the final analysis, the Williamses' blueprint for urban revolution echoed the Chinese military commander Lin Biao's concept of a "people's war" (*renmin zhanzheng*), which positioned Third World peasant guerrillas as a global periphery whose rage and carnage would crush the United States and its allies.[77]

With these connections in mind, the Williamses returned to China in October 1964. During this visit, Chinese officials sent Zhen Kaizhu, Jin Jingyi, and Zhen Jinti, three Chinese cinematographers, to film the couple's travels, footage that was later edited into a full-length documentary. The film's components were fairly basic and conventional; it was organized around different shots of the couple's travels, a sonic backdrop of Chinese classical music, and a male narrator who provided informational tidbits. But together, this assemblage of imagery, music, and voice transmitted particular aspects of the CCP's ideology. In one scene, as the Williamses visit a dam and an electric pumping station, the narrator details the agricultural experimental centers that had been opened since the end of the Chinese Civil War and how this had produced a rise in the number of Chinese scientists. Yet, later on in the film, the viewer is supplied with images of China's rural scenery and Chinese citizens' slow but growing access and use of electrical technology. Together, these romantic representations of Chinese rural life, consumption, and technological modernization conveyed that even with economic modernization, China was not abandoning its rustic traditions and prioritization of the peasantry as the socialist revolution's most important constituency. The film's closing shot was explicitly international, however. As the narrator asserts that Western imperialism was now in retreat, the camera pans across a Chinese communist poster displaying a black person, a Native American, a Latin American, and a Chinese worker standing in solidarity—visual iconography of the Third World anti-imperialist struggle.[78]

The documentary additionally employed aesthetics of sound and visuality to portray China as an ally of black struggle. Visuals of the Williamses and the Chinese landscape are united with the narrator's voice. What takes shape is a cinematic hybrid form, a fusion of China and blackness through sound, image, and the Williamses' bodies. But what is unfortunate is that the Williamses' voices are never made audible; viewers are never made privy to what is being said during the couple's conversations with Chinese citizens. In contrast, the narrator's audibility allows him to serve as the film's paramount authority, a depiction that replicates the domineering dynamics and spectacle of Chinese government-led tours. The film's narrator is thus a metaphorical tour guide, his voice "the crucial mediator between the visitor and the setting. . . . that the lessons of the conducted tour would sink in and that appropriate political conclusions would be drawn."[79]

As the Williamses and the Chinese government championed Afro-Asian solidarity, the Williamses' relationship with the Cuban government soured. China's ideological and geopolitical conflict with the Soviet Union was an important factor. As Soviet allies, Cuban communists and Communist Party of the United States of America members living in Cuba were neither receptive to the Williamses' endorsement of China nor to the couple's increasing criticisms of the Soviet regime. For years the Williamses had criticized the post-Stalin Soviet government for its openness to détente with the United States.[80] "The Moscow-oriented elements in Cuba gained the ascendancy and the new party line was to curse everybody and everything that smelled even faintly Chinese," Robert Williams wrote. "Having just returned from my second trip to Beijing, I found myself a prime target."[81] Cuban communists were also hostile to the Williamses' criticisms of Cuban race relations. Although the Cuban regime had denounced structural racism and eliminated policies of racial segregation and inequality, white Cubans remained disproportionately privileged in the workforce, government, military, and the public sphere. In contrast, black Cubans were relegated to harsher living conditions and lower-paying jobs.[82] For Robert Williams, the reality of Afro-Cuban life illuminated the limitations of white communists' claims about constructing working-class alliance across racial lines: "[Although] many Cuban officials . . . claim to be Socialist, they still have some of the same attitudes, and that is that blacks are to be discriminated against, and power should be in the hands of whites."[83] When probed about racial inequality, Cuban communists conveyed to the Williamses an aversion to openly engaging issues of racial difference. Cubans were not black or white, the communists argued, but first and foremost Cuban.[84] "People did not want to identify with anything African, or Afrocentric," Mabel Williams explained, "The more African, the more kinkier your hair, the farther you were away from government."[85]

Thus in the aftermath of the Williamses' travel to China, the Cuban regime viewed the Williams family less and less as allies in forging revolutionary connections between Cubans and black Americans. Concerned that the Williamses' criticisms of Cuban race relations clashed with the narrative of racial democracy propagated by the Cuban government, Cuban communists and CPUSA members living in Cuba took different steps to silence the Williamses. Firstly, they portrayed the Williamses' criticisms of Cuban racial inequality as not based on critical analysis but rather a preoccupation with skin color; it was argued that the couple's heightened focus on race and investment in black nationalist ideology prevented the Williamses from developing a more nuanced critique of Cuban life and culture.[86] Atrocious lies about the family were also spread.[87] In addition, the Williamses' ties to China were frequently used as ammunition to obstruct the couple's participation in Cuban-sponsored international events.[88] Robert Williams privately expressed exasperation about these multiple attempts to gag his political voice. "Exile is hell when the country you are exiled in is not concerned with your problems. They have completely neutralized and incapacitated me. I'm just staying here as an ornament," he complained. "I've had enough. Shit is shit whether it's red, white or black."[89]

Cuban communists would go to great lengths to curb the Williamses' dissemination of information. *Radio Free Dixie*'s wattage was reduced from its fifty-thousand-watt long-wave transmitter to a meager one-thousand-watt transmitter, which effectively depleted the show's international audience. More important, a group the Williamses believed to be members of the Cuban intelligence unit G-2 forged and circulated two counterfeit editions of the *Crusader*.[90] The first issue framed the Williamses as angry demagogues with blind allegiance to China. Its cover bore a cartoon that was a takeoff of Joe Rosenthal's 1945 Pulitzer Prize–winning photograph that depicts five American soldiers raising the U.S. flag atop Mount Suribachi during the Battle of Iwo Jima in World War II (see figure 3.6). In the image on the forged newsletter though, a mound of deceased men of color, bodies meant to represent the national and ethnic wings of the Third World bloc, replaces the mound of land and war carnage displayed in the original photo. Atop this group of bodies stands a smiling Chinese soldier and an equally happy black man. Lastly, China's flag is perched atop the mound of bodies, its fabric blowing in the wind. Through visual argument, the image suggests that black America and China are climbing on the backs of other revolutionary struggles, exploiting Third World liberation movements and endangering global anti-imperialism. The second counterfeit issue was more explicit, its front page reading, "China Betrays the Cuban Revolution" (see figure 3.7). Beneath this caption is a cartoon with a three-headed Chinese dragon being slain by Fidel Castro, his hands holding a bayonet with the word "Truth" inscribed on its blade. Above the image is a statement purportedly written by Robert Williams that reviles China as a deceptive nation insincere in its solidarity with Asian and African countries: "Surely, a man is entitled to make one big mistake in his lifetime. Well I have made mine. . . . I allowed myself to be deceived by the soft lies and subtle flattery of the leaders of the People's Republic of China."[91]

Ultimately, the Williamses took these attacks on their intellectual and political freedom very seriously. Such efforts, the couple believed, represented "a sinister conspiracy perpetuated to sabotage the militant Afro-American freedom struggle and to rupture the cordial and growing friendship between the Afro-American and Chinese peoples."[92] Hoping to quell this tension between the family and the Cuban regime, the couple reached out to Castro. In a letter to Castro, the Williamses detailed a web of charades being carried out against their family by top-level Cuban bureaucrats and intelligence agents.[93] Castro's government, however, conveyed little empathy for the Williamses' grievances. "The Cuba life is 100% Russian," Robert Williams mused. "Anyone who is Pro-Chinese or black nationalist is considered counterrevolutionary and I am no exception. The Chinese are solid but the white communists will not allow us to accept their aid. So that leaves us nowhere."[94]

In private, the Williamses decided that they could no longer remain in Cuba. Initially Robert and Mabel Williams were set upon returning to the United States. They were consequently very dismayed to learn that the U.S. State Department would not issue them the travel documents required to enter the country unless Robert Williams agreed to face the preexisting kidnapping charges against him. The family's next option was Sweden. The FPCC founder Richard Gibson, now working in Paris for the journal *Revolution*, informed the Williamses that he and several Swedish Marxists were working to bring the Williamses to Sweden for a speaking engagement. Gibson explained that after arriving in Sweden, the Williamses could either remain in exile there or travel elsewhere.[95] But the Williamses were convinced that the Cuban government would do everything in its disposal to prevent the family from leaving Cuba. Consequently, in the family's request to the Cuban minister of foreign relations for permission to travel, the Williamses portrayed the visit to Sweden

The Crusader

MONTHLY NEWSLETTER

ROBERT F. WILLIAMS, Publisher — IN EXILE —
VOL. 8 — No. 2   OCTOBER SPECIAL EDITION 1965

MARSHAL LIN PIAO ON PEOPLE'S WAR

There are a few times in one's life when a man is proud to be a man. I must remark on such a time now. Two years ago when I first visited the People's Republic of China, I saw many impressive sights and met many great people. Mao Tse-tung, Liu Shao-chi, Chou En-lai—the names are a roll call of the greatest of the Chinese heroes who fought against the Japanese aggressors, liberated their homeland, and successfully waged

FIGURE 3.6: Counterfeit issue of the *Crusader* from October 1965. Robert F. Williams Archive, HS 11749. Courtesy of Bentley Historical Library, University of Michigan.

as a brief stay aimed at supplementing their income. The couple, however, privately determined that Sweden would not be their final destination; after arriving they would arrange travel to Canada.[96] The Williamses had established a good relationship with the Canadian embassy in Havana and in confidence made the office aware of the family's predicament. In response, an embassy

The Crusader

MONTHLY NEWSLETTER

ROBERT F. WILLIAMS, Publisher   —IN EXILE—

VOL. 8 — No. 4   April-May 1966

CHINA BETRAYS THE CUBAN REVOLUTION

Surely, a man is entitled to make one big mistake in his lifetime. Well I have made mine. Along with many, many others, I allowed myself to be deceived by the soft lies and subtle flattery of the leaders of the People's Republic of China.

When I was in Peking two years ago, Chairman Mao Tse-tung assured me that the People's Republic of China supported the revolutionary struggles of all nations and peoples and upheld the revolutionary unity of the peoples of the socialist camp and the people of the whole world.

FIGURE 3.7: Counterfeit issue of the *Crusader* from April–May 1966. Robert F. Williams Archive, HS 11750. Courtesy of Bentley Historical Library, University of Michigan.

agent explained how the Williamses might go about obtaining political asylum. They should apply for residence first as "landed immigrants" and then apply for political-asylum status once they were on Canadian soil. The agent added that the couple's application would receive greater favor should they "demonstrate the proper attitude towards China" and renounce their association with the Chinese government.[97] The Williamses responded to the agent's recommendations with skepticism. The prospect of applying for residency as landed immigrants seemed suspicious. Should the Williams family fail to receive political refuge once in Canada, they would then be at serious risk of extradition. Conjecturing that the agent might to be working in collaboration with the U.S. government, the Williamses disregarded the agent's counsel. More bad news was on the way though. The Williamses learned that both Cuban and Swedish officials were delaying a decision to approve the couple's travel to Sweden.[98]

At the end of the day, China was the family's lone option. A discussion with Shen Jian, China's ambassador to Cuba, offered the family a portal of escape.[99] Shen confirmed that if they were willing to relocate to China, the Chinese government would approve and help facilitate the process. "China is your home; stay as long you like," he relayed.[100] For the Williamses, the decline of their relationship with the Cuban political establishment was a sign of the failures of Cuban communism and the brewing tensions between the Soviet and Chinese governments. Both the Soviets and the Cubans, the Williamses ruled, underestimated the agency of antiracist struggles. China, however, was a different story. "I am convinced that there is no place in the communist camp for blacks. In the Chinese camp, yes, but the white communists are between us and them," Robert Williams resolved. "I want to get the hell out of here as soon as possible."[101]

On July 15, 1966, Mabel and Robert Williams traveled to Moscow, the first leg of a journey that would eventually take them to Beijing.[102] The Cuban government was under the impression that the couple planned to stop in China for a brief visit with their boys before traveling to Hanoi to air anti–Vietnam War broadcasts.[103] It would be weeks before the Cubans learned that the family was gone for good.

★

ICONOGRAPHY OF STRUGGLE

The U.S. media and government spun news of the Williams family's relocation. It was alleged, for instance, that they were at the center of an international leftist network that was smuggling guns to U.S. black militants and who were "outside agitators" of the 1965 urban rebellion in Watts, California. Others denounced the fact that the *Crusader* was freely distributed within U.S. borders, arguing that American access to the publication would generate a rise in Chinese communist publications entering the United States. The Williamses' media, one columnist maintained, aided China in waging a "racial campaign against Russia and the United States" and cultivating "a perfectly united and harmonized non-white front under the leadership of China." "The red book of the Communist Party isn't red enough for Williams. He's an advocate of a militant aggressive policy; a policy of total revolution advocated by the Chinese Reds," another reporter charged. "Williams' important position as the titular leader of a Negro revolt in America cannot be underestimated. He is not only the man Fidel Castro looks to . . . but he is also the advisor to the Beijing Government."[104] The Williamses even held the attention of the FBI; numerous branches kept tabs on the family's movements throughout the Williamses' stay in China. Officers noted that while the government perceived the Williams family's links to Cuba as troubling, it was the family's relationship with China that presented the greatest threat. "In Cuba, Robert Williams is looked upon as a calamity that is necessary to endure," one FBI report stated, "[but] the misfortunes of Williams did not begin here, but rather when he persisted in his revolutionary Chinese."[105]

The idea of Robert Williams functioning in some PRC advisory role was an absurdity, to say the least. While he did make several recommendations to Chinese officials about how China could increase its influence among U.S. black activists and was periodically included in government meetings with foreign residents about shifts in U.S. foreign policy, at no point was Williams given direct access to government circles and confidential information. But Williams's self-produced media did play a role in exporting Chinese communism to U.S. radicals, particularly black activists and thinkers. In Beijing the family's media became a significant branch in a larger expatriate-run media enclave that included Anna Louise Strong's *Letters from China* newsletter and Sidney Rittenberg's work as head of Peking Radio's foreign department.[106]

Permitted by government to continue their media pursuits, the Williamses used their media platform in China to condemn the Vietnam War. In August 1965, the U.S. Congress authorized the expansion of the U.S. military's deployment and combat units into South Vietnam. U.S. intervention in the region was prompted by fear of the fall of the U.S.-backed regime of Ngo Dinh Diem in the south. When the National Liberation Front (more widely known as the Viet Cong), a common front of southern Communists opposed to Diem's rule, initiated an armed rebellion against the government in 1960, thousands of their North Vietnamese comrades joined them in a struggle to unify the two sides into one communist government. Fearing that a victory over South Vietnam's government would fuel communist explosions in neighboring Asian countries, particularly in the territories of America's Asian allies, the Kennedy, Johnson, and Nixon administrations escalated U.S. involvement in the conflict throughout the 1960s.[107]

The U.S. government's decision was met by the growth of a global and nationwide U.S. antiwar movement. Thousands of people, particularly U.S. youths, college-aged adults, and students of color, were outraged with the war, many of them opting to demonstrate in protest and refusing to be drafted or to enlist to fight. On college campuses, city streets, and government grounds, activists called for U.S. forces to cease their military operations in Vietnam and elsewhere and respect the sovereignty and human rights of foreign peoples, especially those of formerly colonized populations in Asia and Africa. Mabel and Robert Williams joined in on this call. One of the first steps they took in denouncing U.S. involvement in the war was recording radio messages aimed at black troops stationed in Vietnam. On *Hanoi Hannah*, an English-language propaganda broadcast run by the Vietnamese radio personality Trịnh Thị Ngọ on Radio Hanoi, Robert Williams persuaded black soldiers to abandon their military posts.[108] "How can we defend democracy in the jungles of Vietnam when it doesn't exist in the streets of Washington and Harlem, or the black belt of lower states?" he insisted.[109]

The Williamses' opposition to the U.S. intervention in Vietnam had actually taken shape years earlier, when they were residents of Cuba. In October 1964, the couple traveled to North Vietnam to attend the "International Conference of Solidarity against U.S. Imperialist Aggression and in Defense of Peace." Once in Hanoi, the Williamses were immediately transfixed by the devastation of U.S. military campaigns. Deplaning, they observed trenches and air-raid shelters surrounding the tarmac. "It made me sick," Robert Williams revealed, "to think that a huge nation like the United States was threatening these poor people. . . . While Lyndon Johnson was pouring troops into South Vietnam, Mao Zedong was rushing supplies to the North." But during the Williamses' visit to North Vietnam, an extensive conversation with the North Vietnamese leader Ho Chi Minh made a deep impact on the Williamses' political consciousness. Ho arrived at the banquet with a Vietnamese youth whose face and body were disfigured by a U.S. napalm attack that had burned the majority of his skin. Sensitive to Robert Williams's shock, Ho moralized the child's wounds as "examples of the sacrifices they are willing to make to free themselves from chains of imperialism." Ho went on to recount his first visit to New York City in 1912. There, he witnessed the similarities between U.S. racism and French colonialism. "[In New York] I saw that the same man was responsible for evil," he remarked. However, in Harlem, at a meeting of the Pan-African organization the Universal Negro Improvement Association, Ho drew connections between U.S. black nationalism and Vietnamese independence. For the Williamses, Ho's musings on how a chance encounter in Harlem transported him back to Vietnam's struggles against foreign occupation demonstrated the role of cross-cultural exchanges and an internationalist sensibility as contributing forces to both local and global political struggle. "I now saw the oneness of the liberation struggles of all men, no matter how different their colors or how many tens of thousands of miles separate them," Robert Williams mused. "Just as the desire of black Americans to be independent helped motivate Ho Chi Minh to battle the French, so the courageous example of the Vietnamese in their defiance of U.S. imperialism inspires those of us fighting for freedom in the U.S.A. today."[110]

FIGURE 3.8: "Jianjue zhichi Meiguo renmin fandui Mei diguozhuyi qinlue Yuenan" (Resolutely support the American people in their resistance against American imperialist aggression in Vietnam), 1966. Courtesy of Stefan R. Landsberger Collection, International Institute of Social History (Amsterdam).

In *Listen, Brother!* (1968), a forty-page antiwar pamphlet, the Williamses built on this standpoint. African American troops were serving as "enemy occupiers of an alien land," helping to "make Vietnam the Mississippi of Asia." The couple explained, "Now, you are the brutal cop. The man with the gun. The licensed killer in the colored ghetto. . . . The sight of your uniform . . . [is] like the sight of a brutal thug cop in the ghetto." Vietnam was therefore no different from the poor black American neighborhoods where inhabitants faced daily police harassment, poverty, and dismal conditions of life. "It's America all over again," the Williamses stated. "Back home . . . you will be the 'gooks.' It will be your time to get burnt. It will be your house on fire, your mother burnt or machine-gunned. . . . How in the hell can you . . . bring white man's justice to colored Vietnam . . . while your freedom has been deferred for 400 years?"[111]

The pamphlet made similar arguments through photographs. Images of brutal attacks on black American bodies, which represent a visual record and portrait of U.S. violence, reframe the war within the scope of U.S. race relations. A Newark man being clubbed by the police, white-supremacist groups with Confederate flags standing united with the National Guard, and the most impressionable image of all: a horrifying photograph of a black man shot seventeen times by the Newark police, his body lifeless on a gurney, a hole as wide as a soccer ball separating the right side of his chest from the left, his breastbone and ribcage visible. Surreally juxtaposed beside polemics about the violence of war, the raw mortality represented in these pictures suggests that the carnage of imperialist war and the antiblack violence of U.S. racism are comparable. Image and text together forge an aesthetic transfer of embodiment and oppression between black Americans and the Vietnamese. Racial coalition in the pamphlet thus denotes a shared history of epistemic, ontological, and bodily violence.

But most important, the pamphlet's photographs divert from the conventional male-dominant discourses and representations of Third World anticolonial liberation. Although the pamphlet's title might suggest otherwise, *Listen, Brother!* supplied, to some degree, a visual gender analysis and feminist critique. In the document, black and Vietnamese women are depicted as leading agents of world revolution. In one image a black mother and child are shown lying comfortably on a blanket with the caption, "The greatest joy in life, that of mother and child." However, next to the image is the pamphlet's narrative. In it, the authors figuratively depict the murder of a Vietnamese child by a U.S. napalm attack:

You shiver in your foxhole. It's a drab and barren world. . . . The gentle stir of the tropical wind transmits the rancorous stench of death and decay. Somewhere in the vastness of night a distraught mother struggles to restrain her tormented moans of irrepressible agony. Her brown, thin and calloused hands are useless in the moment of the greatest need of a mother's comforting and life-giving touch. The ghoulish scent of burnt flesh has claimed her greatest joy in life, that of mother and child, the tender touch of mother's loving care is denied. The flaming hell of napalm has masterfully consummated the perfection of sadistic butchers. These are the beneficiaries of racist America's blessing of democracy.

By placing the image alongside the narrative, the Williamses again articulated a transfer of embodiment, this time between the black mother and child framed in the photograph and the Vietnamese mother and child described via the text. On the following page another image affirms this articulation. This photo portrays the funeral of the four young girls killed in the 1963 bombing of the 16th Street Baptist Church in Birmingham, Alabama. The photograph displays the mother of one of the girls, her head cradled in the arms of the man sitting beside her. Tears flow down her face as she observes her daughter's casket from a pew; beside the mother is a paper fan with a picture of her and her daughter's smiling faces.[112] But this photograph is not accompanied by summation or analysis inside the pamphlet. The narrative of the Vietnamese mother and murdered child thus stands in as a caption for the black mother's stricken face.

The Williamses' visual construction of racial mutuality between black and Vietnamese women, however, reinforced a maternalist conception of revolutionary womanhood. In the aforementioned photographs, black and Vietnamese women's struggles against racism, capitalism, and patriarchy were not the linkage that connected them, but rather their efforts to protect their children from the carnage of militaristic white supremacy. Women of color's anti-imperialist and antiracist revolutionary activities were consequently framed through a reductive gendered analogy, as if the only tropes or figures capable of expressing vibrant female radicalism were that of "the mother" or "violated woman." Ultimately, by deploying this "motherist frame," the Williamses perpetuated "dichotomous notions of women's and men's roles," which limited and constrained "the cultural frames of resistance available to" female radical internationalists.[113]

But while these depictions perpetuated narratives of maternal sacrifice, they did not beckon black men to come to the defense of black and Vietnamese women. Other photographs indicated something different. For example, one photograph displays a young black woman being arrested at a demonstration. Angry yet poised, her expression conveys a militant disposition determined not to be shell-shocked by abusive authority. The second image depicts an Afro-

Dominican woman standing in the doorway of her home as a U.S. troop with weapon in hand marches by during America's gunboat occupation of the Dominican Republic in 1965. As the black soldier walks by, the woman stands smiling, unafraid, almost beaming for the camera. And beneath the image is a caption reading, "How colored they look!" The caption can be read one of two ways: either the woman is making the statement, commenting on the incorporation of black subjects within U.S. military interventions, an implicit remark that ties into the pamphlet's general narrative that black involvement in imperialist military campaigns is unconscionable and irreconcilable; or it was the soldier who made the statement, his words conveying his bewilderment at the fact that the territory and people he came to occupy share his skin complexion and racial status.

The cover of *Listen, Brother!*, on the other hand, returned to the original scene of the crime, the 16th Street Baptist Church bombing. Underneath the pamphlet's title is a photograph of citizens attending the victims' funerals. At the shot's center is a close-up of a black woman's face, her impenetrable eyes and somber countenance framed as the pamphlet's cladding (see figure 3.9). Against a backdrop of a crowd of black men whose blurred faces converge around her, the woman's face depicts a stoic anger and revolutionary resolve. If the dark silhouettes surrounding her represent both the everyday masses and then-imminent battalions of anticolonial liberation, this woman is nonetheless at the center, positioned as their guide and the preeminent expression of black struggle. Describing several Chinese propaganda posters, Harriet Evans offers an analysis that is helpful in interrogating the visual politics conveyed in the cover image of *Listen, Brother!* Examining posters that display both Chinese men and women where women "occupy center stage," Evans points out how the displacement of men in the images allows for "the subordination of the men in the visual hierarchy." She continues, "Female authority here is constructed neither through the absence of men nor through positioning men as participants in an equal game but through showing men as spectators of activities from which, temporarily, they are excluded as actors." Evans maintains that although such representations can still be reliant on symbolic meanings about male power, portraying women in such a way "suggest[s] an authority over the context and the skills and aptitudes that form the theme of the poster," a visual discourse that does not fit easily into conventional patriarchal constructions of power and resistance.[114]

A comparable dynamic is displayed on the cover of *Listen, Brother!* By centering the woman's face and expression yet obscuring those of her male comrades, the image suggests that her authority and agency might be constructed on terms not belonging to that of the men who surrounded her. The other

FIGURE 3.9: Cover of Robert F. Williams's *Listen, Brother!* (1968).

photographs of black women in *Listen, Brother!* also tie into such themes, shifting away from dominant stereotypes of black women as sexual temptresses, mammies, and appendages to masculine leadership. They were supplanted with a different trope—the black woman as the image of resistance and revolutionary internationalism, as the subject of black liberation and Third World movements.

Thus, despite its masculine textual narrative and focus on maternalism, *Listen, Brother!* kicked off with a foreword authored by Mae Mallory, the black female activist ally of the Williamses who was framed and charged with kidnapping alongside Robert Williams back in Monroe. Mallory, a former member of the Communist Party of the United States of America and secretary for the militant organization Crusaders for Freedom, had been drawn under Robert Williams's tutelage after hearing him speak on a Harlem radio show in the summer of 1959.[115] And on that August 1961 evening when the Williams family fled their Monroe home, it was Mallory who helped usher them into the night; she later fled to Cleveland to avoid arrest. Unlike the Williamses though, her escape proved unsuccessful. Hence, at the point of the publication of *Listen, Brother!*, her analysis of U.S. empire had, until recently, evolved inside Cleveland and North Carolina prison cells. Opening with her voice consequently rooted *Listen, Brother!* in the national and local context of U.S. racial oppression and gendered black struggle as a conflict waged not simply or solely by men for the rights to manhood but by both black women and men for the rights to being human and free. Furthermore, through its photographic representations of everyday black woman as heroic and resilient and its recognition of black female oppression, *Listen, Brother!* articulated that it was the courage to protect one's own, such as a mother's willingness to defend her child and a woman's determination to protect her community (as Mallory did), that represented the ultimate revolutionary act.

Although still steeped in ideals of maternal sacrifice, the images in *Listen, Brother!* portray black womanhood and motherhood as transgressive and revolutionary, representations that stood in stark contrast to hegemonic depictions of black femininity.[116] And by presenting black women at the forefront of black resistance, the pamphlet somewhat, though not unproblematically, interrogated the inadequacy of discourses that represented anti-imperialist and antiracist struggle merely through the terms of redemptive manhood and masculine protection of femininity. While a good portion of text and language within *Listen, Brother!* was directed at black male troops, the pamphlet's appeal was nonetheless framed around encouraging these soldiers to take on a soul sister outlook and practice. The black American male soldier was persuaded to return home, not for the sake of defending the honor of black women and black children but rather to join them in struggle.

The Williamses' depiction of women of color as maternalist soldiers of anti-imperialism and racial liberation was not new or unusual; Chinese propaganda art also circulated such representations (see figures 3.10 and 3.11). In numerous posters, Vietnamese and black women are portrayed as guerrilla soldiers in combat against an imperialist aggressor. In these images, women are displayed carrying children on their backs, wearing loose clothing, always armed, and exhibiting a determination similar to that of the woman on the cover of *Listen, Brother!* This was a visual rendering of the CCP's gender analysis that maintained that women could only be freed from patriarchal oppression by creating a socialist society where women behaved and lived like men.[117] In the end, both the Williamses and Chinese government's failure to construct a visual imaginary of revolutionary womanhood and female internationalism void

美帝国主义从非洲滚出去

FIGURE 3.10: "Mei diguo zhuyi cong feizhou gun chuqu!" (Get out of Africa, American imperialists!), 1964. Courtesy of the Collection of Pierre-Loïc Lavigne.

FIGURE 3.11: "Bei yapo minzu lianhe qilai jianjue fandui mei diguozhuyi" (Oppressed peoples, unite to resolutely fight against U.S. imperialism), 1964. Courtesy of the Collection of Pierre-Loïc Lavigne.

of children and guns suggests a great deal. It demonstrates just how internalized their cultural beliefs about gender and revolution were. It also showcases how the image of the Third World woman came to stand in for the depiction of all women of color, a discursive signification that homogenized women's different experiences living and negotiating racial capitalism and global patriarchy.[118]

What is also disappointing is that in the closing of *Listen, Brother!*, the Williamses fell back into constructing transnational black politics as a male-dominant political space. Employing a metaphor of music, the Williamses closed the pamphlet by emphasizing the blackness shared by Vietnamese and blacks:

> The brothers and sisters on the corner are singing louder. . . . A Vietnamese is standing in the crowd, she looks just like a soul sister. Charlie doesn't know she is a Vietnamese. To him, what's the difference anyhow, a nigger is a nigger and a gook is a gook. . . . The brothers and sisters are singing louder and louder. . . . The black people start to wake. There is a sea of angry black faces. They are singing loud enough for the world to hear them. . . . They say that on a quiet night if you listen hard enough you can hear the angry black people tugging hard enough at their chains all over America. You can hear them singing to wake the dark people up. . . . Nobody listens to a nigger's

moans . . . nobody, that is, but the brothers. Brother, they are listening. They can hear you . . . everywhere black souls hurt. . . . Listen brother.[119]

Listening here ultimately denoted male activity and male struggle. In this closing representation, women were depicted as heard not through their own formulated practices of transnational expression and interconnection but rather through the soul brothers' forms of communication. But if only the brothers were listening, what were they incapable of hearing, singing, and saying?

Back in the United States, sectors of the American public were listening to the Williamses' polemical call for black soldiers to abandon their posts in the U.S. military. News of Listen, Brother! led the FBI to launch an investigation into whether or not copies of the pamphlet and the Crusader were being circulated among U.S. soldiers, and if so, what impact they were having on black soldiers' mindsets.[120] U.S. black activist circles on the other hand favorably received the pamphlet's antiwar message. Black Student Voice, a newsletter put out by high school–aged black radicals in Detroit, echoed the Williamses' claim that U.S. attacks on Vietnam must be viewed in relation to the historical oppression of African Americans. "The black man's life in America is valued less than a common dog," one young person wrote. "Even today in Vietnam thousands of innocent yellow men, women, and children are being napalmed."[121] Charles Johnson, a member of the Wayne State University–based black nationalist organization UHURU, denounced the war in similar terms: "There ain't no way in the hell that I'm going out like a fool and fight my nonwhite brothers in China, Africa and Latin America."[122] Black journalists also echoed the arguments presented in Listen, Brother! Eddie Ellis, in his article "Violence the Same in Vietnam or in Dixie," criticized civil rights leaders' silence about the war. He argued that with a few exceptions, black leaders were ignoring "the particular relevance the Asian conflict has to the struggle of the black man in the United States." How could black Americans demand an end to U.S. antiblack violence, Ellis insisted, "and at the same time run off and be violent with Mao Zedong, and Ho Chi Minh?"[123]

The Williamses were encouraged by these different black American proclamations of international solidarity. Believing that more young blacks were self-identifying as part of a worldwide struggle, the couple remarked: "There is a great trend developing wherein more and more Afro-Americans are beginning to identify with the liberation forces of the world. The militant black people of racist America are becoming more and more anti-imperialist as well as being anti-racist. They are beginning to understand that the struggles of the world's oppressed peoples complement each other."[124] Through information sharing and discursive representations of Afro-Asian coalition, the Williamses contributed to helping construct these imaginaries. But it should not be overlooked that their efforts to demystify anti-imperialist struggle produced their own counterproductive, mystifying discourse, one that romanticized China-propagated arguments about social development, internationalism, and guerrilla warfare and that relied on problematic masculinist claims about Third World revolution.

Other black travelers struggled to unpack the contradictions of Chinese foreign policy and contend with the demanding and inconsistent conditions of expatriate life in China. There, another veteran of black-radical struggle, Vicki Garvin, joined the couple. As an English-language instructor in Shanghai and a newspaper language "polisher" in Beijing, Garvin built close relationships with students in training to become educators and translators, as well as with hotel workers, diplomats, and other foreign expatriates who called China home. In magnitude though, her encounters differed greatly from those of the Williamses, William Worthy, Shirley Graham Du Bois, and W. E. B. Du Bois. Whereas the latter group generally generated mediated representations of Chinese life for a black public, Garvin produced narratives of black life for Chinese audiences. In so doing she became better versed in Chinese ideological and national understandings, particularly the writings and thought of Mao Zedong. This aided her in translating histories of black American resistance to Chinese language students. Her cross-cultural mediations therefore required a far different methodological and conceptual tool set. Furthermore, as an unmarried black woman and female expatriate, the contradictions of gender vibrant within Chinese life and communist ideology seemed more intensely apparent to her. Consequently, Garvin fashioned a practice and pedagogy of transnational politics, intercultural understanding and exchange, and female radicalism that contrasted with the models posited in *Listen, Brother!* and in Chinese propaganda art. Still, her experiences living in China also convey the difficulty of negotiating the Chinese political terrain. As guests of China, she and other black expatriates' safety was contingent on their assent to and defense of the PRC leadership's ideology, practices, and policies. These radicals consequently found themselves periodically caught in webs of contradiction, where exile required particular silences and omissions.

4

MAOISM AND THE SINIFICATION OF
BLACK POLITICAL STRUGGLE

China's youth, already enriched with the knowledge from their elders
of the bitter past, of class struggle in the pre-liberation days, are now fully
grasping the truth that struggle, not complacency, is always the order of the
day. . . . I have observed with great elation the growth of young teachers and
students I once taught as they studied theory, not for the sake of knowing it,
but to apply it to change the objective situation and their own world outlook.
—VICKI GARVIN

Use the past to serve the present, make the foreign serve China.
—MAO ZEDONG

In a speech to a New York audience, Victoria "Vicki" Ama Garvin recounted her
expatriate life in China. Six years of residency in Shanghai and Beijing offered
her a unique perspective on the country, particularly the transformations being
instituted by the government and everyday working-class citizens and the poor.
Witnessing popular support for the project of rebuilding China in the interest
of its most downtrodden members, Garvin explained, reinvigorated her belief
in the possibility of revolutionizing the United States along similar lines: "I was
inspired by this new society in which working people had acquired hegemony,
abolishing the rule of the few who had controlled all aspects of their lives, and
I looked forward to the day when this would happen in the United States as
well." But she also gently distanced herself from the romantic championing of
Chinese communism that was in vogue among Western New Leftist activists.
"The Chinese people are not superhuman beings," Garvin insisted to the audience. The Chinese people had instead tapped into the need for radical ideology
to be responsive to the shifting historical and political conditions of the times.
"Marxism is not dogma; it too must continue to grow, to meet new needs of a
changing and dynamic society, or it will stagnate and die," she noted. "To this

body of revolutionary working class theory will be added still more names of those who make significant contributions."[1]

Over the course of Garvin's stay in China, Mao Zedong's name was added to this list. Although his writings dated back to the 1920s, foreign translations were not available outside of China until the mid-1960s. But when China's Foreign Language Press began publishing excerpts of Mao's speeches in *Quotations from Chairman Mao* (*Mao zhuxi yulu*), known more commonly as the "little red book," and translated versions of the multivolume *Selected Works of Mao Zedong* (*Maozedong xuanji*), Mao's thought took on an of-the-moment allure among millions of people outside China. Consequently, throughout the decade nearly eleven billion official Mao texts and images were printed and circulated globally. Foreigners' attraction to China and Mao Zedong Thought became even more heightened during China's Great Proletarian Cultural Revolution (GPCR), a mass struggle against revisionism, bureaucratism, and government elitism that dominated Chinese political and social life from 1966 to 1976. For numbers of China enthusiasts, the GPCR signaled both the rebirth of the Chinese Communist Revolution and an example of the revolutionary culture required to upend capitalism and generate a sustainable socialist society. Foreign expatriates in China helped to fuel these perceptions, linking the GPCR to Western social movements, most notably the struggle being waged in the United States. Simultaneously, these expatriates also helped educate Chinese citizens who sought greater understanding of the roots of U.S. political conflict.

The educational spaces helmed by Garvin during her time of residence in China were key sites for such lessons. There, she worked as an English-language instructor to Chinese graduate students, fourth-year university students, and hotel workers, and as a language polisher for *Peking Review*. In these spaces, she observed and participated in important shifts in Chinese life, particularly the increasing importance of Mao's philosophical dogma in the educational system and later the political turbulence of the GPCR. To effectively integrate into this world, Garvin dedicated serious time to understanding the country's political culture and increasing her knowledge of Mao's ideas and writings. In her classroom she used Maoist arguments to prime students for the roles they would play in reshaping the educational sector and Chinese life. She also foregrounded arguments about gender and African American history in her lectures, highlighting historical and conceptual associations between black diasporic and Chinese traditions of resistance.

Revisiting Garvin's atypical experience within the Chinese educational system and the expatriate community to which she and Robert and Mabel Williams were members tenders insight into the unavoidable paradoxes of being a "foreign friend" of China. Like most expatriates, Garvin and the Williamses were attracted by the magnetism of Mao's thought and the enthusiasm of Chinese people regarding the nation's social and economic uplift. Paralyzed by the lure of mass struggle, these expatriates misrepresented the benefits of Mao's leadership. Many turned a blind eye to Mao and other officials' abuse of power and to atrocities incongruous with the rhetoric of people's power articulated by the People's Republic of China (PRC), the most blatant example being the GPCR. In short, considering Garvin's and other expatriates' experiences of residence in China illuminates the slippery political terrain they negotiated as guests of state. Political exile instigated their study and engagement of Mao's political philosophy and played a role in these foreigners' constructive interrogations of U.S. black-radical struggle. Yet, at times, what was missing from their political critique was a balanced examination of the internal struggles and contradictions that were rampant in the Chinese state and society.

★

RED AND EXPERT

Garvin's radicalism was formed and widened as result of years working as a labor organizer in Depression-era Harlem. During the 1940s and 1950s, she was active in the Communist Party of the United States of America (CPUSA), the American League for Peace and Democracy, the National War Labor Board, and the United Office and Professional Workers of America Union. She later joined the National Negro Congress and was a founding member of both the National Negro Labor Council and Paul Robeson's newspaper *Freedom*.[2] McCarthyism, the propect of Soviet Union détente with the U.S. government, and personal disillusionment with the future of American leftist organizations left her demoralized, her political spirit filled with "low morale and pessimism about the U.S. during the 1950s."[3] The CPUSA, for instance, no longer felt connected to grassroots energy but was rather made up primarily of "careerists, opportunists, even enemy agents and counter-revolutionaries," most of whom were "posing as revolutionary leaders" and were "removed from manual labor and everyday struggle."[4] Garvin left the party in 1958. Three years later she abandoned U.S. domestic politics altogether.

Garvin left the United States in early 1961, accepting employment as a secretary for a Nigerian businessman in Lagos. There, she envisioned experiencing a newly independent African nation-state and the wonder of the continent-wide decolonization movement. But within two years she had relocated again, this time to Accra, Ghana, joining an exodus of African American expatriates fascinated with Ghanaian independence and Kwame Nkrumah's leadership.[5] To

FIGURE 4.1: Garvin, date unknown. Courtesy of Lincoln and Miranda Bergman.

earn a living, she worked as an English-language instructor at Accra's Institute of Foreign Languages, where she educated foreign technicians and the children of the ambassadorial bureaucracy.

It was Huang Hua, China's ambassador to Ghana, who opened China's doors to her. Receiving positive feedback about Garvin's teaching from her fellow expatriate Shirley Graham Du Bois, Huang secured Garvin a position instructing lower-level Chinese technicians and Chinese-embassy officials during the evenings.[6] With He Liliang, Huang's spouse, as one of her first students, Garvin's relationship with the family grew. Impressed with Garvin's teaching practices, Huang and He Liliang suggested that Garvin consider relocating to China to help strengthen Chinese teachers' faculties in teaching English. The offer caught her off guard. Garvin admitted that she knew little about China, besides the Western news media's portrayals of the country as economically and culturally backward. She admitted, "There was no explanation of why such conditions existed, nor any exposure or outcry against these foreign countries which had carved out 'spheres of influence.'"[7] China's depiction as "the sick man of Asia" was frequently contrasted to the "'heroic efforts' of the missionaries," Westerners who were characterized as bringing "relief, education and Christianity to the Chinese people."[8] Even though she was skeptical of such representations, what made Garvin consider Huang's offer was that China's negative image in the Western mind corresponded with that of African populations. Both depictions communicated the superiority of Europe and North America and aided in Western imperialism's mutual subjection of African and Asian populations. The possibility of observing firsthand a reality that clashed with the aforementioned images confirmed Garvin's decision. "It was with enthusiasm that I welcomed the opportunity to observe the achievements of the Chinese people and learn something about how they had achieved them," she stated.[9]

Other factors informed her decision. While fellow expatriates W. E. B and Shirley Graham Du Bois had personally informed her of their high regard for China, China's progressive relationship with Nkrumah's government was influential.[10] A serendipitous conversation also proved fruitful in reinforcing that she had made the right choice. During a layover in Cairo, she ran into Malcolm X and informed him of Huang's offer. Malcolm was especially encouraging, pushing Garvin to soak up as much as she could. "Go over there and learn as much as you can because we'll need you in the struggle when you get back," he insisted.[11] But perhaps the primary factor that tipped the balance in favor of Garvin's move to China was the latent breakdown of Nkrumah's government. Within his first few years in office, Nkrumah outlawed strikes; alienated and suppressed miners, cocoa farmers, and workers; and increased his presidential powers to rule by decree, policies that lessened citizens' rights to due process and free speech. Assassination attempts on Nkrumah's life in August 1962 and January 1964 and the persistence of inequality, corruption, and wide political divides within Ghanaian society further illuminated the contradictions of Nkrumah's project of African modernity. The prospect of the government's subversion became a reality in 1966 (Garvin had left Ghana by this point), when Nkrumah was overthrown by a military coup d'état, ironically while he was out of the country on a diplomatic visit to China. Ultimately, Garvin admitted that life in both Lagos and Accra left her a bit cynical about postindependence African governments. Although she "felt more relaxed with [Ghana's and Nigeria's] black majority," it was clear that "independence there was nominal; still neocolonial."[12] Despite the elimination of colonialism and the symbolic value of African independence, many African countries were still prisoners of foreign capital, unequal geopolitical relationships, and local class divisions. And in these countries, according to Garvin, the "black bourgeoisie . . . rule[d] in conjunction with the imperialists." "This was a relatively higher degree of black power," she deduced, "but for whom?"[13] In the end, living in two newly independent African nation-states forced Garvin to concede that capitalism was still undermining African liberation. "Black was beautiful," she remarked, "but the masses [still] didn't have power."[14]

Garvin thus arrived in Shanghai in 1964 with high hopes to witness a people's revolution and socialist society in-action. Throughout her stay, she was housed in the Peace Hotel, a safe-haven for foreign expatriates. One of the few hotels in Shanghai whose bar still included a live jazz band (during the 1950s–1970s, the CCP suppressed most Western-influenced music and popular culture from Chinese life), the hotel offered patrons full service meals, cleaning, and laundry. She was assigned to teach at the Shanghai Foreign Languages Institute (*Shanghai waiguoyu xueyuan*), and was given a salary of 380 yuan, a wage three to four times greater than that paid to a Chinese professor.[15] Founded in December 1949 and originally named the Shanghai Russian School (*Shanghai e wen xuexiao*), the university of nearly four thousand students was the first foreign-language school to be established after the PRC's inauguration. At its launch the school specialized only in Russian language and literature and had a significant number of Soviet instructors; this was a product of China's then-close ties to the Soviet Union and the general trend in Chinese education of replicating the USSR's educational system. By 1952 though, course offerings increased to include English, Burmese, Vietnamese, and Indonesian, and later French, German, Japanese, Arabic, and Spanish. Administrators also divided the program into four primary components: language practice, translation, literary history, and linguistics.[16]

At its founding, the Shanghai Foreign Languages Institute's curriculum was a microcosm of education throughout the country. In 1951 China shifted its universities away from the Western model of postsecondary education that revolved around the combination of liberal arts, sciences, and professional schools. This model was replaced with that of the Soviets, the latter of which was organized around the subdivision of specialized institutes and professional schools. Soviet educators were additionally brought en masse to teach in Chinese institutions, and Chinese students were sent abroad to study in Soviet and Eastern European schools. Educational theory was also imported. *Pedagogy*, a textbook authored by I. A. Kairov, president of the Soviet Academy of Education Sciences, for example, was translated into Chinese and adopted by Chinese educators as the foremost theoretical work of its day. These changes produced what Ruth Hayhoe has described as *yuanxi tiaozheng*: a "reordering of colleges and departments" and a "reordering of knowledge" away from the populist ambitions and rhetoric of the Chinese Communist Revolution. A more bureaucratic, rigidly structured, top-down system of higher education instead was cultivated, which inevitably "reinforced tendencies toward centralization of knowledge and uniformity of thought."[17] This system came to its end in 1960 though, with the suspension of Sino-Soviet relations and the Soviets' subsequent recall of all their educators in 1960, which signified the beginning of new ideological direction in Chinese education.

As one of fifteen new foreign-language specialists entering the institute during the fall term of 1964, Garvin's appointment was part of these shifts. The severe decrease in the institute's faculty after the quick departure of its Soviet staff forced China to redirect its educational resources and focus. Recognizing that the end of Sino-Soviet relations meant China must identify new foreign allies and take on an even larger footprint in foreign relations, Chinese schools and universities were instructed to adopt a more international orientation. Rather than study abroad in the Soviet Union and Eastern Europe, Chinese students were now sent to various Western European countries. Educational offerings were also diversified, particularly foreign languages, whereby the teaching of multiple foreign languages was given equal importance to Russian-language comprehension.[18] China also sought out a new cadre of foreign teachers and translators. Eying foreigners who espoused radical political outlooks yet distanced themselves from the Communist Party of the Soviet Union (CPSU), the PRC had little time to comprehensively vet the ideological consciousness of this new wave of foreign guests. The historian Ann-Marie Brady explains: "A new group of foreign experts was invited to China: people chosen primarily for their professional qualifications rather than their political credentials. They were, in Maoist terms, more 'expert' than 'red.'"[19]

Mao first introduced the idiom of red and expert (you hong you zhuan) in a January 1958 speech. He stressed that service to the country could not be disconnected from business and economic development. In order for China to meets its economic and social objectives, political rectitude and professional skill would have to be unified. Expertise and professional work then had to be guided by correct political consciousness, whereby a person's labor and professional practice would reflect the principles of communism.[20] Thereafter, "red and expert" became a popular concept used by Mao and the CCP, particularly regarding the future of Chinese education. Education, Mao insisted, had to take on a more radical populist purpose; it needed to be redirected toward eliminating elitism, bureaucratism, and economic conservatism and transforming China into a modern, classless society.

In 1959 the defense minister Lin Biao and the People's Liberation Army (PLA) set it upon themselves to popularize Mao's ideas and broaden his appeal among national and international audiences. PLA leaders selected quotations from Mao's writings covering the period of 1926–49 and instructed PLA troops to use the quotations for group study and discussion. These quotations, it was argued, represented the truths of Marxism within the Chinese context, and were composed of idioms that would guide the troops toward victory in warfare and in becoming models of patriotism and national service. Four hundred and twenty-six of these quotations were ultimately compiled into an internal document circulated among the PLA. Reformed in this ideology, the PLA then carried Mao's message to the Chinese public. In May 1964 the internal document was published as the first edition of *Quotations from Chairman Mao*.[21] This was followed by the publication of the *Selected Military Writings by Mao Zedong* (*Maozedong junshi wenxua*) and *Selected Readings from the Works of Mao Zedong* (*Maozedong zhuzuo xuandu*), and later the revision and translation into thirty-six languages of the *Selected Works of Mao Zedong*, five volumes of Mao's writings and speeches.

These publications were central to the cultivation of an immense personality cult around Mao, where he was framed as the embodiment of the "four greats" (*sige weida*)—"the great teacher, great leader, great supreme commander, and great helmsman" (*weida de daoshi, weida de lingxiu, weida de tongshuai, weida de duoshou*). Chinese citizens were consequently instructed to study Mao's philosophy and learn from his and the PLA's example. Formulaic activities were also instituted. Through daily readings (*tiantian du*); fealty dances (*zhong zi wu*); "quotation gymnastics" (*yulu cao*), where people recited Mao's statements while participating in physical exercise; theater performances; and other activities, everyday Chinese citizens engaged in "lively study and application" (*huoxue huoyong*) of Mao's thought.[22]

The PLA's deification of Mao was also premised on distinguishing his philosophical doctrine from prior Marxist ideology. Mao and the CCP had initiated this process in the 1930s, described first as the "Sinification of Marxism" (*Makesi zhuyi de zhongguo hua*), which Mao explained as the effort to "imbu[e] every manifestation of Marxism with China's special characteristics."[23] Although the "Sinification of Marxism" was replaced in 1942 with the official term "Mao Zedong Thought" (*Maozedong sixiang*), both phrases spoke to Mao's "simultaneous interpretation of Chinese history and China's present through Marxist categories and the interpretation of Marxist categories through the specific historical situation of China."[24] Whereas Marxism-Leninism traditionally identified capitalism as a precedent for the establishment of a socialist and later communist society, Mao was hostile toward capitalism. He argued that capitalism represented a foreign force that could not be detached from Western imperialism. He therefore rejected capitalism as a necessary stage for socialism's and communism's development in China. "The Chinese [Communist] Revolution can avoid a capitalist future and can be directly linked with socialism without traversing the old historical path of the Western countries,"

Mao asserted.[25] Furthermore, unlike Soviet Marxism-Leninism, which viewed cities and urban populations as forces that would bring revolutionary ideology to the countryside, Mao preached about "the advantages of backwardness." He maintained that it was groups of peasant origins (*nongmin chusen*) and other underserved populations that would play the dominant role in the Chinese Communist Revolution.[26] Mao's vision of revolutionary politics and praxis for the Chinese context therefore fused Marxism-Leninism with adamant anti-capitalism, unabashed radical nationalism, and celebration of the rural poor, features that distinguished his thought from the Marxism-Leninism of the Soviet regime.

These were not the only ideas through which Mao amended Marxism-Leninism. In Mao's 1957 speech "On the Correct Handling of Contradictions among the People" (*Guanyu zhengque chuli renmin neibu maodun de wenti*), he maintained that despite many Marxists' claims that communism would bring the end of class inequality, it was futile to believe that communism could eradicate all class struggle and ideological conflict. Mao explained, "Contradictions among the people, and how to resolve this problem is a new problem. Historically, Marx and Engels said very little about this problem, and though Lenin referred to it, he only just referred to it. . . . He didn't have time to analyze this problem systematically."[27] Mao's concepts of permanent revolution (*buduan geming*) and protracted struggle (*changqi douzheng*) attended to this gap in Marxism-Leninism. For Mao, generating a true classless society meant cultivating a culture organized around constant ideological debate, class struggle, and revolutionary action; revolution, Mao argued, required everyday people and the government to be in a perpetual state of responding to the new contradictions brought on by systematic change. Mao furthermore strayed away from Karl Marx's focus on objective forces, Vladimir Lenin's prioritization of the Communist Party as the vanguard force of the communist revolution, and both Marx and Lenin's interpretation of the relationship between revolutionary ideology and class affiliation. Mao instead asserted that alongside objective factors, such as the economic mode of production, subjective forces (culture and human consciousness, will, and activity) were decisive factors in historical change. This argument went against Marxism-Leninism's minimization of culture as merely determined by the economic mode of production and class relations. Mao furthermore challenged Marxist claims that social-class affiliation determined the state of a person's political consciousness and that the rural poor were not in the appropriate economic or political state to confront capitalism and cultivate a radical proletarian attitude and practice. Mao responded that class position alone could not be equated with a correct or incorrect political outlook. Rather, what was most vital was the radical ideology and practice that individuals, no matter what their classes, espoused, because it was with this intellectual and political labor that they would transform their environment toward communism.

By the 1960s, to ensure the spread of these ideas, Mao and his followers in government and the PLA emphasized the use of these ideas and concepts in schools and their integration into curricula. A halt was subsequently placed on the distribution and circulation of media, images, and representations not authorized by the CCP. The publishing sector was additionally restructured to devote its resources to printing Mao's writings, what in effect led to a rapid decline and shortage of university and secondary-school textbooks.[28] These changes grew out of Mao's observations of China's young people, a segment that gained from the Chinese Communist Revolution but whose attitudes, Mao believed, were disconnected from the legacy of the revolution and the work of protracted struggle. But Mao also viewed China's young people, as well as the country's poor population, as "blank" (*kongbai de*), meaning untainted by the past, Soviet revisionism, and reactionary outlooks.[29] In Mao's view, these characteristics made young people and the poor the perfect candidates to be galvanized towards the task of altering Chinese life and ensuring a permanent revolution in China. In 1962 the Chinese government responded by inaugurating a socialist education movement (*shehuizhuyi jiaoyu yundong*), more commonly referred to as *siqing yundong* (four cleanups movement), whereby students and faculty were sent to rural areas to learn, work, and engage in *sixiang gaizao* (ideological remolding). They were additionally charged with centering Mao Zedong Thought in their coursework, pedagogy, and knowledge production because such political philosophy would guide them in the national task of creating a socialist economy and polity. Schools were also tasked to shift away from privileging urban elites and academic intellectuals and instead prioritize the inclusion of workers and peasants as students and educators.

As Garvin entered this political and educational context, she was informed that she was to push students "to become ideologically sound and professionally competent, placing politics in the forefront, to develop into worthy successors to the revolution, and to master language as a weapon in the class struggle, nationally and internationally."[30] For her initial year she was the sole instructor for first-year graduate students studying to become English-language teachers, translators, radio announcers, and interpreters. Her second year was spent strengthening the English competency of fourth-year undergraduates. What's more, with several language textbooks furnished by the department, she was entrusted to create each course from shorthand, undertakings that Garvin found challenging: "I thought oh Christ, where do you start?" Her limited understanding of Chinese history and politics and her brief experience as an ed-

FIGURE 4.2: Garvin (back row, fifth from right), students, and a billboard with Karl Marx's image, Shanghai Foreign Languages Institute, 1965. Courtesy of Lincoln and Miranda Bergman.

ucator were reminders of how unprepared she was. Who was she to know how to best prepare Chinese students for the revolutionary work that awaited them? Garvin explained, "Although I had spent many years in Marxist-Leninist study and concrete practice in my own country, I was and still am a product of U.S. society and influenced by bourgeois ideology." Doubtful of her ability to effectively contribute to Mao's national call to action, she mused: "I came to China poorly equipped to fulfill properly the immensely important task of assisting young people through language teaching to become 'red and expert.'"[31] While foreign expatriates were forbidden from purchasing Mao's writings, they were allowed to borrow copies from colleagues and libraries (these regulations were loosened over the course of the decade).[32] Through some means, Garvin obtained both English-translated and Mandarin versions of Mao's writings and immediately delved into them with the aid of Li Ruihua, her interpreter and one of her students. Intense study and engagement, she determined, would enable her to "play a positive role as a teacher in China."[33]

"The Orientation of the Youth Movement" (Qingnian yundong de fangxiang) a speech that Mao delivered to Chinese youths in Yan'an in 1939, was one of the first works Garvin read that offered her helpful themes around which to organize both her class lectures and the overall instructional culture of her classes. In the speech Mao appropriated the May Fourth Movement, demonstrations led by Chinese students in opposition to the Treaty of Versailles in 1919, as a model for the anti-imperialist work required of Chinese youths. Mao explained that class struggle and transition toward communism could only be instigated by "learning the theory of revolution and studying the principles and methods for resisting," and then physically transforming the nation by taking "part in labor," which denoted the ability to unify ideological thinking with political practice.[34] Unpacking the speech's thesis, Garvin wrote: "In his article, 'The Orientation of the Youth Movement,' Chairman Mao described a revolutionary youth as one who is both willing to integrate himself with the broad masses of workers and peasants, and [who] does so in practice."[35] Garvin thus ruled that of supreme import would be that her students consider the politics of their future pedagogy. They would have to dedicate serious time and energy to mulling over the relationship between their teaching and language practice and the daily struggles faced by Chinese people. This meant that class discussions and readings had to be pragmatic—high theory had to be made applicable to material conditions. It also meant continuously reevaluating ideas and methods so that both she and students could learn from mistakes and turn past errors and failures into lessons and achievements.

Another idea that Garvin found fruitful was what Mao described in 1952 as *gu wei jin yong*, to "make the past serve the present."[36] Garvin similarly decided that critical engagement of history would play a major function in her class. Students would be compelled to put historical analysis in conversation with the roles they would play in contemporary class struggle, national development, and world relations. The second half of Mao's dictum, *yang wei zhong yong*, meaning to make "the foreign serve China," became another feature of Garvin's teaching philosophy. Mao's tribute to the Canadian surgeon Norman Bethune, for instance, informed Garvin's understanding of how she, as a non-Chinese educator, could aid Chinese teachers and students in advancing China toward communism. Mao's 1939 essay "In Memory of Norman Bethune" (*jinian Bai Qiuen*) memorialized Bethune's service to China during the country's war of resistance against Japanese imperialism, and the essay encouraged foreigners sympathetic to China to follow Bethune's example.[37] Garvin perceived teaching in similar terms, identifying her classroom as a site for the evolution of her internationalist praxis. Introducing herself to the institute's university body, she laid out this realization: "As we attempt to integrate ourselves into the life and work of the Institute, our experience will be two-sided: receiving as well as giving, learning as well as teaching, thereby enriching our theories with practice. We look forward to a mutually fruitful stay in your country as we help to facilitate communication among peoples through proficient use of foreign languages."[38]

In Garvin's class, English versions of Mao's essays were read and reread, students instructed to practice pronunciation and unpack the meanings and ideology of Mao's words. She soon discerned that while the "students accepted the concepts of 'language as a tool in class struggle' and 'service to the people' as slogans," they "were not fully aware of their practical application." Believing that these theoretical formulations should be perceived in concrete terms, she pushed students to situate the terms and ideas in their own lives and to consider how their "personal and collective class consciousness and world outlook" could be "tied to the content of the texts."[39] The students initially found this approach, the heuristic method, to be extremely difficult; they struggled to come up with personal examples. Hoping to make things easier, Garvin tried a different approach. Before asking the students to offer suggestions about the terminology's practical application, she first used examples from the Chinese Communist Revolution to frame the terms and then encouraged students to debate over the terminology's meanings. Only after these steps would the students be asked to come up with their own examples.

For example, Garvin opened one lecture with Mao's speeches "Serve the People" (*Wei renmin fuwu*, 1944) and "The Foolish Old Man Who Removed Mountains" (*Yugong yishan*, 1945).[40] Then she asked the class to consider the analogies operating in both works. The class determined that at the center of both works was the importance of martyrdom for the sake of protecting the nation and that nothing could outweigh the labor of collective and consistent action and sacrifice over time. The students also resolved that by strengthening their own "'tool' of expertise, the quality and precision of the language as measured by the mastery of grammar, diction, pronunciation," they too could serve the nation and move mountains of inequality and oppression. Garvin subsequently came up with small-scale methods for graduate students to apply and enact this ideology. To "heighten their sense of responsibility," each of them was assigned to a student in the first-year English-language class.[41] The more-advanced student's duty was to instruct and mentor the less-advanced student for one hour daily, working mainly on strengthening listening, reading, and speaking comprehension. For this task Garvin appropriated "Learn from Comrade Lei Feng" (*Xiang Lei Feng tongzhi xuexi*), a 1963 Chinese propaganda campaign that honored the death of a young Chinese soldier. Garvin explained that by raising their professional level and by educating their younger peers, the senior students were following Lei Feng's lead and "serving the people."[42]

Garvin's reliance on these Maoist writings mirrored the general shifts in Chinese education during the period. Summarizing the widespread use of Mao's philosophy in Chinese education, the historian Daniel Leese notes that educators were instructed "to arouse passions by remembering past hardships and to use the historical experiences of the CCP to remember the oppression of the

Chinese nation." He explains, "The catharsis, finally was to be reached by comparing the past favorably to the present, based on the reading of Mao's articles on frugality and proletarian solidarity. This living education was to lead individuals to find the 'source of sweetness' in the correct leadership of the CCP and Mao Zedong."[43] Garvin's course materials reveal, to some extent, the uniformity of teaching conventions of that period, her classroom another venue for the transmission and instrumentalization of Maoist dogma.

But her methods and the classroom culture she promoted were a distant cry from conservative Chinese teacher-student interactions. Describing his experience within the Chinese education system during the late 1950s and early 1960s, the political scientist Dongping Han recollects that students "endured a lot of mental stress. . . . Students' role in the classroom was insignificant, accepting whatever the teachers tried to inject into their minds, following teachers' instructions carefully. . . . Talking, commenting, and discussing in the class were forbidden. . . . *shidao zunyan* (strict teacher's authority) was the order of the day."[44] In contrast, Garvin's class was organized around reflexivity, self-criticism, and productive valuation. She and her students were equal in their right to engage in constructive discussion as long as it was oriented toward advancing their ideological outlook and educational practice. Following Mao's argument about the importance of learning from the masses, Garvin pushed students to recognize that they had just as much to learn from one another as from her. "Each cadre must learn to be a pupil before assuming the role of 'leader,' so as to accumulate knowledge to be summarized and systematized into theories to guide the masses," she relayed.[45] Garvin's efforts to facilitate the classroom as a site to forge intellectual and political community were also enhanced by her willingness to allow students to publically evaluate her pedagogy. She wrote, "Teaching is a process of continual learning expedited by criticism and self-criticism. Periodically I scheduled sessions at which students were invited to criticize any and all aspects of our work, including my own performance. I profited greatly from their suggestions and criticisms."[46]

★

THE DUAL CHARACTER OF BLACK RESISTANCE

From the students' assessments Garvin discovered that they were interested in learning about capitalism's impact on U.S. life, particularly on African Americans. The students additionally sought "concrete information and facts about imperialism" rather than "just imperialism is bad" explanations. After considering the students' requests, she decided that she could teach a course on

African American history and the politics of black resistance in the United States, a class that would entail a high degree of reading, writing, and speaking English. A subsequent conversation with the department chair confirmed the class's appeal. However, the chair also relayed that the course syllabus and readings would be subject to the department's approval. While the process of getting the course approved was not extremely difficult, it did relay the ideological divides growing between China and the Soviet Union. Several books and pamphlets that Garvin proposed to use were rejected solely because they were CPUSA- and CPSU-affiliated publications, works that the department rebuffed as products of Soviet revisionism. "But the facts are correct," she countered. However, the department was unrelenting in its restrictions.[47]

Compelled to locate writings more agreeable with the CCP's political line, Garvin reviewed Mao's writings. His speech "On the Correct Handling of Contradictions among the People" was particularly influential in composing her lectures. In his analysis of contradictions, Mao relayed that social movements must face two different types of social contradictions, "those between ourselves and the enemy and those among the people." While Mao classified dissension "among the people" as a "non-antagonistic contradiction," he ruled that it nonetheless held the possibility of escalating into an "antagonistic contradiction" and fundamental struggle between enemies if not "properly handled." The means to prevent such a conflict was through the "democratic method of resolving contradictions," which he defined as a process of "persuasion and education." Through education, parties could flesh out the "dual character" of social struggles and political classes—that is, the "revolutionary and conciliationist side to its character"—and through persuasion they could then share, teach, and implement these lessons among other groups.[48]

This speech, most especially Mao's point about the dual character of social movements and political struggles, became a dominant portal through which Garvin taught African American history. She remarked, "[Mao] has repeatedly warned us of U.S. imperialism's dual tactics—the carrot and the club" and "the continuous ideological struggle between the two opposing political lines, resistance and capitulation that exist in every people's movement." Garvin then went on to situate these ideas within the context of U.S. black political movements. In American politics, "the carrot and the club" represented the dual character and repressive tactics of U.S. hegemony, whereas "resistance and capitulation" characterized the revolutionary and conciliationist sides of black social movements. She explained that historically, the Black Liberation Movement was divided between two tendencies—one side adamantly resistive to class and racial oppression, whose increasing frustration, political activism, self-defensive responses, and efforts to be self-determinate were met with state coercion and violence (i.e., "the club"); and the other side more reactionary in its political outlook, willing to compromise and relinquish radical critique and confrontation for gradual social change, marginal social access, and reconciliation with the forces of their oppression (i.e., "the carrot").

Garvin built on these themes in her first lecture series, The Struggle between Two Lines among Afro-Americans, the lecture's title appropriating Mao's dualistic, "among the people" framework. Garvin opened by examining the culture of enslaved Africans and their violent rejection of the U.S. slave economy and racial system. In her historical summation, she highlighted how slave insurrections helped collectivize enslaved Africans into a revolutionary social force. This resistance represented the first wave of African radicalism in the Americas and was the precursor to all future forms of black militancy. "The truth is that the Negro people as a whole have never accepted their inferior position," she explained to the students. "From the early days of enslavement they have been in revolt."[49] The rebellions of the enslaved took on organized forms through the militancy of Maroon societies, the slave liberator Harriet Tubman, the Haitian revolution led by Toussaint L'Ouverture, and the insurrections organized by Nat Turner, Gabriel Prosser, and John Brown.

Garvin, however, pointed out that such revolutionary rejections of racial capitalism did not compose all black politics. "Inevitably two lines emerged," she remarked about the different approaches of black resistance. U.S. and European abolitionist movements represented the early reformist tendencies of black political struggle—these wings' gradualist approach, tactical accommodations, and compromises with the structure of power contrasting with the radical, revolutionary line of resistance. The differences between these two ideological lines, according to Garvin, represented the "important struggle" over "compromise or resistance."[50] She highlighted the abolitionists Frederick Douglass and William Lloyd Garrison as best conveying the distinct poles of this struggle during the late nineteenth century. Garrison's "narrow expression of moral indignation," Garvin asserted, "was one-sided," "not based on class analysis," "paternalistic," and "failed to take account of all the existing contradictions between the north and south." Douglass in contrast was anti-imperialist, critical of capitalism, and supportive of equal rights for women, workers, and black self-defense. Douglass therefore embodied the more progressive of the two activists and thinkers because his radical vision of social and political life, unlike Garrison's, did not correspond with that of liberal democracy and global capitalism. Douglass rather viewed the abolition of slavery as tied to the fight against all forms of exploitation and dehumanization, what effectively meant a struggle against capitalism's mutual forms of subjection and exploitation.[51]

These same dichotomies were present when Garvin transitioned into assessing the contemporary state of black American activism. Returning to the analogy of "the carrot and the club," she maintained that civil rights legislation, most notably the landmark Civil Rights Act of 1964, which outlawed then-dominant public forms of racial discrimination, and the Voting Rights Act of 1965, which prohibited discrimination in voting, were "pathetic compromise[s]." These government responses to antiblack oppression, she elaborated, were "limited in scope and coverage" because they failed to actively identify and transform the dominant structural forces of white supremacy and capitalist exploitation. In her view, the legislation did not represent a genuine concern and commitment to upending the psychological, political, and economic impact of racism and inequality; the legislation was rather an effort to "slow down the momentum of the Negro liberation movement."[52] Garvin explained, "The U.S. ruling class was then dangling an emaciated carrot before the awakening black people, attempting to entice them from the streets to the courtrooms."[53] She also criticized elements of the Civil Rights Movement, particularly the NAACP and Urban League, for sanctioning the U.S. government's feeble response to U.S. racial oppression. By constantly focusing on reform rather than revolution and turning a deaf ear to the international scene, these civil rights organizations' program of action was incapable of achieving democracy and quality of life for the U.S. poor and calling into question the U.S. government's imperialist activities throughout the world. Garvin asserted that in "confin[ing] their activities to the home front" and "regard[ing] the fight for Negro rights as a domestic family affair," these organizations were being "utilized to support U.S. foreign policy," actions that left them "aloof from international issues" and which helped "shield the true nature of U.S. exploitation."[54]

Garvin ruled that the reform-based approach of the Civil Rights Movement's more moderate wings was no match for "the mounting challenge of the newly-emerging left forces" of black political activism. The latter contingent were antiracist and anticapitalist in their political stance and were not invested in being integrated into American life; they rather were focused on achieving economic and social equality and upending the chokehold of U.S. elites on the U.S. economy and the world. It was this wing of the Black Freedom Struggle, Garvin ruled, that consequently "represented the best interests of the overwhelming majority of American blacks" because U.S. black radicals understood that "the Negro liberation movement is an important part of the worldwide anti-imperialist struggle."[55] These movements' political work was therefore advanced by their efforts to build solidarity with non-U.S. antiracist and anti-imperialist movements. Thus for instance, the Chinese Communist

Revolution, among other foreign struggles, was equipping African American activists "with their most decisive weapon—genuine Marxist-Leninist ideology to wage victorious struggles against colonialism and neo-colonialism. . . . The leadership of China is singling out U.S. imperialism as the main enemy of the world."[56] Garvin also described the Vietnamese forces fighting against the U.S. military as the analog to the black American struggle for liberation. "Whereas internationally Vietnam represents the Achilles heel of America's vulnerable foreign policy today, the Negro question is its counterpart domestically," Garvin lectured.[57] Lastly, she closed the lecture series by arguing that the divides between the Black Freedom Struggle's militant fringe force and its moderate wings was reaching its breaking point. It represented "the last ideological struggle" of the Black Freedom Movement, the differences separating these sides having ultimately evolved into an "antagonistic contradiction" over "the subjective outlook of the black masses."[58]

Fundamentally, Garvin's lectures framed black political ideology as oscillating between socialist and bourgeois ideologies—that is, between an impulse to crush capitalism and white supremacy and engender a new system of social and economic life, and an impulse to reform capitalism and liberal democracy to include African Americans and other racial minorities. Douglass, Tubman, Brown, and L'Ouverture were identified as the precedents of black radical traditions, as the predecessors to the Cold War global movement against capital and white supremacy. Garrison and the abolitionist movement, however, were represented as the more capitulary wings of black political ideology. Garrison's efforts to abolish slavery therefore tied into various civil rights organizations' platform of integrating African Americans into U.S. national life. Although these organizations criticized liberal democracy, they nonetheless remained faithful to the promise of liberal democracy, believing that racial and social egalitarianism could exist alongside capitalism's expansion.

Garvin's lectures offered students an entry point into African American political struggle; student papers, essay outlines, and notes reveal broad comprehension and interest in the African American history, political traditions, and contemporary state of U.S. black politics and culture. But it can't be overlooked that Garvin simplified this history's complexity. Important ideological differences and the diversity of black perspectives were in some measure flattened out. She did not elaborate much on the gender oppression, intraideological differences and struggles, class dynamics, and the different historical contexts that shaped black activists' varying and distinct political ideologies and arguments. In short, the history through which she summarized African American politics and history presented a far more homogenous picture than what was actually true. But it was effective in translating African American history and the challenges facing blacks in the Cold War context to a group of young-adult-aged Chinese students. Garvin's teaching furthermore linked the two racial groups' political struggles conceptually in a way that made sense.

To enable students to draw their own conclusions, Garvin thought it also crucial for them to dedicate time outside the classroom to considering this history. Once a week, class time was spent discussing the topics and themes found in the pages of newspapers, periodicals, and unrestricted news releases. Garvin hoped that reading these publications aloud and discussing their content might ensure her students full comprehension of the facts in context as well as strengthen their understanding of differences in language, grammar, sentence structure, and style. Student debates and dramatization of the texts made these activities social and moreover entertaining. The group would then consider the positions offered within these debates and performances "with [the] aim of strengthening their ability to defend a given position and to refute incorrect views."[59] "We experimented and did a lot of things," Garvin remarked. "I had very much of free hand to give them a practice of teaching and helping others."[60]

Such experimentation was not an easy task. Garvin sensed this frequently among female students. In their dispositions, she periodically discerned a hesitancy to take on leading roles in class discussions, debates, and dramatic improvisations. "Girl students were overly shy, easily embarrassed and reluctant to be extremely active," Garvin noted. She attributed this to "hangovers from the past society in which the role of women was gravely restricted" and when women were prevented access to education.[61] It was the result of "thousands of years of oppression, physically and mentally under reactionary doctrine, rules and customs which deemed them inferior and useless."[62] Deciding to deal with this issue head-on, Garvin devoted numerous lectures to examining women's struggles in both the Chinese and African American contexts. In these lectures, she examined how discourses of female inferiority and practices of male supremacy and female subordination functioned in both the United States and China. Students were also required to facilitate some of these lessons, female students specifically assigned to play primary roles in organizing and leading the teachings and discussions.

From their readings, the students ascertained that the Chinese government had taken some steps in remedying the inequality and injustice faced by Chinese women. Article 6 of its 1949 Common Program provisional constitution stipulated that "women shall enjoy equal rights with men in political, economic, cultural, educational, and social life" and gave legal protections for marriage and divorce. In the aftermath, some women gained greater access to employment and leadership positions and were given status equal to that of men in the per capita calculation of what rations a household should receive. Female-led associations such as the All China Women's Federation played a chief role in implementing these measures, working to increase women's access to contraception and to quality education. One result was the slow growth of women entering higher education, which increased from 17.9 percent in 1947 to 24.6 percent in 1956, a large portion of these women majoring in medicine, social sciences, teaching, and foreign languages.[63] Students also examined Chinese women's campaigns to extend facilities for childcare, laundries, and other services to reduce the time-consuming drudgery of household responsibilities. Students discussed and considered the strengths of China's New Marriage Law of 1950 (xin hunyin fa), legislation that promoted marriage equality and monogamy, and that outlawed concubinage, child betrothal, infanticide, and exaction of payment or gifts as a condition for marriage. By banning marriage by proxy, the law declared that all Chinese marriages would be based on the free choice of partners, meaning that both marrying parties had to consent to marriage. In conversations with the students, Garvin affirmed the law's importance in reshaping Chinese gender relations and advancing the rights of Chinese women. It was helping to "bring democracy into the family unit," she stated. She also lauded the increase of women in Chinese higher education. In her view, more and more were being "educated and trained to play a full role in production, family affairs, and all aspects of society in preparation for their full development on a country-wide basis." She elaborated, "[I was] tremendously impressed . . . by remarkable changes and gains they [women] had made. . . . What they have won was by no means due to generosity or compassion of ruling class. It took decades of persistent struggle ideologically and with arms to transform China's social system to one of socialism and to lay the basis for emancipation of women."[64]

Garvin and the students also acknowledged though that more had to be done to ensure the extension and protection of Chinese women's rights. The aforementioned advancements, they admitted, did not erase the gender imbalance, patriarchal relations, and chauvinist attitudes that mired schools, labor, land reform, and overall Chinese life. For instance, despite the protections given to married women and women's growing access to higher education and the work sector, marriage remained patrilocal, professional fields continued to favor men, and women's educational attainment still was not on par with men. The government moreover skirted around taking direct responsibility for remedying this inequality, relegating the responsibility of advancing women's rights to CCP-led women's organizations and often evading the issue by asserting that only a communist revolution would produce women's liberation.[65]

Garvin's students additionally examined the connections between Chinese and American women's struggles, in time coming to distinguish black women's struggles from that of middle-class U.S. women. From their discussions, Garvin ascertained that the majority of images of U.S. women that the students had seen were representations cultivated by marketers and advertisements, depictions of U.S. women as avid consumers and obedient housewives. "The average American woman by no means conforms to the glowing image which U.S. propaganda organs seek to project. She is neither happy, contented, care-free nor basking in luxury," Garvin relayed to the group. But she also distinguished working-class black women's struggles from that of other American women. Pointing to the specific gender, class, and racial oppression experienced by U.S. black women, Garvin maintained: "Millions of working class Negro women have historically shouldered a major share of responsibility and leadership, including that of armed resistance. . . . Many Negro women have remained firm and courageous in constant battle against their oppressors."[66] Whiteness and class privilege, the students learned, provided many middle-class women with status and advantages unavailable to working-class black women. But Garvin also impressed on the students the importance of not simply likening black women's oppression to that endured by Chinese women. While both group's experiences were products of patriarchy, capitalism, and racism, they were still structured and took shape in uneven, heterogeneous ways.

Garvin's point was that U.S. black female radicalism could not be simply translated within the idioms and ideology of Chinese communism, nor within the terms of Chinese women's struggles. African American women's political agency, like that of black radicalism in general, she explained, was the result of a distinct historical struggle for black autonomy, self-determination, collective being, and definition on their own terms. Thus, while it was imperative for black women and Chinese women to perceive themselves as leading political agents in the struggle against capitalism, white supremacy, and sexism, it was also important for them to acknowledge the differences in cultivating radical feminist practice in different national contexts—that is, to differentiate black American radicalism from Chinese communism. This did not mean essentializing Chinese and black women's histories as disconnected from other transgressive movements and histories; rather, it meant perceiving the differences between Chinese feminist and black feminist radical practices and histories and noting their inability to be bound by the conceptual parameters of a universalist discourse of feminism. Garvin thus encouraged her female students to mobilize their own subjectivities and the histories of female struggle in different national and geographical contexts as means to cultivate their own radical, feminist politics. Female students were persuaded "to develop self-confidence" and "to exploit their capacity to become truly equal in the service of China's socialized construction."[67]

To encourage further initiative and creativity, Garvin assigned a project where each student was to produce a critical research paper and presentation on a particular facet of African American history. The students' papers covered a range of topics and themes, with titles including "Nineteenth Century Negro Struggles for Freedom," "Role of Fascist and Racist Organizations in Suppressing Negroes," "Negro-White Unity in the Struggle for Negro Rights," "Ideology and Tactics of the Main Organizations Fighting for Negro Rights in the Twentieth Century," and "Youth and the Negro Struggle." Garvin was extremely impressed with this work, commenting: "The chapters they wrote could certainly have been used in the U.S. for some education." These papers culminated with a student-led presentation at a conference of English-language educators and language students in May 1965. A summation of all the students' research, "The History of the Negro in the U.S.," was subsequently formed out of information taken from each student's paper. "We really made this a collective thing," Garvin explained about the lecture's intensive and extensive preparation.[68] What started as a class-constructed outline went through four drafts of writing and revision, where "every sentence and paragraph [was] analyzed for language, structure, accuracy, clarity and ideology."[69]

At the conference, the presenters—two students elected by their classmates—took center stage. "Although the Chinese and the Afro-Americans are separated by the Pacific Ocean, they are fighting against their common enemy—U.S. imperialism," the students opined in the presentation's opening. "We Chinese students are deeply concerned about the plight and the struggle of the U.S. Negroes and many are eager to know something more on this question." They then went on to examine the history of race in the United States, the divides distinguishing black political leadership, and the contemporary conditions that structured black lives. To some extent their summation replicated the ideas supplied by Garvin in her lectures, situating the diversity of black political viewpoints within a dualist capitulation-versus-resistance framework and positioning the U.S. Black Freedom Movement as part of a world anti-imperialist struggle. "The mounting struggle of the Negroes for equality and freedom is of paramount importance both nationally and internationally. It lays bare the inner link between the internal reactionary policy and the aggressive foreign policy of the U.S. government," they explained. "It helps check U.S. fascism and reaction at home and weakens the ideological and material potential of the United States in carrying out its policy of aggression abroad."[70] Once the students finished giving the presentation, audience members were permitted to ask questions; each of Garvin's students was required to answer at least one question in English, an endeavor that forced them to come up with an impromptu answer and demonstrate proficiency. Garvin then closed the question-and-answer session with her own thoughts, summing up her admiration of the students' work. "Guided by the Communist Party's slogan to become 'red and expert,' and inspired by the recent reforms in teaching methods in our department, the teachers in my class agreed to exercise initiative by undertaking this lecture which I had previously committed myself to give," she stated. "My students, I am confident, have acquired the foundation from which to earn the title, 'revolutionary successors,' both red and expert."[71]

★

CHAMPIONING THE REVOLUTION

Two years into her stay, Garvin's run as a college instructor was put on hold. The onset of the GPCR brought classes at the Shanghai Foreign Languages Institute, along with the majority of China's urban educational institutions, to a standstill. Universities and schools were a primary site where the GPCR's clashes and struggles were waged. Dissatisfaction with the educational system and the elite class backgrounds of students and faculty had been brewing for some time. The sociologist Julia Kwong explains that this was a period when "educational opportunities shrank. . . . The number of courses proliferated and the curriculum often included materials students considered irrelevant to later job requirements. The students' workload was heavy. In this unsympathetic atmosphere, many workers and peasants' children did badly and were expelled. To these students, the schools, especially the good ones, were 'little pagodas' (ivory towers) nurturing the lucky few."[72] When students and faculty erupted against administration leadership at Beijing University on May 28, 1966, it was partially a response to what was viewed as bourgeois domination of education. These criticisms spread to educational institutions throughout the country; numerous campus populations spoke out against the revisionist, elitist, and bureaucratic practices of educational leaders and intellectuals. By July of that year urban universities' and secondary schools' classes came to a screeching halt, the majority remaining closed for the next two to three years. This resulted in a severe drop in student enrollment; from 1966 to 1969 there was no new enrollment in higher education.[73]

The suspension of classes at the Shanghai Foreign Languages Institute and widespread educational disruptions in the city forced most foreign students and staff to return to their home countries. Garvin initially remained at the Shanghai Peace Hotel. Frustrated and bored, she instructed English classes for hotel personnel. For no salary, she taught six classes per day, six days a week, to receptionists, shopkeepers, elevator operators, doormen, waitresses, housemaids, and stewards until authorities relocated her and other Shanghai expatriate residents to Beijing. "I really felt that I was useful," she commented.[74]

From Beijing, Garvin paid close attention to the GPCR's developments. "Obviously there were many things that were going wrong," she acknowledged, citing the anarchy and destruction of property by the Red Guards. Still, she remained empathetic toward the Red Guards and the GPCR's call for citizens to enact permanent revolution; she attributed some of the Red Guards' intemperance to immaturity and misinterpretation of Mao's directives. For Garvin, the GPCR's violent excesses did not outweigh the positive shifts it was engendering: "In every revolution, some people are killed, including innocent ones. This can't be avoided. . . . No matter what a Party decrees, it cannot stop every individual slaughter." Garvin though was impressed with how the revolution offered her students a context to take responsibility for constructing a new society and opportunities to "create new theory rising out of their own experiences."[75] This was visible in several students' work in agricultural collectives. She lauded these students for "plunging themselves into state affairs[,] . . . acquiring firsthand experiences and steeling themselves in the crucible of acute class struggle." She concluded that their "direct participation in the Great Cultural Revolution has provided the means through which theory, the thought of Mao Tse-tung, is linked with practice."[76]

Garvin was not alone in her admiration of the GPCR. In fact, the most pertinent other black American endorsement came from then-China residents Mabel and Robert Williams. After relocating to Beijing in July 1966, just months into the GPCR, the couple claimed to a friend: "The Cultural Revolution . . . will have a profound impact on the future of our world. It is a great opportunity to live through and to observe such an historic event."[77] Denouncing Western media coverage of the GPCR as "slander, distortion and deliberate misinformation," Robert Williams authored an editorial in hopes of providing black Americans with a more objective account of what was transpiring in China. "As an American black man, it is a rare opportunity to stand in the midst of the truth of history, to know fact rather than fiction and to witness one of the greatest social experiments of this age," he wrote. Williams specifically pointed to the ways the revolution stimulated working-class and working-poor participation in rural schools and the military. Curricula had formerly given greater value to "bourgeois intellectualism" and "personal advantage" rather than the social function education could play in uplifting the poor. Williams asserted that the GPCR's reformation of education was eliminating such class distinctions and divisions: "[The schools now] stress service to the people, internationalism and the virtues of perseverance." He also praised the PLA for choosing Mao's leadership and the will of the Chinese people over the CCP. The PLA was no longer the state's edifice of violence and coercion but now lived, worked, and studied "side by side with the people," offering the world a military model that challenged "the capitalist concept of an army's role in society."[78] For Williams, these shifts demonstrated that China was fighting to become a society that prized selflessness and sacrifice first and foremost over all other human practices. It was this aspect, he maintained, that should be carried over into the U.S. political struggle. "If a man can rid himself of selfishness, this will abolish most of the evil of the world, but this is the most difficult fight of man, to be selfless," he remarked. "We have to instill in our people in the ghetto that they have to build a selfless society, a collective society."[79]

In personal correspondence and other forums of media, Mabel and Robert Williams broadened Mao's appeal among their radical colleagues and comrades. Over the course of their exile they had cemented ties with many of the socialist militants and revolutionary nationalists who found expression in the call for Black Power.[80] Ultimately, the couple's sanctuary in China and continued editing of the *Crusader*, which by then frequently closed with citations from Mao's writings, increased China's mystique among this generation of American radicals. Many of the Williamses' supporters in the United States, for instance, grilled the couple about "the ideas of Mao and how it applies to them as young blacks" and requested copies of the little red book and "Red Guard pins with Mao's picture" (see figure 4.3).[81] Others confirmed that the Williamses' ties to China were altering black attitudes about the country. While one person maintained that "African Americans will accept or reject China mostly by your statements and your happiness in living with them," another suggested that the Williamses' ties to China might prompt more African American political organizations and leaders to emulate the model of partnership and tutelage embodied in Sino-African relations.[82] Another person stated that it would be of great benefit to black radicals and youths to have access to Chinese educational and technical institutions. Because it was through the Williamses "that over 95% of the African Americans [would] know and accept China," the person wrote, it was vital that the Williamses help facilitate "China as a haven for those black youths who want to continue their education."[83] Others informed the Williamses that the family's engagement with China had led them to adopt a Maoist political line. One wrote, "Mao Zedong's thought has no color and is indispensable to any revolutionary fighter. . . . Without that international movement, we are certainly doomed to failure, and, as Chairman Mao has warned, the struggle will be a long one."[84] Someone else stated that among black radicals, "the attitude towards China becomes the demarcation line be-

FIGURE 4.3: Mao signs Robert Williams's copy of *Quotations from Chairman Mao Zedong*. Robert F. Williams Archive, HS 1091. Courtesy of Bentley Historical Library, University of Michigan.

tween revolutionaries and enemies of revolution."[85] Another person was more direct: "Fuck it man, I'm for Mao."[86]

These messages speak to how Mao's cult of personality transgressed national borders. They also reveal a fairly uncomplicated framing of China that was to some extent enabled by the Williamses' and other expatriates' idealistic portrayals of the country. This was a consequence of several factors. First, the inability to read or speak Mandarin prevented some expatriate residents from comprehensively engaging people and sources of information outside the government's control. Most of the information shared by Western expatriates was obtained from government contacts and fellow expatriates. Robert Williams's editorial on the GPCR, for instance, was composed from data and personal stories he acquired while traveling with a contingent of foreign expatriates on a nationwide tour organized by China's Foreign Experts Bureau. Keep in mind this was a state-regulated tour devoid of opinions and encounters that strayed from the Central Cultural Revolution Group's main line.[87]

Ultimately, the Chinese government went to enormous lengths to influence and sanitize Western expatriates' impressions of China. Those Western foreigners who were deemed as influential and important by the state were afforded comfortable accommodations, private transportation, spending allowances, lavish gifts, and meals where they dined in foreigner-only facilities, all at the government's expense. Some of them were also given the status of "foreign experts" (*waiguo zhuanjia*), a title referring to their privileged access to some government information and denoting that they had gained some level of trust from political officials. The Williams family, for instance, was housed in a compound run by the China Peace Committee. The complex had once served as the Italian embassy and moreover was home to a dynamic community of leftists who took flight to China to escape political repression in their home countries.[88] Staffed by private drivers and housekeepers, it was one of several buildings where foreigners lived, residences that were ultimately disconnected from ordinary Chinese communities. While most of these housing complexes were less extravagant than that of the Williamses' residence, the buildings' remoteness and privileged conditions led Chinese citizens to dub them as "golden ghettos" (*jinse de pinminku*).[89]

But amid these luxuries were government techniques of persuasion, manipulation, and surveillance. In 1964 the Chinese government instituted new regulations that limited foreign residents' movements and activities and that more effectively increased their isolation from Chinese life. Not all, but some foreigners were required to carry identification booklets with them. If seeking to travel outside of their area of residence, many also had to apply for travel permits that listed the places where they were allowed to visit; for the most part, these foreigners were only permitted to participate in such sightseeing when on government-organized group tours. Of course, this wasn't the case for every foreigner; foreign educators like Garvin experienced less surveillance because their work and residency was steeped in the activities and processes of everyday Chinese life. They thus traveled and moved around with, to some degree, greater freedom than prominent guests of state such as the Williams family. But for the most part, the Western expatriate community was under close watch. Personal handlers, drivers, and secret agents tracked foreigners' daily movements and kept tabs on foreigners' opinions, personal relationships, and mail correspondence. And this climate of supervision and scrutiny produced mistrust within the expatriate community, with some members alleging that the government had sanctioned other members to spy and keep tabs on other expatriates.[90]

This is all to say that Garvin and the Williamses' ambivalence regarding publically addressing the GPCR's perilous conditions was not just the result of misinformation and ignorance on their part; it was most likely prompted by the government's iron hand. During this period, the Western expatriate community in China split on what kind of political stance to take about the GPCR and the domination of Mao's ideological clique over the CCP. Many expatriates refrained from becoming too actively involved in the debates surrounding the GPCR, some articulating support for Mao while privately arguing that they had neither enough information nor background to grasp the struggle's complexity. Others threw themselves into the GPCR's turmoil, exporting its mantra through writings and translations of Chinese articles. Small factions even formed foreigners-only rebel groups, collectives that publically aligned with the GPCR. These foreigners produced *dazibao* (big character posters) and requested permission to be allowed to live in similar meager conditions as Chinese farmers and workers. Other members of the expatriate community privately criticized such requests. In their view, such actions by fellow expatriates communicated more an attempt to posture revolutionary credentials and ideology than an articulation of true interest and commitment to the revolution's ideals.[91] This group of expatriates maintained that the GPCR was distinctly a Chinese social struggle, one that Western radicals could learn from, but nonetheless a movement that most foreign residents should study from a distance rather than from within its midst. Numerous expatriates did not heed this advice though. For example, those foreigners who were publically critical of the revolution and Mao's leadership were accused of being Soviet revisionists and U.S. spies. They faced harassment, house arrest, detainment, and solitary confinement; some of these people were not released from imprisonment until the mid to late 1970s. Such antiforeign sentiment also led to the censuring and terrorization of Chinese citizens known for being close with foreign residents, as well as the burning and destroying of several diplomatic missions.[92]

It was therefore in neither Garvin's nor the Williamses' interest to publically criticize the GPCR, as their safety was highly dependent on their ability to effectively negotiate the Chinese political terrain. When the Red Guards paraded teachers of the Williamses' sons down streets, both Robert and Mabel Williams privately challenged other expatriates about this treatment. However, their media propaganda did not reflect such criticisms. "What was happening in China was an internal affair," they rationalized. "Our job was to focus on the affairs of black Americans. You can't fight everybody's battles."[93] Still decades later, Robert Williams conceded that the GPCR was mired by immense turmoil and violence. "It just turned into anarchy," he stated.[94]

For Garvin, on the other hand, the inconsistencies of Mao's personality cult became more apparent after she relocated to Beijing. There, she worked as an editor and language polisher for the Foreign Languages Press and *Peking*

Review, joining a contingent of foreigners who helped translate and refine Chinese news reports. Most of her work involved correcting grammar, punctuation, and spelling, work tasks that she identified as being of menial scale. What discouraged her most though was that she was not permitted to question, challenge, or revise the content of these submissions. For instance, when editing articles about agriculture and industry, Garvin frequently felt that she lacked the necessary expertise regarding these subjects to ensure that the article's writers were employing the correct terminology. She also disagreed with the articles' constant exaltation of Mao. When she replaced statements such as "thanks to Chairman Mao," with "thanks to Chairman Mao and the party," her superiors scolded her for glossing over Mao's supreme value to the country and restored her corrections to the original phrasing. Consequently, in contrast to the praise Garvin once showed Mao in her Shanghai classroom, in Beijing she privately grew weary of the chairman's extreme lionization. "I understand the role of leadership but obviously he didn't do all of this by himself; he did this *through* the party," she stressed in later decades.[95]

As Garvin worked to reconcile her anxieties about Mao's cult of personality, the Chinese government seized on the rising number of urban rebellions in the United States to reassert China's support for black liberation. Over the course of the 1960s, racial confrontation and civil unrest against white violence led to the spread of racial uprisings in U.S. cities and underserved black communities. This insurgency was a response to decades of police brutality and injustice, underemployment and labor exploitation, and lack of access to quality housing, food, health care, education, and public services. Chinese media covered these episodes, frequently likening U.S. black resistance to anticolonial struggles in Vietnam and Angola. Elevating black Americans' struggles to the fold of world revolution, China stressed that the U.S. government was "now waging two race wars—one against Negroes at home, the other against Asians in Vietnam."[96]

This support was reiterated when Mao issued a statement in April 1968 that repudiated Martin Luther King Jr.'s assassination. Mao's proclamation also called attention to black antiwar activism, insisting that over the second half of the 1960s, African American political consciousness had risen steadily. Such could be seen through the "tremendous aid and inspiration" that black activism was providing "to the struggle of the Vietnamese people."[97] In conjunction with the statement, the Chinese government published several propaganda posters that reinforced the message that racial and social turmoil had led black Americans to the point of armed warfare against American institutions of power. One poster featuring Mao's statement in full also displayed an annotated map that detailed the spread of urban rebellions in the United States (see figure 4.4). Each rebellion is noted with an image of a flame, a representation that linked the poster with Chinese posters detailing other "world revolutionary hot spots," including Palestine, Vietnam, Burma, and Paris.[98] The depiction stipulates that the flames of revolution were bringing U.S. democracy and imperialism to a standstill, the upsurge in black violence, revolt, and transgression mushrooming to all pockets of the country. Via the image, blackness was framed as the antithesis of U.S. tyranny, namely as the central force capable of instituting U.S. social justice. Another poster built on this theme, displaying a multiracial collective of U.S. youths led by a black man and woman, the two of them armed with rifles of liberation and torches of liberty. In the distance stood the burning U.S. capitol, which denoted the failure of liberal democracy and civil rights legislation to stem the tide of social discontent.

At the Shanghai Foreign Languages Institute, a rally was held to celebrate King's life and the increasing fervor of black American militancy. In a speech to the attendees, Garvin coupled black liberation with Mao's ideas about power. "The slogan, 'Black Power,' has already become a battle cry and the truth that 'political power grows out of the barrel of a gun' is being grasped by ever-increasing numbers of revolutionaries," she explained. She closed by re-emphasizing the ideological importance of radical internationalism to the Black Freedom Movement: "Let the black people of the United States take fresh heart in the knowledge that they are not alone, not without friends and allies at home and abroad."[99] Afterward she participated in a march of what she estimated to be thousands of Chinese who assembled in the downpour of heavy rain, waving red banners and chanting: "Oppressed nations and peoples of the world unite! . . . Support our black brothers and sisters!" Electrified by this immense expression of solidarity, Garvin recounted: "I felt ten feet tall to be in China at that particular time."[100]

Amid this charged political environment, Garvin cultivated a life. In 1966 she met Leibel Bergman, a white American from San Francisco and a veteran communist organizer who broke with the CPUSA and the Progressive Labor Party in the mid-1950s to later cofound the New Left organization the Revolutionary Union in the late 1960s. The death of his spouse, Anne, in 1963, after a two-year battle with bone cancer, and Bergman's decreasing faith in various communist organizations however left him somewhat despondent with the state of U.S. radicalism by the midpoint of the 1960s. Thus, when he was offered the chance to live and work in China for two years, he jumped at the opportunity. With his two eldest sons, Bergman traveled to China in 1965 to teach at Beijing's Institute for International Relations.[101]

In Shanghai, Bergman was introduced to Garvin, and the two soon grew extremely fond of one another. Within a year they were in love and in 1967 they

支持美国黑人抗暴斗争的声明

（一九六八年四月十六日）

美国黑人抗暴斗争形势简图

FIGURE 4.4: "Zhichi Meiguo heiren kangbao douzheng de sheng ming/Meiguo heiren kangbao douzheng xingshi jiantu" (Statement in support of Black American's antiviolence struggle/A situation sketch of Black American's antiviolence struggle), 1968. Courtesy of Ann Tompkins (Tang Fandi) and Lincoln Cushing Chinese Poster Collection, C. V. Starr East Asian Library, University of California, Berkeley. Also published in Tompkins and Cushing, *Chinese Posters*. Digital image courtesy Lincoln Cushing/Docs Populi.

were married in an elaborate Red Guard ceremony, their interracial marriage a feat largely impossible in many U.S. states at that time. In comparison to many of their expatriate colleagues, the couple's daily lifestyle was particularly modest. Garvin and Bergman's compound housed mainly Chinese families. It thus lacked paid help and only had access to hot water for bathing once a week.[102] But in this community Garvin found tranquility. "I felt much more comfortable in that kind of environment," she commented. "It gave me a different type of experience beyond teaching."[103]

Garvin also took serious pride in participating in *laodong* (labor and work), seasonal volunteer labor, and homestays in rural communities.[104] In 1968 university students and faculty were sent to rural areas to be reformed through labor, what was referred to as *laodong gaizao*, or *laogai* for short. On farms and in communes, they worked and lived alongside peasants and agricultural laborers in institutions that came to be known as the May Seventh Cadre Schools, named after Mao's 1966 GPCR directive that intellectuals, Red Guards, and urban youths be dispatched from cities to farms and factories to undergo ideological reeducation and manual labor. Over the course of the next decade, more than sixteen million youths were sent to the countryside, the city of Shanghai registering the highest percentage.[105] Laogai built on the practice of *laodong jiaoyang* (labor reeducation), which was organized around the idea that rural life and labor would teach proletarian politics to elites, intellectuals, and urban populations and create more-equitable learning spaces and sites of production. Garvin volunteered to participate in such work, toiling on a vegetable farm where she cut and sorted potatoes and pulled grain. Despite believing that she "was probably more of hindrance than a help," she worked hard to contribute to the commune and ended up building close relationships with several residents.[106] And even after leaving China in 1970, she returned to visit this community in later years, her comfort among them a reminder of the ties she forged with her students in Shanghai.

Ultimately, Garvin's teaching practices and her overall experience in China illuminate an ideological bridge between her own ideas and Mao Zedong Thought. For Mao, schools and universities were central sites to politicize the attitudes of the working-class and poor masses and incite them toward transforming Chinese life. He believed that the masses were not simply awaiting the knowledge that would lead them to liberation; they rather already carried in them the spontaneous consciousness and seeds for revolution. It was therefore crucial to refigure education so learning spaces could exist not just in schools but also in other sites of daily life. In these collective spaces, people could experience individual sacrifice and engage in service and nation building. Nonetheless, as the GPCR proved, Mao and his political allies' rhetoric of labor and education also sanctioned extreme violence and persecution. At its worst, it helped to legitimize a ruthless, extrajudicial means of harassment, surveillance, and unrest that brought Chinese life to a standstill.

Still, Garvin and Mao shared similar ideas about the role of education in building community and politicizing people toward an antibourgeois, populist perspective. Like Mao's numerous social experiments during his reign of

FIGURE 4.5: Garvin (center) and a group of young women, China, 1978. Courtesy of Lincoln and Miranda Bergman.

power, Garvin decided that her classroom exercises would be modeled around taking risks. And while students inspired her "with their qualities of being 'red'—their enthusiasm, hard work and initiative, self-reliance, and collective work," from her they ascertained the importance of "master[ing] the English language as a tool in promoting understanding, communication, and advancement of the class struggle and socialism."[107] "I loved the students very dearly," she recollected decades later.[108] Such love and compassion were central to her pedagogy; Garvin positioned teaching and learning as radical political spaces, as crucial sites for the making of transnational politics and the advancement class struggle, feminism, internationalism, and socialism. And in contrast to black radical and Chinese communist propaganda that situated revolutionary politics within tropes of guerrilla warfare and traveling political exile, Garvin's framework positioned the teacher and the student as the subjects of radical internationalism and transgressive anti-imperialist resistance. Through use of both Chinese and U.S. media, she situated black American and Chinese struggle alongside one another, not simply as analogous but also as starting points of communication to broaden the two culture's understandings of one another.

After returning to the United States, she drew on these experiences as a member of the U.S.-China People's Friendship Association (USCPFA). Established in New York City in 1971, USCPFA fashioned itself as an organization helping to facilitate greater U.S. awareness and cultural connections with China. Garvin contributed by organizing speaking engagements, public dis-

FIGURE 4.6: Garvin (standing, tenth from the left) and a travel delegation of City College of New York students and alumni in Tiananmen Square, Beijing, August 1992. Courtesy of Lincoln and Miranda Bergman.

cussions, and creative events and by serving on the editorial committee of USCPFA's journal, *New China*. She also traveled on behalf of the organization, speaking about the struggles of Chinese peasants and the GPCR's successes in raising Chinese citizens' political consciousness.[109] Lastly, Garvin helped plan travel tours of China. Via these tours, many U.S. activists visited China; one of the first delegations included the Black Panther Party members Huey Newton, Elaine Brown, and Robert Leonard Bay; the Young Lords member Pablo "Yoruba" Guzman; the former Progressive Labor Party leader Bill Epton; the civil rights leader Hosea Williams; the *Fanshen* author William Hinton; and the Revolutionary Union leaders Bob Avakian and Leibel Bergman.[110]

Although only a handful of black American nationalists and Marxist-Leninists took part in such tours, growing numbers of them championed China for its support of African liberation and contributions to African infrastructure development. Yet over the course of the 1970s, it became increasingly difficult for black American activists to reconcile the Chinese government's rightward political shift. As China built railways and roads linking Tanzania and Zambia, dispatched tens of thousands of doctors and engineers to Burkina Faso and Cameroon, and armed and trained Angolan and Mozambican guerrillas, it opened itself to rapprochement with the United States and later military alliance with apartheid South Africa, signs of the decline of China's claims of proletarian world revolution.

Coda

*Rapprochement and the Decline of
China's World Revolution*

America's involvement in the war in Vietnam united the
entire socialist world and the nonaligned Third World against the
United States. . . . But that entire structure of political alignments
was upset by President Nixon's visit to the People's Republic of China
in February 1972. . . . The international posture of China was radically
changing, and no one . . . knew what to think. The press photographs
showing Mao Tse-Tung and Richard Nixon shaking hands testified
to a meeting that no revolutionary would have ever imagined.
— KATHLEEN CLEAVER

The whole Chinese Revolution may go down to defeat for a while. We
may lose everything. But never mind. If we are defeated here, you in Africa
will learn from our mistakes, and you will develop your own Mao Zedong,
and you will learn to do it better. And so in the end, we shall succeed.
—ZHOU ENLAI

On the morning of February 21, 1972, President Richard Nixon and the first
lady, Pat Nixon, walked down the airstairs of Air Force One, where a Chinese
delegation, led by Premier Zhou Enlai, awaited them. Decades earlier Nixon
denounced the PRC government, stating that if China seized Taiwan, "the next
frontier would be the coast of California." In subsequent years he also rejected
the idea of U.S.-China rapprochement, asserting that recognizing China would
be "detrimental to the cause of freedom and peace."[1] But by 1972, this rhetoric
appeared hollow as the first couple journeyed from Guam to Shanghai before
finally arriving at Beijing Capital International Airport. There, Nixon's anticommunist cloak was replaced by the First Lady's plush scarlet-colored over-
coat, an appendage that symbolically signaled the U.S. government's push for
détente with Red China. The news cameras did not miss a beat. On televisions

all over the world, people watched Nixon graciously shake Zhou's hand before being whisked away for a private meeting with Chairman Mao Zedong.

Five years earlier, while campaigning for the 1968 presidential election, Nixon had called for the improvement of U.S.-China relations in an October 1967 article in *Foreign Affairs*. In this article, he stressed the strategic importance of building partnerships with America's Asian neighbors. In revisionist fashion, he played down America's invasive activities within the Asia Pacific region, maintaining that the United States had "abandoned its colonial role" and was now a "protector" of Asian sovereignty. Nixon ruled that consequently, the world was witnessing the rise of a "new Asia" that was "becoming Western without ceasing to be Asian." But he added that such transformation was futile without China's inclusion. While the country and its government represented "Asia's most immediate threat," it was nonetheless vital to "pull China back into the family of nations[,] . . . back into the world community."[2] Nixon closed by likening China to America's most economically impoverished, disenfranchised urban communities. According to him, both were severely in need of regulation, pacification, and managed assimilation. With a hint of bigotry and paternalism, he employed a racial metaphor. He implied that the East was black: "Dealing with Red China is something like trying to cope with the more explosive ghetto elements in our own country. In each case a potentially destructive force has to be curbed; in each case an outlaw element has to be brought within the law; in each case dialogues have to be opened; in each case aggression has to be restrained while education proceeds; and, not least, in neither case can we afford to let those now self-exiled from society stay exiled forever."[3] Thereafter, with the exceptions of an interview with *Time* magazine and a few other instances, Nixon saved this commentary for closed circles.[4] But throughout 1970 his administration privately sought the reestablishment of relations with China and took strides in facilitating a communicative space more in line with this goal.[5] As Nixon relayed to his chief of staff, H. R. Haldeman, in 1971, one year prior to the visit that would shake global geopolitics, U.S. rapprochement with China could "change the world balance" and "shatter old alignments."[6]

The Nixon administration's interest in cementing talks with China grew out of the shifting geopolitical environment of the late 1960s, particularly the U.S. government's efforts to end its military campaign in Vietnam, decrease its military commitments in Asia, and stifle both Japan's economic growth and the Soviet Union's growing military and nuclear power. While the Tet Offensive in 1968 displayed the U.S. military's vulnerabilities and potential defeat in Vietnam, the intensification of both the Soviet's military arsenal and Japan's trade surplus with the United States conveyed to the Nixon administration the necessity of locating new allies and security partners in curbing Soviet and Japanese expansion in Asia Pacific. Although a U.S.-backed coup in Cambodia in April 1970 damaged the credibility of Nixon's claims of reducing the U.S. presence in Asia, by the early 1970s other actions signified both Chinese and U.S. interest in détente. As U.S. forces gradually withdrew troops from Vietnam and rhetorically committed to decreasing their military presence in Japan, South Korea, and certain parts of Southeast Asia, Mao openly commented that a visit to China by a leading U.S. emissary might improve the two countries' strained relations. Mao's statements seemed even more credible after the Chinese government invited the U.S. table-tennis team to visit China to play against their Chinese counterparts in April 1971.[7]

Although not privy to all of the details of Nixon's discussions and covert outreach to China, the U.S. State Department was also considering the prospect of U.S.-China reconciliation.[8] In the process, it took into consideration the knowledge and perspectives of foreign residents of China, most notably Robert F. Williams. In fact, it was this China-friendly political atmosphere that aided the Williams family's pursuit to return to the United States. After the Williamses conveyed willingness to address Robert Williams's criminal charges, the couple successfully arranged one-way passports good for a single journey with the U.S. Justice and State Departments.[9] And so it was that in the autumn of 1969 the Williams family returned to the United States, thus bringing to a close their eight-year hiatus in political exile (see figure C.1). Wearing a blue Chinese suit similar to that worn by Mao and the Chinese leader Sun Yatsen, Robert Williams walked the tarmac of Detroit Metropolitan Airport with fist raised high in the Black Power salute. Alongside him were local police and federal agents tasked with transporting him to a federal hearing to face his warrant for kidnapping. According to the FBI director J. Edgar Hoover, Williams remained a "highly influential black extremist" still requiring close surveillance.[10] After being released on bail and a personal recognizance bond, Williams discovered that the agency had seized his belongings and photocopied his diary; he later learned that they had given close attention to all entries recorded during the years of 1966 through 1969, the period of his residence in China.

Months later, after twice dodging federal subpoenas, Williams was required to testify about the family's abroad experiences before a Senate subcommittee. Although evading many of the committee's questions, he nonetheless spoke highly of the People's Republic of China (PRC), disputing the conventional wisdom that the Chinese aspired to conquer U.S. minds and hearts. The State Department viewed Williams's opinions as particularly valuable and subsequently blocked the subcommittee's attempt to release his testimony and diary excerpts to the news media. One reporter remarked, "They see Williams as a

FIGURE C.1: Robert Williams (right) and his attorney, Milton Henry, just minutes after Williams's return to the United States, Detroit, September 12, 1969. Courtesy of AP Photo.

bridge to China. The department's argument against publication of Williams' testimony is that it would upset his use as a conduit to send and receive messages from top Chinese officials."[11] In January 1970, Harry E. T. Thayer, the deputy director of the State Department's Office of Asian Communist Affairs, contacted Robert Williams to obtain his opinions about the normalization of U.S.-China relations. Williams suggested the department begin by reshaping popular American discourses about China. He explained that the U.S. government's statements of support for Taiwan and media references to "'the Chinese threat,' 'the Chinese enemy,' etc." hindered progressive U.S.-China exchange. "The PRC is 'practical' . . . and recognizes we have the Taiwan connection, but our frequent references to it are gratuitous and only irritating to the Chinese," Thayer reported learning from Williams. Williams also counseled that U.S. foreign policy stop "pushing its status as the great 'Pacific power,'" "cease announcing China-related steps publicly before . . . inform[ing] the Chinese privately," and stop "specify[ing] limits on what we [the United States] will permit" in East Asia. Such practices, Williams explained, "make the Chinese appear in the eyes of others . . . as 'beggars.'"[12] While it is unknown with what value the State Department regarded Williams's views, the department did deem it important to keep an open line of communication with him. In the months that followed, Allen S. Whiting, a former RAND Corporation analyst, a State Department employee, and a key China-affairs adviser to Henry Kissinger, then the national security advisor, helped broker the department's efforts to learn more from Williams. Employed also as a professor of political science at the University of Michigan, Whiting helped Williams secure a Ford Foundation Fellowship grant and research position at the university's Center for China Studies.[13]

Elements of the U.S. Left were alarmed by the government's outreach to Williams and consequently viewed his homecoming with some skepticism. Rumors were even circulated that the Williams family's reentry into U.S. life was the consequence of Robert Williams's acceptance of a government-approved deal. At the People's Peace Conference in Michigan, for instance, Williams was jeered for his criticisms of Cuban race relations and privately accused of being a CIA plant, stories that in all likelihood were initiated by the FBI or CIA.[14] Other people alleged that Williams had proffered information and his personal diaries for his family's safe passage back into the United States. A journalist summed up the cloud of suspicion that hung over Williams's head: "His resurfacing at the center as an expert on China and an advocate of the recognition of the Peking government is as mysterious as the special treatment the Nixon administration has accorded him since his return."[15] Robert Williams refuted these allegations as "vicious attacks on [his] character." He furthermore countered that he did not voluntarily surrender his diaries and only stood before the Senate subcommittee because he was mandated to do so.[16] Even after Robert Williams's death in 1996, Mabel Williams continued to frown upon such accusations. "He went to the embassy to file for a passport to return home," she remarked. "He didn't get a deal. He never made a deal."[17]

No information substantiates the claims that the Williams family's homecoming was the result of a deal with the government as a trade for information. Instead, what government documents and family archives confirm is that the Williamses leveraged Nixon's growing openness to U.S.-China détente and the family's experiences in China as means to temper both the State and Justice Departments' opposition to Robert Williams's return. Prior to receiving their one-way passports, the Williamses' attorney and friend, Conrad Lynn, reached out to the Nixon administration regarding Robert Williams's interest in returning to the United States. After hearing back from the administration, Lynn disclosed to the Williams family: "The spot the Nixon government is on now precludes any sustained prosecution of you. An entire group of lawyers have long concluded that the kidnapping indictment is dead. . . . You under-estimate the intelligence of the administration. They do not want any martyrs on their hands now. Their very best tactic would be to ignore you altogether."[18] Nixon personally confirmed this attitude in a letter to the State Department where he instructed the department to inform the Williamses that they would be neither intimidated nor harassed by the U.S. government in their process of returning home.[19] Thus, while the evidence does relay, to some extent, rhe-torical cooperation on the Nixon administration's part, it does not corroborate the charges that Robert Williams was offered or accepted a government deal. "If I secured a deal, I sure don't know anything about it," Williams maintained to his dying day.[20]

In any case, the State Department's outreach to Williams coincided with the Chinese government's embryonic openness to alignment with the United States. Throughout the late 1960s and early 1970s, the political divide between China and the Soviet Union worsened. The Soviets' invasion of Czechoslovakia in August 1968 and the Soviet leader Leonid Brezhnev's justification of this act one month later (where he declared Moscow's willingness to intervene in any uprising against socialism or effort to upend Soviet hegemony) conveyed the Soviets' intentions to not allow their communist power base to be diminished by liberalization efforts in satellites states or by the growing influence of other communist governments. Soviet tensions with China, however, became violent in March of 1969. On Zhenbao (Damansky) Island, located on the Ussuri River on the border separating the Soviet Union and China, a Chinese ambush of Soviet troops turned into full-scale conflict. Although the clashes only lasted six months and never expanded deep into Soviet or Chinese territory, they signified a great deal about the decline of Sino-Soviet relations. Throughout the conflict, the PRC rationalized their actions as in defense of Chinese sover-eignty and in rejection of Soviet occupation. China's leadership asserted that Soviet claims over what China perceived to be Chinese territory, as well as the USSR's actions in Czechoslovakia, confirmed that the Soviet Union was now an imperialist power more dangerous the United States. Fearing future Soviet and Japanese encirclement of China, elements of China's leadership, Mao most no-tably, concluded that détente with the United States would back both the USSR and Japan into a geopolitical corner and drastically alter Asia Pacific's political landscape in favor of China.

When it was announced in late July 1971 that Henry Kissinger had secretly traveled to Beijing to meet with Zhou and arrange an official visit by Nixon, var-ious black Americans were wary of the prospect of U.S.-China détente. What seemed to be the latent reversal of America's anti-China policy illuminated to some people the bankruptcy of the U.S. anticommunist crusade and American foreign policy. In black newspapers, Nixon was denounced as a "sellout" and "spoiled child who . . . lost the game," whereas China's leadership was heralded for helping to institute the "birth of a new era" in international relations, one demonstrating the fact that "it was hard to ignore six hundred million folks."[21] One reporter even scouted around Harlem in search of community members' opinions. Nixon was "a phony and a hypocrite," remarked a schoolteacher. The teacher also commented that as "the architect of the anticommunist climate in America," Nixon had contributed to the repressive political atmosphere that led to the seizure of William Worthy's passport a decade earlier. A city clerk, however, supplied the best excerpt. Revisiting the racial analogy that Nixon had used about China in his 1967 *Foreign Affairs* editorial, the clerk asked: "Why the hell doesn't he [Nixon] visit Watts, Harlem, and the South Side, instead of going all the way to China?"[22]

This outlook reverberated through black political circles. The civil rights activist Charles Evers, for instance, stressed that the Nixon administration's outreach to China was misdirected; the still ongoing Vietnam War deserved higher prioritization. "We've got young poor whites and blacks dying in Vietnam and he is going to the ballet in China," Evers opined.[23] Vernon Jordan, the executive director of the National Urban League, asserted: "Black people rightly want to know why this nation can perform such fancy footwork in its foreign relations but seems to be so unyielding in its domestic policies." Echoing the Harlem clerk's statements, Jordan lambasted Nixon for visiting the wrong place. "Just as visits to Peking and Shanghai will give policy makers an insight into the realities of life in China, so too would visits to Harlem, or visits to St. Louis' miles of abandoned downtown buildings," Jordan contended. "Like the Chinese government, black Americans have been ignored and unrecognized."[24] These arguments expressed a common theme. Establishing relations with China should not supersede addressing the errors of U.S. intervention abroad, the general welfare of working-class and working-poor Americans, and the structural crises and fiscal problems apparent in America's urban metropolises.

Other black Americans, conversely, perceived China's diplomatic gambit as signifying a cosmic shift in China's claims of world revolution. "[What will be its] impact on Afro-American-Chinese relations?" the congressman Charles Rangel queried.[25] The Black Panther Eldridge Cleaver answered Rangel's question by ruling that U.S.-China détente would have a negative effect on black struggle. "Any reconciliation between the United States and Communist China would do no good for black people," Cleaver surmised.[26] A *New York Amsterdam News* writer seconded Cleaver's viewpoint, criticizing China's leaders for giving Nixon wiggle room to repair America's international image. "It's too bad that the Republic of China [sic] would allow itself to be used in this way," the journalist wrote.[27] On the other hand, while the *Chicago Defender* editorialist Warner Saunders agreed that the "warming of relations between China and the USA may carry with it significant meaning for black and other poor minorities," he doubted the validity of China's claims of racial connection with people of African descent. "I am fully aware that yellow is not brown and brown is not black," he remarked. Saunders also acknowledged that whether or not the Chinese government was more progressive than the United States was still up for debate. "I don't know whether they [Chinese citizens] are forced to endure that system or whether they want it freely. Mao Zedong, their leader[,] says they really love it that way," he cynically commented before sarcastically concluding: "But of course, Nixon tells us, and everybody else, that we 'love our system.'"[28]

Condemnation though wasn't the primary feature of all black American viewpoints about détente. Some people presumed Nixon's travel to be a sign of U.S. acquiescence that anti-imperialist movements worldwide might exploit to their advantage. To an audience in a Manhattan ballroom, the former Progressive Labor Party leader Bill Epton insisted: "Nixon has made overtures to the Chinese from a position of weakness. It is Nixon who wants to come to China; China did not make overtures to Nixon." He continued, "There is no fear that the Chinese government will 'sell out,' and members of the Left in the U.S. should have no fear of this."[29] One journalist held a similar view, countering that China's engagement of the United States had to be understood as a classic example of realpolitik: "Other oppressed people aren't asking for their freedom; they are going out and struggling for it." The journalist asserted, "The Chinese people didn't bow out and plead for recognition. Nixon . . . yielded to POWER." China, he concluded, was actually providing black Americans with a useful example of international resistance against U.S. hegemony. "China took what was rightfully theirs," he maintained. "We must start thinking along similar lines."[30] The congresswoman Shirley Chisholm similarly tagged the détente as a "clever political move."[31] The civil rights activist Hosea Williams on the other hand described it as working not just in China's advantage but also potentially for blacks: "With the vast amount of influence China has throughout Africa, this strengthens the struggle of black Americans against racism among the Third World nations. I am certain that with China's influence among many Afro nations, there will be no gates opening to America unless the country is willing to lessen the pressure against blacks."[32]

But some of the most insightful commentary about the impact of U.S.-China détente on black revolutionary movements could be found in the newsletter of the North Carolina–based black-nationalist collective the Youth Organization for Black Unity. In a series of articles for the newsletter, the writer Chuck

Hopkins raised important questions: "For some the emergence of China as a strong world force has been looked upon favorably in the struggle to combat European capitalism and imperialism. What does this apparent thaw in relations mean? Has the U.S. succeeded in liberalizing the revolutionary policies of China? Can the struggling masses of Africans continue to look to China as a bastion of support?"[33] Hopkins's personal judgment was that China was not evading the cause of African struggle and was merely using the U.S. détente as means to strengthen its voice within world affairs. He ruled, "To the contrary, this represents but another step in China's long march to become the most powerful rear-base to the world's racist and anti-imperialist forces."[34] But Hopkins also maintained that his confidence in China would not prevent him from critically scrutinizing China's future activities, particularly its relations with African governments and liberation armies. He admitted that China's growing closeness to the U.S. government might end up superseding and subverting China's support for national liberation movements elsewhere. "There are basically two criteria which revolutionaries might employ to judge the success of Nixon and his clique," Hopkins forewarned. "These are the extent to which they are able to impose restrictions on China's support of the African struggle, and the degree to which they succeed in drawing China into the tentacles of the world capitalism economy."[35]

Hopkins's remarks hammered at the point made by the former Black Panther Party member Kathleen Cleaver in the epigraph—how were people to comprehend the redirection of China's foreign-policy ideology? Fundamentally, Nixon's visit to China and the reopening of U.S.-China relations did not generate an all-out reversal in black radicals' evaluations of the PRC. In fact, the late 1960s and early 1970s had witnessed the rapid ascent of Mao Zedong Thought among American communist parties and socialist-oriented black-nationalist organizations. Black and brown revolutionary nationalist organizations of the 1960s, such as the Revolutionary Action Movement, the Black Panther Party for Self-Defense, the Black Workers Congress, the Young Lords Party, and the Cleveland Workers Action Committee, and later Pan-African Marxist-Leninist groups of the 1970s, including the Youth Organization for Black Unity, Malcolm X Liberation University, the African Liberation Support Committee, and the Congress of African People, were drawn into China's ideological orbit.[36] Other black activists were introduced to Mao Zedong Thought after joining Marxist-Leninist organizations such as the Progressive Labor Party, the California Communist League (which later became the Communist Labor Party), Students for a Democratic Society and its offshoot the Revolutionary Union (originally the Bay Area Revolution Union, and which ultimately became the Revolutionary Communist Party), and the October League (which later split into the Communist Party Marxist-Leninist).[37] Among these circles, copies of *Quotations from Chairman Mao Zedong* and pro-China magazines such as *Peking Review*, *China Reconstructs*, *Black America*, and the *Liberator* became standard reading, trends that led the black Marxist luminary and October League member Harry Haywood to conclude: "China's great legacy is cause for great optimism for the future."[38]

But with Sino-U.S. rapprochement and the signing of the U.S.-China Shanghai Communiqué, China's geopolitical agenda, chiefly its activities in Africa, continued to stir up concern. From 1961 to 1971, China extended aid to sixteen African countries. Although the Great Proletarian Cultural Revolution (GPCR) cut short these relations from 1966 to 1969, thereafter these ties flourished. From 1971 to 1976, China became the largest communist provider of aid to Africa, giving US$1.8 billion, a large portion of which was loans, to twenty-eight states, an amount that exceeded the USSR's US$1 billion to twenty states. This five-year total dwarfed the US$700 million worth of aid that China provided to Africa over course of the 1950s and 1960s. China's investment was repaid in full with African support for China's admission as one of the five permanent members of the UN Security Council in 1971. African countries' votes were decisive, representing 34 percent of the ballots tallied in favor of seating the Chinese delegation over Taiwan and ending America's long-standing strategy of preventing the PRC from participating in the United Nations.[39]

Although Chinese aid to Africa never matched that supplied by the United States and the Soviet Union during the Cold War, China emphasized that as a developing country its agrarian model of social revolution had more in common economically and ideologically with African anticolonial movements. As the second epigraph conveys, in the eyes of Zhou and various Chinese-government insiders, the battles waged by African political movements against foreign occupation and economic exploitation were a mirror image of the crusade of the Chinese Communist Party (CCP). These arguments stretched the truth. But they helped to frame perceptions of China as an avid backer of African armed struggle and economic sovereignty. At military schools in Beijing and Nanjing as well as in locations furnished by the governments of Tanzania, Ghana, and Congo-Brazzaville, People's Liberation Army soldiers trained insurgent groups, liberation armies, and dissident-led rebellion forces from Algeria, Botswana, Burundi, Cameroon, the Democratic Republic of Congo (formerly Zaire), Ghana, Kenya, Malawi, Niger, Nigeria, and South Africa.[40] But it was primarily China's relations with Tanzania and its support of liberation struggles in several countries that drew African American attention and concern.

Decolonized of British rule in 1961, Tanzania was a success story of African independence. Alongside the deep interest in the Ujamaa socialism and co-operative economics articulated by the Tanzanian president, Julius Nyerere, the country's support for various African liberation struggles contributed to making Tanzania a Mecca-like destination for black American expatriates.[41] In any case, as one of the most Chinese oriented of all nations during the 1960s and 1970s, Tanzania gained a great deal from its relations with China. In return for China's unfettered access to Tanzanian ports along the Indian Ocean, Tanzania received a disproportionate percentage of Chinese loans. In 1964, of China's US$156 million spent on loans, Tanzanian infrastructure projects received almost a quarter of the total amount.[42] One year later, the two governments signed the Sino-Tanzanian Treaty of Friendship and launched an economic- and political-assistance program that lasted for more than a decade. Chinese loans were responsible for projects such as the establishment of a shipping line that exported Tanzanian cotton into China, a naval base in Dar es Salaam, and a jet airstrip in Ngerengere, all designed by Chinese engineers. Chinese instructors also trained the Tanzanian army, navy, and air force.

But it was China's agreement to finance and construct the Tanzania Zambia Railway Authority, a 1,160-mile railroad project that connected Zambia's copper belt to Tanzania's ports, that came to be China's flagship project in the continent. After Great Britain, the United States, the USSR, the World Bank, and the United Nations refused to fund the railway, China stepped in with an interest-free loan of somewhere between US$400 and $450 million, requiring repayment over the span of thirty years after an initial five-year grace period. The railway, it was argued, would untangle Zambia from its dependency on earlier established transportation systems to the south, routes dominated primarily by Rhodesia and South Africa, and open up the region to new investment and trade. Running from Dar es Salaam to Kapiri Mposhi, and constructed by what is estimated at more than thirty thousand Chinese workers, the Tanzania Zambia Railway Authority was completed in 1975, two years ahead of schedule.[43]

Various black American nationalists and leftists expressed admiration for the railway, describing it as a development project that would alter the geopolitical landscape of southern Africa. It was "the greatest ever . . . Communist overseas aid project," according to a journalist for the *African World*, a venture that was producing a "[great] leap forward in African development."[44] Another writer proclaimed, "Tanzania's friendship and solidarity with China has scared the imperialist powers led by the USA into seeking rapprochement with China. They are scared by China's aid to Tanzania."[45] Other activists though were concerned over the drawbacks of Chinese aid, particularly how these trade agreements worked to an uneven extent in China's favor. For example, China's ability to dump surplus goods in African nations had a tumultuous impact on local

African products and businesses. "The inflow of Chinese goods will endanger industries already established in recipient countries," one member of the Youth Organization for Black Unity explained. "African recipient countries are often in the difficult position of virtually having to take whatever is available. Thus shops in Dar es Salaam are full of unsold 'make-weight' Chinese goods. . . . The influx of simple industrial goods tends to inhibit the recipient country from establishing that sort of industry within its borders."[46] Several Tanzania-based black American expatriates even alleged that Chinese management and workers were ironfisted in their conduct toward Tanzanians on work sites, subjecting Tanzanians workers to unsafe conditions and harsh treatment, as well as periodically refusing to hire Tanzanian laborers.[47]

These misgivings about the inequality of Sino-African relations were heightened by China's foreign policy shift to the right. Many China supporters couldn't believe that the Chinese government denounced an unsuccessful Marxist youth rebellion against Ceylon's (Sri Lanka) government in April 1971; the latter government's repressive response to the rebellion led to the deaths of thousands of Ceylonese people, the majority of whom were poor dissidents fighting in opposition to government neglect. Two years later, China was silent about a CIA-backed coup in Chile that resulted in the ousting and subsequent suicide of the country's president, and the propping up of the reactionary, U.S.-supported regime of Augusto Pinochet. The Chinese government repeated this silence years later when it failed to support national liberation movements in Puerto Rico, Oman, Palestine, Bangladesh, and Portugal.

Still, what tempered some foreign radicals' all-out abandonment of faith in the Chinese government was China's military support for anticolonial liberation struggles in Portugal's African empire (Mozambique, Guinea-Bissau, and Angola) and political movements against white-minority rule in Namibia, South Africa, and Zimbabwe (Rhodesia). Although numerous activists disapproved of China's close relations with the Zairian president Joseph Mobutu Sese Seko (the military leader who led a CIA- and Belgium-sponsored coup against Patrice Lumumba's government), China's endorsement of African independence, economic sovereignty, and black-majority rule held sway. China funneled money through the Organization of African Unity in support of African liberation movements and supplied military support and aid to guerrilla liberation armies, most notably in Zimbabwe, South Africa, Mozambique, and Angola. But more and more, China's aid to these struggles was no longer premised around anti-imperialism and Third World internationalism. By the 1970s, which liberation movement or political party China supported was primarily determined by which group was least pro-Soviet in orientation and whose victory would best hinder Soviet influence and geopolitical objectives in

Africa. This came to represent a vital feature of Chinese, and, to a lesser extent, Soviet, strategies regarding Africa: aid only those liberation movements that would check and potentially diminish the rival's power.

Regarding China's standing among radical activists worldwide, the straw that broke the camel's back was China's involvement in the Angolan political conflict. In April 1969, Nixon and Kissinger directed the National Security Council Interdepartmental Group for Africa (a collective composed of representatives from the State Department, the Department of Defense, and the CIA) to produce a comprehensive review of U.S. policy toward southern Africa, specifically concerning U.S. interests in Rhodesia, South Africa, Namibia, the Portuguese territories, and adjacent African states. The completed seventy-page study, *National Security Study Memorandum 39* (known as NSSM 39), stressed the necessity of protecting and maintaining U.S. economic and military hegemony in the region. Of chief concern was U.S. access to South African gold, coal and raw materials, Angolan oil, Rhodesian chrome and minerals, and bases and ports along the Cape of Good Hope and Indian Ocean, as well as the ability of the U.S. government and American corporations to outsource the production and sale of Western technology, textiles, military hardware, and private arms within the region. The report asserted that Soviet and Chinese influence in the region, as well as violent revolutions and immediate black-majority rule, could ruin U.S. access to these territories and resources. But the report advised that despite these challenges, the U.S. government should avoid military intervention and work to prevent open warfare in the region. Nixon's administration was also encouraged to refrain from voicing public criticism of South Africa's and Rhodesia's racial injustices, the belief being that such statements could adversely impact America's alliances with these regimes. The report maintained that the United States should rather (1) push for the continuation of white-minority rule in southern Africa with gradual integration of the black majority; and (2) extend aid to Portugal in its colonial wars while also developing relations with those liberation movements that, if placed in power, would maintain the current economic and anticommunist status quo.[48]

The implementation of these policies, first by Nixon's government and later by that of his successor, Gerald Ford, struck a sour chord when Portugal's fascist government was overthrown by a military coup d'état in April 1974. The defeat of Prime Minister Marcello Caetano's regime spelled disaster for Portugal's colonial empire, effectively opening the doors for the immediate independence of Guinea-Bissau (which in fact had already declared its independence six months earlier), Cape Verde, Mozambique, and Angola. In Angola, however, the removal of Portuguese forces and the establishment of Angolan independence were followed by a civil war between the country's three leading guerrilla liberation groups and political parties: Movemento Popular de Libertação de Angola (MPLA; Popular Movement for the Liberation of Angola), led by Antonio Agostinho Neto; Frente Nacional de Libertação de Angola (FNLA; National Front for the Liberation of Angola), led by Holden Roberto; and an FNLA splinter group, União Nacional para a Independência Total de Angola (UNITA; National Union for the Total Independence of Angola), established by Jonas Savimbi. Each of these three parties declared itself as Angola's sole governing force. Yet in time UNITA and FNLA united against the MPLA.

Ford and Kissinger (then the secretary of state) worried over losing access to the military base in the Azores Islands, and control of Angolan oil, iron, uranium, phosphates, and diamond mining to the MPLA, a Soviet ally. Ford's administration also feared that if the MPLA obtained power, its communist influence might bleed into neighboring countries and have a devastating impact on American and Western influence in southern Africa. Ford and Kissinger consequently mobilized a multinational force to defeat the MPLA. Aided by Mobutu Sese Seko's Zairian army, the South African military, a band of well-paid Portuguese Angolan and French mercenaries, the CIA, and over $75 million of U.S. aid, FNLA and UNITA were charged with routing the MPLA. These actions did not surprise many black radicals, the majority of them rationalizing the United States and South Africa's responses as attempts to secure and maintain their imperialist, exploitative interests in southern Africa. But the greatest surprise was that China was providing support, weapons, and military instructor training to FNLA troops in Zaire. How could a government that had premised itself as the global leader of anti-imperialist, proletarian internationalism align with apartheid South Africa and imperialist America?

During the 1960s China had provided support to all three groups—the MPLA, UNITA, and FNLA. Yet by the 1970s the PRC rejected the MPLA for its pro-Soviet and urban-based orientation.[49] China's opposition to the MPLA, the party viewed unanimously as the leading revolutionary anti-imperialist force in Angola, nonetheless flew in the face of ubiquitous Chinese portrayals of Angolan anticolonialism as the African counterpart to the Chinese Communist Revolution.[50] The differences distinguishing the MPLA from UNITA and FNLA, at least ideologically, should have led the PRC to lean in the MPLA's direction. The MPLA's membership was interracial (composed of blacks, mixed-race people, and people of European ancestry), a factor of the party's ability to transcend tribal and ethnic differences. The MPLA also advocated an explicitly revolutionary Marxist position, organizing workers, peasants, women, and youths into mass organizations, a trait that gained the party support from Cuba and the Soviet Union. Furthermore, the MPLA's ideology informed its nonmilitary activities. Identifying the necessity of establishing local institutions that could fulfill the everyday needs of the masses, the MPLA established schools, cooperatives, hospitals, and other social services. UNITA and the FNLA, in contrast, were anticommunist, Western sustained, and supportive of upholding traditional ethnic divides and class divisions. While the FNLA's headquarters in Zaire left members disconnected from daily Angolan life, the collaboration between the Portuguese colonial military and UNITA revealed its reactionary position regarding Angolan self-determination.[51] What's more, China's alliance with the United States and South Africa in defeating the MPLA contradicted the PRC's decades-long denials of relations with South Africa. Throughout the 1960s, China's leaders maintained that they had ended all economic and trade ties to Pretoria, a response to the latter government's oppressive treatment of black South Africans and Namibians. But in actuality China was increasing its trade with the country over the period.[52]

China's anti-MPLA alliance, then, with the United States and apartheid South Africa confirmed the Chinese government's decisive ideological and geopolitical shift. It was now positioned on the side of Western imperialism, which demonstrated the collapse of Mao's claims of global revolutionary struggle and the irrevocable materialization of the union first stimulated by Nixon and Zhou's handshake.

China's actions garnered serious backlash among African American radicals. One of the most intriguing works to document these criticisms was The Facts on Angola (1976), a fifty-seven-page booklet edited by the black Marxist Gerald Horne in conjunction with MPLA representatives. The document was published by the National Anti-imperialist Movement in Solidarity with African Liberation, a Communist Party of the United States of America auxiliary organization established in 1973 by a broad coalition of activists representing different ideological stripes. The Facts on Angola was moreover composed of articles and materials from a variety of national and political sources (including Somalia, Angola, Tanzania, Zambia, Algeria, France, the Soviet Union, Great Britain, Guinea, and the United States). Inside the booklet, several articles called out the duplicity of China's leaders and the rose-colored tinge of black radicals who continued to champion Chinese communism. An article Horne authored for the Daily World denounced China's "shameful betrayal" and criticized Maoist-leaning black activists for their undying support of China and uncritical, "blind anti-Sovietism." U.S. fascination with Maoism, he insisted, was not revolutionary; it was instead bourgeois, exclusivist, unconcerned about national interests, and dogmatic, characteristics that displayed "the bankruptcy of Maoism." China was "no more than the 'Trojan horse' of imperialism," Horne remarked.[53] In speeches and other publications, the national executive secretary of the National Anti-imperialist Movement in Solidarity with African

Liberation, Anthony Monteiro, articulated a similar viewpoint, remarking that the Angolan crisis exposed that "the U.S. and China share a common position." He added that these revelations weakened the ideological currency of Mao Zedong Thought as a tool for radical praxis and struggle in the United States. "Peking finds itself in an embarrassing position," Monteiro concluded.[54]

In his autobiography, Kissinger commented that during his and Nixon's discussions with Mao and Zhou in 1972, Mao poked fun at the dogma surrounding his writings, as well as at foreigners' celebration of his ideas. Kissinger noted, "Mao laughed uproariously at the implication that anyone might have taken seriously a slogan that had been scrawled for decades on public surfaces all over China."[55] Considering Mao's claims of Third World alliance and world revolution against capitalism and imperialism, what were China's Western supporters to make of this? Was Mao's statement to Nixon and Kissinger a deceptive tactic to charm his guests or did his smile signify the end of China's rhetoric of proletarian internationalism and his joy regarding this founding of an international anti-Soviet Union front? Nearly a decade before Mao's meeting with Nixon and Kissinger, Mao alluded to the potential demise of China's influence as promoter of world revolution, ironically on the same night that he first publically articulated his support for the African American struggle. As mentioned earlier, on the eve of Mao's transmission of his August 1963 "Statement Supporting the Afro-American in Their Just Struggle against Racial Discrimination by U.S. Imperialism," he met with a delegation of African guerrillas and revolutionary nationalists to formally read the speech, as well as articulate China's support for African liberation. According to Sidney Rittenberg, a former CCP insider who attended this meeting, one of the visitors informed Mao that Soviet desertion of the visitor's particular African struggle left him questioning China's motives in aiding African movements. "Will the red star over Tiananmen Square in China go out?" the person asked Mao. Considering the shifts in foreign policy that China would implement in the 1970s, Mao's response was telling. "Can I guarantee to you that China won't betray the revolution? Right now I can't give you that guarantee. . . . No, I don't think we have solved this question," Mao replied. "We understand the seriousness of this problem, but we don't know how to handle it yet."[56]

Ultimately, the shifts in Chinese foreign policy during the 1970s were an ominous sign. As China sacrificed revolutionary ideology for pragmatism, its rhetoric of worldwide, protracted struggle seemed unconvincing. In a short time, several of China's allies, Albania most notably, distanced themselves from the PRC's rightward shift.[57] For those China supporters who still believed in the PRC's radical rhetoric though, it was the government's ties to the regimes of Muammar al-Gaddafi in Libya and the Shah of Iran, Mohammad Reza Pahlavi, and later China's 1979 invasion of Vietnam and support for the despotic Pol Pot–led Khmer Rouge government during the Cambodian-Vietnamese War, that illuminated the fickleness of China's claims of anti-imperialism.

These changes were definitively solidified after the deaths of both Mao and Zhou in 1976 and the rise of new Chinese leadership headed first by Hua Guofeng and subsequently by Deng Xiaoping. Deng severed ties with Mao's notion of permanent class struggle, Third World revolution, and a centrally planned economy. Deng instead focused on shifting China toward *Zhongguotese shehuizhuyi* (socialism with Chinese characteristics), namely a socialist-market economy organized around a combination of state-owned enterprises and special economic zones open for foreign investment and free trade. This policy and that of *si ge xiandaihua* (the four modernizations, which called for advancing science and technology, the mechanization of agriculture, urban industry, and the military) ultimately came to define both Deng's administration and China's adoption of capitalism over subsequent decades.

The demise of China's explicit anticapitalist stance marked the beginning of the end of the country's symbolic claims of antiracist solidarity. Following the signing of the U.S.-China communiqué, which outlined the normalization of relations between the two governments, America's chief allies (Great Britain, Japan, and West Germany) followed suit in strengthening ties with the PRC and loosening their connections with Taiwan. Furthermore, during the 1980s Deng's government and the CCP distanced themselves from the calamity of the GPCR, placing a majority of the blame on the deceased Mao. While championing Mao's contributions, they simultaneously drew distinctions between the communist China of the past and the one that was entering the global arena after Mao's death and the collapse of his leftist following.

Although a small number of black radicals ventured on travel expeditions to China in later years, it was predominantly a different group of black Americans who were attracted to China and to whom the PRC reached out over the course of the 1980s and subsequent decades. These relations were sparked by a different impetus than that of solidifying Third World internationalist solidarity. This time it was China's shifting economic policy that became the dominant prism through which China's relations with black foreigners was framed, imagined, and invested with meaning. By 1980 even *Black Enterprise* was reporting that the Chinese government was "actively courting black businessmen . . . to become part of the more than $1.2 billion export businesses that U.S. firms now do with China yearly."[58]

Nonetheless, the relations forged between China and U.S. black radicals were not easily erased. In 1975 the writer John Oliver Killens traveled to China with a delegation of educators. Upon entering the country, Killens immedi-

中、非人民情谊深

FIGURE C.2: "Zhong, Fei renmin qingyi shen" (The feelings of friendship between the peoples of China and Africa are deep), 1972. Courtesy of Stefan R. Landsberger Collection, International Institute of Social History (Amsterdam).

ately felt a rush of excitement and anxiety: "Was I building myself for one more great disappointment? Was it true? Had they [the Chinese] really *put it together*? Could Afro-Americans gather hope and inspiration from this experiment? . . . If they [the Chinese] had overcome, why not every man?" Thereafter, various encounters demonstrated some of the unique features of Chinese life. Besides finding value in Chinese citizens'"healthy respect for honest labor and the peasantry," Killens was also intrigued to learn that the Chinese education and higher learning were using African American literature to educate Chinese students in English language and U.S. culture. China's investment in cross-cultural exchange with black populations was further emphasized to Killens by African students who conveyed their appreciation for the opportunities to study in China, by African politicians who spoke highly of Chinese investment in African development projects, and by the number of billboards Killens noticed displaying images of Afro-Chinese solidarity. One billboard stood out—it portrayed an African woman with her baby and two doctors, one Chinese and the other African (see figure C.2). While the mother and child represented, respectively, the continent and the need for patriotic defense of the continent's future, the juxtaposition of the black and Chinese doctors suggested that to nurture and sustain the continent's health required international partnerships. By training Africans in medical care and extending health-care assistance to

African peoples, Chinese aid, the billboard relayed, was helping to safeguard the lifeblood of Africa. But the image's subtle paternalism was clear. While the Chinese government was comfortable portraying itself as an ally, supporter, and defender of African sovereignty, it rarely, if ever, inversely depicted African nations in similar terms—that is, as defenders of China and as populations with something important to teach to China.

These contradictions did not evade Killens. He commented in an essay about the prohibitive features of his travels, such as his hosts' unwillingness to allow his travel delegation to visit Chinese prisons and what he described as the "obvious contradiction" of "industry-caused air pollution" produced by Chinese coal mines. Even so, he admitted that much of what motivated his travel to China was his interest in considering how China's Great Proletarian Cultural Revolution measured up to the Black Freedom Movement. African Americans' struggle for justice, better living conditions, and autonomy over their lives and communities, Killens confessed, seemed "to be dying on the vine." However, Killens's experiences in China reignited his belief that the fight for black liberation was not on its deathbed. Most pertinently, Mao and the CCP's message of protracted struggle struck a chord. Killens remarked, "If I understood the Chinese people's answers to my questions, their position is that a revolution never ceases." Moreover, hearing narratives of the Chinese people's long march against feudalism, foreign occupation, and imperialism, Killens was reminded of James Weldon Johnson's "Lift Every Voice and Sing" ("we have come over a way that with tears has been watered") and Martin Luther King Jr.'s comments about the long struggle for black freedom ("we have come a long, long way . . . but we have a long way to go" and "we have reached the mountain top, but we have not yet reached the promised land"). Ultimately, acknowledging Chinese people's resolve over the long course of history offered Killens a productive intellectual space to reconcile his disappointment with the failures and shortcomings of the U.S. Black Freedom Struggle. It was the realization of "how far the [Chinese] people had come in such a short space of time" that again made Killens "believe in the old slave-song fragment that became the theme song of the [Civil Rights] Movement . . . : WE SHALL OVERCOME."[59]

As with several of the people whose stories fill these pages, travel encounters in China transported Killens back to the scene of his subjection, to the struggles that awaited his participation and cultural labor. While his tour of China is another reminder of the seductiveness of the Chinese state's organized spectacles and performances of the nation, Killens's commentary also demonstrates the mysterious power that China's history of transgression and the Chinese people's firm determination held over some foreign visitors. Moreover in writing, Killens sketched an image of China that likened it to black

America. Similar to the representations supplied by other black radical travelers though, Killen's depiction was not simply an attempt to render China a more accurate portrayal and assessment. It was a call to arms. In his essay, China became a symbol of the long journey and contradictions that black radicalism needed to prepare for.

The eminent historian John Hope Franklin also offered striking reflections after he traveled to China to give a series of lectures in 1979. A discussion with audience members revealed what Franklin described as an "intense interest in the American government's racial policy and radical or deviant facets of the black movement." He was moreover amazed at various Chinese audience members' familiarity with Cold War African American radical history. Despite finding fault with their lack of knowledge about the less militant wings of black politics, Franklin "was struck by the fact that . . . they knew even the obscure utterances of black radicals," including Angela Davis, the Black Panther Party, and W. E. B. Du Bois.[60] Why were black radicals the main protagonists of these Chinese people's understandings of American political struggle? What led to their specific imaginaries of the U.S. black movement? In a similar vein as black radical travelers' problematic, yet significant, outlooks on the Chinese Communist Revolution, Chinese citizens formulated perspectives on U.S. social struggle. These Chinese people's imaginaries of black resistance, as Franklin pointed out, lacked awareness of the complexity and diversity of U.S. black political activity. But these people, nonetheless, clearly found value and pride in certain aspects of U.S. black political struggle; enough so to make a significant impression on Franklin. While this book has mainly been concerned with black radical imaginings of China, an interesting question is how did the corresponding side of these relations—Chinese citizens—alternatively imagine and represent the Black Freedom Struggle? Franklin's audience offers one possible entry point.

Postscript

WEAVING THROUGH SAN HUAN LU

> China's observers tend overwhelmingly to attribute the successes and
> failures of the Chinese revolution to individual leading figures. . . . [This
> has] resulted in the neglect and even denial of the new social subjectivities
> created through this process. . . . A reactivation of China's legacy provides
> an opening for the development of a future politics. This opening is not a
> simple doorway back to the twentieth century, but a starting point.
> —WANG HUI, *The End of Revolution*

> After all is said and done build a new route to China
> if they'll have you. Who will survive in America?
> —GIL SCOTT-HERON

Writing a book about political traffic between black Americans and China conjured up my memories living in Beijing as an exchange student. There, I received housing, meals, and genuine love and recognition from a middle-class Chinese family—my host parents, who were engineers, and my host brother, a college student. In conversations with them I was often asked about U.S. life, particularly about my family and African American culture and history. Much of what my host family and neighborhood friends knew revolved around professional basketball (Qiaodan!) and popular culture (Maike'er Jiekexun!). And in turn, I learned a great deal about them.

A conversation that stands out was one night my host mother and father briefly detailed their family's and friends' personal travails during the Great Proletarian Cultural Revolution. During the early 1970s, they and hundreds of thousands of other students and youths left their homes, families, and educations to live in rural areas and experience *sixiang gaizao* (ideological remolding): to learn what it would mean to surrender property, dwell in economically underserved areas, and work as common laborers alongside the poor. The idea was that in these educational and professional spaces, young people could give up their social and material privilege and learn from those people below them

FIGURE PS.1: The author, host family, and friends, September 1997.

in the class hierarchy. While my host parents absorbed important lessons during these experiences, they commented that some of their peers endured mistreatment, substandard living conditions, and repression from rural bureaucrats and oppressive peasant leaders.

As I grew closer to my host family, neighbors, and schoolmates, I indulged in media and cultural practices that perpetuated racist images of Chinese people. Weaving my bicycle through the multitude of cyclists and ramblers that filled the intersection of San Huan Lu (Third Ring Road), I bobbed my head to the sonic currents transmitted through my Discman headphones, singing and gaining pleasure from the rapper Redman "the Funk Dr. Spock's" claims that drug usage made him "so chinky-eyed," he "saw people waving on the map." Rarely, if ever, did I think to myself how such lyrics, and moreover the embodied sensations that I drew from them, to some extent flew in the face of the relations that I was developing in my daily life. Simultaneously, in the homes of some of the people whom I shared my time with were tubes of Darlie toothpaste, which until 1985 was known more widely as "Darkie" toothpaste, its logo displaying a buffoonish black character in top hat and bow tie, which can be likened to a turn-of-the-twentieth-century minstrel performer. To this day it still carries the name of *hei ren yagao*, which translates to "black man's toothpaste," and its logo now features an image that calls to mind the Jewish comedian and blackface performer Al "the jazz singer" Jolson.

While these representations signified the different ways modalities of race are constitutive of and enacted in globalization, less explicitly, my location and exchange in China were a sign of race's currency across national and cultural borders. My observations and participation in Beijing life were a micronarrative of China's shifting visions and project of political modernity, late moments in the country's transformation from Maoist social revolution driven by the will of the nation's most backward and downtrodden to a market economy organized around the promotion of advanced culture, productive forces, population (i.e., *san ge daibiao*, "the three represents"), and harmonious society (*hexie shehui*). My time there represented another stage in China's integration into global capitalism—China both in dispute and colluding with U.S. power. As I and other U.S. students navigated *hutong* alleys, practicing Mandarin on street vendors and other young people, skyscrapers were being erected throughout the city, edifices and intended paragons of the city's evolving cosmopolitan sensibility. Moreover, on Wangfujing Street McDonald's and Kentucky Fried Chicken were filled. There, droves of middle-class and elite Chinese youths (at that time such Western fast-food meals for a family could cost up to one-sixth of a worker's monthly salary) sat for hours eating Big Macs and seaweed-seasoned fries and discussing the music of Yanni (Greece), the Backstreet Boys (United States), and Na Ying (China). In time, hip-hop culture (*xiha*) would also travel to Chinese cities, offering a productive creative outlet for political critique, play, and cultural rebellion by young people disenchanted with China's economic growth and the rapidly increasing divide between China's rural majority and its rising middle class. Concurrently, while growing use of the Internet and social media would provide some Chinese publics with sites to reemphasize neonationalist conceptions of China, it would supply other netizens with alternative spaces to celebrate Chineseness and call attention to the national and international processes structuring and transforming everyday life. Ultimately, such cacophonous engagement and transmutation of local and nonlocal products and practices conveyed a far more vibrant Chinese cultural landscape than that depicted by both Western and Chinese media as China's transition "from *tu* to *yang*"—that is, from rustic and backward to modern, foreign, and Western.[1]

We Americans were an important component of this complex, evolving matrix of cultural traffic. Our presence within Chinese secondary schools and higher education and the movement of our bodies on streets and in courtyards epitomized a great deal; as cultural ambassadors of U.S. public diplomacy, we contributed to the image of improved U.S.-China relations, China's growing regard and influence among international circles, and U.S. business, government, and education's increasing investments in China. To many working-class and poor Chinese, though, we were reminders of Western privilege, U.S.

encroachment, and continued foreign extraterritoriality in East Asia. As a black exchange student I was also a symbol of China's own multicultural project, a daily avowal and public display of China's own engagement with the global politics of difference. Alongside, although unequally, the numbers of African university students and immigrant laborers I met in restaurants and areas of leisure, my residence and study represented a distinct kind of racial project facilitated by the Chinese state and negotiated—more often than not amicably, but at some moments in a volatile manner—by me, other black people in China, and Chinese citizens.

I left China concerned with how regimes of representation and power travel and take shape in different environments, particularly with how ideologies of race are articulated in media, the movement of bodies, and cultural production, and to whose ends. I wondered how the image on the plastic coating of those toothpaste tubes and in Redman's metaphor tied into a longer history of geopolitics, global flow, and cultural representation, and if there were circuits of African American and Chinese encounters that refuted such depictions. In time I learned about such histories, that one central period for their formation was during the Cold War when a handful of African American radicals looked upon China with great regard and when China's leadership reached out to black liberation movements worldwide. Each group attempted to reframe both itself and its relation to the other with media, blackness being worked to racialize Chinese communism and to put socialist-leaning Asian liberation movements in conversation with activists of African descent—examples of the new subjectivities to which the intellectual Wang Hui alludes in the first epigraph. But as Wang also suggests, engaging this history compels me (and hopefully you as well) to consider the relationship between the Cold War state of global affairs that predated my birth and the neoliberal systems of social injustice, destruction, violence, and death that currently encompass life in the United States, China, and other places, albeit in different and uneven ways. Two brief examples, although unrelated, convey some aspects of this.

In the fall of 2011, numbers of Chinese netizens voiced support for Chen Guangcheng, a blind Shandong attorney and peasant activist known for challenging Chinese authorities' abuse of rural populations through the government's one-child policy and other state-sanctioned acts. Chen's dissent had been met with severe government suppression and house arrest. Sidestepping government control and censorship of media, his supporters took to the Internet, posting pictures of themselves dressed in a similar manner as Chen (wearing dark sunglasses comparable to those worn daily by the activist and political prisoner) and creating stickers calling for Chen's immediate release.

Eventually, after a dramatic escape from house arrest, Chen and his family fled to the U.S. embassy, where they negotiated political refuge.

On the other side of the globe, the February 2012 murder of Florida teen Trayvon Martin by the self-appointed neighborhood-watch coordinator of the community where Martin's father's fiancée resided was a reminder of the lack of value that U.S. society places on black life. Dressed in a hooded sweatshirt and returning home from purchasing snacks from a convenience store, the unarmed African American high school student was profiled as a potential assailant or burglar. Angered over the tragedy of Martin's slaying, and, moreover, the larger culture of extrajudicial vigilantism, police harassment and killing, media representations, and structural oppression that sanction the incarceration, repression, and murder of black life, thousands of people sprung into action. They created online petitions, posted photos of themselves wearing hooded sweatshirts, and organized "million hoody marches."[2] Martin's family, however, did not obtain justice from the U.S. court system. A mostly white jury found Martin's murderer not guilty. Moreover, as this killer walked free and as Florida kept intact the "Stand Your Ground" law which prevented this murderer and other nonblack killers of unarmed black people from answering for their crimes, police officers, and the mayor and police chief of a major U.S. metropolis one thousand miles north, were defending their "stop and frisk" activities against black and Latino residents—a citywide "preventative" crime measure whose central instrument of enforcement is racially profiling, harassing, and detaining black and brown New Yorkers.

It is important to highlight that the violence exhibited on Martin and Chen are not exceptions to the rule but examples of the indiscriminate and exploitative impact of neoliberalism and genocidal suppression in both the United States and China. The Chinese government's efforts to squash Chen mirror its heavy-handed subdual of movements led by oppressed migrant workers and ethnic and racial minorities, primarily Tibetans and Uyghur Muslims. Casting its crackdown on the latter groups as part of the "fight against terrorism," the government has used the escalating global war on terror as a pretext for curbing ethnic minorities' freedom of speech, travel, religion, language use and instruction, and expression of cultural identity. Moreover, in an economy where manufacturing and cheap labor reign, migrant workers in China have become permanent second-class citizens, an urban working class vulnerable to the abusive, profit-at-all-costs agenda of domestic and foreign conglomerates that through graft and corruption operate, for the most part, with impunity. Lacking government protection and support, migrant workers endure lives where they have little, if any, formal access to quality education, housing, and health care. And they have been hit the hardest by the country's rising unemployment, urban-rural divides, and skyrocketing cost of living. Fear of a broad-based oppositional movement composed of these populations has thus led the Chinese state to go to all lengths to stem the tide of public demonstrations, riots, and media and online criticism—anything that calls into question the government's collusion with multinational capitalism.

Martin's slaying and the U.S. criminal justice system's failure to effectively prosecute his murderer, on the other hand, illuminate what the legal scholar Michelle Alexander refers to as America's "New Jim Crow," a contemporary system of racial and social control that disproportionately targets poor and working-class African Americans and Latinos. Alexander argues that the prison-industrial complex and the war on drugs, along with job discrimination; disqualification from health, housing, and educational benefits; and an inequitable court system, have functioned as mechanisms of control and discipline against the upsurge in 1960s black protest and the threat of interracial, interethnic dissidence. Following Alexander's line of argument and analysis, the racial profiling and extrajudicial killings of Martin and thousands of other people of color, as well as the escalating number of black and brown people in U.S. prisons and whose communities lack access to basic services and quality of life, are part of American neoliberalism's coercive suppression and punishment of the lower strata of U.S. society.[3]

Thus, while it can't be denied that Martin's and Chen's movements of support showcase the power of creatively refunctioning media and cultural symbols as means to build solidarity and coalition against systematic oppression, the most striking parallel between contemporary China and the United States is the general militarization and corporatization of both states against a budding, subjugated class of disenfranchised and destitute subjects. The imperative that the poet Gil Scott-Heron astutely summarized forty years ago as the question of "who will survive in America" consequently never seemed as timely and widespread as now. The "America" that Scott-Heron criticized encompasses the world, still neatly veiled within modernity's rhetoric of progress, democratization, and the near-successful completion of the globalization process. In reality, the malady of undeterred free trade, militarization, and government excess pursues all facets of social life to the detriment of human development and sustainability. What's more, Scott-Heron's skepticism at the prospect of the Chinese government as an alternative "route" to a progressive world formation now rings unequivocally true. In the United States, China, and elsewhere, the landscape displays capitalism, draconian state and corporate measures, increasing militarism, vast class disparities and warfare, fundamentalist neo-national movements, and neoliberalism's resilience and relentless expansion.

One of the central premises of this book is that systems of domination are not only rooted in the colonization of mind and body, human and natural resources, and forms of being and knowing. The expansion and mass accumulation of capital and the dehumanization of social life and existence have also been legitimated and extended through distortion of communication and information and through regulation and control of people's mobility. In sum, controlling and manipulating data, ideas, representations, and intelligence, and moreover people's ability to freely move, travel, and experience cultural contact and coalition with communities different from their own, are essential components of empire in the United States, China, and elsewhere.

There are distinctive differences between the public spheres in China and the United States, most particularly regarding the different forms of coercion, censorship, and state machinery and control that regulate dissent in each, as well as the different politics and means of protest that have been engendered in these countries. Nonetheless, political imagining is vital in both contexts. Every day people devote mental and creative labor toward the joyful, frustrating, and necessary art of struggle and possibility. These practices provide us with contexts for critical engagement of our consciousness and for envisioning and constructing different formations of human relations and daily life. Shifts in our perspective on the size, scope, and differences of our conditions may help engender qualitative changes in the struggles and social formations to which we identify and participate and the forms through which we strategize and mount resistance and cultivate alternative modes of life, community, and connection. These shifts can also prompt us to confront our social locations as well as the traditions and regimes of dead generations that dominate and live among us, the continued hope in institutions that have historically worked to the detriment of our existence and sustainability. Social movements are galvanizing people toward these kinds of perspectives and praxis. Martin's and Chen's supporters are indexes of a growing sensibility regarding the worldwide impact of neoliberalism, their work and critical thinking a reminder of the bridge that first connected black radicals and China's revolution—the long march against global capitalism, an ongoing struggle whose end point is still to be determined.

Glossary

baihua qifang baijia zhengming (百花齐放, 百家争鸣): let one hundred flowers bloom and one hundred schools of thought contend

baihua yundong (百花运动): Hundred Flowers Campaign

baquan zhuyi (霸权主义): hegemonism

Beijing kaoya (北京 烤鸭): Beijing roast duck

buduan geming (不断革命): permanent revolution

changqi douzheng (长期斗争): protracted struggle

changzheng (长征): the Long March

chanzu (缠足): foot binding

cong qunzhong, xiang qunzhong (从群众, 向群众): from the masses, to the masses

Dadao Mei di! Dadao Su xiu! (打倒美帝! 打倒蘇修!): Down with American imperialists and Soviet revisionists!

da yue jin (大跃进): the Great Leap Forward

dazibao (大字报): big character posters

dongfang hong (东方红): the East is Red

fan xiu, fan di (反修反帝): oppose revisionism, oppose imperialism

geming weiyuanhui (革命委员会): revolutionary committees

Guanyu zhengque chuli renmin neibu maodun de wenti (关于正确处理人民内部矛盾的问题): On the Correct Handling of Contradictions among the People

gui cheng (鬼城): ghost city or town

gu wei jin yong, yang wei Zhong yong (古为今用, 洋为中用): make the past serve the present, make the foreign serve China

Hai Rui ba guan (海瑞罢官): Hai Rui Dismissed from Office

Hanhua (汉化): Sinification or Sinicization; the influence of the Chinese state and society

Hanzu (汉族): Han ethnic group

heigui (黑鬼): black devils

heinu zhongzu (黑奴种族): the black slave race

hexie shehui (和谐社会): harmonious society

hong weibing (红卫兵): Red Guards

hou (猴): monkey

huang (黄): yellow

Huangdi (黄帝): Yellow Emperor

Huanghe (黄河): Yellow River

Huangzhong (黄中): Yellow Center

huoxue huoyong (活学活用): lively study and application

hutong (胡同): narrow streets or alleys generally associated with northern Chinese cities

jianjue zhichi Meiguo heiren de zhengyi douzheng (坚决支持美国黑人的正义斗争): resolutely support the just struggle of the Afro-American people

jiaoyang (教养): to educate; to nurture; to train

jiedao banshi chu (街道办事处): street committees

jinian Bai Qiuen (紀念白求恩): In Memory of Norman Bethune

jinse de pinminku (金色的贫民窟): golden ghettos

kongbai de (空白的): blank

kunlun (崑崙): derogatory term used to describe enslaved African and Southeast Asian populations in China during the Tang era (618–906 C.E.)

laodong (劳动): labor; work; toil

laodong gaizao (劳动改造) / laogai (劳改): labor reform

laogai dui (劳改 队): labor reform camp; thought reform camp

Maike'er Jiekexun (迈克尔 杰克逊): Michael Jackson

Makesi zhuyi de zhongguo hua (马克思主义的中国化): Sinification of Marxism; making Marxism Chinese

Maozedong junshi wenxuan (毛泽东军事文选): Selected Military Writings by Mao Zedong

Maozedong sixiang (毛泽东思想): Mao Zedong Thought

Maozedong xuanji (毛泽东选集): Selected Works of Mao Zedong

Maozedong zhuzuo xuandu (毛泽东著作选读): Selected Readings from the Works of Mao Zedong

Mao zhuxi yulu (毛主席语录): Quotations from Chairman Mao

nongmin chusen (农民出身): peasant origins

nongye hezoushe (农业合奏社): agricultural cooperatives

pao da siling bu (炮打司令部): bombard the headquarters

qian dasao fangzi zhaodai xin keren (前打扫房子招待新客人): cleaning the house before entertaining new guests

qiangda de huang zhong ren (强大的黄种人): powerful yellow race

Qiaodan (乔丹): Jordan (i.e., Michael Jordan)

qilai (起来): to stand up; to rise up

Qingnian yundong de fangxiang (青年运动的方向): The Orientation of the Youth Movement

qunzhong luxian (群众路线): mass line

renmin gongshe (人民公社): people's communes

renmin zhanzheng (人民战争): people's war

ruanwo (软卧): soft sleeper

ruanzuo (软座): soft seat

san dou yi duo (三斗一多): three struggles, one increase

san ge daibiao (三个代表): the three represents

san ge shijie de lilun (三个世界的理论): the three worlds theory

San Huan Lu (三环路): Third Ring Road

Shanghai e wen xuexiao (上海俄文学校): Shanghai Russian School

Shanghai waiguoyu xueyuan (上海外国语学院): Shanghai Foreign Languages Institute

shaoshu minzu (少数民族): ethnic minorities

shehuizhuyi jiaoyu yundong (社会主义教育运动): socialist education movement

shidao zunyan (师道尊严): respect for teaching profession; strict teacher's authority

shijie geming (世界革命): world revolution

sige weida (四个伟大): the four greats

sige xiandaihua (四个现代化): the four modernizations

sijiu (四旧): the four olds (old ideas, old culture, old customs, and old habits)

si qing yundong (四清运动): four cleanups movement

sixiang gaizao (思想改造): ideological remolding

Sun Wukong (孙悟空): the Monkey King

tiantian du (天天读): daily readings

waiguo pengyou (外国 朋友): foreign friend

waiguo zhuanjia (外国专家): foreign experts

waijiao shiwu (外交事务): diplomatic affairs

weida de daoshi, weida de lingxiu, weida de tongshuai, weida de duoshou (伟大的导师, 伟大的领袖, 伟大的统帅, 伟大的舵手): the great teacher, great leader, great supreme commander, and great helmsman

Wei renmin fuwu (为人民服务): Serve the People

wuchan jieji wenhua dageming (无产阶级文化大革命): Great Proletarian Cultural Revolution

xia hai (下海): jumping into the sea

Xiang Lei Feng tongzhi xuexi (祥雷锋同志学习): Learn from Comrade Lei Feng

xiha (嘻哈):hip hop

xi nao (洗脑): brainwash (to wash a brain)

xin minzhu geming (新 民主 革命): new democratic revolution

xiuzheng zhuyi (修正主义): revisionism

xiyou ji (西遊記): Journey to the West

xuanchuan hua (宣传画): propaganda poster

yibiandao zhengce (一边倒政策): lean-to-one-side policy

yingwo (硬卧): hard sleeper

yingzuo (硬座): hard seat

Yiyongjun jinxingqu (义勇军进行曲): March of the Volunteers

you hong you zhuan (又红又专): red and expert

youyi (友谊): friendship

yuanxi tiaozheng (院系调整): reordering of colleges and departments

Yugong yishan (愚公移山): The Foolish Old Man Who Removed Mountains

yulu cao (语录操): quotation gymnastics

Zhongguo (中国): China; the Middle Kingdom

Zhongguotese shehuizhuyi (中国特色社会主义): socialism with Chinese characteristics

zhongjian didai (中间地带): intermediate zones

zhong zi wu (忠字舞): fealty or loyalty dance

zu (组): group

Notes

INTRODUCTION. MARCH OF THE VOLUNTEERS

1. At the concert, Robeson also sang non-American folk songs in French, Russian, Spanish, Yiddish, and German, among other languages. He remarked to a journalist, "[These] songs were composed by men trying to make work easier, trying to find a way out. . . . When I sing, 'let my people go,' . . . it is no longer just a Negro song—it is a symbol of those seeking freedom." Dorn, "Paul Robeson Told Me," 131.

2. Liu Liangmo, a Chinese immigrant and activist whose weekly column in the *Pittsburgh Courier* detailed interesting facts about Chinese life and struggle, taught Robeson the song. See Liu, "Paul Robeson"; and G. Robinson, "Internationalism and Justice."

3. Author's translation.

4. "Paul Robeson: A Voice That Inspired China," *China Today*, January 15, 2009. Keynote Records released a full-scale album of Robeson singing this song and other Chinese resistance anthems in 1941.

5. See G. Robinson, "Internationalism and Justice," 266–72.

6. See Gallicchio, *The African American Encounter with Japan and China*, 164–65, 174–78; Jenkins, "Two Sleeping Giants"; and Jones, *Yellow Music*, 1–7.

7. Dorn, "Paul Robeson Told Me," 131.

8. Downing, *Radical Media*, v, xi.

9. This book does not avoid cultural criticism of the political and cultural meanings through which people interpreted and represented the Cold War. In fact, my intention is to acknowledge and unpack *the limits of representation*—that representation is a practice that never supplies unspoiled replica of that which is represented, which is never simply objective, and which always signifies differential and unequal power dynamics between the inscriber/author and the represented, as well as the roles inscription, depiction, and knowledge production have played in subjugating and displacing nonelite perspectives and legitimizing and magnifying the agency and ideas of predominantly elite speakers. Numerous scholars have taken a similar approach. See Appy, *Cold War Constructions*; Hixson, *Parting the Curtain*; Kwon, *The Other Cold War*; Lucas, *Freedom's War*; E. May, *Homeward Bound*; L. May, *Recasting America*; Melley, *Empire of Conspiracy*; Nadel,

Containment Culture; Saunders, *The Cultural Cold War* and *Who Paid the Piper?*; and Whitfield, *The Culture of the Cold War*.

10. Redding, *Turncoats, Traitors, and Fellow Travelers*, 21.

11. Luce, "The American Century." Luce's statement, to some degree, conveyed what is at the heart of Michael Hardt and Antonio Negri's more recent concept of "Empire." This idea theorizes the new languages and means of hegemony instituted by the United States, corporate globalization, and other institutions over the course of the twentieth century, most dominantly in the aftermath of World War II. The authors explain that during this period a "new global form of sovereignty" was shaped that has "no territorial center of power" and that "does not rely on fixed boundaries or barriers." They elaborate: "It is a *decentered* and *deterritorializing* apparatus of rule that progressively incorporates the entire global realm within its open, expanding frontiers." Hardt and Negri, *Empire*, xii (emphasis added). In addition, for more on the "grand area" vision of America's post–World War II economic and geopolitical trajectory, see Shoup, "Shaping the Postwar World."

12. Works that frame the Civil Rights and Black Power movements as composing a "long movement"—that is, a framework that periodizes them through a longer temporal and spatial frame—include Biondi, *To Stand and Fight*; Bush, *We Are Not What We Seem*; Countryman, *Up South*; Joseph, *Waiting 'til the Midnight Hour*; King, *Civil Rights and the Idea of Freedom*; Marable, *Race, Reform, and Rebellion*; W. Martin, *No Coward Soldiers*; Ransby, *Ella Baker and the Black Freedom Movement*; Singh, *Black Is a Country*; Smethurst, *The Black Arts Movement*; Tyson, *Radio Free Dixie*; and Weisbrot, *Freedom Bound*. For a critique of this tendency in historiography, see Cha-Jua and Lang, "The 'Long Movement' as Vampire."

13. On "racial capitalism," see C. Robinson, *Black Marxism*, 2.

14. Elbaum, "What Legacy from the Radical Internationalism of 1968?," 37.

15. Indeed, the person who coined the neologism of the *Cold War*, George Orwell, a British writer and the author of dystopian novel *1984* (1949), perceived the post–World War II global context as composed of power contests that exceeded the conventional U.S.-Soviet rivalry narrative. In an article published just months after America's atomic bombing of Hiroshima and Nagasaki, Orwell denounced the emerging nuclear arsenals of the United States and the Soviet Union. The shift in the technologies of interstate conflict indicated the development of the "kind of world-view, the kind of beliefs, and the social structure that would probably prevail in a state which was at once unconquerable and in a permanent state of 'cold war' with its neighbors." Orwell clairvoyantly concluded the polemic by challenging bipolar framings of the emerging global order: "More and more obviously the surface of the earth is being parceled off into three great empires, each self-contained and cut off from contact with the outer world, and each ruled, under one disguise or another, by a self-elected oligarchy. . . . The third of the three super-states—East Asia, dominated by China—is still potential rather than actual." George Orwell, "You and Atomic Bomb," *Tribune* (London), October 19, 1945.

16. "The map to a new world is in the imagination," the historian Robin D. G. Kelley explains. It "transport[s] us to another place, compel[s] us to relive horrors and, more

importantly, enable[s] us to imagine a new society." Kelley, *Freedom Dreams*, 2, 9. Kelley's use of "the imagination" is also evident in a number of works that encourage the reconceptualization of Benedict Anderson's concept of the "imagined community," which was pivotal in theorizing the imagination as a political practice. Anderson pointed to role of language, technology, print media, the novel, the census, maps, and museums in Western constructions of the nation-state. But Anderson's narrative of the rise of modern nationalism disregards nationalism's development in non-Western locations; postcolonial Asia and Africa are not deeply taken into account. Anderson is also primarily concerned with national territories. Consequently, after absorbing his argument readers are left with the imagination as an analytic primarily for one historically contingent type of formation, through which politics, cultural membership, and solidarity were shaped and formed. Political communities and formations that don't correspond simply with national territorial spaces are given little attention. See B. Anderson, *Imagined Communities*. For critiques of Anderson's concept, see Chakrabarty, *Provincializing Europe*, 172–79; and Christopher Lee, "Introduction," *Making a World after Empire*, 23–24.

17. For other works that consider the significance of travel within black constructions and articulations of modernity, identity, community, and internationalism see K. Baldwin, *Beyond the Color Line and the Iron Curtain*; Bolster, *Black Jacks*; J. Brown, *Babylon Girls*; Cohn and Platzer, *Black Men of the Sea*; Dunbar, *Black Regions of the Imagination*; Edwards, *The Practice of Diaspora*; Elam and Jackson, *Black Cultural Traffic*; Fish, "Voices of Restless (Dis)Continuity"; Gilroy, *The Black Atlantic*; Griffin and Fish, *A Stranger in the Village*; Gruesser, "Afro-American Travel Literature and Africanist Discourse"; Mason, "Travel as Metaphor and Reality in Afro-American Women's Autobiography, 1850–1972"; C. Phillips, *The European Tribe*; Von Eschen, *Satchmo Blows Up the World*; and C. Young, *Soul Power*.

18. Iriye, "Culture and International History," 245 (emphasis added). Iriye elaborates, "All realities in a way are imagined realities, products of forces and movements that are mediated through human consciousness." Iriye is one of several scholars on U.S. relations with East Asia who have called for Western historians and international relations scholarship to give greater consideration to: (1) comparative analysis, particularly the Asian side of these relations (what Michael H. Hunt and Steven I. Levine tag the "Asian context," and Paul A. Cohen, describing U.S.-China relations, identifies as a "China-centered" approach); and (2) the cultural and philosophical contexts of diplomacy between the United States and East Asian countries, specifically the different and intersecting cultural assumptions and understandings that have informed these international and cross-cultural interactions. See G. Chang, "Are There Other Ways to Think about the 'Great Interregnum'?"; P. Cohen, *Discovering History in China*; Hunt and Levine, "The Revolutionary Challenge to Early U.S. Cold War Policy in Asia"; Iriye, *Cultural Internationalism and World Order*; and Qing, *From Allies to Enemies*.

19. See *Race, The Floating Signifier*; also see Hall, *Representation*, 225–76.

20. Rhodes, *Framing the Black Panthers*, 5.

21. Benjamin, *Reflections*, 223, 230.

22. Gitelman, *Scripts, Grooves and Writing Machines*, 11; Gallo, *Mexican Modernity*, 20.

23. Curtin, "Organizing Difference on Global TV," 338.

24. I am thinking here of the intellectual offerings of James Baldwin, Frantz Fanon, and Aimé Césaire. Baldwin acknowledged how U.S. nationality and his subject position as an "American" clouded his perception of Algerian racial oppression in France. "I was still operating, unconsciously, within the *American framework*," he remarked. "Not only was I operating within *the American frame of reference*, I was also a member of American colony, and we were, in general, slow to pick up on what was going on around us." Fanon, on the other hand, explained how anticolonial media helped to produce a revolutionary, anticolonial listening public. The Algerian liberation movement's radio station, for example, he explained, combated French colonialism by offering listeners a collective political and conceptual space to condemn French occupation and imagine and enunciate a self-determinate, independent Algeria. Through sonic waves, these listeners and the station's broadcasters were "at one with the nation in its struggle"—that is, able "to assume the new national formulation" and collective consciousness rooted in French colonialism's elimination and Algerian nationalist awakening. Césaire, lastly, emphasized how media ingrained audiences with ethical, humanist, and internationalist responsibilities. By transforming regional signs into global signifiers available for plural usage and signification, media enabled local discourses to take on larger meanings and forge transcultural connections. Employing "Hitler" as a global signifier of the injustice experienced by different groups, Césaire explained: "When I turn on my radio, when I hear that Negroes have been lynched in America, I say that we have been lied to: Hitler is not dead; when I turn on my radio, when I hear that Jews have been insulted, mistreated, persecuted, I say that we have been lied to: Hitler is not dead; when, finally, I turn on my radio and hear that in Africa forced labor has been inaugurated and legalized, I say that we have certainly been lied to: Hitler is not dead." J. Baldwin, *No Name in the Street*, 37 (emphasis added); Fanon, *A Dying Colonialism*, 88; and Césaire quoted in Fanon, *Black Skin, White Masks*, 90.

25. Chow, *Woman and Chinese Modernity*, 26–27.

26. X. Chen, *Occidentalism*, 3. Chen divides "occidentalism" into two different types: "official occidentalism" and "anti-official occidentalism." While the former refers to the state and the ruling elite's use of discourses and images of the West to justify domestic political repression of Chinese publics, the latter describes Chinese representations of the West as means for resistance against such domestic oppression. It is the former to which I refer. Chen's concept builds on and is critical of Edward Said's concept of "orientalism," (Said, *Orientalism*) which describes constructions of Asia as a central arm of European and the U.S. intellectual and economic imperialism. For Chen and other scholars such as Arif Dirlik, the limitations of Said's concept is its focus solely on Eurocentric conceptualizations of Asia and the world while giving little attention to Asia's complicity in such constructions and Asians' distinct representations of both themselves and the West. Dirlik's engagement of Asian intellectuals' "self-orientalism" of Asia and Chen's analysis of Chinese reification of the "occident" and the East-West

divide therefore offer constructive analytics to problematize the constructions of China fashioned by black radicals and the Chinese state. See Dirlik, "Chinese History and the Question of Orientalism."

27. Chen Jian, *Mao's China and the Cold War*, 15.

28. Such articulations, the scholar Michelle Ann Stephens explains, compose a "black masculine global imaginary," whose "vision[s] of the race's *transnationalism* [have] . . . been projected onto the black male body." See Stephens, *Black Empire*, 18.

29. Stephens, *Black Empire*, 14.

30. On representations of Asia within Cold War American media and culture, see, for instance, Herzstein, *Henry R. Luce, Time, and the American Crusade in Asia*; Hunt, "East Asia in Henry Luce's American Century"; Jun, *Race for Citizenship*; Klein, *Cold War Orientalism*; McAlister, *Epic Encounters*; Neils, *China Images in the Life and Times of Henry Luce*; Perlmutter, *Picturing China in the American Press*; and J. Wu, *Radicals on the Road*.

31. Nikhil Pal Singh has noted this shortcoming. He calls out Cold War historiography for too frequently dividing "the world into international and domestic spheres in which questions of race and cultural difference are at best local and residual concerns." Singh, "Culture/Wars," 474. For works on African American involvement in Cold War foreign affairs and the Civil Rights Movement's international ramifications and activism, see C. Anderson, *Eyes off the Prize*; Anthony, *Max Yergan*; Borstelmann, *The Cold War and the Color Line*; Clemons, *African Americans in Global Affairs*; Dudziak, *Cold War Civil Rights*; Krenn, *The African American Voice in U.S. Foreign Policy since World War II* and *Black Diplomacy*; Kruse and Tuck, *Fog of War*; Layton, *International Politics and Civil Rights Policies in the United States, 1941–1960*; Plummer, *Rising Wind* and *Window on Freedom*; Savage, *Broadcasting Freedom*; and Slate, *Colored Cosmopolitanism*.

32. See Bush, *The End of White World Supremacy*; Daulatzai, *Black Star, Crescent Moon*; Gaines, *African Americans in Ghana*; Horne, *Black and Red, The End of Empires*, and *Race War!*; Singh, *Black Is a Country*; Slate, *Black Power beyond Borders*; Von Eschen, *Race against Empire* and *Satchmo Blows Up the World*; West, Martin, and Wilkins, *From Toussaint to Tupac*; J. Wu, *Radicals on the Road*; and C. Young, *Soul Power*.

33. C. Young, *Soul Power*, 9. Also see Elbaum, *Revolution in the Air*; Maeda, *Chains of Babylon*; Ogbar, *Black Power*; Oropeza, ¡*Raza Sí! ¡Guerra No!*; and Pulido, *Black, Brown, Yellow, and Left*.

34. Two important works that come to mind are Cedric Robinson's classic *Black Marxism* and Brent Hayes Edwards's *The Practice of Diaspora*.

35. Carole Boyce Davies, Barbara Ransby, and Gerald Horne provide biographies of the Trinidadian Marxist Claudia Jones and the African American radicals Eslanda Goode Robeson and Shirley Graham Du Bois. Cheryl Higashida explores several female leftist writers' internationalism, whereas Dayo Gore, Jeane Theoharis, Komozi Woodard, Kimberly Springer, and Erik McDuffie consider women leftists' grassroots organizing, leadership, and participation in Cold War Communist and anti-imperialist campaigns. All of this scholarship conveys the multifaceted and intersectional dimensions of Cold War black feminism. Correspondingly, Michelle Stevens, Steve Estes, Hazel

Carby, Tracy Matthews, and others have illuminated the overarching presence of masculinism and patriarchy within African American radical political activism and thinking. See Carby, *Race Men*; Collier-Thomas and Franklin, *Sisters in the Struggle*; Davies, *Claudia Jones*; Davies, *Left of Marx*, 8; Estes, *I Am a Man!*; Gillman and Weinbaum, *Next to the Color Line*; Gore, *Radicalism at the Crossroads*; Gore, Theoharis, and Woodard, *Want to Start a Revolution?*; Guy-Sheftall, "Speaking for Ourselves"; Higashida, *Black Internationalist Feminism*; Horne, *Race Woman*; Matthews, "'No One Ever Asks What a Man's Role in the Revolution Is'"; McDuffie, *Sojourning for Freedom*, 9; Ransby, *Eslanda*; Smith, *The Truth That Never Hurts*; Stephens, *Black Empire*; Springer, *Living for the Revolution*; S. Ward, "The Third World Women's Alliance"; Welch, "Gender and Power in the Black Diaspora" and "Spokesman of the Oppressed?"; and J. Wu, *Radicals on the Road*. On Third World women's activism, see Alexander and Mohanty, *Feminist Genealogies, Colonial Legacies, Democratic Futures*; Brah, *Cartographies of Diaspora*; Grewal and Kaplan, *Scattered Hegemonies*; Mohanty, *Feminism without Borders*; Perez, *The Decolonial Imaginary*; and Sandoval, *Methodology of the Oppressed*.

36. On the gendered dynamics of American empire and the Cold War, and American foreign policy's role in shaping U.S. culture, see, for example, Kaplan, *The Anarchy of Empire in the Making of U.S. Culture*; and E. May, *Homeward Bound*.

37. Kuumba, *Gender and Social Movements*, 20.

38. In a special issue of *positions* that focuses on Afro-Asian connections, Nikhil Pal Singh and Andrew Jones make a similar point. They assert that "the departmentalization of historical and theoretical work along national and supraregional lines" has led to little cross-disciplinary exchange between East Asian studies and African American studies. See Jones and Singh, "Guest Editors' Introduction," 3.

39. For political science and international relations scholarship, see Caute, *The Fellow Travelers*; Hollander, *Political Pilgrims*; Chin-Chuan Lee, *Voices of China*; and Passin, *China's Cultural Diplomacy*. For East Asian studies works that examine Cold War Chinese political culture, see Andrews, *Painters and Politics in the People's Republic of China, 1949–1979*; Chiu and Zheng, *Art and China's Revolution*; Cook, *Mao's Little Red Book*; Cushing and Tompkins, *Chinese Posters*; Evans and Donald, *Picturing Power in the People's Republic of China*; Kraus, *Pianos and Politics in China*; Landsberger, *Chinese Propaganda Posters*; Landsberger and van der Heijden, *Chinese Posters*; Leese, *Mao Cult*; Mittler, *A Continuous Revolution*; and Wei and Brock, *Mr. Science and Chairman Mao's Cultural Revolution*.

40. See R. Alexander, *Maoism in the Developed World* and *Maoism in the Developing World*; Elbaum, *Revolution in the Air*; Fields, *Trotskyism and Maoism*; Gallicchio, *The African American Encounter with Japan and China*; Green, *Black Yanks in the Pacific*; Kelley and Esch, "Black Like Mao"; Mullen, *Afro-Orientalism*; Mullen and Ho, *Afro-Asia*; Prashad, *Everybody Was Kung-Fu Fighting*; and Raphael-Hernandez and Steen, *AfroAsian Encounters*. More recently, black relations and representations with Asia have been theorized through the concept of "the Black Pacific," a broadening of Paul Gilroy's "Black Atlantic" framework. See Horne, *Race War!* and "The Revenge of the Black Pacific?"; Jones and Singh, "Guest Editors' Introduction"; Okiro, "Toward a Black Pacific"; Onishi, "The New Negro of the Pacific"; and Taketani, "The Cartography of the Black Pacific."

41. See Brady, *Making the Foreign Serve China*, "Red and Expert," and "'Treat Insiders and Outsiders Differently'"; Brady and Brown, *Foreigners and Foreign Institutions in Republican China*; Burgess, "Mao in Zanzibar"; Fennell, "Preliminary Thoughts on Race and Foreign Policy" and "A Tale of Two Obits"; Y. Gao, "W.E.B. Du Bois and Shirley Graham Du Bois in Maoist China"; Matthew D. Johnson, "From Peace to the Panthers"; Monson, *Africa's Freedom Railway*; and J. Wu, *Radicals on the Road*, 4–5.

42. Spivak, *Nationalism and the Imagination*, 47.

43. Eagleton, "Adrienne Rich, Location and the Body," 299.

44. Du Bois, *The Autobiography of W.E.B. Du Bois*, 47.

I. THE 1950S: LOSING CHINA, WINNING CHINA

1. The historian Nigel Harris has criticized using the term *alliance* to describe the CCP and GMD political relationship, explaining that the link did not benefit the CCP and was more the product of Soviet decree than CCP strategizing. "In China, 'alliance' meant something different. It was not a relationship between social classes, nor was it an alliance of the parties of the exploited, the workers and peasants," Harris states. "It was an agreement to subordinate a party which aspired to lead the working class to a party which aimed to lead Chinese capital and landlords." Harris, *The Mandate of Heaven*, 14.

2. See Karl, *Mao Zedong and China in the Twentieth Century*, 15–34.

3. See Harris, *The Mandate of Heaven*; and Isaacs, *The Tragedy of the Chinese Revolution*.

4. See Chang, "The Impact of Presidential Statements on Press Editorials Regarding U.S. Policy, 1950–1984" and "The News and U.S.-China Policy"; Haygood, "Henry Luce's Anti-communist Legacy"; Isaacs, *Scratches on Our Minds*; Kuznitz, *Public Opinion and Foreign Policy*; Liu, "An Analysis of the *New York Times* Editorial Attitude toward the Representation of Communist China in the United Nations"; and Yu and Riffe, "Chiang and Mao in U.S. News Magazines."

5. Koen, *The China Lobby in American Politics*, 50.

6. Fairbank, *The United States and China*, 319. For an overview of more-nuanced Western literature and media coverage on China during the period, see Hayford, "Mao's Journeys to the West." Also see Jespersen, *American Images of China, 1931–1949*.

7. Barnouw, *The Image Empire*, 99.

8. On the Bandung conference see Jansen, *Afro-Asia and Non-alignment*; Kahin, *The Asian-African Conference*; Kimche, *The Afro-Asian Movement*; Christopher Lee, *Making a World after Empire*; Prashad, *The Darker Nations*; Singham and Hune, *Non-alignment in an Age of Alignments*.

9. "Speech by Premier Chou En-Lai to the Political Committee of the Asian-African Conference, April 23, 1955," *New York Times*, April 25, 1955.

10. See Shinn and Eisenman, *China and Africa*, 35–36, 59.

11. On waishi, see Brady, *Making the Foreign Serve China*, "Red and Expert," and "'Treat Insiders and Outsiders Differently.'"

12. See Nadel, *Containment Culture*; also see Lucas, *Freedom's War*; and Saunders, *The Cultural Cold War*.

13. Kennan, "Moscow Embassy Telegram #511, February 22, 1946," 63. This posture was further stipulated in government memos, the most notable including Kennan's article, "The Sources of Soviet Conduct"; the State Department official Paul Nitze's national security policy paper NSC-68; and President Harry Truman's "Truman Doctrine."

14. Du Bois, *The Autobiography of W.E.B. Du Bois*, 388.

15. Von Eschen "Who's the Real Ambassador?," 112.

16. See Dudziak, *Cold War Civil Rights*, 79–83.

17. Southern Democrats briefly seceded from Truman's liberal racial policies to form the Dixiecrats, a party that smeared civil rights activists and leftist radicals as communist collaborators and Soviet stooges. Simultaneously, African American war veterans returned to their homelands to be attacked and murdered by racist militias who accused them of being closeted subversives. Unions, such as the Congress of Industrial Organizations, purged from their ranks members accused or known to have communist or socialist ideological leanings. For more on containment culture's impact on black politics, see Borstelmann, *The Cold War and the Color Line*; Dudziak, *Cold War Civil Rights*; Plummer, *Rising Wind*; Singh, *Black Is a Country*; and Von Eschen, *Race against Empire*.

18. Borstelmann, *The Cold War and the Color Line*, 66. In the aftermath, W. E. B. and Shirley Graham Du Bois, Paul and Eslanda Robeson, Josephine Baker, Claudia Jones, C. L. R. James, and W. Alphaeus Hunton, among others, were branded persona non grata and saw their international activism and mobility curtailed. See Davies, *Left of Marx*; Dudziak, *Cold War Civil Rights*, 61–78; Horne, *Black and Red*; Ransby, *Eslanda*; and Von Eschen, *Race against Empire*.

19. Hero, "American Negroes and U.S. Foreign Policy," 12.

20. On U.S. "Yellow Peril" discourse, see Hamamoto, *Monitored Peril*; R. Lee, *Orientals*; E. Lee, *At America's Gates*; Xing, *Asian America through the Lens*; and Yoshihara, *Embracing the East*.

21. "Ike Charges Treason in Coddling of Reds," *New York Daily News*, October 4, 1952; and U.S. Department of State, "Memorandum of Discussion of the 237th Meeting of the National Security Council."

22. See Borstelmann, *The Cold War and the Color Line*, 81.

23. In 1950 the *Chicago Defender* editor Lucius Harper acknowledged that the Chinese communists were the far more favorable choice in leading China's population. The U.S. government's support of the GMD, he explained, demonstrated its "fear of the spread of Communism" and willingness to go "to the rescue of a government against the best interests of the people." Newspaper readers of the *Afro-American* also criticized the country's closed-door policy toward China. While one person condemned the State Department for keeping "the door to China closed too long to the detriment of American people," another rationalized that the American government could not "ignore Communist China like a headache that will go away if we don't talk about it." "China was never ours to lose," another person commented. "What we did destroy was the friendship of the Chinese people by the arrogant attitude of our diplomats and businessmen on the color question. We are making the same mistake in our disdainful 'white is right' approach."

Lastly, the writer James Baldwin, though no fan of communism, reasoned that China's opposition to the United States was a consequence of Western domination of Asia. "There's no point in being offended at their [China's] lack of generosity in wishing to impose their image of the world on the world," he wrote to his editor in 1956. "This is precisely what Europe did to them and, as far as they are concerned, this is almost the entire history of European civilization." Lucius Harper, "Some Sidelights on the Korean War," *Chicago Defender*, August 5, 1950; "What AFRO Readers Say," *Baltimore Afro-American*, January 19, 1957, 4; "What AFRO Readers Say," *Baltimore Afro-American*, January 1, 1957, 4; "What Afro Readers Say," *Washington Afro-American*, December 7, 1954, 4; Baldwin and Stein, *Native Sons*, 100–101.

24. Ransby, *Eslanda*, 197–201.

25. Hughes, "Consider Me."

1. RUMINATIONS ON EASTERN PASSAGE

1. See Wu C., *Journey to the West* and *Monkey Nobel of China*.

2. Strong and Keyssar, *Right in Her Soul*, 322.

3. Ironically, the figure of the monkey is venerated in both Chinese and African American historical traditions. Within Chinese mythology and customs, Hou, the monkey, is known as a saintly deity and practical joker, representing the ninth creature in the zodiac system. In African American folklore, the signifying monkey is a trickster figure whose origins lie in Yoruba mythology and the deity of Eshu Elegbara, messenger of the gods, protector of travelers, and most importantly the divine mediator who dwells at the crossroads.

4. Du Bois, *The Autobiography of W.E.B. Du Bois*, 49; Du Bois, "The Vast Miracle of China Today," 191.

5. Du Bois, "The Vast Miracle of China Today," 190.

6. Graham Du Bois, *His Day Is Marching On*, 278.

7. The historian Gerald Horne also points to the trip's impact on Graham Du Bois's feminist outlook. See Horne, *Race Woman*, 160.

8. Graham Du Bois, *His Day Is Marching On*, 294.

9. Graham Du Bois, "China's Expansions Make It 'The Land of Tomorrow,'" *Pittsburgh Courier*, April 11, 1959, B2.

10. Porter, *The Problem of the Future World*, 4–5. Notwithstanding the differences between Porter's and my reading of Du Bois's outreach to China, Porter's final chapter is intriguing and rich. Two useful concepts he employs are Julianne Malveaux and Regina Green's argument about "the paradox of loyalty" and M. Jacqui Alexander's category of the "suspect citizen." For Porter they help to describe Du Bois's mediated responses to the political alienation he experienced among U.S. political circles as a result of 1950s Cold War anticommunism. Positioned as a "suspect citizen"—a person whose citizenship and nationality were deemed to warrant doubt and coercive regulation—Du Bois perceived how black liberals' pursuit of racial democracy was

predicated on their abandonment of an explicit anticolonial and anti-imperialist position and their support of U.S. foreign policy. Porter explains that within this context Du Bois realized that blacks were faced with a "paradox of loyalty"—the ways membership in the nation-state demanded their consent and participation in U.S. global hegemony. For Porter, "these restrictive aspects of national citizenship" best frame the simultaneous processes of inclusion and exclusion through which black people are incorporated into the nation and implicated in projects of U.S. empire. See Porter, *The Problem of the Future World*, 147–48, 166.

11. There has only been modest contemplation of Du Bois's fascination with Chinese communism. The literary historian Bill Mullen has pointed to the novel *Dark Princess* (1928) as a central Du Boisian text that proposes the union of Pan-African and Pan-Asian anticolonial political sensibilities. While *Dark Princess* provides a productive vantage point to unpack Du Bois's interwar contentions about Afro-Asian internationalism, in the context of the Cold War, the novel's revelations are limited. Considering that it was published more than three decades before Du Bois's death in 1963 illuminates that *Dark Princess* did not fully correspond to the scholarly giant's outlook during his later years. See Mullen, "Du Bois, Dark Princess, and the Afro-Asian International"; also see Mullen, *Afro-Orientalism*, 1–42. In addition, Du Bois's thought and activism has also received attention in Chinese scholarship. See Juguo, "Du Bois' Quest for Solution to the American 'Negro Problem'", "The Thought of William E. B. Du Bois in Comparison with Booker T. Washington," and "W. E. B. Du Bois and the Pan-African Movement"; Xiaoyang and Yanhong, "On W.E.B. Du Bois's 'Double-Consciousness' and Its Influence on Black American Literature."

12. The Council on African Affairs advocated immediate decolonization of African colonies and opposition to Western corporations' exploitation of colonial nations' natural resources. The Peace Information Center on the other hand was devoted to petitioning governments, most specifically the United States, to cease development of nuclear weapons and take an explicit foreign policy against using such weaponry. By the fall of 1950, financial constraints and governmental pressure led the Peace Information Center to be dissolved. Similarly, the Council on African Affairs disbanded in 1955 after having spent two years defending itself against similar federal charges of subversion. See Porter, *The Problem of the Future World*, 157–61; Von Eschen, *Race against Empire*.

13. Du Bois, *The Autobiography of W.E.B. Du Bois*, 369.

14. Du Bois, *The Autobiography of W.E.B. Du Bois*, 393, 370.

15. Du Bois, *The Autobiography of W.E.B. Du Bois*, 393, 395

16. Du Bois, "The American Negro in My Time," in Du Bois and Aptheker, *Writings by W.E.B. Du Bois in Periodicals Edited by Others*, 194–95 (originally published in *United Asia* [Bombay], March 5, 1953, 155–59).

17. Du Bois, "Socialism and Democracy," in Du Bois and Aptheker, *Writings by W.E.B. Du Bois in Periodicals Edited by Others*, 278 (originally published in *American Socialist*, January 1957, 6–9).

18. Horne, *Race Woman*, 145–49.

19. Interview of David Graham Du Bois, National Visionary Leadership Project interviews and conference collection (AFC 2004/007), Archive of Folk Culture, American Folklife Center, Library of Congress, Washington, D.C. (the interview can also be viewed at: http://www.visionaryproject.org/duboisdavid).

20. Horne, *Race Woman*, 123.

21. Du Bois, *The Autobiography of W.E.B. Du Bois*, 11.

22. Graham Du Bois, *His Day Is Marching On*, 276.

23. David Graham Du Bois remarked that the people he met rarely exhibited overt racial discrimination or prejudice toward him; however, one encounter stood out. A young Chinese girl gasped when she saw him, appalled at his skin color. Immediately, a superior slapped the child and chastised her. In all probability, the adult deemed the girl's reaction an embarrassment, her gasp disrespectful to a state guest. "Apparently she had never seen anything that looked like me," Graham Du Bois revealed. "I felt sorry for the child." But according to Graham Du Bois, this one occurrence was the exception; at no other point during his time in China did he feel that his skin-color was an issue. Impressed with the social developments he witnessed, Graham Du Bois returned to the United States more firmly committed to the project of building communism stateside. Of the trip, he commented: "It was an extraordinary opportunity and it had an enormous impact on me and on my life and on my subsequent years." See Interview of David Graham Du Bois, National Visionary Leadership Project (see endnote 20).

24. Du Bois, *The Autobiography of W.E.B. Du Bois*, 45.

25. Du Bois, untitled article, *The Crisis* 35 (February 1928): 39.

26. Du Bois, "The Winds of Time: Christmas Contrasts," *Chicago Defender*, December 29, 1945, 13.

27. Du Bois, "The Winds of Time: Conference on China," *Chicago Defender*, January 10, 1948, 15.

28. Du Bois, "Colonialism and the Russian Revolution," in Du Bois and Aptheker, *Writings by W.E.B. Du Bois in Periodicals Edited by Others*, 277 (originally published in *New World Review*, November 1956, 18–21).

29. Du Bois, "Normal U.S.-China Relations," in Du Bois and Aptheker, *Writings by W.E.B. Du Bois in Periodicals Edited by Other*, 223 (originally published in *New World Review*, August 1954, 13–15); Du Bois, "The Winds of Time: the Future of the Colonies," *Chicago Defender*, May 19, 1945.

30. Du Bois, *The Autobiography of W.E.B. Du Bois*, 47.

31. Du Bois, *The Autobiography of W.E.B. Du Bois*, 47.

32. Du Bois, "Normal U.S.-China Relations," in Du Bois and Aptheker, *Writings by W.E.B. Du Bois in Periodicals Edited by Other*, 222–23.

33. Du Bois, "China and Africa." This work is also found in Du Bois, *The Autobiography of W.E.B. Du Bois*, 405–8.

34. Du Bois, *The Autobiography of W.E.B. Du Bois*, 406. Du Bois's rhetoric ("Africa does not ask alms from China. . . . It asks friendship and sympathy") intersected with Chinese foreign policy discourse. "Friendship projects" were a central component of Cold

War Sino-African relations, particularly Chinese-financed and -constructed infrastructure projects in Africa. "Friendship roads, friendship ports and friendship buildings sprang up all over the continent," one historian notes. See P. Snow, *The Star Raft*, 166; also see Monson, *Africa's Freedom Railway*, 26–29.

35. Mao, "The Situation in the Summer of 1957 (July 1957)," 482.

36. Dirlik, *Marxism in the Chinese Revolution*, 78. Also see Elbaum, "What Legacy from the Radical Internationalism of 1968?"

37. Du Bois, *Black Folk*, 383.

38. Du Bois, "Africa and Afro-America," in Du Bois and Aptheker, *Writings by W.E.B. Du Bois in Periodicals Edited by Others*, 220 (emphasis added; originally published in the *Spotlight on Africa: Newsletter* from the Council on African Affairs in 1956).

39. Du Bois, "The Bandung Conference," in Du Bois and Aptheker, *Writings by W.E.B. Du Bois in Periodicals Edited by Others*, 236; Du Bois, "Pan-Colored," in Du Bois and Aptheker, *Writings by W.E.B. Du Bois in Periodicals Edited by Others*, 225 (originally published in *Spotlight on Africa*, January 1955).

40. See Cooppan, "Moving on Down the Line," 36. Regarding Du Bois's fondness for comparative examples, Paul Gilroy notes that Du Bois throughout his life "moved beyond simply using European history to generate comparative examples. . . . Instead of this one-way traffic, a systematic account of the interconnections between Africa, Europe, and the Americas emerged." Gilroy, *The Black Atlantic*, 121.

41. Shinn and Eisenman, *China and Africa*, 64.

42. There has been wide debate over the number of deaths caused by the GLF. Some scholars defend them. Others argue that they are too high and not reflective of reality but rather the social construction of famine as a discourse and the anti-Maoist ideological outlook of the intellectual field. For the former view, see Chang and Halliday, *Mao*; Y. Chen, "When Food Became Scarce"; Dikötter, *Mao's Great Famine*; Hershatter, *The Gender of Memory*; Thaxton, *Catastrophe and Contention in Rural China*; and Yang, *Tombstone*. For the latter view, see Gao, *The Battle for China's Past*; and Patnaik, "On Famine and Measuring 'Famine Deaths.'"

43. See MacFarquhar, *The Hundred Flowers and the Chinese Intellectual*.

44. For more on the expatriate community's participation in this culture of disinformation, see Brady, *Making the Foreign Serve China*, 117–20.

45. Du Bois, *The Autobiography of W.E.B. Du Bois*, 49.

46. Graham Du Bois, *His Day Is Marching On*, 293.

47. Du Bois, *The Autobiography of W.E.B. Du Bois*, 50, 47.

48. Du Bois, *The Autobiography of W.E.B. Du Bois*, 45, 50, 53.

49. Du Bois, *The Autobiography of W.E.B. Du Bois*, 44, 51 (emphasis added).

50. Steve Estes explains the primacy of masculinism in the dominant ideology and rhetoric of the Civil Rights Movement: "Masculine rhetoric uses the traditional power wielded by men to woo supporters and attack opponents. It rallies supporters to a cause by urging them to be manly or to support traditional ideas of manhood. It challenges opponents by feminizing them, and therefore linking them to weakness. When political

leaders harness the power of masculinism to forward their agendas, they often simplify complex issues into binary oppositions, placing themselves and their allies in the dominant position." Estes, *I Am a Man!*, 7–8.

51. Du Bois, *The Autobiography of W.E.B. Du Bois*, 48, 52.

52. For more on this, see Carby, *Race Men*; and Gillman and Weinbaum, *Next to the Color Line*.

53. Lee and Stefanowska, *Biographical Dictionary of Chinese Women*, 302–3. Also see Sheridan, *Chinese Warlord*.

54. Lee and Stefanowska, *Biographical Dictionary of Chinese Women*, 450–55.

55. Graham Du Bois, *His Day Is Marching On*, 279; this quote is also found in Graham Du Bois, "China's Expansions Make It 'The Land of Tomorrow.'"

56. Graham Du Bois, "China's Expansions Make It 'The Land of Tomorrow.'"

57. Graham Du Bois, *His Day Is Marching On*, 287.

58. Graham Du Bois spells Bei Guangli's name as "Pei Kwang-li," which is the Wade Giles spelling of this particular name. Bei was clearly a top tour guide used by the Chinese government. The Swedish leftist and writer Jan Myrdal (son of the economist Gunnar Myrdal) mentioned being guided around by Bei during a 1962 trip to China. See Myrdal, *Report from a Chinese Village*, 35.

59. Graham Du Bois, *His Day Is Marching On*, 295.

60. For more on Tang Mingzhao, see Renqiu, *To Save China, to Save Ourselves*, 192; Haiming, *The Transnational History of a Chinese Family*, 197–98; Ji, *The Man on Mao's Right*, 35–36.

61. When Graham Du Bois refers to these different people, their names are spelled with Wade Giles spelling: Ding Xilin is "Ting His-lin"; Zhu Boshen is "Chu Po-shen"; Bei Guangli is "Pei Kwang-li"; and Wang Huifang is "Wong Huei-fang." See Graham Du Bois, *His Day Is Marching On*, 282.

62. On China's practices of managing foreigners' travels, what Hollander refers to as governmental "techniques of hospitality," see Brady, *Making the Foreign Serve China*, 94–136; Hollander, *Political Pilgrims*, 278–499.

63. Brady, *Making the Foreign Serve China*, 94.

64. Hollander, *Political Pilgrims*, 372, 355.

65. Chen J., *Mao's China and the Cold War*, 11.

66. Emmanuel John Hevi, a Ghanaian student who studied in China from 1960 to 1962, detailed the process through which the PRC preselected Chinese citizens to participate in these tours and in rallies and ceremonies championing foreign movements. He wrote, "I have since witnessed several other similar rallies, and, what is more, I have learnt how they are organized. The Party orders that it wants fifty, seventy or a hundred thousand persons to attend such-and-such a rally; and the heads of street committees, factories and other establishments select the people who are to attend. When you are selected, attendance is compulsory, but when you are not selected you have no right to attend. Each group of participants is under an individual who alone is authorized to act as slogan-leader, the slogans being approved by the Party for the occasion. . . . At the

rally you watch your group leader and applaud when he does, shout when he does. In the whole show there is not a single trace of spontaneity which should mark the public demonstration of people who, moved by a common sentiment into words and action rally together to put that sentiment into words and action." Hevi, *An African Student in China*, 160–61.

67. Graham Du Bois, *His Day Is Marching On*, 282.

68. See Knaus, *Orphans of the Cold War*.

69. For more on the Tibetan rebellion of 1959, see Chen J., "The Tibetan Rebellion of 1959 and China's Changing Relations with India and the Soviet Union"; Conboy and Morrison, *The CIA's Secret War in Tibet*.

70. See Graham Du Bois, *His Day Is Marching On*, 289; Du Bois, *The Autobiography of W.E.B. Du Bois*, 48.

71. Du Bois, "Let Us Have Freedom in America," in Du Bois and Aptheker, *Writings by W.E.B. Du Bois in Periodicals Edited by Others*, 317 (originally published in *Worker* [New York], March 6, 1960, 8, 9, 11); Du Bois, *The Autobiography of W.E.B. Du Bois*, 51, 53 (emphasis added). Du Bois also discussed his China travels in the essay "Our Visit to China," *China Pictorial*, March 20, 1959.

72. Graham Du Bois, *His Day Is Marching On*, 276 (emphasis added).

73. Pratt, *Imperial Eyes*, 198, 228, 200–201.

74. Nudelman, "Trip to Hanoi: Antiwar Travel and International Consciousness," 241.

75. Du Bois, *Color and Democracy*, 540.

76. See Sanders, "Afterword: The Black Flame Then and Now," 249.

77. Quite a number of people have detailed the stylistic innovations of Du Bois's writing, particularly how he blended various genres of writing and forms of cultural composition—personal and public history, fiction, poetic verse, autobiography, musical composition, sociology, and ethnography. Such methods, according to Paul Gilroy, worked to interpellate the reader into "different registers of address" and "the intensity of feeling" that "exploration of racialized experienced demanded." Gilroy, *The Black Atlantic*, 115.

78. Du Bois, *Worlds of Color*, 23. Subsequent citations to pages in *Worlds of Color* will appear in the text.

79. In *Worlds of Color*, Du Bignon has a conversation with one of her colleagues where her peer rejects the view that African Americans must align their political strivings with anticolonial movements abroad. "Our problem is simpler. We want to be Americans," the colleague states, reinforcing the idea of antiracist struggle as primarily concerned with black American access to the benefits of U.S. citizenship. Du Bignon, however, shoots this proposal down. "No. Becoming Americans does not mean automatic settlement of our problems. It means sharing the problems of Americans," she states. "We must emerge into the greater world before we become Americans." Du Bois, *Worlds of Color*, 66.

80. Du Bois's essay "Worlds of Color" was first published in the journal *Foreign Affairs* in 1925 and revised that same year for Alain Locke's landmark anthology, *The New Negro*. The essay details Du Bois's travels to the Iberian Peninsula and several West African countries and his participation in several Pan-African Congresses. But more sig-

nificantly, the essay unpacks the shifts in Western imperialism in the years following World War I that have helped produce a colonial class of civil servants and colonized elites and a growing colonial intellectual and worker-led anti-imperialist movement. Brent Hayes Edwards notes that in both Du Bois's essay and the novel *Worlds of Color*, Du Bois "pushes towards a 'planetary' perspective" that "revises the 'color line' in terms of global imperialism and class dynamics." The novel, Edwards concludes, therefore simultaneously operates as a formal dialectic "after-thought" to the article and a fictionalized characterization of Du Bois's "last 'romance' with internationalism." Edwards, "Late Romance," 128–29.

81. K. Baldwin, *Beyond the Color Line and the Iron Curtain*, 162, 163.

82. Clifford, *Routes*, 5.

83. "The East" as a trope for the radicalization of a person's thought and politics is echoed throughout the novel. At the tail end of Mansart's journey, he leaves Asia and sails "east into the sunset again to discover America, in his own thought and through the thinking and doing of other folk." Later, it is this idea that a Brit imparts to Mansart's grandson: "The center of the world is undoubtedly moving East. We must move with it—in thought certainly, if not body." Du Bois, *Worlds of Color*, 43, 189.

84. Said, *Orientalism*, 222; Said, "Orientalism Reconsidered," 103.

85. Glissant, *Poetics of Relation*, 142.

86. This section of the novel is composed from Du Bois's editorials in the *Pittsburgh Courier* that documented his train ride from the Soviet Union into China during the winter months of 1936, and "Yellow Sea," an essay that he authored after this 1936 trip to China. See Du Bois, "Forum, Fact and Opinion: Moscow to Lake Baikal," *Pittsburgh Courier*, January 23, 1937, 11; and Du Bois, "Forum, Fact and Opinion: Manchuria," *Pittsburgh Courier*, February 6, 1937, 6.

87. Hollander, *Political Pilgrims*, 310.

88. Gilroy, *The Black Atlantic*, 133.

89. Referencing Du Bois's 1936 train ride through northern China, David Levering Lewis agrees that Du Bois's assessment of the train bleeds of "racial romanticism." See Lewis, *W.E.B. Du Bois*, 604.

90. Hollander, *Political Pilgrims*, 311.

91. Du Bois, *The Souls of Black Folk*, 37.

92. Mohanty, "Feminist Encounters," 84, 89.

93. Žižek juxtaposes "symbolic identification" with "imaginary identification," the latter of which he describes as the problematic attempt to identify with the Other through discourses and claims of imitation and resemblance. Žižek, *The Sublime Object of Ideology*, 109.

94. Mansart's conversation with the Chinese intellectuals was most likely based on discussions Du Bois participated in during his own 1936 travel to China. At the Chinese Bankers' Club, Du Bois spoke with a group of intellectuals and business professionals, discussions that he described in subsequent accounts as "a most illuminating conversation." The group mostly talked about how China planned to get from under the yolk

and "spell of Europe." What Du Bois identified as a transformative moment though came when he specifically questioned them about their hatred for Japan. Revisiting the conversation in later decades, Du Bois took account of the narrowness of his question and his knowledge of China. Recalling the dialogue twenty-five years later, he commented: "We talked three hours but it was nearly a quarter of a century before I realized how much we did not say." Du Bois, "Normal U.S.-China Relations," in Du Bois and Aptheker, *Writings by W.E.B. Du Bois in Periodicals Edited by Other*, 222; Du Bois, *The Autobiography of W.E.B. Du Bois*, 46. Lewis also describes this discussion, noting similar contradictions within Du Bois's questions: "Their presumptuous guest had turned a blind eye to the bitter paradox that just as China was regaining a modicum of political cohesion and instituted economic reforms, the Japanese had trumped the British as masters of gunboat imperialism." Lewis, *W.E.B. Du Bois*, 606. Du Bois, in his later years, clearly regretted his failure to acknowledge the depths of Japanese aggression and repression in China. According to Sidney Rittenberg (a U.S. Marxist, former China expatriate, and CCP insider), when Du Bois visited China in 1959, at a small gathering hosted by Premier Zhou Enlai, Du Bois began the event by apologizing for his decades-earlier support for Japan. "The last time I was in China I supported the Japanese, because I mistakenly thought the Japanese were going to rally the Asian peoples against imperialism," Du Bois remarked. "I was wrong." Rittenberg recounted, "The Chinese there really appreciated that." Author phone interview with Sidney Rittenberg, August 15, 2013.

95. This ultimately takes shape within Mansart's lineage, through the love affair and romantic relationship between his grandson Adelbert Mansart and the Vietnamese revolutionary Dao Thu. Dao represents Du Bois's attempt to rework what Edward Said describes as Orientalism's patriarchal "sexual promise"—she embodies the defender of the East, a figure of Asian revolutionary freedom fighting that counters Du Bois's frequent masculinist depiction of Chinese Communism but that also conveys his continued reliance on a male-female, heterosexual framework of internationalism. Adelbert and Dao's lives become intertwined when he helps her evade French authorities after she murders a Vietnamese official who is working in cahoots with the French government to repeal Vietnam's independence. Falling in love with Dao, Adelbert accepts when Dao's comrades beseech him to take an unusual assignment. Like Sun Wukong the Monkey King, Adelbert is charged with the mission of accompanying Dao Thu on her return journey to Vietnam. However, to do so Adelbert has to surrender his U.S. citizenship and be commissioned as a French colonial official so that he and Dao can travel through Africa under the auspices of French diplomacy. In Adelbert and Dao's marriage, future offspring, and impending residence in Ghana—the country in which the Du Boises also went into exile—Du Bois again charts a path toward the dream and hope of socialism, anti-imperialism and racial equality. Together, Adelbert and Dao embody "the rising east," Du Bois' proposal of Asian-African kinship and alliance. Moreover, this time it is Africa that supplies the possibility of traveling east. Dao's comrades advise the newly engaged couple: "Perhaps the shortest way to Vietnam and to Indonesia and China is through Africa." Du Bois, *Worlds of Color*, 205.

96. "Peking Meeting Commemorates Centennial of Birth of Dr. W.E.B. Du Bois," *Peking Review*, March 1, 1968, 26–27. Graham Du Bois would go on to establish an ongoing relationship with the Chinese government, periodically visiting and taking residence there until her own death in 1976. For more on her relationship with China after Du Bois's death, see Horne, *Race Woman*, 223–38, 258–62.

97. "Peking Meeting Commemorates Centennial of Birth of Dr. W.E.B. Du Bois." Also see Graham Du Bois, *His Day Is Marching On*, 286; and Young and Green, "Harbinger to Nixon," 125–28.

2. A PASSPORT AIN'T WORTH A CENT

1. §6, 65 Stat. 993, codified at 50 USC. § 785 and Passports Miscellaneous Amendments, 21 Fed. Reg. 336 (Jan. 17, 1956) (amending 22 C.F.R. § 51.136).

2. See Jaffe, "The Right to Travel," 17–28; and Kahn, "International Travel and the U.S. Constitution."

3. Worthy's activism has not received comprehensive analysis in academic scholarship. The works that devote some attention to him include Broussard, *African American Foreign Correspondents*, 156–83; Broussard and Cooley, "William Worthy, Jr."; P. Joseph, *Waiting 'til the Midnight Hour*, 45–51; and Phillips, "'Did the Battlefield Kill Jim Crow?,'" 154, 163–65, 197.

4. William Worthy, "Dr. Du Bois Back," *Baltimore Afro-American*, July 7, 1959, 10.

5. William Worthy, "Racial Arrogance Gave Birth to Red China: Worthy Looks at 'Color' in China," *Washington Afro-American*, January 29, 1957, 6 (also published in *Baltimore Afro-American*, February 2, 1957, 1, 2).

6. See "Bill Worthy's Mother Dies," *Baltimore Afro-American*, September 15, 1956, 5; "Dr. William Worthy, Sr. Obituary," *Journal of the National Medical Association* 46, no. 5 (September 1954): 370; Fox, *The Guardian of Boston*, 266; Worthy Sr., "Retirement of Dr. William Augustus Hinton"; and Worthy Sr., *The Story of the Two First Colored Nurses to Train in the Boston City Hospital*.

7. See Alfred Friendly Jr., "Chips on His Shoulders," *Harvard Crimson*, April 19, 1957, http://www.thecrimson.com, accessed March 11, 2011; Jensen, "William Worthy, '42"; and Jonathan J. Ledecky, "A Man Worth Heeding," *Harvard Crimson*, April 28, 1977, http://www.thecrimson.com, accessed March 11, 2011.

8. The historian Chen Jian has challenged the dominant historical assessment of China's reasons for entering the Korean crisis. Previous historians, most notably Allen S. Whiting's *China Crosses the Yalu* (1960), argued that China's primary purpose in entering the fray was to ensure the safety of the Chinese-Korean border from the imminent threat of U.S. incursion and influence. Chen, on the other hand, employing Chinese documents and archives unavailable to Whiting and other scholars, supplies a counternarrative. He explains that China's entry into the Korean War was determined by more-complicated factors than just protecting China's security interests. Of vital importance to China's leadership was their belief that securing the war's outcome in favor of North

Korea might impact China's domestic and international interests, particularly the CCP's influence at home and abroad. See Chen J., *China's Road to Korean War*.

9. See Halliday and Cumings, *Korea*, 159, 197. Regarding the number of casualties during the war, see Cumings, *The Origins of the Korean War*, 770; Fehrenbach, *This Kind of War*, 46; and Halliday and Cumings, *Korea*, 11, 200.

10. The desegregation of the U.S. military built on earlier shifts produced by World War II. During the war opportunities in government and nongovernmental initiatives abroad led to increased African American employment overseas as aid workers, technicians, medical-service personnel, educators, and engineers. This expansion of what the government perceived as cultural workers who would repair America's image abroad was also aided by the government's selection of several African Americans to serve as national voices within the international arena, most centrally as ambassadors and alternate UN delegates. Black musicians, entertainers, and artists were also sent on government-sponsored international tours. The image of U.S. racial progress was lastly circulated through State Department–packaged junkets featuring images and narratives of black American achievement and enjoyment of middle-class life; these junkets were strategically placed in U.S. embassies, particularly in Asian and African territories. See Borstelmann, *The Cold War and the Color Line*; Plummer, *Rising Wind*; Von Eschen, *Satchmo Blows Up the World*.

11. Phillips, *War! What Is It Good For?*, 114.

12. See Dudziak, *Cold War Civil Rights*, 85–87; Robin, *The Making of the Cold War Enemy*, 166; and Widener, "Seoul City Sue and the Bugout Blues," 56–57. Truman's legislation and the onset of the war did not drastically alter the reality of segregation and class inequality in the U.S. armed forces. Draft exemptions for educated persons and those from well-to-do and well-connected families resulted in a fighting force composed mainly of undereducated, working-class, and working-poor whites and racial minorities. Furthermore, despite Truman's order, the army remained a segregated space. Black troops were assigned to all-black units commanded by white officers. Soldiers of color were denied access to leadership positions, advanced training schools, intelligence outfits, promotions, and combat duty equal to their white counterparts. Instead, they were relegated to the less prominent, low-grade, and humiliating military duties, what served as a reminder of their inferior status. Such segregation and discrimination did not only operate within military assignments but also within the military's medical practices. Blood transported and used for transfusions was labeled according to race. Furthermore, although the integration of the armed services did facilitate an increase in opportunities for interracial military bonding and interaction, it was mired by the pervasiveness of white-supremacist ideology. For some white soldiers, being trained and having to fight alongside black and Latino troops reinforced their bigotry, which led to disputes and divisions along racial and ethnic lines. Sexual relations and partnerships forged between U.S. troops and Korean women also brought to the fore matters of race; many soldiers returned to the United States with Asian wives and children, real-life examples of interracial coalition and miscegenation that more benighted Americans found difficult

to accept. See Borstelmann, *The Cold War and the Color Line*, 81–82; and Plummer, *Rising Wind*, 204–9.

13. On African American involvement in the Korean War, see Bowers, Hammond, and MacGarrigle, *Black Soldier, White Army*; Bussey, *Firefight at Yechon*; Dalfiume, *Desegregation of the U.S. Armed Forces*; Donnelly, *We Can Do It*; Edgerton, *Hidden Heroism*; Kinkead, *In Every War but One*; Phillips, *War! What Is It Good For?*; and Scipio, *Last of the Black Regulars*.

14. Horne, *Race Woman*, 146.

15. Robeson and Foner, *Paul Robeson Speaks*, 252. The war's racial overtones are also examined in Green, *Black Yanks in the Pacific*, 110–36; Phillips, "'Did the Battlefield Kill Jim Crow?'"; Plummer, *Rising Wind*, 206–9; and Widener, "Seoul City Sue and the Bugout Blues." On the differences distinguishing rhetoric of *war of color* versus that of *race war*, see Widener, "Seoul City Sue and the Bugout Blues," 62.

16. William Worthy, "Asiatic World Breaking Chains: Korean Debacle Bound to Open Eyes of U.S. GIs," *Washington Afro-American*, August 18, 1953, 2.

17. William Worthy, "No Pretty Outlook," *Afro-American*, April 10, 1954, 4.

18. Worthy, "Asiatic World Breaking Chains," 2.

19. See Charles Davis, "POWs Return with Bitter Memories of Red Prisons," *Washington Afro-American*, August 25, 1953, 1; Douglass Hall, "Major's Memory of Prison Vivid" and "Prison Taught GIs to Love Democracy," *Washington Afro-American*, August 25, 1953, 13. Also see Julia Hock, "Raincheck on Peace," *Washington Afro-American*, August 18, 1953, 5.

20. Worthy, "Asiatic World Breaking Chains," 2; William Worthy, "Are All of Our Spokesmen Tongue-Tied?," *Washington Afro-American*, February 16, 1954, 4.

21. Worthy, "Are All of Our Spokesmen Tongue-Tied?" 4.

22. See Jowett, "Brainwashing." In postwar accounts, Chinese generals and military persons attest to China's policy of leniency toward POWs. They remark that while harsh physical mistreatment, murder, and theft of prisoners' goods did occur at the hands of Chinese troops and commanders, higher-up officials condemned such actions. Other historians, however, have challenged such claims. For the generals' claims, see Li, Millet, and Yu, *Mao's Generals Remember Korea*, 77–85.

23. In recent years several people have argued that the motives behind the indoctrination lectures were mainly practical and strategic, aimed more at instilling order and discipline among the prisoners, instigating political discord and divides between them, and making use of idle time than at producing radical ideological transformations of the prisoners' outlooks. In *Mao's Generals Remember Korea*, Lieutenant General Du Ping, the director of the political department of the Chinese People's Volunteer Force, stated that the lectures were aimed at "destroying the cohesion of the enemy forces." The historian Garth Jowett affirms this argument, stating that there is "little evidence that these discussions were seriously intended to bring about a massive shift in opinion; rather they served to occupy the POWs' time in nonproductive ways." He concludes that the Chinese military's intent was not "to convert the majority of prisoners to communism" but rather to create "enough confusion and doubts in the minds of prisoners to reduce

the potential for large-scale conflict and escape attempts in the prison camps." He also points out that those U.S. POWs who did collaborate with the Chinese mainly did so out of desperation and for the sake of survival and self-protection. Li, Millet, and Yu, *Mao's Generals Remember Korea*, 77; Jowett, "Brainwashing," 207–8 (particularly "Statements from Figure 10.2"). On laogai dui, see H. Wu, "The Labor-Reform Camps in the PRC."

24. Quoted by Wu Henian, a Chinese camp counselor in the POW camp, in Shuibo Wang's film *They Chose China* (2005).

25. Carlson, *Remembered Prisoners of a Forgotten War*, 195–202.

26. Edward Hunter, "Brainwashing Tactics Forced Chinese into Ranks of Communist Party," *Miami Herald*, September 19, 1950; Robin, *The Making of the Cold War Enemy*, 167. Also see Hunter's *Brainwashing and Brain-washing in Red China*.

27. Hunter, *Brainwashing*, 5–6; *Communist Psychological Warfare (Brainwashing)*. The credibility of Hunter's claims was enhanced by his reliance on arguments from studies authored by government- and corporate-financed think tanks. For example, some of his evidence came from Nathan Leites and Elsa Bernaut's *Ritual of Liquidation* (1954), a RAND Corporation study that examined the Soviet Union's psychological and psychiatric practices of indoctrination and propaganda during the 1930s. See Robin, *The Making of the Cold War Enemy*, 167–68.

28. Biderman, *March to Calumny*, 1.

29. See "Case History Histories of Those 21: What Their Lives Show," *Newsweek*, January 18, 1954, 52–57; "Communist Brainwashing—Are We Prepared?," *New Republic*, June 8, 1953, 5–6; "Korea: The Sorriest Bunch," *Newsweek*, February 8, 1954, 40; "Korean Puzzle: Americans Who Stay," *US News & World Report*, October 9, 1953, 38; "One Who Won't Return," *Time*, October 26, 1953, 27; "The Prisoners," *Commonweal*, October 16, 1953, 29; "Race POWs Stay with Communists," *Pittsburgh Courier*, January 2, 1954, 1; Victor Riesel, "Brainwashed Ex-GIs Used for Propaganda in South," *Milwaukee Sentinel*, August 16, 1954, 14; William A. Ulman, "The GI's Who Fell for the Reds," *Saturday Evening Post*, March 6, 1954, 64. Also see Clifford, *In the Presence of My Enemies*; Kornfeder, *Brainwashing and Senator McCarthy*; Lifton, *Thought Reform and the Psychology of Totalism*; Meerloo, *The Rape of the Mind*; Schein, *Coercive Persuasion*; Swarup, *Brain-washing in Red China*; Tsui, *From Academic Freedom to Brainwashing*; and Winance, *The Communist Persuasion*.

30. Kinkhead, "Have We Let Our Sons Down?"; and Mayer "Why Did So Many G.I. Captives Give In?", 56.

31. Borstelmann, *The Cold War and the Color Line*, 81.

32. Jacobson and Gonzalez, *What Have They Built You to Do?*, 119. The writer Harold Issacs's 1958 comments best typified this view: "The fictionally evil Fu Manchu could hardly compete with a real-life Chinese Communist commissar. . . . All the qualities attributed to the 'evil and untrustworthy Oriental' come into their own in the new circumstances. They are drawn upon particularly to reinforce one of the most power of all 'new' images emerging, the image of the Chinese as *brainwashers*. . . . It was clear that great power was already attached to the mystique which gave the Chinese such extraordinary skill in the use of these weapons of mental and emotional torture. It obviously

was going to outstrip by far anything attributed to the Russians. . . . For the Chinese there was a whole battery of relevant qualities to draw upon . . . : their inhuman cruelty, for one thing, and at its service, their inscrutability, their deviousness, their subtlety, and their devilish cleverness." See Isaacs, *Scratches on Our Minds*, 218.

33. The 1962 film version of Richard Condon's literary thriller, *The Manchurian Candidate* (1959), about a Korean War veteran brainwashed by Chinese and Soviet scientists to become a communist assassin, brought brainwashing and anti-China politics to the screen. On Cold War films whose story lines revolved around communist "brainwashing," see Carlson, *Remembered Prisoners of a Forgotten War*, 14; Carruthers, "'The Manchurian Candidate' (1962) and the Cold War Brainwashing Scare"; Carruthers, "Redeeming the Captives"; and Charles Young, "Missing Action."

34. Jacobson and Gonzalez, *What Have They Built You to Do?*, 15, 39.

35. Plummer, *Rising Wind*, 205. On African American soldiers in segregated units during the Korean War, see Borstlemann, *The Cold War and the Color Line*, 82; Mershon and Schlossman, *Foxholes and Color Lines*, 220–24; Rishell, *With a Black Platoon in Combat*, 52; Widener, "Seoul City Sue and the Bugout Blues," 58.

36. Widener, "Seoul City Sue and the Bugout Blues," 68. One black POW, Richard Barnes, echoed the claims of the different treatment nonwhite and white prisoners received in the camps: "If you were a white man you would get six months in solitary for an offense for which a Negro would be unpunished. It was no accident." See "Reds Set Up Race Barriers," *Pittsburgh Courier*, August 22, 1953, 16.

37. Sixty-one countries signed the pledge, including the United States, in August 1949. China later declared its recognition of the pledge on July 13, 1952. Regarding the issue of repatriation, article 118 of the agreement stated: "As soon as a war ends, prisoners of war must be released and repatriated without any delay." But although the agreement declared repatriation as a POW's right, it asserted in article 7 that while a POW could return home, he or she was not required to return to their country of citizenship.

38. On the twenty-one POWs, see Adams, Adams, and Carlson, *An American Dream*; Carlson, *Remembered Prisoners of a Forgotten War*; Levine, "Twenty-One GIs Who Chose Tyranny"; Moshkin, *Turncoat*; Palsey, *21 Stayed*; and Zweiback, "The 21 'Turncoat GIs'?"; as well as Shuibo Wang's film *They Chose China*.

39. "Korean Puzzle: Americans Who Stay," *U.S. News & World Report*, October 9, 1953, 38–40.

40. For more on Adams, Sullivan, and White, see Adams, Adams, and Carlson, *An American Dream*; Carlson, *Remembered Prisoners of a Forgotten War*, 202–12; and Palsey, *21 Stayed*.

41. Margaret C. Smith, "Washington and You: Fate of Pro-Reds in Korea Proof of Folly," *Lewiston Daily Sun*, January 27, 1954, 4.

42. Plummer, *Rising Wind*, 209.

43. Riesel, "Brainwashed Ex-GIs Used for Propaganda in South," 14.

44. What is important to note though is that the postwar surveys authored by these behavioral scientists and various army-funded research centers supported their arguments by evading analysis of the racial and ethnic composition of American POWs,

ignoring how social stratification and racial differences and ideologies were steeped in the cultures of the U.S. military and the prison camps. See Robin, *Making of the Cold War Enemy*, 163, 173; Widener, "Seoul City Sue and the Bugout Blues," 67.

45. Hunter, *Brainwashing*, 89, 91–92.

46. Charles Young, "Missing Action," 52, 55.

47. Carlson, *Remembered Prisoners of a Forgotten War*, 9. These arguments were compounded by psychologists' assertions that Americans with sufficient strength of character withstood brainwashing. The cultural historian Alan Nadel explains, "The fight against brainwashing, in other words, was internal, a struggle not with the forces of evil but with the temptation to succumb to one's own weakness." Nadel, "Cold War Television and the Technology of Brainwashing," 156. Contrasting the image of the weak-willed American to that of the stout American loyalist helped affirm a hypermasculine image of American patriotism and military service. During the Cold War the image of "the soldier" was represented as the ideal national subject. While the racial integration of the armed services meant that the cultural configuration of the soldier must now include nonwhite bodies, "the soldier" was nonetheless still identified as male and hypermasculine. Depictions of soldiers were thus foreground in articulations of mastery, physicality, violence, patriotism, obedience, and loyalty, where the soldier became the locus of male power par excellence. This fixed construction meant that "the infantrymen came to symbolize manhood . . . [and were] catapulted into the role of saviors of the nation," an image that ultimately came to be the "template for postwar manhood." P. Jackson, *One of the Boys*, 8; Faludi, *Stiffed*, 16. Measured against this icon, the "brainwashed" and "collaborating" soldier came to represent failed character, failed Americanness, and failed manhood; this soldier was identified as being neurotic, maladjusted, alienated, easily compromised, and of grave risk to American national security. The depiction of the American patriot as the personification of ideal manhood and the brainwashed American Communist as its antithesis was therefore a central feature of the postwar discourse of "hard masculinity." Ultimately, defending America was identified as a masculine "Cold Warrior" endeavor against the veiled, feminine penetration by foreign communism. See, for example, S. Clark, *Cold Warriors*, 2; and Cuordileone, *Manhood and American Political Culture in the Cold War*, viii–vx, 67.

48. Borstelmann, *The Cold War and the Color Line*, 82; Jacobson and Gonzalez, *What Have They Built You to Do?*, 124. This racial calculus was brought to television in *Look Up and Live: The Broken Pitcher* (1962). The drama follows the struggles of three American soldiers imprisoned in China; a moral dilemma arises for the sole black member of the trio (Ossie Davis) when he is offered freedom in return for the life of another soldier (Hugh Reilly), who has lost his mind. Through Davis's character, black Americans were again positioned as defenders of the nation against Chinese communism. This made-for-television movie and, moreover, the general representation of Asian communism in Cold War American popular culture fit into a Cold War American supranational project of cultural hegemony that Heonik Kwon, Melanie McAlister, Christina Klein, and others describe as "American Orientalism." The authors pinpoint the constitutive role

of discourses of cultural pluralism and racial liberalism within Cold War American representations of Asia, where both racist and anticommunist rhetoric and strategies coalesced with arguments about racial and cultural tolerance. The authors conclude that how Asian populations were represented and stereotyped in American culture during the Cold War cannot be disassociated from the politics of black-white U.S. race relations and the growth of postwar racial liberalism. "U.S. representation . . . especially those since 1945, have been consistently obsessed with the problem of domestic diversity," McAlister states. "Thus in the postwar period, the us-them dichotomies of Orientalism have been fractured by the reality of a multiracial nation. . . . There was never a simple, racial 'us' in America, even when, as was generally the case, whiteness was privileged in discourses of Americanness." McAlister, *Epic Encounters*, 11. Also see Klein, *Cold War Orientalism*; and Kwon, *The Other Cold War*, 57–80.

49. William Worthy, "POWs Two Years Later: The Other Side of the Coin," *Washington Afro-American*, March 8, 1955, 10.

50. For more on Camp 5, see Basset and Carlson, *And the Wind Blew Cold*, 40–71; Cunningham, *No Mercy, No Leniency*, 54–75; Lech, *Broken Soldiers*, 67–110; and Spiller, "Appendix B: Prisoner of War Camps in North Korea," in Spiller, *American POWs in Korea*, 168.

51. William Worthy, "POWs Two Years Later: They Wept Bitter Tears," *Baltimore Afro-American Magazine Section*, January 8, 1955, 3; also see "Reds Duped More White Than Tan GIs," *Washington Afro-American*, August 18, 1953, 1, 2.

52. William Worthy, "Some POWs Desert 'Land of Jim Crow,'" *Washington Afro-American*, August 11, 1953, 3.

53. Worthy, "POWs Two Years Later: They Wept Bitter Tears," 3.

54. Li, Millet, and Yu, *Mao's Generals Remember Korea*, 78, 80.

55. Worthy, "POWs Two Years Later: The Other Side of the Coin," 10.

56. The church was not the only space where prisoners and Chinese authorities interacted in a cooperative and amicable manner. Upon the prisoners' recommendations, camp authorities transformed a former factory into a recreation hall, baseball field, and clubhouse with sports equipment and games. Both prisoners and camp authorities used the equipment, competing against one another in periodic athletic contests and pickup games. This culminated in 1952 with an inter-camp POW athletic competition with uniforms, music, medals, and opening and closing ceremonies to match, a media spectacle that the Chinese government propagated to emphasize the supposed humane conditions of its prison camps.

57. William Worthy, "POWs Two Years Later: The Lord Will Make a Way Somehow," *Baltimore Afro-American Magazine Section*, February 8, 1955, 6; Douglass Hall, "Set Up Underground Church: POWs Worshipped Despite Rebuffs," *Baltimore Afro-American*, August 29, 1953, 13.

58. Biderman, *March to Calumny*, 60–61; Widener, "Seoul City Sue and the Bugout Blues," 68.

59. Worthy, "POWs Two Years Later: The Lord Will Make a Way Somehow," 6.

60. Worthy, "Some POWs Desert 'Land of Jim Crow,'" 3.

61. Dikötter, "Racial Identities in China." Other examples of yellow's use in constructions of the Chinese nation include China's Yellow River (*Huanghe*) and discourses of China as the "Yellow Center" (*Huangzhong*). See and M. D. Johnson, *Race and Racism in the Chinas*; and Sautman, "Myths of Descent, Racial Nationalism and Ethnic Minorities in the People's Republic of China."

62. Dikötter, "Racial Discourses in China," 33, 20.

63. On kunlun and premodern interactions between Africans and Chinese, see Wyatt, *The Blacks of Premodern China*. Others have examined aspects of this history. J. J. L. Duyvendak, for example, pointed to Duan Chenghi's assortment of tales from the ninth century, *Youyang Zazu* (Miscellaneous morsels from Youyang), as the first Chinese work to refer to the African continent. Duyvendak, *China's Discovery in Africa*, 12. Also see Schafer, *The Golden Peaches of Samarkand*; Wilensky, "The Magical Kunlun and 'Devil Slaves'"; Yun, *The Coolie Speaks*, 171–73; and Zhang, "Gudai Zhongguo yu Feizhou zhi jiaotong."

64. On blacks as a "slave race" and "devils," see Dikötter, *The Discourse of Race in China*, 15–17; also see Dikötter, "Racial Identities in China." It should be noted that during the first few decades of the twentieth century Chinese academicians and scholars such as Chen Darong, Chen Yinghuang, and Du Yaqan positioned Africans as underdeveloped human beings. For instance, Chen Yinghuang, China's first professor of anthropology, laid out this kind of racial taxonomy in a 1918 textbook. He wrote, "Anthropology studies all races, from the Chinese and English down to the dwarf slave and the black slave." Du Yaquan's *Great Dictionary of Zoology* (1923) similarly contended that the "black race . . . have a shameful and inferior way of thinking, and have no capacity to shine in history." Chen D., *Dongwu yu rensheng*; Chen Yinghuang, *Renleixue*, 5 (also cited in Dikötter, *The Construction of Racial Identities in China and Japan*," 7, 21); Du, *Dongwuxue da cidian*, 15 (also cited in Dikötter, "Racial Identities in China," 408).

65. Worthy, "POWs Two Years Later: The Other Side of the Coin," 10.

66. Kinkead, *In Every War but One*, 17. On black former POWs' efforts to defend themselves against such accusations of collaboration, see, for instance, Carlson, *Remembered Prisoners of a Forgotten War*; Latty, *We Were There*; Spiller, *American POWs in Korea*; J. Thompson, *True Colors*; and Thomas Ward Jr., "Detachment Number 1: African-American Prisoners at Camp 5 during the Korean Conflict," Virginia Military Institute, www.vmi.edu /archives. Accessed March 11, 2011.

67. Worthy, "POWs Two Years Later: The Lord Will Make a Way Somehow," 6.

68. Adams, Adams, and Carlson, *An American Dream*, 32–33, 54. Morris R. Wills, Adams's fellow POW and, later, his fellow China resident, makes a similar point about the identities of the prison camp's lecturers. See Moshkin, *Turncoat*, 53.

69. Shuibo Wang, *They Chose China* (2005).

70. "Peking Chinese International Service in English: POW Statements on Korean War by Pfc. Harold M. Dunn, Pfc. Clarence C. Adams, and Pfc. Thomas R. Barnes," March 20, 1953, Sound Recording 263-BK-492, Audio Recordings of Monitored Broadcasts from Asia, compiled 1949 – 1960, Records of the Central Intelligence Agency, Record Group 263, National Archives at College Park, MD (hereafter NACP). Also see

"Peking Chinese International Service in English, POW Messages: Pvt. Joseph G. Kepipi, Pfc. Clarence C. Adams, and Trooper E.G. Beckerly," November 17, 1951, Sound Recording 263-BK-220, Audio Recordings of Monitored Broadcasts from Asia, compiled 1949–1960, Records of the Central Intelligence Agency, Record Group 263, NACP.

71. Adams, Adams, and Carlson, *An American Dream*, 59. Adams was not alone in his description of the camp as a site of profound transformation. Morris Wills, the POW, also described his own maturation and evolution in the camp: "I filled the vacuum left by my own government by taking an interest in China, Chinese and communism—by reading and by developing a friendship with the Chinese. It opened a way forward; I found another path out." Quoted in Moshkin, *Turncoat*, 59.

72. Zweiback, "The 21 'Turncoat GIs?,'" 358 (emphasis added).

73. Worthy, "Some POWs Desert 'Land of Jim Crow,'" 3.

74. The biographer Cecil Mark Inman and the historians T. R. Fehrenbach and William L. White suggest that the figure is somewhere between 58 and 60 percent, a number that includes the troops killed after capture, from untreated wounds, from the long march northward, and those whose fates were never clearly determined. Fehrenbach, *This Kind of War*, 444; Inman, *A Celebration of Life*, 129–30; and White, *The Captives of Korea*, 265.

75. Worthy, "Asiatic World Breaking Chains," 2.

76. Worthy, "POWs Two Years Later: The Other Side of the Coin," 10.

77. Worthy, "Some POWs Desert 'Land of Jim Crow,'" 3; Worthy, "Asiatic World Breaking Chains," 2.

78. Worthy, "Our Disgrace in Indo-China," 77, 82.

79. William Worthy, "Tale of Two Cities: One Has Got to Go," *Baltimore Afro-American*, March 20, 1956, 9; William Worthy, "Worthy Finds Montgomery Is Moscow (Russia), U.S.," *Baltimore Afro-American*, March 5, 1956, 12.

80. "Letter from Unnamed Source to Foreign Service Official," June 22, 1956, folder "030.2a Invitations to U.S. Correspondents to visit Mainland China Department of State," folder "William Worthy Trip 1957," decimal files 1954–1957 (container 22), Bureau of Far Eastern Affairs, Office of Chinese Affairs, Records of the Department of State, Record Group 59, NACP.

81. See "AFRO Newsman Now a Nieman Fellow," *Washington Afro-American*, June 12, 1956, 5; "Eleven Are Selected Nieman Fellows: 5 Foreign Newspaper Men Named Associates for a Year's Study at Harvard—the List of Fellows," *New York Times*, June 7, 1956; and "Pulitzer Prize Winner J. A. Lewis among 11 Receiving Nieman Grants," *Harvard Crimson*, June 12, 1956, http://www.thecrimson.com, accessed March 11, 2011.

82. "Confidential Memo from unnamed source," folder "030.2a Invitations to U.S. Correspondents to visit Mainland China Department of State," decimal files 1954–1957 (container 22), Bureau of Far Eastern Affairs, Office of Chinese Affairs, Records of the Department of State, Record Group 59, NACP.

83. "Why Bill Worthy Went to Red China," *Baltimore Afro-American*, January 5, 1957, 1, 2.

84. "U.S. Newsmen Visit Peiping," *Milwaukee Journal*, December 27, 1956, 7.

85. "State Department Awaits Report from Hong Kong," *Modesto Bee*, December 24,

1956, 5; Wilmot Hercher, "Reporter Defies China-Visit Ban," *Washington Post*, December 25, 1956, A12. Upon the counsel of the ACLU, Worthy authored and swore, in compliance with the law, a disclaimer that absolved the State Department of all responsibility for the safety of his person or property while he was in China. See "Mr. Worthy's Mission," *Baltimore Afro-American*, January 5, 1957, 1, 2.

86. "Ralph N. Clough, Director of the Office of Chinese Affairs, to Mr. Robertson," folder "030.2a Invitations to U.S. Correspondents to visit Mainland China Department of State," decimal files 1954–1957 (container 22), Bureau of Far Eastern Affairs, Office of Chinese Affairs, Records of the Department of State, Record Group 59, NACP.

87. "Press Release Draft," December 27, 1956, folder "030.2a Invitations to U.S. Correspondents to visit Mainland China Department of State," decimal files 1954–1957 (container 22), Bureau of Far Eastern Affairs, Office of Chinese Affairs, Records of the Department of State, Record Group 59, NACP; also see "Three Reporters Lose Passports," *Lewiston Daily Sun*, December 29, 1956, 4.

88. William Worthy, "Bill Worthy Talks to Red Premier," *Baltimore Afro-American*, January 22, 1957, 1, 12; "Clearing Up the Travel Ban," *St. Petersburg Times*, February 9, 1957, 4.

89. "Memo: Effect of Chou En-lai's Recent Southeast Asian Tour on Our Problems Generally and on Overseas Chinese," January 3, 1957, folder "Tours by Communist Chinese, Jan-April 1957," decimal files 1954–1957 (container 22), Bureau of Far Eastern Affairs, Office of Chinese Affairs, Records of the Department of State, Record Group 59, NACP.

90. "Worthy Calls His Passport Fight 'A Showdown' on Press Rights: Hits China Recognition Stand," *Harvard Crimson*, February 18, 1957, http://www.thecrimson.com, accessed March 11, 2011; also see "Worthy Emphasizes Decreasing of Tensions in Communist China," *Harvard Crimson*, March 6, 1957, http://www.thecrimson.com, accessed March 11, 2011.

91. Ann Lolordo, "UPI Recalls William Worthy's trip to China—Before It Was Popular," *Washington Afro-American*, May 1, 1979, 5.

92. "The Newspaper Curtain," *Harvard Crimson*, February 13, 1957, http://www.thecrimson.com, accessed March 11, 2011.

93. Richard Hughes, "What 'Dateline Peiping' Means," *New York Times*, June 23, 1957, 191.

94. Milton Bracker, "Defiant Newsman Back from China," *New York Times*, February 11, 1957, 8.

95. William Worthy, "Weekly Press Leads Fight for Freedom—Worthy Says," *Baltimore Afro-American*, March 26, 1957, 20. On CBS's show *World News Roundup*, Worthy broadcast from Beijing that there were indications from Zhou's camp that several of the Americans imprisoned in China might soon be released due to good behavior. Worthy's forecast proved correct; two months later, in March 1957, Mackensen was freed. See "Peiping Frees U.S. Missionary at End of 5-Year Prison Term; Rev. Paul J. Mackensen Jr., Last of Lutherans Held—No Word on His Return, Eisenhower Studies Ban," *New York Times*, March 8, 1957, 5; and "Red China Seen Freeing Some U.S. Prisoners," *Hartford Courant*, January 1, 1957.

96. Worthy, "Racial Arrogance Gave Birth to Red China," 6.

97. Adams, Adams, and Carlson, *An American Dream*, 74–76.

98. *Jet*, April 17, 1958, 5; *Jet*, May 8, 1958, 4.

99. William Worthy, "No Campus Romances in Red China Universities," *Washington Afro-American*, March 19, 1957, 1.

100. Worthy, "Racial Arrogance Gave Birth to Red China," 1.

101. "Who would blame a Chinese worker for being hostile to African students when he, who toils to contribute to their scholarship funds, is left half-starving on evil-smelling cabbage while the foreigners eat good food in almost unlimited quantities?" asked the student Emmanuel John Hevi. Hevi, *An African Student in China*, 132.

102. Hevi, *An African Student in China*, 162–63; Shinn and Eisenman, *China and Africa*, 218.

103. Hevi explained, "Boy-meets-girl affairs are perfectly permissible in China granting [it is a] Chinese boy and Chinese girl or European boy and Chinese girl, but where it is [an] African boy trying to meet Chinese girl then there is a whole lot of noise and fuss. . . . The Party does not allow marriage between Chinese women and foreign men, I was told. . . . But I knew a European student in Peking University who married a Chinese. There was a colored student in the People's University who had married a Chinese. . . . He was one of the American soldiers taken prisoner during the Korean War. . . . In his case the Chinese could not well have refused him a wife since he would have found it difficult to import one. In view of these facts it is difficult to discover whether the Chinese really do not want inter-marriage or whether they invented that rule to block any serious amorous advances by Africans." Hevi, *An African Student in China*, 174–75.

104. See Adie, "Chinese Policy Towards Africa," 55; Hevi, *An African Student in China*, 139–41; and Teufel, "China's Approach to Africa," 469.

105. Worthy, "Reporting in Communist China," 10, 11. In the article, Worthy employs the Wade Giles spellings of these officers' names: Yen Shao Hua, Madame Kong Peng, Chen Hui, and Sse Yun.

106. Worthy, "Weekly Press Leads Fight for Freedom—Worthy Says," 20.

107. During Worthy's layover in Budapest he was instructed by the U.S. consul Richard R. Selby Jr. to surrender his passport. Worthy, however, refused to do so. In the aftermath the State Department issued an order that his passport should not be seized or invalidated by any other customs officers. See "Worthy in Hungary," *Baltimore Afro-American*, February 9, 1957, 1, 2.

108. "Letter from Frances G. Knight, Director of Passport Office, to William Worthy," March 29, 1957, folder "William Worthy Trip 1957," decimal files 1954–1957 (container 22), Bureau of Far Eastern Affairs, Office of Chinese Affairs, Records of the Department of State, Record Group 59, NACP.

109. "Why Bill Worthy Went to Red China," 2.

110. "U.S. Passport Policy Faces New Assault in Worthy Cause," *Chicago Defender*, April 19, 1958, 9.

111. See "Dulles Suggests Press Employ Non-American to Enter China," *Baltimore Afro-*

American, May 21, 1957, 6; "Same Mr. Cartwright," *Washington Afro-American*, April 16, 1957, 4; and "Worthy Says Cartwright Clouded Issue of Newspaperman's Rights," *Harvard Crimson*, April 11, 1957, http://www.thecrimson.com, accessed March 11, 2011.

112. "William Kuntsler, ACLU Attorney, to State Department (government letter 12/30-PR23A)," December 30, 1957, folder "William Worthy Trip 1957," decimal files 1954–1957 (container 22), Bureau of Far Eastern Affairs, Office of Chinese Affairs, Records of the Department of State, Record Group 59, NACP.

113. In Worthy's case, the federal court distanced its ruling from the Supreme Court's *Kent v. Dulles* (1958) decision, an earlier decision that ruled in favor of the painter Rockwell Kent's appeal against the State Department's decision to deny him a passport because of his alleged Communist Party membership. That judgment outlawed the secretary of state from using the beliefs, associations, or character of an applicant as reasons to deny a passport or not issue a passport. Justice William O. Douglas, writing the majority opinion, explained: "The right to travel is a part of the 'liberty' of which the citizen cannot be deprived. . . . Freedom of movement across frontiers in either direction, and inside frontiers as well, was a part of our heritage. . . . It may be as close to the heart of the individual as the choice of what he eats, or wears, or reads." *Kent v. Dulles*, the first case to make a distinction between "the freedom of movement" and "the right to travel abroad," and to more importantly rule that the right to travel was a citizen's inalienable right, set limitations on the powers of the secretary of state. See Rockwell Kent v. John Foster Dulles, 357 U.S. 116, 126, 78 S.Ct. 1113, 2 L.Ed. 2d. 1204 (1958).

114. See William Worthy, Jr. v. Christian A. Herter, Secretary of State 270 F.2d 905, 106 App. D.C. 153 (D.C. Cir. 1959).

115. J. Russell Wiggins, the executive editor of *Washington Post* and *Times Herald*, in an open session of the Senate's Constitutional Rights Subcommittee requested that the Senate overrule the State Department's mandate on the news media's travel to China. On behalf of the American Society of Newspaper Editors, Wiggins asserted: "Members of the newspaper profession probably have differing views on the wisdom generally of increasing cultural exchanges with Red China, but they are nearly of one mind as possible on the dangers of closing any corner of the globe to reporters and on the general wisdom of forcing the American people to rely upon government sources, rumors and conjecture." See "Congress Gets Protest by Newsmen on Prohibition of Travel to Red China," *Hartford Courant*, March 30, 1957, 1A. Various people seconded Wiggins's view; this included journalist Roscoe Drummond and the Minnesota senator Hubert Humphrey. See Roscoe Drummond, "Ban on Red China Travel Harmful to U.S. Press," *Hartford Courant*, January 13, 1957, 3B; "Worthy to Be Witness," *Baltimore Afro-American*, February 12, 1957, 6.

116. Senator Thomas Carey Hennings Jr., the chairman of the Senate Judiciary Committee's subcommittee on constitutional rights, defended Worthy. "[The State Department's actions are] contrary to our nation's bests interests," Hennings argued. "The right to travel, not only within this country, but beyond its borders is one of the natural

rights of a free man or woman." The broadcast journalist Edward R. Murrow was of similar mind; he asserted that Worthy's appeal spoke to "the public's right to be informed." See "Worthy to Be Witness," 6; Barnouw, *The Image Empire*, 99.

117. See "What Afro Readers Say," *Washington Afro-American*, May 7, 1957, 4. The criticisms of Worthy came from both academics and journalists. After hearing Worthy speak, Knight Biggerstaff, chair of Cornell University's History Department and Department of Far Eastern Studies, slighted Worthy for his opposition to the government's political line. While he praised Worthy's analysis of Chinese politics, Biggerstaff felt that the newsman had become the ACLU's "guinea pig and accessory" and disparaged him for "bristling with the righteousness of his cause and reveling in his martyrdom." See "Report from R.A. Aylward about Worthy's Visit to Cornell University," April, 16, 1957, folder "William Worthy Trip 1957," decimal files 1954–1957 (container 22), Bureau of Far Eastern Affairs, Office of Chinese Affairs, Records of the Department of State, Record Group 59, NACP. Similarly, the journalist Holmes Alexander denounced Worthy's defense as "a whining complaint" that represented "the threadbare argument of racial discrimination" and "another masked attack by the Communist conspiracy upon our American system, this time upon the passport instrument." See Holmes Alexander, "On the Political Front," *Reading Eagle*, August 14, 1957, 10.

118. The *Militant* reporter George Lavan lamented, "The Big Business Press, which loves to contrast 'free' status with that of controlled papers in other countries, has docilely submitted to the State Department's ukase with only a few editorial mutterings. It is quite in keeping with the mentality of the lords of the press in this country." See "Pulitzer Prize for Worthy?," *Baltimore Afro-American*, January 22, 1957, 1, 4. Worthy was also critical of the dominant news media's failure to publically support his cause. He maintained that the American press had "forfeited its right to criticize the Communist press for being government controlled." But he remained very optimistic about the power of the press, arguing that it was up to the African American press to "restore the shattered damage of freedom of the press" and not "bow to the edict of the State Department." He concluded, "In this atmosphere of subdued McCarthyism, colored people have become the custodians of the things for which American democracy stands." See "Press Too Indifferent, Says Newsman," *Times Daily*, April 8, 1957, 2; Worthy, "Weekly Press Leads Fight for Freedom—Worthy Says," *Baltimore Afro-American*, March 26, 1957, 20; William Worthy, "'McCarthyism Was Rejected'—Worthy," *Washington Afro-American*, May 7, 1957, 1. Readers of black newspapers, however, remained avid in their support of Worthy's constitutional rights to free movement, travel, and reporting from abroad. See, for instance, "What AFRO Readers Say: Letter from Howard Harris," *Baltimore Afro-American*, February 23, 1957, 4; "What AFRO Readers Say: Letter from James Ford," *Baltimore Afro-American*, March 30, 1957, 4; and "What AFRO Readers Say: Letter from William Patterson," *Baltimore Afro-American*, March 26, 1957.

119. Kahn, "International Travel and the U.S. Constitution," 46. The confiscation of Americans' passports throughout the Cold War illuminates what Egidio Reale and Louis Jaffe have referred to as "the passport problem": the question of whether a passport is

primarily an identity card, statement of nationality, and right of travel obliged to all nationals or most chiefly an instrument of state control that reified the boundaries of the nation. The writer James Baldwin highlighted this point when he queried (regarding the seizure of W. E. B. Du Bois's passport): "One of the questions his situation raises is the question of just what a passport is: is it a privilege allowed the government for *some* citizens? . . . Or is it the right of *all* citizens?" Reale, "The Passport Question," 506–9; Jaffe, "The Right to Travel"; Baldwin and Stein, *Native Sons*, 103. Also see Krueger, "Passports in the Twenty-First Century"; Salter, "Passports, Mobility, and Security"; and Torpey, *The Invention of the Passport*.

120. "Larger Question," *Sarasota Herald-Tribune*, December 30, 1956, 4; "Congress Gets Protest By Newsmen on Prohibition of Travel to Red China," *Hartford Courant*, March 30, 1957, 1A.

121. William Worthy, "The Case of Cuba against Uncle Sam," *Baltimore Afro-American*, April 25, 1961, E4.

122. Fitzhugh S. M. Mullan, "Cuban Travel," *Harvard Crimson*, November 15, 1963, http://www.thecrimson.com, accessed March 11, 2011; "U.S. Is Accused of News Control," *New York Times*, October 12, 1962, 12.

123. Fair Play for Cuba Committee, "Cuba: A Declaration of Conscience by Afro-Americans," *Baltimore Afro-American*, April 29, 1961, 10.

124. "Bulletin," *Sumter Daily Item*, September 29, 1961, 5B.

125. Worthy, "The Red Chinese American Negro," 132.

126. Worthy, "Africa, Truth and the Right to Travel," 118.

127. Phil Ochs, "The Ballad of William Worthy," in *The Best of Broadside 1962–1988*; Langston Hughes, "No Regrets and No Fears," *Chicago Defender*, October 17, 1953, 11.

II. THE 1960S: THE EAST IS RED AND BLACK

1. Worthy, "The American Negro Is Dead," 126, 168. Worthy amended remarks made by Indonesian President Sukarno (Soekarno) in March 1933, who stated: "If the Banteng of Indonesia can work together with the Sphinx of Egypt, with the Nandi Ox of India, with the Dragon of China, with the champions of freedom of other countries—if the Indonesian Banteng is able to work together with all the enemies of international capitalism and imperialism throughout the world—ah, then the days of international imperialism will soon be numbered!" See Sukarno, "Ment'japai Indonesia Merdeka" (Achieving an Independent Indonesia) in *Dibawah Bendera Revolusi*, 296–97.

2. Kelley and Esch, "Black Like Mao," 8.

3. "China vs. Russia—Racial Exploitation?," *New York Amsterdam News*, August 31, 1963, 9.

4. Chen J., *Mao's China and the Cold War*, 5.

5. See Lüthi, *The Sino-Soviet Split*.

6. See Freeberne, "Racial Issues and the Sino-Soviet."

7. Quoted in "Peking Says Kennedy Uses Fascist Tactics on Negroes," *Sun*, August 13, 1963, 2.

8. Ralph McGill, "Chinese Agitators and Race Riots: Is Mao Stirring Unrest in U.S.?," *Boston Globe*, September 14, 1964, 10.

9. Freeberne, "Racial Issues and the Sino-Soviet," 411.

10. Law, *Chinese Foreign Aid*, 47–48; and in Bräutigam, *Chinese Aid and African Development*, 39.

11. See Mao Zedong, "Talks with African Friends." Even prior to Mao's August 1963 statement, race, anticolonialism, and Third World solidarity were significant features of Chinese foreign policy. In July 1960, China's government declared its support for Prime Minister Patrice Lumumba and the Congo's plight against Belgian neocolonialism and U.S. imperialism. After Lumumba's murder in January 1961 by a force made up of Congolese opposition, the CIA, and Belgian intelligence, the PRC government condemned the assassination and offered its support to the Congo, a now-divided nation where different parties claimed themselves as the country's rightful leaders. International support was also conveyed through activities in different countries. As a group of black Americans stormed the UN's general assembly to protest Lumumba's murder and Western encroachment on Congolese sovereignty and self-determination, 700,000 Chinese people converged in Beijing's Tiananmen Square to praise Lumumba's leadership. Another interesting fact is that prior to his killing, Lumumba had a camaraderie with the Xinhua News Agency reporter Wang Shu and Chen Jianking, China's ambassador to Egypt. After Lumumba's assassination, the playwright Li Huang was inspired by these friendships to author a drama in tribute to the Congolese liberation movement and to anticolonial African armed struggles. *Winter on the Equator* (*Chidao dongtian*), an opera written by Huang and Zhu Zhuyi (the latter was a playwright and director who had served in the Chinese navy alongside East African soldiers), was directed by Zheng Fenyi and performed in Shanghai by Chinese performers. The production was later renamed *War Drums on the Equator* (*Chidao zhuangu*). See *Sino-African Friendship: 50 Year Anniversary*, China Central Television, Fall 2007; X. Chen, "Remembering War and Revolution on the Maoist Stage," 132; and Li H., *War Drums on the Equator*.

12. Sauvy, "Trois mondes, une planète."

13. On the Third World project, see Prashad, *The Darker Nations*.

14. Mao, "Chairman Mao's Theory on the Differentiation of the Three Worlds Is a Major Contribution to Marxism-Leninism."

15. See Brady, *Making the Foreign Serve China*, 125.

16. Many people cite the commencement of the GPCR as beginning in November 1965 with a number of polemics orchestrated by Jiang Qing, Mao's wife, with the assistance of several Shanghai intellectuals, against *Hai Rui Dismissed from Office* (*Hai Rui ba guan*), a popular play written by Wu Han. At the crux of the critiques were allegations that the play was a subtle condemnation of Mao's leadership and evocation of his dismissal from office. The debates and criticisms generated by Jiang Qing's attack on Wu

Han were moreover used as a platform to publically question, denounce, and remove from office several senior party officials with whom Mao was struggling for control over the CCP. For more on the GPCR, see Clark, *The Cultural Revolution*; Esherick, Pickowicz, and Walder, *The Chinese Cultural Revolution as History*.

17. Liu Shaoqi died in 1969; his death was most likely brought on by the regular physical abuse he received at public denunciation meetings and by the government's denial of adequate medicine and medical attention for him. After allegedly attempting to lead a coup to oust Mao from power, Lin Biao was killed in a mysterious plane crash in Mongolia as he and his family attempted to flee China in 1971. Deng Xiaoping was more fortunate. He was purged to a rural factory in Jiangxi province, where he worked until his return to politics in 1974. After Mao's death in 1976, Deng went on to become China's supreme leader.

18. Jones's statement is from an untitled and unpublished draft report made to the Committee of Asian and Afro-Caribbean Organisations. The document is found among her papers, which are housed in the Schomburg Library in New York in The Claudia Jones Memorial Collection. See Ella Rule, "Claudia Jones, Communist," *Lalkar*, accessed June 2, 2013, www.lalkar.org/issues/contents/mar2010/claudia.html. Jones's visit to China is documented in Davies, *Left of Marx*, 126–27, 226–28. To see Jones's poem, "Thoughts on Visiting Yenan/Yenan: Cradle of Revolution," see Davies, *Claudia Jones*, 202–3.

3. SOUL BROTHERS AND SOUL SISTERS OF THE EAST

1. Williams's oceanic metaphor in "An Ocean's Roar of Peace" intersects with a stanza in one of Mao's letters. Mao wrote: "The Four Seas are rising, clouds and waters raging, the Five Continents are rocking, wind and thunder roaring. Our force is irresistible." Williams's poem also calls to mind the *xia hai* (jumping into the sea) fables of ancient Chinese poetry that celebrated sailors' courage at sea. In contemporary China, *xia hai* is now a colloquial term that denotes risking for great gain within markets and commerce. For Williams's poem, see *Crusader* 4, no. 2 (June–July 1962): 7. For Mao's letter, see Mao, "Reply to Comrade Kuo Mo-jo (Guo Moruo)." On xia hai, see C. Hsu, *Creating Market Socialism*, 18; and Yardely, *Brave Dragons*, 96.

2. Zuo Zhongling, "To Robert Williams," special edition, *Crusader* 6, no. 2 (October 1964): 10.

3. On Robert and Mabel Williams, see R. Cohen, *Black Crusader*; Mullen, *Afro-Orientalism*; Rodriguez, "'De la Esclavitud Yanqui a la Libertad Cubana'"; Rucker, "Crusader in Exile"; Stephens, "Narrating Acts of Resistance" and "'Praise the Lord and Pass the Ammunition'"; Tyson, *Radio Free Dixie*; Williams and Williams, *Robert and Mabel Williams Resource Guide*; and Williams, *Negroes with Guns*.

4. Mabel Williams, phone interview with the author, October 4, 2009.

5. Evans, "'Comrade Sisters,'" 65.

6. Achille Mbembe's description of African political cartoons similarly sums up how

the Williamses fashioned media aesthetics as instruments of political and cultural warfare. "The pictographic sign does not belong solely in the field of 'seeing'; it also falls in that of 'speaking,'" Mbembe explains. "It is in itself a figure of speech, and this speech expresses itself, not only for itself or as a mode of describing, narrating, and representing reality, but also as a particular strategy of persuasion, even violence." Mbembe, *On the Postcolony*, 142.

7. Commenting on Chinese propaganda posters' impact on U.S. black radicals, scholar Kathleen Cleaver, the former Black Panther Party communications secretary, makes a grand point: "Because China is so far away, we saw very few posters. What was influential was a style, a Chinese style that we absorbed from just a few posters. . . . There was a sense that Chinese art was reaching out to the African liberation movement and to the black liberation movement, at the same time that we were getting in touch with their art." Cushing and Tompkins, "Kathleen Cleaver Interview by Lincoln Cushing, August 2006," in *Chinese Posters*, 19.

8. Tyson, *Radio Free Dixie*, 79, 86.

9. On the Detroit Race Riot, see Capeci and Wilkerson, *Layered Violence*; Shogun and Craig, *The Detroit Race Riot*; and H. Thompson, *Whose Detroit?*

10. See Robert F. Williams's FBI Freedom of Information file; also see Tyson, "Robert F. Williams, 'Black Power' and the Roots of the African American Freedom Struggle," 549.

11. Wanda Sabir, "The Political Awakening of Mabel Williams, Wife of the Author of 'Negroes with Guns,'" *San Francisco Bayview*, March 17, 2004.

12. Sabir, "The Political Awakening of Mabel Williams, Wife of the Author of 'Negroes with Guns.'"

13. See Tyson, *Radio Free Dixie*, 102–36.

14. Williams, *Negroes with Guns*, 63.

15. See Dirks, "Between Threat and Reality"; Hill, *The Deacons for Defense*; Wendt, *The Spirit and the Shotgun*.

16. The NAACP took serious steps at discrediting Robert Williams and tarnishing his image. Besides framing Williams's advocacy of armed self-defense as an attempt by communist organizations to infiltrate the NAACP, the organization also turned to notable members such as Thurgood Marshall, Martin Luther King Jr., Jackie Robinson, and Daisy Bates to publically denounce Williams. See Tyson, *Radio Free Dixie*, 160–64; and "Robert F. Williams, 'Black Power' and the Roots of the African American Freedom Struggle," 557–59.

17. Historian Tim Tyson notes that early in Robert Williams's life, he displayed an interest for world affairs and sharing newspaper reports with community members. Tyson explains that as a child and young man, Williams was a "political interpreter of the world," particularly among Monroe's railroad men. Years later as an adult, Williams was informed by the Marine Corps that he "showed an aptitude for information services" after he completed a series of aptitude tests. Alongside Williams's knack for poetry, these early indications of a passion and propensity for journalism and media

suggest that the Williamses' pursuit of truth through news coverage and propaganda was not by happenstance. See Tyson, *Radio Free Dixie*, 25, 72.

18. "The Fourth Estate: Sambo Journalism," *Crusader* 8, no. 2 (January 1967): 1–3; *Crusader* 1, no. 9 (August 22, 1959).

19. Mabel Williams, phone interview with the author, October 4, 2009.

20. Williams, "Testimony of Robert F. Williams," 9.

21. Williams, *Negroes with Guns*, 72.

22. "What Is the American Radical?," *Crusader* 1, no. 2 (July 4, 1959): 2.

23. *Crusader* 1, no. 38 (March 19, 1960): 1; *Crusader* 1, no. 28 (January 9, 1960): 1.

24. See Cubillas, "Robert Williams."

25. "Cuba: Fidel & the U.S. Negro," *Time*, June 6, 1960.

26. Westad, *The Global Cold War*, 171.

27. See Brock and Fuertes, *Between Race and Empire*; Guridy, *Forging Diaspora*; Plummer, "Castro in Harlem"; and Cynthia Young, *Soul Power*.

28. See Louis, Rust, and Rust, *Joe Louis*.

29. "NAACP Leader in Cuba to Learn What U.S. Fears," *Fair Play*, July 8, 1960, 4.

30. Tyson, *Radio Free Dixie*, 225.

31. *Crusader* 1, no. 51 (June 18, 1960).

32. The group included Julian Mayfield, Sarah Wright, John Henrik Clarke, LeRoi Jones (Amiri Baraka), Dr. Ana Codero, Ed Clark, and Harold Cruse, among others. They traveled to Cuba to participate in the anniversary celebration of the 26th of July Movement, which honored the 1953 revolt in the Oriente province, where more than a hundred Cubans captured the Moncada Barracks in Santiago de Cuba, distributed arms to the Cuban population, and launched a national revolt that overthrew the military dictatorship of Fulgencio Batista. See Rodriguez, "'De la Esclavitud Yanqui a la Libertad Cubana,'" 65; and Woodard, *A Nation within a Nation*, 52.

33. "100 Attend Meeting Despite Cancellation of Church Hall," *Michigan Fair Play Newsletter* 1, no. 1 (March 1961): 1, Robert F. Williams Papers, Bentley Historical Library, University of Michigan, Ann Arbor (hereafter RWP), box 9, folder "FBI Files 1955–1972."

34. Cubillas, "Robert Williams," 74. In a UN Security Council debate over the Bay of Pigs attack, Cuba's foreign minister, Raul Roa, referenced a statement made by Robert Williams, where the latter comically suggested that if the American government was so interested in "liberating" colonized peoples, it should also send troops, mercenaries, and weapons to liberate black Southerners from the racial tyranny of white-supremacist militia groups such as the Ku Klux Klan. See Roa, "Speech to the Security Council, April 18, 1961," 220.

35. The Freedom Riders were civil rights activists who traveled on interstate buses throughout Southern states to challenge the federal government and Southern states' failure to enforce interstate laws outlawing segregation on interstate buses as well as in the restaurants and restrooms of interstate bus terminals. See Arsenault, *Freedom Riders*.

36. See Tyson, *Radio Free Dixie*, 272–81.

37. Williams, *Negroes with Guns*, 104.

38. A Michigan contingent of students and activists visited the Williamses in Cuba in 1963. Among them were General Baker, Luke Tripp, Charles Simmons, Charles Johnson, and John Watson, a group who went on to establish two important Black Power Movement organizations: UHURU and the League of Revolutionary Workers. In the same year the Williamses were also visited by Max Stanford (Muhammad Ahmad), a revolutionary nationalist who established the Revolutionary Action Movement with Robert Williams as the organization's premier-in-exile. See Mullen, *Afro-Orientalism*, 81–82, 85–86; Ahmad, *We Will Return in the Whirlwind*, 95–166, 237–86.

39. *Crusader* 1, no. 4 (December 23, 1961).

40. Mabel Williams, phone interview with the author, October 4, 2009.

41. In Canada, Anne and Vernel Olsen, two members of Fair Play for Cuba, ran and facilitated the North American distribution arm of the Williamses' propaganda. Each month the Williamses mailed the Olsens bulk issues of the *Crusader* and recordings of *Radio Free Dixie*. The Olsens then mass-duplicated the newsletters and recordings and snuck these articles into the United States from Toronto, Vancouver, and Montreal. For more on the Olsens, see Tyson, *Radio Free Dixie*, 284, 288, 290; and Wright and Wylie, *Our Place in the Sun*, 10.

42. Mabel Williams, phone interview with the author, October 4, 2009.

43. *Crusader* 4, no. 2 (August 1962): 1; *Crusader* 10, no. 2 (Summer 1969): 1.

44. Mabel Williams, phone interview with author, October 4, 2009.

45. *Crusader* 4, no. 2 (August 1962): 4; Sandra Dickson and Churchill Roberts's documentary *Negroes with Guns: Rob Williams and Black Power* (2004).

46. Williams, *Listen, Brother!*, 14.

47. "Letter from Robert Williams," RWP, box 1, folder "Undated Correspondence, 1959–1967."

48. "Undated Letter from Robert and Mabel Williams," RWP, box 1, folder "Undated Correspondence, 1959–1967"; *Crusader* 1, no. 15 (October 3, 1959).

49. Mao, "Problems of War and Strategy (November 6, 1938)."

50. Sidney Rittenberg recounts being called in by Mao to polish the English of Mao's original statement in support of African American struggle. Rittenberg states that he and the U.S. expatriate Frank Coe were privately brought into Mao's chambers at the state council meeting place to "go over the English text of the letter" and offer their "opinion of the contents." The major change that the two men recommended was the "addition of American Indians to the list Mao had offered of American ethnic groups struggling for equality." Rittenberg later confirmed his participation in the speech's completion during an interview with me. See Rittenberg and Bennett, *The Man Who Stayed Behind*, 268–71; Sidney Rittenberg, phone interview with the author, August 15, 2013.

51. Mao, *Statement Supporting the Afro-American People in Their Just Struggle against Racial Discrimination by U.S. Imperialism.*

52. Allan L. Otten, "Mao's Bark and Bite: U.S. Analysts Discount China Threat to Peace Despite Rising Militancy," *Wall Street Journal*, September 17, 1963, 1.

53. Mao, "On New Democracy (January 1940)"; Mao, *Talks at the Yan'an Forum on Literature and Art*, May 1942.

54. On *xuanchuan hua*, see Andrews, *Painters and Politics in the People's Republic of China, 1949–1979*; Chiu and Zheng, *Art and China's Revolution*; Cushing and Tompkins, *Chinese Posters*; Evans and Donald, *Picturing Power in the People's Republic of China*; Landsberger, *Chinese Propaganda Posters*; and Landsberger and van der Heijden, *Chinese Posters*. The Chinese government's growing investment in the aesthetics of socialist-realist art, however, hindered many Chinese artists' talents, creative output, and political views. Pictorial art that did not correspond with the CCP's mandate was deemed as bourgeois and obstructing national development. Artistic styles and techniques that did not suit the party's mission and standard were consequently eradicated, with the CCP instituting controls on the kinds of works artists could produce. For more, see Andrews, *Painters and Politics in the People's Republic of China, 1949–1979*.

55. See Cushing and Tompkins, *Chinese Posters*, 10.

56. The Western expatriates attending the rally included Anna Louise Strong, Sidney Rittenberg, Frank Coe, Talitha Gerlach, Dr. George Hatem, Bertha Hinton, and Dorise Nielsen. Coe, a former American government official who fled the United States after being blacklisted as an alleged communist and Soviet spy, spoke at the rally. He connected the growing militancy of the Civil Rights Movement to the radical energy of the Chinese Communist Revolution: "The American Negroes were naturally stirred when 650 million Chinese people won their freedom." The Marxist-Leninist journalist Anna Louise Strong's comments at the rally were later aired on the radio. She encouraged black Americans to look to China as "an example that shows that racial discrimination and inequality can be abolished." But she added that like the Chinese, the Civil Rights Movement needed to articulate an explicitly anticapitalist stance. "The experience of the Chinese people," she argued, "suggests that the American Negro will not gain full benefits under the present social system in America." See "Frank Coe Speech to Beijing Rally in Support of Afro-American Struggle, August 12, 1963," ALS-Works-Mss26-1-481, Anna Louise Strong Papers, National Library, Beijing, China (hereafter ALSP); "Anna Louise Strong on the American Negroes' Struggle—August 19, 1963," ALS-Works-Mss26-1-481, ALSP.

57. "Cable from Robert and Mabel Williams," box 1, folder "Undated Correspondence, 1959–1967," RWP.

58. Stanley Karnow, "Red China Lauds Rioting Negroes as Good Students of Mao's Thought," *Washington Post*, August 9, 1967, A21.

59. Tad Szulc, "Expatriate, on Cuban Radio, Calls on U.S. Negroes to Meet Violence with Violence," *New York Times*, July 28, 1964, 13; also see "American Negro Backed," *New York Times*, August 13, 1963, 21; "China's Red Leader Hits U.S. Bias," *New York Amsterdam News*, August 17, 1963, 42; "Mao 'Backs' Negroes," *Hartford Courant*, August 9, 1963, 1; "Mao Text," *Christian Science Monitor*, August 15, 1963, 16; "Red China Offers U.S. Negroes Its Support," *Chicago Daily Defender*, August 12, 1963, 13; Tad Szulc, "Antiwhite Drive by Peking Is Seen: Chinese Blow at U.S. Held Move to Gain Worldwide Support of Colored," *New York Times*, August 13, 1963, 1, 21.

60. Peter Kumpa, "Peking Applauds Violence, Encourages U.S. Negroes," *Baltimore*

Sun, April 7, 1968, 3; Jack Anderson, "Red China's Plot against the U.S.," *Boston Globe*, October 20, 1963, D14.

61. See William Worthy, "The Red Chinese American Negro," 174.

62. M. S. Handler, "Peking Rebuffed on Right's March: Wilkins Replies to Cable by Defending U.S. Policies," *New York Times*, August 23, 1963, 12.

63. "China vs. Russia Racial Exploitation?," *New York Amsterdam News*, August 31, 1963, 9.

64. Worthy, "The Red Chinese American Negro," 173–74.

65. Joel A. Rogers, "History Shows," *Pittsburgh Courier*, August 10, 1963, 11. William Worthy seconded Rogers's view, agreeing that China's outreach was a tactical maneuver aimed at gaining "propaganda ascendency over Moscow" and articulating "effective support for anti-colonial movements." See Worthy, "The Red Chinese American Negro," 132.

66. See Robert F. Williams's FBI Freedom of Information file; "U.S. Government Memorandum to FBI Director, November 4, 1963," in Robert F. Williams' Federal Bureau of Investigation file obtained through the Freedom of Information Act (hereafter Williams FBI file FOIA); and "U.S. Negro Leader Arrives in Peking," *New China New Agency*, September 25, 1963.

67. "China: America's Shades of Waterloo," *Crusader* 6, no. 3 (March 1965): 5–7; and "China: New Hope of Oppressed Humanity," *Crusader* 5, no. 2 (February 1964): 6–7.

68. Special edition, *Crusader* 6, no. 2 (October 1964).

69. "China," *Crusader* 5, no. 3 (March–April 1964): 8.

70. "Letter from Fu Jhu Tih, Undated," RWP, box 7, folder "Correspondence (in Chinese) 1963–1967" (note: Fu Jhu Tih is the Wade-Giles spelling of the man's name; Fu Ru Tie is the spelling in Pinyin); "To Our Friends, the American Negro: Children in Care of American Negro Leader, Robert F. Williams," *Crusader* 5, no. 3 (March–April 1964): 6.

71. "The East Is Red: 650 Million Soul Brothers Cable Support," *Crusader* 6, no. 1 (July–August 1964): 5.

72. "A Herd of Sheep Led by Wolves," *Crusader* 6, no. 4 (April–May 1965): 1–2.

73. *Crusader* 5, no. 2 (February 1964): 1.

74. Nadel, *Containment Culture*, 14; also see Chaloupka, *Knowing Nukes*.

75. "FBI Files—Section 8, 1967: Radio Free Dixie Transcript, August 21, 1965," RWP, box 9.

76. "Chapter 13: Neither a Capitalist nor a Socialist Uncle Tom," 455–56, RWP, box 12, folder "Personal Memoir Manuscript."

77. In *Long Live the Victory of the People's War!* (1965), Lin Biao states: "Taking the entire globe, if North America and Western Europe can be called 'the cities of the world,' then Asia, Africa and Latin America constitute the 'rural areas of the world.'" Lin, "Long Live the Victory of the People's War," 24.

78. "Robert Williams in China 1964, Reels 1, 2, & 3," RWP, box 14, folder "Videocassettes."

79. Hollander, *Political Pilgrims*, 377.

80. A 1959 issue of the *Crusader* included an editorial, written as if it were a letter to the

Soviet Premier Nikita Khrushchev after the announcement of Khrushchev's impending visit to the United States. The letter advised radicals worldwide that the American government's invitation to Khrushchev demonstrated the restructuring of American and Soviet foreign policy and the Soviet's growing conciliatory attitude toward U.S. capitalism. "You know before you got the bomb, you were no more than dirt under their feet," the Williamses remarked about the Soviet regime. "Mr. K [Khrushchev], it seems that H-bombs really create bridges of acceptance between people. Maybe if you could loan the poor downtrodden American Negroes a few, he too would be dined and invited to the stately mansion of a racist governor like Luther Hodges of North Carolina." The Williamses' criticisms of Soviet attempts to induce peaceful coexistence with the United States were echoed in 1964 when Robert championed China's successful testing of its first nuclear weapon. He argued that China's ability to develop its own nuclear capability, most especially after the desertion of Soviet technicians, represented the development of "a people's bomb, a freedom bomb of the oppressed." Robert Williams explained, "It is also the Afro-American's bomb, because the Chinese people are blood brothers to the Afro-American and all those who fight against racism and imperialism." See "An Open Letter to Mr. 'K,'" *Crusader* 1, no. 8 (August 15, 1959): 1; "Speech: Delivered at the International Conference for Solidarity with the People of Vietnam against U.S. Imperialist Aggression for the Defense of Peace," Hanoi, Democratic Republic of Vietnam, November 25–29, 1964, *Crusader* 6, no. 3 (March 1965): 5; "Hallelujah: The Meek Shall Inherit the Earth," special edition, *Crusader* 6, no. 2 (October 1964): 8–9.

81. "Chapter 13: Neither a Capitalist nor a Socialist Uncle Tom," 445–46, 450, RWP, box 12, folder "Personal Memoir Manuscript."

82. The Williamses found such racial underrepresentation to be the case even in their place of employment. "I went into Radio Havana," Robert asserted. "It looked like Mississippi. They asked me what did I mean when I said it looked like Mississippi, and I told them because all the faces in the station were white." See Williams, "Testimony of Robert F. Williams," 4. On issues of race in Cuba, see Helg, *Our Rightful Share*; and Sawyer, *Racial Politics in Post-revolutionary Cuba*.

83. Williams, "Testimony of Robert F. Williams," 92.

84. This kind of thinking, along with other factors, led the government to abolish Afro-Cuban organizations and social clubs and oppose Afro-Cuban religious and cultural practices such as Santería, Palo Mayombe, and Abakuà. From Afro-Cuban musicians, the Williamses learned that *plantes*, the Abakuà's musical and spiritual ceremonies, had been banned and that some musicians were barred from playing jazz, rhythm and blues, and gospel music in public venues. These acts by Castro were part of a larger wave of state policies, where the Cuban government closed many of venues and cabaret entertainment spaces where popular music was played and enjoyed. See C. Moore, *Castro, the Blacks and Africa*, 121, 265, and *Pichón*, 221; and Carlos Moore, phone interview with the author, March 20, 2009. On the role of music and culture in the decades after the Cuban Revolution and Castro's policies regarding music's role in cultivating a so-

cialist Cuban society, see Acosta, *Cubano Be, Cubano Bop*; R. Moore, *Music and Revolution*; and Orovio, *Cuban Music from A to Z*.

85. Mabel Williams, phone interview with the author, October 4, 2009.

86. "Letter to Reggie L.," RWP, box 1, folder "Undated Correspondence, 1959–1967." In another isolated incident, Robert Williams felt the brunt of the Cuban government's antiblack disposition. In November 1962, a black-nationalist organization, the Provisional Government of the African-American Captive Nation (PGAACN), asked Williams to become the group's prime minister from exile. With members in Los Angeles, New York, New Jersey, and Philadelphia, PGAACN intended to run black candidates for local offices and to establish an independent African American republic in thirteen southeastern states. Williams initially accepted the position, but was later persuaded by the Cuban authorities to resign. The Cubans' position was that PGAACN's political outlook did not sit well with Cuba's model of revolution. Williams divulged, "The Cuban party called me in and . . . asked me not to participate in that because they had a big black population in Oriente and if they came out in support of this and if they showed interest, then the black people in the Oriente province may want to do the same thing." Months later, he secretly accepted leadership of another U.S.-based black revolutionary organization, the Revolutionary Action Movement. This time he kept the news of his new position to himself. He explained, "Such incidents convinced me that, if black Americans were ever to turn to revolutionary violence, we would have to do it on our own. . . . We don't have to beg Cuba or any other country for token handouts." See "Chapter 13: Neither a Capitalist nor a Socialist Uncle Tom, pg. 457," RWP, box 12, folder "Personal Memoir Manuscript." On Robert Williams's exchanges with PGAACN and the Revolutionary Action Movement, see Ahmad, *We Will Return in the Whirlwind*; Williams, "Testimony of Robert F. Williams," 45–48; and "Ofuntola Oserjeman Khing-Adefunmi (President of PGAACN) & Gisenga Latunji (Serje Khing) Letter to Robert Williams, November 25, 1962, (Exhibit 37A)," in Williams, "Testimony of Robert F. Williams," 77.

87. One such lie alleged that the Williams family's exile in Cuba was prompted by Robert Williams's attempt to evade a rape charge. See Williams, "Testimony of Robert F. Williams," 45; R. Cohen, *Black Crusader*, 222.

88. An example of such obstruction is the Tricontinental Conference of January 1966. Convened in Havana, the conference was organized by the Organization for Solidarity for the People of Africa and Asia, and brought delegates from African, Asian, and Latin American nations. Robert Williams was identified by several of the conference attendees, particularly members of African delegations, as a voice they hoped to hear from over the course of the conference. But the conference organizers provided the Williams family with little-to-no information regarding the conference. Robert Williams was allowed entry only after several delegates asked of his whereabouts. Inside the conference, an African delegate privately informed Robert Williams that Williams' mistreatment was a result of his pro-China outlook: "If you weren't so friendly with the Chinese, you wouldn't be having so many problems." See "Chapter 13: Neither a Capitalist nor a Socialist Uncle Tom, pg. 462," RWP, box 12, folder "Personal Memoir Manuscript."

89. "Letter to Unknown Person," RWP, box 1, folder "Undated Correspondence, 1959–1967."

90. The main factors pointing to Cuban involvement was that the bogus issues carried a postmark available only in the Cuban government's bulk mailings. Robert Williams also pointed out that the cover displayed the *Crusader's* old imprint and subheading, which suggested to him that those individuals involved had knowledge of the newsletter's past format and had used images from past issues to forge the counterfeit edition. While Williams' suspicions seem plausible, CIA involvement also seems highly possible. See "Crusader Forged: Counterfeiters Strike Again," *Crusader* 8, no. 4 (May 1967); and "Letter from Anna Olson, February 6, 1966," RWP, box 1, folder "Correspondence, February–April 1966."

91. "COUNTERFEIT: *The Crusader* 8, No. 2 (Special Edition October 1965)," RWP, box 5, folder "The Crusader July 1963–1969"; and "COUNTERFEIT: *Crusader* 8, No. 4 (April–May 1966), RWP, box 5, folder "The Crusader July 1963–1969."

92. "Letter from Robert Williams, February 7, 1966," RWP, box 1, folder "Correspondence, February–April 1966."

93. In the letter to Castro, Robert Williams alleged that several Cubans had impeded and sabotaged the Williams family's efforts to produce and distribute propaganda. Williams identified political leaders such as Major Manuel Piñeiro Losada, the chief of intelligence; Captain Osmány Ciendfuegos Gorriarán, secretary-general of the Tricontinental Conference; Captain Emilio Aragonés, personal aide to Fidel Castro; and Major René Vallejo, Castro's personal physician and confidant. Robert Williams also charged that several of these Cuban officials had prevented his wife from traveling to Canada to attend to the Williamses' business affairs. "Letter to Fidel Castro, August 28, 1966," RWP, box 1, "Correspondence, July–August 1966"; C. Moore, *Castro, the Blacks and Africa*, 265.

94. "Letter to Unknown Person," RWP, box 1, folder "Undated Correspondence, 1959–1967."

95. "Letter from Richard Gibson, February 1, 1966," RWP, box 1, folder "Correspondence, February–April 1966."

96. See "Letter to Frank, March 17, 1966," RWP, box 1, folder "Correspondence, May–June 1966."

97. "Chapter 13: Neither a Capitalist nor a Socialist Uncle Tom," 459, RWP, box 12, folder "Personal Memoir Manuscript."

98. This is discussed in "Letter from Robert Williams, March 27, 1966," RWP, box 1, folder "Correspondence, February–April 1966."

99. For more on Shen Jian, see "The Spy Who Helped the Chinese Communist Party Conquer China," *Epoch Times*, November 27, 2011, www.theepochtimes.com, accessed February 10, 2012.

100. "Chapter 13: Neither a Capitalist nor a Socialist Uncle Tom," 459, 467, RWP, box 12, folder "Personal Memoir Manuscript."

101. "Undated letter," RWP, box 1, folder "Undated Correspondence, 1959–1967."

102. The Williamses' sons, Bobby and John, were already in China at the point of their

parents' travel there in July 1966. In September 1964, the couple sent the two boys to Beijing to continue their academic studies. "Letter to Ricky, January 14, 1966," RWP, box 1, folder "Correspondence: Undated and January 1966."

103. Williams, "Testimony of Robert F. Williams," 115.

104. George Roberts, "Castro Arming Southern Negroes," *National Police Gazette*, July 1965; Robert C. Baker, "Letter to the Editor: Origin of Those Race Riots," *Chicago Defender*, August 12, 1967; "China vs. Russia Racial Exploitation?," *New York Amsterdam News*, August 31, 1963; "China: The Black Expatriate," *Newsweek*, April 22, 1968.

105. "Civil Rights Division 1955–1970," RWP, box 9, folder "FBI Files."

106. See Strong and Keyssar, *Right in Her Soul*; and Rittenberg and Bennett, *The Man Who Stayed Behind*.

107. See Westad, *The Global Cold War*, 180–90.

108. Regarding "Hanoi Hannah," see Alter, *Vietnam Protest Theatre*, 34; Philip Shenon, "Ho Chi Minh City Journal: Hanoi Hannah Looks Back, with Few Regrets," *New York Times*, November 26, 1994; Tom Tiede, "'Hanoi Hannah' Talks to GIs," *Playground Daily News*, January 6, 1966, 5.

109. "Hanoi Domestic Service in English, Recorded Talk by Robert F. Williams," October 12, 1965, Sound Recording no. 263-FB-43, Records of the Central Intelligence Agency, Record Group 263, (NACP). Robert Williams was not the only black expatriate in China to record such messages aimed at black troops stationed in Vietnam. Now residing in Beijing, Clarence Adams, the former Korean War prisoner and nonrepatriate, broadcast similar statements on Hanoi Hannah. See "Hanoi Domestic Service in English, Recorded Talk by Clarence Adams," July 30, 1965, Sound Recording no. 263-BV-1559, Records of the Central Intelligence Agency, Record Group 263, NACP; and "Hanoi Domestic Service in English, Recorded Talk by Clarence Adams," October 5, 1965, Sound Recording no. 263-BV-1546–1547, Records of the Central Intelligence Agency, Record Group 263, NACP.

110. See "Chapter 13: Neither a Capitalist nor a Socialist Uncle Tom," 445–448, RWP, box 12, folder "Personal Memoir Manuscript." Also see Rittenberg, *The Man Who Stayed Behind*, 282–84; and Strong and Keyssar, *Right in Her Soul*, 322–24. On Ho Chi Minh's travels, see Quinn-Judge, *Ho Chi Minh*.

111. Williams, *Listen, Brother!*, 7, 10–11, 26.

112. Williams, *Listen, Brother!*, 8–10.

113. Kuumba, *Gender and Social Movements*, 19.

114. Evans, "'Comrade Sisters,'" 68.

115. See Tyson, *Radio Free Dixie*, 189–90.

116. See Lumsden, "Good Mothers with Guns," 907.

117. See Davin, "Gendered Mao," 204.

118. To discern how male-dominant narratives functioned in Chinese propaganda art, see Andrews, *Painters and Politics in the People's Republic of China*; and Evans, "'Comrade Sisters.'" The visual politics of postwar black-radical media and art, black nationalists, and American popular culture also relied on hypermasculine images of black

resistance. See, for instance, Courtright, "Rhetoric of the Gun"; Doss, "Imaging the Panthers" and "Revolutionary Art Is a Tool of Liberation"; Hughey, "Black Aesthetics and Panther Rhetoric"; Josephs, "Whose Revolution Is This?"; and Wendt, *The Spirit and the Shotgun*, and "'They Found Out That We Really Are Men.'"

119. Williams, *Listen, Brother!*, 37–39.

120. "Section 14 Serials 315–379, 1969–1970," RWP, box 9, folder "FBI Civil Rights Division 1955–1970."

121. "Support Bro. Rob!," *Black Student Voice* 1, no. 3, no date.

122. Worthy, "The Red Chinese American Negro," 175.

123. Eddie Ellis, "Violence the Same in Vietnam or in Dixie," *Chicago Defender*, March 5, 1966, 7.

124. *Crusader* 8, no. 4 (May 1967): 1.

4. MAOISM AND THE SINIFICATION OF BLACK POLITICAL STRUGGLE

1. "Red Star over China: A Discussion by Vicki Garvin—January 11, 1972," 1–3, Vicki Garvin Papers, Schomburg Center for Research in Black Culture, New York Public Library, New York (hereafter VGP) box 1, folder "Vicki Garvin Writings and Speeches on China 1970s–1980s."

2. For more on Garvin's activism during the 1940s and 1950s, see Biondi, *To Stand and Fight*; Campbell, *Middle Passages*; and Gore, "From Communist Politics to Black Power," and *Radicalism at the Crossroads*. Garvin also receives some attention in Gaines, *American Africans in Ghana*; and Joseph, *Waiting 'til the Midnight Hour*.

3. "Talk at Chicago State, May 1979," 1–2, VGP, box 2, folder "Writings and Speeches on China."

4. "Unnamed," 4, VGP, box 2, folder "Vicki Garvin Original Drafts/Notes."

5. For a historicization of the African American expatriate community in Ghana, see Gaines, *American Africans in Ghana*.

6. It is fitting that Huang Hua was the person to introduce Garvin to educating Chinese people in English and English-language instruction. A former translator and interpreter, Huang had risen in China's political ranks as a result of his strong proficiency in English and his attentiveness to diplomacy. He went from serving as an interpreter for the American journalist Edgar Snow and translating Snow's notes into Chinese (actions that helped produce Snow's well-known book *Red Star over China* [1937]) to participating in the Korean War armistice talks in 1953, the Geneva Conference in 1954, and preliminary exchanges between U.S. and Chinese delegations in Warsaw in 1959. Huang later became China's ambassador to Ghana, Egypt, and Canada, and he played a pivotal role in restoring China's diplomatic relations with the United States as China's first permanent representative to the United Nations and as a part of the five-man Chinese body that, with the former U.S. secretary of state and national security advisor Henry Kissinger, arranged Nixon's historic 1972 summit with Zhou Enlai and Mao Zedong. See David Barboza, "Huang Hua, 97, a Diplomat Who Served China, Dies," *New York*

Times, November 24, 2010; and Martin Childs, "Huang Hua: Politician and Diplomat Who Played a Leading Role in Bringing China out of International Isolation," *Independent* (United Kingdom), *December 7*, 2010.

7. "Speech, unknown date," VGP, box 1, folder "Vicki Garvin Writings and Speeches on China 1970s–1980s."

8. "Red Star over China," VGP.

9. "Vickie Garvin: Candidate at Large, National Steering Committee," VGP, box 1, folder "U.S.-China Friendship Association."

10. See Idun-Arkhurst, *Ghana's Relations with China*; Larkin, *China and Africa, 1949–1970*; Rotberg, *China into Africa*; and Taylor, *China and Africa*.

11. Vicki Garvin, interview with Lincoln Bergman, disc 3 (undated), Oak Park, IL, Freedom Archives Collection, San Francisco.

12. "Unnamed," 3, VGP, box 2, folder "Vicki Garvin Original Drafts/Notes."

13. "Red Star over China," 2, VGP.

14. "Unnamed," 3, VGP, box 2, folder "Vicki Garvin Original Drafts/Notes."

15. See Brady, *Making the Foreign Serve China*, 91, 133.

16. See "History at a Glance," Shanghai International Studies University, accessed March 10, 2012, http://en.shisu.edu.cn/enabout/2011/2011,enabout,000664.shtml.

17. Hayhoe, *China's Universities 1985–1995*, 83, 77, 79, 90. The most dominant symbol of this inequality in education was the establishment of a national examination system, the idea being that a competitive assessment would produce a workforce of specialists capable of modernizing China to the standards of Western societies. These exams, however, reinforced the privileges of well-to-do urban youths with more previous educational background and professional access than that of rural poor populations. Some Chinese intellectuals criticized this inequality and the PRC's full-scale adoption of Soviet educational methods.

18. Hayhoe, *China's Universities 1985–1995*, 98–99.

19. Brady, *Making the Foreign Serve China*, 131.

20. See Mao, "Red and Expert (January 31, 1958)."

21. See Cook, *Mao's Little Red Book*, and "Third World Maoism."

22. Leese, *Mao Cult*, 23, 87.

23. Mao quoted in Knight, *Rethinking Mao*, 209. Rebecca Karl, on the other hand, points out the shortcoming of simplifying Mao Zedong Thought as the "'sinification' of Marxism, or the making of Marxism Chinese." She explains, "This formulation is inadequate, however, as it takes Marxism as a unified dogma and considers Chinese as a settled cultural predisposition. Marxism was (and continues to be) a much-contested matter, and, in the 1930s, 'Chinese' was the subject of intense struggle." Karl, *Mao Zedong and China in the 20th Century*, 53.

24. Karl, *Mao Zedong and China in the 20th Century*, 53. Also see Apter and Saich, *Revolutionary Discourse in Mao's Republic*; and Wylie, *The Emergence of Maoism*.

25. Mao, "On Contradiction (August 1937)," 332.

26. Meisner, *Mao Zedong*, 86.

27. Mao, "On the Correct Handling of Contradictions among the People (February 27, 1957)"; also quoted in Schram, *The Thought of Mao Tse-Tung*, 151–52.

28. Leese, *Mao Cult*, 122.

29. Meisner, *Mao Zedong*, 149.

30. "Summary of Teaching Experiences in the PRC, July 18, 1966," 1–2, VGP, box 1, folder "Lesson Plans China."

31. "Summary of Teaching Experiences in the PRC, July 18, 1966," VGP.

32. Leese, *Mao Cult*, 99–120.

33. "Summary of Teaching Experiences in the PRC, July 18, 1966," VGP

34. Mao, "The Orientation of the Youth Movement (May 4, 1939)," 246.

35. "Speech/Note to Students September 1964," VGP, box 1, folder "Vicki Garvin Speeches in China."

36. See T. Chen, "Use the Past to Serve the Present," 208.

37. Mao, "In Memory of Norman Bethune (December 21, 1939)."

38. "Speech/Notes to Students, September 1964," VGP,

39. "Summary of Teaching Experience in the PRC, July 18, 1966," 3, VGP.

40. Several scholars have noted that "Serve the People," "The Foolish Old Man Who Removed Mountains," and "In Memory of Norman Bethune," were three of the most widely read and cited articles by Mao. This trilogy of essays, commonly referred to as the "three old articles" (*lao san pian*), were frequently referred to in Chinese classrooms. See Cheng Y., *Creating the New Man*, 62–63; Cleverley, *In the Lap of Tigers*, 99; and Shapiro, *Mao's War Against Nature*, 102.

41. "Summary of Teaching Experience in the PRC, July 18, 1966," 3, VGP.

42. "Speech of Vicki Garvin, April 1968," 2, VGP, box 1, folder "Vicki Garvin Speeches in China."

43. Leese, *Mao Cult*, 100–101.

44. Han, *The Unknown Cultural Revolution*, 30–31.

45. "Red Star over China," 5, VGP.

46. "Summary of Teaching Experience in the PRC, July 18, 1966," 17, VGP.

47. Garvin, interview with Bergman, disc 3.

48. Mao, "On the Correct Handling of Contradictions among the People (February 27, 1957)."

49. "The Negro Liberation Movement and the 1964 Election," 10, VGP, box 1, folder "Lesson Plans China."

50. "The Struggle between Two Lines among Afro-Americans," 5, VGP, box 1, folder "Lesson Plans China."

51. "Struggle between Two Lines within Abolitionist United Front," 2, 4, VGP, box 1, folder "Lesson Plans China."

52. "The Negro Liberation Movement and the 1964 Election," 8, 13, VGP.

53. "Speech of Vicki Garvin, April 1968," 2–3, VGP.

54. "The Negro Liberation Movement," 5, VGP, box 1, folder "Lesson Plans China";

Vicki Garvin, "Comparisons of Position of Martin L. King and Robert Williams (as of 1964)," 2, VGP, box 1, folder "Lesson Plans China."

55. "Speech of Vicki Garvin, April 1968," 2–3, VGP.

56. "The Negro Liberation Movement," 1, VGP.

57. "Speech of Vicki Garvin, April 1968," 2, VGP.

58. "The Struggle between Two Lines among Afro-Americans," 6, VGP.

59. "Summary of Teaching Experience in the PRC, July 18, 1966," 6, 10, VGP.

60. Garvin, interview with Bergman, disc 3.

61. "Summary of Teaching Experience in the PRC, July 18, 1966," 5, VGP.

62. Women of China Speech," 2, VGP, box 1, Folder "U.S. China Friendship Association."

63. Hayhoe, China's Universities 1985–1995, 88–89.

64. "Women of China Speech," 7, 3, VGP.

65. See Davin, "Gendered Mao," 204–11.

66. "International Women's Day," 7, 1, VGP, box 1, folder "Lesson Plans China."

67. "Summary of Teaching Experience in the PRC, July 18, 1966," 5, VGP.

68. Garvin, interview with Bergman, disc 3; some students' essays and paper outlines can be found in folder "Papers on U.S. Black History," VGP, box 2.

69. "Comments at Students Lecture, May 1965," 3, VGP, box 2, folder "Papers on U.S. Black History."

70. "Racial Discrimination in the United States Lecture, May 1965," 1, 4, VGP, box 2, folder "Papers on U.S. Black History."

71. "Summary of Teaching Experience in the PRC, July 18, 1966," 1–2, 17, VGP.

72. Kwong, Cultural Revolution in China's School, May 1966–April 1969, 14.

73. Hayhoe, China's Universities 1985–1995, 100.

74. Garvin, interview with Bergman, disc 3.

75. "Red Star over China," 7–8, VGP.

76. "Remarks of Comrade Garvin (English Dept.) at a Meeting to Celebrate the Formation of the Great Alliance of Students at the Shanghai Institute of Foreign Languages, September 25, 1967," 1-2, VGP, box 1, folder "Vicki Garvin Speeches in China."

77. Robert F. Williams, "Letter to Bernie, February 13, 1967," Robert F. Williams Papers, Bentley Historical Library, University of Michigan, Ann Arbor (hereafter RWP), box 1, folder "Correspondence, Undated and January 1967."

78. Robert F. Williams, "An Afro-American in China," 1–11, RWP, box 2, "Correspondence, January 1969."

79. Robert C. Maynard, "Struggle of Black People Was Developing—Williams Says Duty Called Him Back," Washington Post, September 15, 1969.

80. These relations culminated in Robert Williams's acceptance of the role of president in exile of first the Revolutionary Action Movement in 1963, a revolutionary and paramilitary organization with cells spread out across the United States, and in 1968 the Republic of New Afrika, a black separatist organization that advocated the creation of

an independent African American republic in several southeastern U.S. states. For more on the Revolutionary Action Movement and the Republic of New Afrika, see Ahmad, *We Will Return in the Whirlwind*, 95–166, and "Revolutionary Action Movement (RAM)"; Kelley, *Freedom Dreams*, 60–109; Kelley and Esch, "Black Like Mao"; and Mullen, *Afro-Orientalism*, 85–104.

81. "Letter from Goyo Pirsen, April 2, 1967," RWP, box 1, folder "Correspondence, March–April 1967"; "Letter from Viola Parker of the North Carolina Student Nonviolent Coordinating Committee, June 21, 1967," RWP, box 1, folder "Correspondence, May–June 1967."

82. "Letter from Robert Brock, October 4, 1967," RWP, box 1, folder "Correspondence, October 1967."

83. "Letter from Students for Pan Africa Association, September 10, 1967," RWP, box 1, folder "Correspondence, July–September 1967"; "Letter from Len Holt, April 2, 1967," RWP, box 1, folder "Correspondence, March–April 1967."

84. "Letter from Richard Gibson, July 27, 1967," RWP, box 1, folder "Correspondence, July–September 1967."

85. "Letter from Carlos Moore, February 4, 1967," RWP, box 1, folder "Correspondence, Undated and January 1967."

86. "Letter from Progressive Workers Movement (Toronto, Ontario)," RWP, box 1, folder "Correspondence, Undated and Jan 1967."

87. See Brady, *Making the Foreign Serve China*, 157.

88. The Williamses' neighbors included Anna Louise Strong; Sai Onji, a former member of the Japanese imperial family who sympathized with the PRC; the Chilean artist Jose Venturelli; the New Zealand writer Rewi Alley; and the Sudanese freedom fighter Ahmed Kheir.

89. Brady, *Making the Foreign Serve China*, 131.

90. Brady, *Making the Foreign Serve China*, 101–2, 130–32.

91. Lincoln Bergman, the stepson of Vicki Garvin who also lived and worked in China as an educator during the mid-1960s, described such requests as "chauvinistic and 'plus royaliste que la roi,' i.e., more Maoist than Mao." Lincoln Bergman, interview with the author, January 9, 2012.

92. See Brady, "Red and Expert" and *Making the Foreign Serve China*, 143–75. Also see Brady, *Friend of China*; Grey, *Hostage in Peking*; S. Han, *My House Has Two Doors*; Milton and Milton, *The Wind Will Not Subside*; and Rittenberg and Bennett, *The Man Who Stayed Behind*.

93. John Williams, interview with the author, October 4, 2009.

94. "Unnamed Article," RWP, box 12, folder "Biographical Material."

95. Garvin, interview with Bergman, disc 3 (emphasis added).

96. Quoted in Murrey Marder, "Rioting in U.S. Provides Red World With Huge Propaganda Windfall," *Washington Post*, July 29, 1967, A4; also see Harriet Schwartz, "Communist Views on Negro Collide: Peking Says Force Will End 'Ghetto'—Soviets Wary," *New York Times*, August 1, 1964, 11.

97. Mao, *Statement in Support of the Afro-American Struggle against Violent Repression*, April 16, 1968.

98. Cushing and Tompkins, *Chinese Posters*, 97.

99. "Speech of Vicki Garvin, April 1968," 4, 6, VGP.

100. Garvin, "China and Black Americans," 23; Garvin, interview with Bergman, disc 3.

101. Lincoln Bergman, "Introduction," in Bergman, *Will We Remember?*, 7; Lincoln Bergman, interview with the author, January 9, 2012; Miranda Bergman, interview with the author, March 15, 2012. On Leibel Bergman, see Avakian, *From Ike to Mao and Beyond*, 188–373; and Leibel Bergman, *I Cannot See Their Faces and Keep Silent*.

102. See "Civil Rights Division 1955–1970: Section 14 Serials 315–379, 1969–1970," RWP, box 9, folder "FBI Files."

103. Garvin, interview with Bergman, disc 4.

104. Garvin, interview with Bergman, disc 3.

105. See MacFarquhar and Schoenhals, *Mao's Last Revolution*, 251.

106. Garvin, interview with Bergman, disc 3.

107. "Comments at Students Lecture," 3, VGP. Letters from Garvin's former students also emphasize her impact on their consciousness. See "Letters from Students at Shanghai International Studies University, 550 Dalian Road, Shanghai 200083 China, 1992," VGP, box 1, folder "Correspondence China."

108. Garvin, interview with Bergman, disc 3.

109. See Victoria Ama Garvin's FBI file, "U.S. Department of Justice, FBI Document, October 25, 1972," 1–7, available through the Freedom of Information Act.

110. See Guzman, "Visit to China"; Newton, *Revolutionary Suicide*, 348, 352.

CODA. THE 1970S: RAPPROCHEMENT AND THE DECLINE
OF CHINA'S WORLD REVOLUTION

1. "A Speech by Richard M. Nixon during the California Senate Campaign, September 18, 1950," in *China and U.S. Foreign Policy* (Washington, DC: Congressional Quarterly, 1971), 19; Hugh Sidey, "The Presidency: 'Thirsting to Get to China,'" *Life*, April 30, 1971, 4.

2. Nixon, "Asia after Viet Nam," 112–13, 119, 121–23.

3. Nixon, "Asia after Viet Nam," 123.

4. See "'I Did Not Want the Hot Words of TV' and Other Presidential Reflections in a Crisis Week," *Time*, October 5, 1970. Also, in a 1969 memo to Kissinger, Nixon stated: "I think we should give every encouragement to the attitude that this Administration is 'exploring possibilities of rapprochement [sic] with the Chinese.'" "Memorandum from President Nixon to His Assistant for National Security Affairs (Kissinger)," Nixon Presidential Materials, NSC Files, Box 341, Subject Files, HAK/President Memoranda, 1969–1970. National Archives at College Park, MD (hereafter NACP). Nixon's handwritten notes from meetings held January 20–21, 1969, also touched on the subject of rapprochement. He wrote, "Chinese Communists: Short range—no change. Long range—we do not want 800,000,000 living in angry isolation. We want contact—will

be interested in Warsaw meetings. Republic of China—cooperative member of international community and member of Pacific community." See Nixon Presidential Materials, White House Special Files, President's Office Files, box 1, President's Handwriting File, January 1969, NACP. Portions of these documents can also be viewed at https://history.state.gov/historicaldocuments/frus1969-76v17/d3, accessed February 11, 2012.

5. The most glaring example was the U.S. State Department's ease of restrictions on both American travel to China and Chinese travel to the United States, as well as the department's termination of the twenty-two-year trade embargo against China.

6. "Haldeman Daily Notes, July 13–19, 1971," White House Special Files, box 44, Haldeman Papers Project, NACP. Also see Haldeman, *The Haldeman Diaries*, 318–24.

7. On the influence of the Vietnam War, as well as U.S.-Japan and U.S.-U.S.S.R. relations, on Sino-American rapprochement, see Schaller, "Détente and the Strategic Triangle, or, 'Drinking your Mao Tai and Having Your Vodka, Too.'"

8. See Karl, *Mao Zedong and China in the Twentieth Century*, 152.

9. See Robert F. Williams Papers, Bentley Historical Library, University of Michigan, Ann Arbor (hereafter RWP), box 9, folder "FBI Files, Section 9–1968–1969." In a letter to the attorney William Kuntsler, Robert Williams confirmed obtaining a "limited passport" and announced his future return to the United States. See Robert Williams, "Letter to William Kuntsler, November 7, 1968," RWP, box 2, folder "Correspondence, September–December 1968." For more on this arrangement, see "Memo 510, July 22, 1969," RWP, box 9, folder "FBI Civil Rights Division 1955–1970"; and "Letter from J. Edgar Hoover," June 10, 1970, from Robert F. Williams's FBI file, obtained from the Freedom of Information Act (hereafter FBI file FOIA).

10. "Letter from Director J. Edgar Hoover to Detroit office, RE: Robert F. Williams, Racial Matters-Black Nationalists," July 30, 1970, Robert Williams's FBI file FOIA.

11. Paul Scott, "Black Revolutionary Protected," March 11, 1971, from an unnamed periodical, found in RWP, box 9, folder "FBI Files, Section 14 Serials 315–379, 1969–1970." Apparently, the Chinese government also thought Williams might be able to aid in improving China's image in the U.S. According to Robert Williams, Premier Zhou Enlai personally encouraged Williams to leverage his knowledge to help China normalize its relations with the United States. Williams, however, privately admitted that he was extremely apprehensive about speaking publically about such themes, fearing that his opinions might "disrupt or aggravate" China's diplomatic goals. See Gwendolyn Hall, "A Tribute to Robert F. William: A Towering Figure in the Civil Rights Movement, October 1996," RWP, box 12, folder "Biographical Material: Gwendolyn Hall"; "Undated Memo," RWP, box 9, folder "FBI Files: Section 16–1971."

12. "State Department 1961–1973: Department of State Memorandum of Conversation, RE: Williams on China, participants: Henry E.T. Thayer and Robert F. Williams," January 12, 1970, 1–8, RWP, box 11, folder "State Department Documents 1961–1973."

13. Robert F. Williams, "Letter to Allen Whiting, March 3, 1970," RWP, box 12, folder "Center for Chinese Studies Fellowship 1970–1973." In this letter, Robert Williams alludes to fact that Whiting is assisting him in obtaining the position by reaching out

to Professor Rhoads Murphey, the director of the Center for Chinese Studies, on Williams's behalf.

14. Tommy Jacobs, "Portrait of the Exile . . . in His Own Land," *Michigan Daily*, October 17, 1971, 19–23; "Letter from Jane Barrett, Undated," RWP, box 1, folder "Undated Correspondence."

15. Scott, "Black Revolutionary Protected."

16. Robert F. Williams, "Personal Notes on Senate Internal Committee," RWP, box 1, folder "Undated Correspondence."

17. Mabel Williams, phone interview with the author, October 4, 2009.

18. "Letter from Conrad Lynn, July 22, 1969," RWP, box 2, folder "Correspondence, July–August 1969."

19. "Letter from President Richard Nixon, July 8, 1969," RWP, box 11, folder "State Department Documents 1961–1973"; "Letter from Dwight Burgess, American Consulate, July 10, 1969," RWP, box 2, folder "Correspondence, July–August 1969."

20. Mabel Williams, phone interview with the author, October 4, 2009.

21. "Birth of a New Era," *Chicago Defender*, November 4, 1971, 21; Warner Saunders, "Red China: It's Hard to Ignore 600 Million Folks," *Chicago Defender*, April 13, 1971, 8.

22. Chuck Andrews, "A Week That Changed the World, or Sellout?," *New York Amsterdam News*, March 4, 1972, A3.

23. "Evers: Nixon Trip a Joke," *Chicago Defender*, February 29, 1972, 12.

24. Vernon Jordan, "Nixon to China: What about Harlem?," *New York Amsterdam News*, March 4, 1972, A5.

25. Andrews, "A Week That Changed the World, or Sellout?," A3.

26. Cleaver, "Back to Africa," 244.

27. "Tricky Dick in China," *New York Amsterdam News*, March 4, 1972, A4.

28. Warner Saunders, "Better China, U.S. Relations May Help Blacks," *Chicago Defender*, August 10, 1971, 8; Saunders, "Red China," 8.

29. "William Epton: Travel to Communist China, Fall 1971," October 27, 1971, 1–23, U.S. Department of Justice, FBI, New York, Bill Epton's FBI file FOIA.

30. Roger Clendening, "Another View of Nixon China Visit," *New York Amsterdam News*, July 22, 1972, A5.

31. Andrews, "A Week That Changed the World, or Sellout?," A3.

32. Faith Christmas, "Calls China Visit a 'Repentant' Act," *Chicago Defender*, February 24, 1972, 5; also see "Hosea Williams Offers Nixon 'Tips' on Chinese Visit," *Chicago Defender*, December 21, 1971, 8.

33. Chuck Hopkins, "Inside the News: China Wins Diplomatic Victory," SOBU Newsletter, May 1, 1971, 1.

34. Chuck Hopkins, "Nixon Tries Desperate Diplomacy," *African World*, August 7, 1971, 1, 3, 9. Also see Chuck Hopkins, "Nixon's Trip: A Victory Won by Chairman Mao," *African World*, March 4, 1972.

35. Hopkins, "Inside the News," 1, 2.

36. The Maoist ideology of the revolutionary nationalist organizations of the 1960s

was homegrown, a result of Marxism-Leninism's impact on black-nationalist circles and the altering, more-revolutionary and militant tide of antiracist political activism during the second half of the decade. The Pan-African Marxist-Leninist groups of the 1970s, on the other hand, were drawn towards Maoism as a result of the African leaders Kwame Nkrumah's, Julius Nyerere's, and Amílcar Cabral's China leanings and socialist thought, as well as due to the declining currency of black power ideology. See Frazier, "The Congress of African People"; Kelley, *Freedom Dreams*, 60–109; Kelley and Esch, "Black Like Mao"; Mullen, *Afro-Orientalism*; Ratcliff, "Liberation at the End of a Pen"; Johnson, *Revolutionaries to Race Leaders*; and Wilkins, "'In the Belly of the Beast.'"

37. See R. Alexander, *Maoism in the Developed World*; Elbaum, *Revolution in the Air*; and Fields, *Trotskyism and Maoism*.

38. Haywood, *Black Bolshevik*, 643.

39. Shinn and Eisenman, *China and Africa*, 40–41; Alden and Alves, "History and Identity in the Construction of China's Africa Policy," 51; Le Pere and Shelton, *China, Africa and South Africa*, 56.

40. See Alden and Alves, "History and Identity in the Construction of China's Africa Policy," 49; Brady, *Making the Foreign Serve China*, 127; Schatten, *Communism in Africa*; Shinn and Eisenman, *China and Africa*, 39; and Snow, *The Star Raft*.

41. See Markel, "'We Are Not Tourists'"; and Wilkins, "'In the Belly of the Beast.'"

42. Yu, "China's Role in Africa," 108. Also see Yu, "Sino-African Relations."

43. See Hsu, "Zanzibar and Its Chinese Communities"; Monson, *Africa's Freedom Railway*; Shinn and Eisenman, *China and Africa*, 261; and Yu, "China's Role in Africa."

44. "Tanzania's Enemies Attack Anti-imperialist Policies," *African World*, July 22, 1972, 4, 15.

45. Winston Berry, "United Nations Report—Communication Network Needed," *African World*, May 15, 1971. Robert Williams also wrote about the Tanzania Zambia Railway's importance in *The Call*, the journal published by the Afro-Asian Writers Bureau. While visiting Tanzania for several months in 1968 and 1969, Williams embarked on a ten-day 1,470-mile round-trip motorcycle adventure from Dar es Salaam to Zambia, traveling along the partially completed railway. He modeled the ride after "the long marches of the young Red Guards" and "the cross country treks of China's youth." Throughout the trip several encounters shed light on the significance of Chinese aid. In the village of Bulongwa (located in Tanzania's Iringa region), Tanzanians expressed their appreciation for Mao's writings and for China's investment in Tanzanian development. And along the railway, he observed Chinese engineers and Tanzanian and Zambian workers lay down the railways' initial pieces, images that ultimately led him to conclude that "Africa's potential will be unlimited." Williams, "An Afro-American in Africa," 21, 22.

46. "Alternative to Imperialists: Chinese Aid to Africa," *African World*, September 16, 1972, 12, 16.

47. This was detailed in correspondence to Robert Williams, where Al Haynes maintained: "The Chinese are stealing the corporation blind!" See "Correspondence, February 1969: Letter from Al Haynes (Muhammad Zaid), February 5, 1969," RWP, box

2, folder "September–December 1968." Jamie Monson also asserts that the overly-optimistic representations of Chinese-Tanzanian relations and China's role in funding the railway were complicated by numerous factors, such as: the railways' demanding work conditions; the high and overbearing regulation, hierarchal labor structure, and work bureaucracy enforced by Chinese management and engineers; the different work ethics and cultural understandings about work held by Chinese and African laborers; distrust by the communities living alongside the railway; and at some instances limited cultural exchange and communication between Chinese and African laborers. See Monson, *Africa's Freedom Railway*.

48. See El-Khawas and Cohen, *The Kissinger Study of Southern Africa*.

49. Alden and Alves, "History and Identity in the Construction of China's Africa Policy," 50.

50. See S. Jackson, "China's Third World Foreign Policy," 393.

51. See Westad, *The Global Cold War*, 207–37.

52. Shinn and Eisenman, *China and Africa*, 344.

53. *The Facts on Angola*, 34. Also see Gerald Horne, "Trojan Horse for Imperialism in Angola," *Daily World*, January 8, 1976, 6.

54. Monteiro, "Angola," 10. Monteiro, however, also insisted that these developments not nullify the anti-imperialist movement developing in the United States, a struggle linking communists with nationalists and peace activists. U.S. activists, Monteiro ruled, though, should bear in mind that they had a "special responsibility" to the worldwide struggle. He stressed that dwelling in the belly of the capitalism meant acknowledging that imperialist "oppression is carried out in *our* names." "The people of this country are rapidly coming to realize that freedom is indivisible, that a nation which oppresses others cannot itself be free," Monteiro stated. Monteiro, *Africa and the USA*, 10, 7.

55. Kissinger, *On China*, 262.

56. Rittenberg and Bennett, *The Man Who Stayed Behind*, 271–72.

57. The Albanian labor leader Enver Hoxha lambasted Mao's three worlds theory as a "racist thesis" that reductively disregarded "the fact that in the 'Third World' there are oppressed and oppressors, the proletariat and the enslaved, poverty-stricken and destitute peasantry, on the one hand, and the capitalists and landowners, who exploit and fleece the people." Hoxha, *Imperialism and the Revolution*. Also see Cook, "Third World Maoism," 298.

58. *Black Enterprise*, October 1980, 2.

59. Killens, "Black Man in the New China," 31, 33, 36, 41, 37.

60. Franklin, *Mirror to America*, 285–87.

POSTSCRIPT. WEAVING THROUGH SAN HUAN LU

1. Yan, "McDonalds in Beijing," 41.

2. See Mina, "A Tale of Two Memes."

3. See Michelle Alexander, *The New Jim Crow*.

Bibliography

ARCHIVES

Anna Louise Strong Papers, National Library, Beijing, China (ALSP)
Federal Bureau of Investigation file obtained through the Freedom of Information Act (FBI file FOIA)
National Archives at College Park, MD (NACP)
Robert F. Williams Papers, Bentley Historical Library, University of Michigan, Ann Arbor (RWP)
Vicki Garvin Papers, Schomburg Center for Research in Black Culture, New York Public Library, New York (VGP)

INTERVIEWS

Lincoln Bergman, January 9 and March 15, 2012, San Francisco, CA
Miranda Bergman, March 15, 2012, San Francisco, CA
Carlos Moore, March 20, 2009, phone
Sidney Rittenberg, August 15, 2013, phone
John Williams, October 2, 2009, Detroit, MI; October 4, 2009, phone
Mabel Williams, October 4, 2009, phone

PUBLICATIONS

Acosta, Leonardo. *Cubano Be, Cubano Bop: One Hundred Years of Jazz in Cuba.* Washington, DC: Smithsonian Books, 2003.
Adams, Clarence, Della Adams, and Lewis Carlson. *An American Dream: The Life of an African American Soldier and POW Who Spent Twelve Years in Communist China.* Amherst: University of Massachusetts Press, 2007.
Adie, W. A. C. "Chinese Policy Towards Africa." In *The Soviet Bloc, China and Africa*, ed. Sven Hamrell and Carl Gösta Widstrand, 43–63. Uppsala: Scandinavian Institute of African Affairs, 1964.

Ahmad, Muhammad [Maxwell Stanford Jr.]. "Revolutionary Action Movement (RAM): A Case Study of Revolutionary Movement in Western Capitalist Society." MA thesis, Atlanta University, 1986.

———. *We Will Return in the Whirlwind: Black Radical Organizations 1960–1975*. Chicago: Charles H. Kerr Publishing Company, 2007.

Alden, Chris, and Cristina Alves. "History and Identity in the Construction of China's Africa Policy." *Review of African Political Economy* 35, no. 115 (2008): 43–58.

Alexander, Michelle. *The New Jim Crow: Mass Incarceration in the Age of Colorblindness*. New York: New Press, 2010.

Alexander, M. Jacqui, and Chandra Mohanty, eds. *Feminist Genealogies, Colonial Legacies, Democratic Futures*. New York: Routledge, 1997.

Alexander, Robert. *Maoism in the Developed World*. New York: Praeger Publishers, 2001.

———. *Maoism in the Developing World*. New York: Praeger Publishers, 1999.

Alter, Nora M. *Vietnam Protest Theatre: The Television War on Stage*. Bloomington: Indiana University Press, 1996.

Anderson, Benedict. *Imagined Communities: Reflections on the Origin and Spread of Nationalism*. London: Verso, 1993.

Anderson, Carol. *Eyes off the Prize: The United Nations and the African-American Struggle for Human Rights, 1944–1955*. Cambridge, UK: Cambridge University Press, 2003.

Andrews, Julia F. *Painters and Politics in the People's Republic of China, 1949–1979*. Berkeley: University of California Press and the Center for Chinese Studies, University of Michigan, 1994.

Anthony, David Henry. *Max Yergan: Race Man, Internationalist, Cold Warrior*. New York: New York University Press, 2006.

Appy, Christian G., ed. *Cold War Constructions: The Political Culture of United States Imperialism, 1945–1966*. Amherst: University of Massachusetts Press, 2000.

Apter, David E., and Tony Saich. *Revolutionary Discourse in Mao's Republic*. Cambridge, MA: Harvard University Press, 1994.

Arsenault, Raymond. *Freedom Riders: 1961 and the Struggle for Racial Justice*. New York: Oxford University Press, 2006.

Avakian, Bob. *From Ike to Mao and Beyond: My Journey from Mainstream America to Revolutionary Communist*. Chicago: Insight Press, 2005.

Baldwin, James. *No Name in the Street*. New York: Vintage Books, 2007.

Baldwin, James, and Sol Stein. *Native Sons*. New York: Random House, 2004.

Baldwin, Kate. *Beyond the Color Line and the Iron Curtain: Reading Encounters between Black and Red, 1922–1963*. Durham, NC: Duke University Press, 2002.

Barnouw, Erik. *The Image Empire: A History of Broadcasting in the United States, from 1953*. Oxford: Oxford University Press, 1977.

Basset, Richard M., with Lewis H. Carlson. *And the Wind Blew Cold: The Story of American POW in North Korea*. Kent, OH: Kent State University Press, 2002.

Baughman, James L. *Henry R. Luce and the Rise of the American News Media*. Boston: Twayne, 1987.

Benjamin, Walter. *Reflections: Essays, Aphorisms, Autobiographical Writings.* Ed. P. Demetz. Trans. E. Jephcott. New York: Schocken Books, 1986.

Bergman, Leibel. *I Cannot See Their Faces and Keep Silent.* Saint Paul, MN: Prometheus Press, 1946.

Bergman, Lincoln, ed. *Will We Remember? Poems by Leibel Bergman.* Chicago: Friends of Leibel Bergman, 1984.

The Best of Broadside 1962–1988: Anthems of the American Underground from the Pages of Broadside Magazine, five-disc sound recording. Washington, DC: Smithsonian Folkways Recordings, 2000.

Biderman, Albert. *March to Calumny: The Story of the American POWs in the Korean War.* New York: Macmillan, 1963.

Biondi, Martha. *To Stand and Fight: The Struggle for Civil Rights in Postwar New York City.* Cambridge, MA: Harvard University Press, 2003.

Bolster, Jeffrey. *Black Jacks: African American Seamen in the Age of the Sail.* Cambridge, MA: Harvard University Press, 1997.

Borstelmann, Thomas. *The Cold War and the Color Line: American Race Relations in the Global Arena.* Cambridge, MA: Harvard University Press, 2003.

Bowers, William, William M. Hammond, and George L. MacGarrigle. *Black Soldier, White Army: The 24th Infantry Regiment in Korea.* Washington, DC: Center of Military History, United States Army, 1996.

Brady, Anne-Marie. *Friend of China: The Myth of Rewi Alley.* New York: Routledge, 2002.

———. *Making the Foreign Serve China: Managing Foreigners in the People's Republic.* Lanham, MD: Rowman and Littlefield, 2003.

———. "Red and Expert: China's 'Foreign Friends' in the Great Proletarian Cultural Revolution, 1966–1969." In *China's Great Proletarian Cultural Revolution: Master Narratives and Post-Mao Counternarratives,* ed. Woei Lien Chong, 93–138. Lanham, MD: Rowman and Littlefield, 2002.

———. "'Treat Insiders and Outsiders Differently': The Use and Control of Foreigners in the PRC." *The China Quarterly,* no. 164 (December 2000): 943–64.

Brady, Anne-Marie, and Douglas Brown. *Foreigners and Foreign Institutions in Republican China.* London: Routledge, 2013.

Brah, Avtar. *Cartographies of Diaspora: Contesting Identities.* London: Routledge, 1996.

Bräutigam, Deborah. *Chinese Aid and African Development: Exporting Green Revolution.* New York: St. Martins Press, 1998.

Brock, Lisa, and Digna Castañeda Fuertes, eds. *Between Race and Empire: African-Americans and Cubans before the Cuban Revolution.* Philadelphia: Temple University Press, 1998.

Broussard, Jinx C. *African American Foreign Correspondents: A History.* Baton Rouge: Louisiana State University Press, 2013.

Broussard, Jinx C., and Skye Chance Cooley. "William Worthy, Jr.: The Man and the Mission." *Journalism Studies* 10, no. 3 (2009): 386–400.

Brown, Jayna. *Babylon Girls: Black Women Performers and the Shaping of the Modern.* Durham, NC: Duke University Press, 2008.

Burgess, G. Thomas. "Mao in Zanzibar: Nationalism, Discipline, and the (De)Construction of Afro-Asian Solidarities." In *Making a World after Empire: The Bandung Moment and Its Political Afterlives*, ed. Christopher Lee, 196–234. Athens: Ohio University Press, 2010.

Bush, Roderick. *The End of White World Supremacy: Black Internationalism and the Problem of the Color Line*. Philadelphia: Temple University Press, 2009.

———. *We Are Not What We Seem: Black Nationalism and Class Struggle in the American Century*. New York: New York University Press, 1999.

Bussey, Charles M. *Firefight at Yechon: Courage and Racism in the Korean War*. Lincoln: University of Nebraska Press, 1991.

Campbell, James. *Middle Passages: African American Journeys to Africa, 1787–2005*. New York: Penguin, 2006.

Capeci, Dominic, and Martha Wilkerson. *Layered Violence: The Detroit Rioters of 1943*. Jackson: University Press of Mississippi, 1991.

Carby, Hazel V. *Race Men*. Cambridge, MA: Harvard University Press, 1998.

Carlson, Lewis. *Remembered Prisoners of a Forgotten War: An Oral History of Korean War POWs*. New York: Hawthorne Books, 2002.

Carruthers, Susan L. "'The Manchurian Candidate' (1962) and the Cold War Brainwashing Scare." *Historical Journal of Film, Radio and Television* 18, no. 1 (1998): 75–94.

———. "Redeeming the Captives: Hollywood and the Brainwashing of America's Prisoners of War in Korea." *Film History* 10, no. 3 (1998): 275–94.

Caute, David. *The Fellow Travelers: A Postscript to the Enlightenment*. London: Wiedenfeld and Nicholson, 1974.

Cha-Jua, Sundiata Keita, and Clarence Lang. "The 'Long Movement' as Vampire: Temporal and Spatial Fallacies in Recent Black Freedom Studies." *The Journal of African-American History* 92, no. 2 (Spring 2007): 265–88.

Chakrabarty, Dipesh. *Provincializing Europe: Postcolonial Thought and Historical Difference*. Princeton, NJ: Princeton University Press, 2000.

Chaloupka, William. *Knowing Nukes: The Politics and Culture of the Atom*. Minneapolis: University of Minnesota Press, 1992.

Chang, Gordon H. "Are There Other Ways to Think about the 'Great Interregnum'?" *Journal of American-East Asian Relations* 7 (Spring–Summer 1998): 117–22.

Chang, Tsan-Kuo. "The Impact of Presidential Statements on Press Editorials Regarding U.S. Policy, 1950–1984." *Communication Research* 16, no. 4 (1989): 486–509.

———. "The News and U.S.-China Policy: Symbols in Newspapers and Documents." *Journalism Quarterly* 65, no. 2 (1988): 320–27.

Chen Darong. *Dongwu yu rensheng* [Animals and life]. Shanghai: Shangwu yingshuguan, 1916.

Chen Jian. *China's Road to the Korean War: The Making of the Sino-American Confrontation*. New York: Columbia University Press, 1994.

———. *Mao's China and the Cold War*. Chapel Hill: University of North Carolina Press, 2000.

———. "The Tibetan Rebellion of 1959 and China's Changing Relations with India and the Soviet Union." *Journal of Cold War Studies* 8, no. 3 (Summer 2006): 54–101.

Chen, Tina Mai. "Use the Past to Serve the Present: The Foreign to Serve China." In *Words and Their Stories: Essays on the Language of the Chinese Revolution*, ed. Ban Wang, 205–26. Boston: Brill, 2011.

Chen, Xiaomei. *Occidentalism: A Theory of Counter-Discourse in Post-Mao China*. 2nd ed. Lanham, MD: Rowman and Littlefield, 2002.

———. "Remembering War and Revolution on the Maoist Stage." In *Cold War Literature: Writing the Global Conflict*, ed. Andrew Hammond, 131–45. London: Routledge, 2006.

Chen Yinghuang, *Renleixue* [Anthropology]. Shanghai: Shangwu yingshuguan, 1918.

Chen, Yixin. "When Food Became Scarce: Life and Death in Chinese." *The Journal of the Historical Society* 10, no. 2 (June 2010): 117–65.

Cheng, Yinghong. *Creating the New Man: From Enlightenment Ideals to Socialist Realities*. Honolulu: University of Hawaii Press, 2009.

Chiu, Melissa, and Zheng Shengtian, eds. *Art and China's Revolution*. New York: Asia Society; New Haven, CT: Yale University Press, 2008.

Chow, Rey. *Woman and Chinese Modernity: The Politics of Reading between West and East*. Minneapolis: University of Minnesota Press, 1991.

Clark, Paul. *The Cultural Revolution: A History*. Cambridge, UK: Cambridge University Press, 2008.

Clark, Suzanne. *Cold Warriors: Manliness on Trial in the Rhetoric of the West*. Carbondale: Southern Illinois University Press, 2000.

Cleaver, Kathleen. "Back to Africa: The Evolution of the International Section of the Black Panther Party (1969–1972)." In *The Black Panther Party Reconsidered*, ed. Charles E. Jones, 211–54. Baltimore, MD: Black Classic Press, 1998.

Clemons, Michael. *African Americans in Global Affairs: Contemporary Perspectives*. Lebanon, NH: Northeastern University Press, 2010.

Cleverley, John. *In the Lap of Tigers: The Communist Labor University of Jiangxi Province*. Boston, MA: Rowman and Littlefield, 2000.

Clifford, James. *Routes: Travel and Translation in the Late Twentieth Century*. Cambridge, MA: Harvard University Press, 1997.

Clifford, John W. *In the Presence of My Enemies*. New York: W. W. Norton, 1963.

Cohen, Paul A. *Discovering History in China*. New York: Columbia University Press, 1984.

Cohen, Robert Carl. *Black Crusader: A Biography of Robert Franklin Williams*. Secaucus, NJ: Lyle Stuart, 1972.

Cohn, Michael, and Michael K. Platzer. *Black Men of the Sea*. New York: Dodd, Mead, 1978.

Collier-Thomas, Bettye, and V. P. Franklin, eds. *Sisters in the Struggle: African American Women in the Civil Rights–Black Power Movement*. New York: New York University Press, 2001.

Communist Psychological Warfare (Brainwashing): Consultation with Edward Hunter, Author and

Foreign Correspondent. Committee on Un-American Activities, House of Representatives, 85th Cong., 2d Session, March 13, 1958. Washington, DC: United States Government Printing Office, 1958.

Conboy, Kenneth, and James Morrison. *The CIA's Secret War in Tibet.* Lawrence: University Press of Kansas, 2002.

Cook, Alexander C. *Mao's Little Red Book: A Global History.* New York: Cambridge University Press, 2014.

———. "Third World Maoism." In *A Critical Introduction to Mao,* ed. Timothy Cheek, 288–312. New York: Cambridge University Press, 2010.

Cooppan, Vilashini. "Moving on Down the Line: Domestic Science, Transnational Politics, and Gendered Allegory in Du Bois." In *Next to the Color Line: Gender, Sexuality, and W.E.B. Du Bois,* ed. Susan Kay Gillman and Alys Eve Weinbaum, 35–68. Minneapolis: University of Minnesota Press, 2007.

Countryman, Matthew. *Up South: Civil Rights and Black Power in Philadelphia.* Philadelphia: University of Pennsylvania Press, 2007.

Courtright, John. "Rhetoric of the Gun: An Analysis of the Rhetorical Modifications of the Black Panther Party." *Journal of Black Studies* 4 (March 1974): 249–67.

Cubillas, Vicente. "Robert Williams: De la esclavitud Yanqui a la libertad Cubana" [Robert Williams: From Yanqui slavery to Cuban liberty]. *Bohemia* (1961): 74–77.

Cumings, Bruce. *The Origins of the Korean War.* Vol. 2, *The Roaring of the Cataract, 1947–1950.* Princeton, NJ: Princeton University Press, 1990.

Cunningham, Cyril. *No Mercy, No Leniency: Communist Mistreatment of British Prisoners of War in Korea.* London: Leo Cooper, 2000.

Cuordileone, K. A. *Manhood and American Political Culture in the Cold War.* New York: Routledge, 2005.

Curtin, Michael. "Organizing Difference on Global TV: Television History and Cultural Geography." In *Television Histories: Shaping Collective Memory in the Media Age,* ed. Gary R. Edgerton and Peter C. Rollins, 333–56. Lexington: University Press of Kentucky.

Cushing, Lincoln, and Ann Tompkins. *Chinese Posters: Art from the Great Proletarian Cultural Revolution.* San Francisco: Chronicle Books, 2007.

Dalfiume, Richard M. *Desegregation of the U.S. Armed Forces: Fighting on Two Fronts, 1939–1953.* Columbia: University of Missouri Press, 1969.

Daulatzai, Sohail. *Black Star, Crescent Moon: The Muslim International and Black Freedom beyond America.* Minneapolis: University of Minnesota Press, 2012.

Davies, Carol Boyce. *Left of Marx: The Political Life of Black Communist Claudia Jones.* Durham, NC: Duke University Press, 2007.

———, ed. *Claudia Jones: Beyond Containment.* Boulder, CO: Lynne Rienner Publishers, 2011.

Davin, Delia. "Gendered Mao: Mao, Maoism, and Women." In *A Critical Introduction to Mao,* ed. Timothy Cheek, 196–218. New York: Cambridge University Press, 2010.

Dikötter, Frank, ed. *The Construction of Racial Identities in China and Japan.* Honolulu: University of Hawaii Press, 1997.

———. *The Discourse of Race in China.* Stanford, CA: Stanford University Press, 1992.

———. *Mao's Great Famine: The History of China's Most Devastating Catastrophe, 1958–62.* New York: Walker, 2010.

———. "Racial Discourses in China: Continuities and Permutations." In *The Construction of Racial Identities in China and Japan*, ed. Frank Dikötter, 12–33. Honolulu: University of Hawaii Press, 1997.

———. "Racial Identities in China: Context and Meaning." *The China Quarterly*, no. 138 (June 1994): 404–12.

Dirks, Annelieke. "Between Threat and Reality: The National Association for the Advancement of Colored People and the Emergence of Armed Self-Defense in Clarksdale and Natchez, Mississippi, 1960–1965." *Journal for the Study of Radicalism* 1, no. 1 (2007): 71–79.

Dirlik, Arif. "Chinese History and the Question of Orientalism." *History and Theory* 35, no. 4 (1996): 96–118.

———. *Marxism in the Chinese Revolution.* Oxford: Rowman and Littlefield, 2005.

Donnelly, William M. *We Can Do It: The 503rd Field Artillery Battalion in the Korean War.* Washington, DC: U.S. Army Center for Military History, 2000.

Dorn, Julia. "Paul Robeson Told Me." In *Paul Robeson Speaks: Writings, Speeches, Interviews, 1918–1974*, ed. Philip Sheldon, 130–32. New York: Kensington Publishing Company, 2002.

Doss, Erica. "Imaging the Panthers: Representing Black Power and Masculinity, 1970–1990s." *Prospects: Annual of American Cultural Studies* 23 (October 1998): 483–516.

———. "Revolutionary Art Is a Tool of Liberation: Emory Douglas and the Protest Aesthetics at the *Black Panther*." In *Liberation, Imagination, and the Black Panther Party: A New Look at the Panthers and Their Legacy*, ed. Kathleen Cleaver and George Katsiaficas, 175–87. New York: Routledge, 2001.

Downing, John D. H., with Tamara V. Ford, Genève Gil, and Laura Stein. *Radical Media: Rebellious Communication and Social Movements.* London: Sage, 2001.

Du Bois, W. E. B. *The Autobiography of W.E.B. Du Bois: A Soliloquy on Viewing My Life from the Last Decade of Its First Century.* New York: International Publishers, 1968.

———. *Black Folk: Then and Now.* New York: H. Holt and Company, 1939.

———. "China and Africa." *Peking Review*, March 3, 1959.

———. *Color and Democracy: Colonies and Peace.* New York: Harcourt, Brace and Company, 1945.

———. *Dark Princess: A Romance.* Jackson: Banner Books and University Press of Mississippi, 1995.

———. *The Souls of Black Folk.* Boston: Bedford Books, 1997.

———. "The Vast Miracle of China Today: A Report on a Ten-Week Visit to the People's Republic of China." In *W. E. B. Du Bois on Asia: Crossing the World Color Line*, ed. Bill Mullen and Cathryn Watson, 190–95. Jackson: University Press of Mississippi, 2005.

———. *Worlds of Color: The Black Flame Trilogy, Book Three.* Vol. 13 of *The Oxford W. E. B. Du Bois*, ed. Henry Louis Gates Jr. New York: Oxford University Press, 2007.

———. "Worlds of Color." *Foreign Affairs* 3, no. 3 (1925): 423–44.

———. "Yellow Sea." In *W. E. B. Du Bois on Asia: Crossing the World Color Line*, ed. Bill Mullen and Cathryn Watson, 83-87. Jackson: University Press of Mississippi, 2005.

Du Bois, W. E. B., and Herbert Aptheker. *Writings by W.E.B. Du Bois in Periodicals Edited by Others*. Vol. 4, 1945–1961. Millwood, NY: Kraus-Thomson Organization, 1982.

Dudziak, Mary L. *Cold War Civil Rights: Race and the Image of American Democracy*. Princeton, NJ: Princeton University Press, 2002.

Dunbar, Eve. *Black Regions of the Imagination: African American Writers between the Nation and the World*. Philadelphia: Temple University Press, 2013.

Du Yaquan, ed. *Dongwuxue da cidian* [Great dictionary of zoology]. Shanghai: Shangwu yinshuguan, 1927.

Duyvendak, Jan Julius Lodewijk. *China's Discovery in Africa: Lectures Given at the University on January 22 and 23rd, 1947*. London: Arthur Probsthain, 1949.

Eagleton, Mary. "Adrienne Rich, Location and the Body." *Journal of Gender Studies* 9, no. 3 (November 2000): 299–312.

Edgerton, Robert B. *Hidden Heroism: Black Soldiers in America's Wars*. Boulder, CO: Westview Press, 2001.

Edwards, Brent Hayes. "Late Romance." In *Next to the Color Line: Gender, Sexuality, and W.E.B. DuBois*, ed. Susan Gillman and Alys Eve Weinbaum, 124–49. Minneapolis: University of Minnesota Press, 2007.

———. *The Practice of Diaspora: Literature, Translation, and the Rise of Black Internationalism*. Cambridge, MA: Harvard University Press, 2003.

Elam, Harry Justin, Jr., and Kennell Jackson, eds. *Black Cultural Traffic: Crossroads in Global Performance and Popular Culture*. Ann Arbor: University of Michigan Press, 2005.

Elbaum, Max. *Revolution in the Air: Sixties Radicals Turn to Lenin, Mao and Che*. New York: Verso, 2002.

———. "What Legacy from the Radical Internationalism of 1968?" *Radical History Review*, no. 82 (Winter 2002): 37–64.

El-Khawas, Mohamed A., and Barry Cohen, eds. *The Kissinger Study of Southern Africa: National Security Study Memorandum 39*. Westport, CT: Lawrence Hill and Company, 1976.

Esherick, Joseph W., Paul G. Pickowicz, and Andrew G. Walder, eds. *The Chinese Cultural Revolution as History*. Stanford, CA: Stanford University Press, 2006.

Estes, Steve. *I Am a Man! Race, Manhood, and the Civil Rights Movement*. Chapel Hill: University of North Carolina Press, 2005.

Evans, Harriet. "'Comrade Sisters': Gendered Bodies and Spaces." In *Picturing Power in the People's Republic of China*, ed. Harriet Evans and Stephanie Donald, 63–78. Lanham, MD: Rowman and Littlefield, 1999.

Evans, Harriet, and Stephanie Donald, eds. *Picturing Power in the People's Republic of China: Posters of the Cultural Revolution*. Lanham, MD: Rowman and Littlefield, 1999.

The Facts on Angola: News Reports from the Press from the U.S.A., France, Somalia, Tanzania, Algeria, the U.S.S.R., Guinea and Other Countries. New York: National Anti-imperialist Movement in Solidarity with the African Liberation New York Committee, 1976.

Fairbank, John King. *The United States and China.* Cambridge, MA: Harvard University Press, 1958.

Faludi, Susan. *Stiffed: The Betrayal of the American Man.* New York: Harper Perennial, 2000.

Fanon, Frantz. *Black Skin, White Masks.* New York: Grove Press, 1967.

———. *A Dying Colonialism.* New York: Monthly Review Press, 1965.

Fehrenbach, T. R. *This Kind of War: A Study in Unpreparedness.* New York: Macmillan, 1963.

Fennell, Vera L. "Preliminary Thoughts on Race and Foreign Policy: Sino-African Solidarity in Three Keys." Global R(ace) E(thnicity) M(igration) Seminars and Pedagogical Lunches, University of Minnesota, October 3, 2007. Accessed March 11, 2010, www.globalrem.umn.edu/video/fennell0708.php.

———. "A Tale of Two Obits: Reading the Cold War through the Obituaries of W. E. B. Du Bois and Chairman Mao Tse-tung." *International Journal of Communication* 7 (2013): 1–20.

Fields, A. Belden. *Trotskyism and Maoism: Theory and Practice in France and the United States.* New York: Praeger Publishers, 1989.

Fish, Cheryl. "Voices of Restless (Dis)Continuity: The Significance of Travel for Free Black Women in Antebellum Americas." *Women's Studies* 26, no. 5 (Summer 1997): 475–95.

Fox, Stephen R. *The Guardian of Boston: William Monroe Trotter.* New York: Atheneum, 1970.

Franklin, John Hope. *Mirror to America: The Autobiography of John Hope Franklin.* New York: Farrar, Straus, and Giroux, 2005.

Frazier, Robeson Taj P. "The Congress of African People: Baraka, Brother Mao, and the Year of '74." *Souls* 8, no. 3 (2006): 142–59.

Freeberne, Michael. "Racial Issues and the Sino-Soviet." *Asian Survey* 5, no. 8 (August 1965): 408–16.

Gaines, Kevin. *African Americans in Ghana: Black Expatriates and the Civil Rights Era.* Chapel Hill: University of North Carolina Press, 2006.

Gallicchio, Marc. *The African American Encounter with Japan and China: Black Internationalism in Asia, 1895–1945.* Chapel Hill: University of North Carolina Press, 2000.

Gallo, Rubén. *Mexican Modernity: The Avant-Garde and the Technological Revolution.* Cambridge, MA: MIT Press, 2005.

Gao, Mobo. *The Battle for China's Past: Mao and the Cultural Revolution.* Ann Arbor, MI: Pluto Press, 2008.

Gao, Yunxiang. "W.E.B. Du Bois and Shirley Graham Du Bois in Maoist China." *Du Bois Review: Social Science Research on Race* 10, no. 1 (Spring 2013): 59–85.

Garvin, Vicki. "China and Black Americans." *New China* 1, no. 3 (Fall 1975): 23.

Gillman, Susan Kay, and Alys Eve Weinbaum, eds. *Next to the Color Line: Gender, Sexuality, and W.E.B. Du Bois.* Minneapolis: University of Minnesota Press, 2007.

Gilroy, Paul. *The Black Atlantic: Modernity and Double Consciousness.* Cambridge, MA: Harvard University Press, 1993.

Gitelman, Lisa. *Scripts, Grooves, and Writing Machines: Representing Technology in the Edison Era.* Stanford, CA: Stanford University Press, 1999.

Glissant, Édouard. *Poetics of Relation*. Translated by Betsy Wing. Ann Arbor: University of Michigan Press, 1997.

Gore, Dayo. "From Communist Politics to Black Power: The Visionary Politics and Transnational Solidarities of Victoria 'Vicki' Ama Garvin." In *Want to Start a Revolution? Radical Black Women in the Black Freedom Struggle*, ed. Dayo Gore, Jeanne Theoharis, and Komozi Woodard, 71–94. New York: New York University Press, 2009.

———. *Radicalism at the Crossroads: African American Women Activists in the Cold War*. New York: New York University Press, 2011.

Gore, Dayo, Jeanne Theoharis, and Komozi Woodard, eds. *Want to Start a Revolution? Radical Black Women in the Black Freedom Struggle*. New York: New York University Press, 2009.

Graham Du Bois, Shirley. *His Day Is Marching On: A Memoir of W. E. B. Du Bois*. New York: J. B. Lippincott, 1971.

Green, Michael Cullen. *Black Yanks in the Pacific: Race in the Making of American Military Empire after World War II*. Ithaca, NY: Cornell University Press, 2010.

Grewal, Inderpal, and Caren Kaplan. *Scattered Hegemonies: Postmodernity and Transnational Feminist Practices*. Minneapolis: University of Minnesota Press, 1994.

Grey, Anthony. *Hostage in Peking*. London: Michael Joseph, 1970.

Griffin, Farah J., and Cheryl J. Fish, eds. *A Stranger in the Village: Two Centuries of African-American Travel Writing*. Boston: Beacon Press, 1998.

Gruesser, John C. "Afro-American Travel Literature and Africanist Discourse." *Black American Literature Forum* 24, no. 1 (Spring 1990): 5–20.

Guridy, Frank Andre. *Forging Diaspora: Afro-Cubans and African Americans in a World of Empire and Jim Crow*. Chapel Hill: University of North Carolina Press, 2010.

Guy-Sheftall, Beverly. "Speaking for Ourselves: Feminisms in the African Diaspora." In *Decolonizing the Academy: African Diaspora Studies*, ed. Carole Boyce Davies, 27–43. Trenton, NJ: Africa World Press, 2003.

Guzman, Pablo. "Visit to China." *Palante* 3, no. 20 (n.d.).

Haiming Li. *The Transnational History of a Chinese Family: Immigrant Letters, Family Business, and Reverse Migration*. New Brunswick, NJ: Rutgers University Press, 2005.

Haldeman, H. R. *The Haldeman Diaries*. New York: G. P. Putnam's, 1994.

Hall, Stuart, ed. *Representation: Cultural Representation and Signifying Practices*. London: Sage. 1997.

Halliday, Jon, and Bruce Cumings. *Korea: The Unknown War*. New York: Pantheon Books, 1988.

Hamamoto, Darrell. *Monitored Peril: Asian Americans and the Politics of TV Representation*. Minneapolis: University of Minnesota Press, 1994.

Han, Dongping. *The Unknown Cultural Revolution: Life and Change in a Chinese Village*. New York: Monthly Review Press, 2008.

Han, Suyin. *My House Has Two Doors*. London: Jonathan Cape, 1980.

Hardt, Michael, and Antonio Negri. *Empire*. Cambridge, MA: Harvard University Press, 2000.

Harris, Nigel. *The Mandate of Heaven: Marx and Mao in Modern China*. New York: Quartet Books, 1979.

Hayford, Charles W. "Mao's Journeys to the West: Meanings Made of Mao." In *A Critical Introduction to Mao*, ed. Timothy Cheek, 313–31. New York: Cambridge University Press, 2010.

Haygood, Daniel Marshall. "Henry Luce's Anti-communist Legacy: An Analysis of US News Magazines' Coverage of China's Cultural Revolution." *Journalism History* 35, no. 2 (2009): 98–105.

Hayhoe, Ruth. *China's Universities 1985–1995: A Century of Cultural Conflict*. New York: Garland Publishing, 1996.

Haywood, Harry. *Black Bolshevik: Autobiography of an Afro-American Communist*. Chicago: Liberator Press, 1978.

Helg, Aline. *Our Rightful Share: The Afro-Cuban Struggle for Equality, 1886–1912*. Chapel Hill: University of North Carolina Press, 1995.

Hero, Alfred O., Jr. "American Negroes and U.S. Foreign Policy: 1937–1967." In *The African American Voice in U.S. Foreign Policy since World War II*, ed. Michael L. Krenn, 2–34. New York: Garland Publishing, 1998.

Hershatter, Gail. *The Gender of Memory: Rural Women and China's Collective Past*. Berkeley: University of California Press, 2011.

Herzstein, Robert E. *Henry R. Luce, Time, and the American Crusade in Asia*. Cambridge, UK: Cambridge University Press, 2005.

Hevi, Emmanuel J. *An African Student in China*. London: Pall Mall Press, 1963.

Higashida, Cheryl. *Black Internationalist Feminism: Women Writers of the Black Left*. Champaign: University of Illinois Press, 2011.

Hill, Lance. *The Deacons for Defense: Armed Resistance and the Civil Rights Movement*. Chapel Hill: University of North Carolina Press, 2004.

Hinton, William. *Fanshen: A Documentary of Revolution in a Chinese Village*. New York: Monthly Review Press, 1966.

Hixson, Walter L. *Parting the Curtain: Propaganda, Culture, and the Cold War, 1945–1961*. London: Macmillan, 1997.

Hollander, Paul. *Political Pilgrims: Travels of Western Intellectuals to the Soviet Union, China, and Cuba*. New York: Oxford University Press, 1981.

Horne, Gerald. *Black and Red: W.E.B. Du Bois and the Afro-American Response to the Cold War, 1944–1963*. Albany: State University of New York Press, 1986.

——. *The End of Empires: African Americans and India*. Philadelphia: Temple University Press, 2008.

——. *Race War! White Supremacy and the Japanese Attack on the British Empire*. New York: New York University Press, 2003.

——. *Race Woman: The Lives of Shirley Graham Du Bois*. New York: New York University Press, 2000.

——. "The Revenge of the Black Pacific?" *Callaloo* 24, no. 1 (2001): 94–96.

Hoxha, Enver. *Imperialism and the Revolution*. Chicago: World View, 1979.

Hsu, Carolyn L. *Creating Market Socialism: How Ordinary People Are Shaping Class and Status in China*. Durham, NC: Duke University Press, 2007.

Hsu, Elizabeth. "Zanzibar and Its Chinese Communities." *Populations, Space and Place* 13, no. 2 (2007): 113–23.

Hughes, Langston. "Consider Me." In *The Collected Poems of Langston Hughes*, ed. Arnold Rampersad, 385–86. New York: Alfred A. Knopf, 1994.

Hughey, Matthew. "Black Aesthetics and Panther Rhetoric: A Critical Decoding of Black Masculinity in *The Black Panther*, 1967–80." *Critical Sociology* 35, no. 1 (2009): 29–56.

Hunt, Michael H. "East Asia in Henry Luce's American Century." *Diplomatic History* 23 (1999): 321–53.

Hunt, Michael H., and Steven I. Levine. "The Revolutionary Challenge to Early U.S. Cold War Policy in Asia." In *The Great Powers in East Asia, 1953–1960*, ed. Warren I. Cohen and Akira Iriye, 12–34. New York: Columbia University Press, 1990.

Hunter, Edward. *Brainwashing: The Story of Men Who Defied It*. New York: Farrar, Straus, and Cudahy, 1956.

———. *Brain-washing in Red China: The Calculated Destruction of Men's Minds*. New York: Vanguard Press, 1951.

Idun-Arkhurst, Isaac. *Ghana's Relations with China*. Johannesburg: South African Institute of International Affairs, 2008.

Inman, Cecil Mark. *A Celebration of Life: An Ex-POW's 54 Year Journey*. Maitland, FL: Xulon Press, 2006.

Iriye, Akira. "Culture and International History." In *Explaining the History of American Foreign Relations*, 2nd ed., ed. Michael Hogan and Thomas G. Paterson, 241–56. Cambridge, UK: Cambridge University Press, 2004.

———. *Culture Internationalism and the World Order*. Baltimore, MD: John Hopkins University Press, 1997.

Isaacs, Harold. *Scratches on Our Minds: American Views of China and India*. New York: John Day Co., 1958.

———. *The Tragedy of the Chinese Revolution*. Stanford, CA: Stanford University Press, 1951.

Jackson, Paul. *One of the Boys: Homosexuals in the Military in World War II*. Montreal: McGill-Queen's University Press, 2004.

Jackson, Steven F. "China's Third World Foreign Policy: The Case of Angola and Mozambique, 1961–93." *The China Quarterly*, no. 142 (June 1995): 388–422.

Jacobson, Matthew Frye, and Gaspar Gonzalez. *What Have They Built You to Do? The Manchurian Candidate and Cold War America*. Minneapolis: University of Minnesota Press, 2006.

Jaffe, Louis L. "The Right to Travel: The Passport Problem." *Foreign Affairs* 35, no. 1 (1956): 17–28.

Jansen, G. H. *Afro-Asia and Non-alignment*. London: Faber and Faber, 1966.

Jenkins, Destin K. "Two Sleeping Giants: African American Perceptions of China, 1900–1939." Senior thesis, Columbia University, April 2010.

Jensen, Phyllis Graber. "William Worthy, '42: Journalist, Civil Rights Activist, Remains

as Vigilant as Ever." *Bates Magazine*, Fall 1995. http://abacus.bates.edu/pubs/mag/95
-Fall/worthy.html.

Jespersen, T. Christopher. *American Images of China, 1931–1949*. Stanford, CA: Stanford
University Press, 1996.

Ji Chaozhu. *The Man on Mao's Right: From Harvard Yard to Tiananmen Square, My Life inside
China's Foreign Ministry*. New York: Random House, 2008.

Johnson, Cedric. *Revolutionaries to Race Leaders: Black Power and the Making of African American Politics*. Minneapolis: University of Minnesota Press, 2007.

Johnson, Matthew D. "From Peace to the Panthers: PRC Engagement with African-
American Transnational Networks, 1949–1979." *Past and Present* 218 (2013): 233–57.

Johnson, M. Dujon. *Race and Racism in the Chinas: Chinese Racial Attitudes Toward Africans and
African-Americans*. Bloomington, IN: Author House, 2007.

Jones, Andrew F. *Yellow Music: Media Culture and Colonial Modernity in the Chinese Jazz Age*.
Durham, NC: Duke University Press, 2001.

Jones, Andrew F., and Nikhil Pal Singh. "Guest Editors' Introduction." *positions* 11, no.
1 (2003): 1–9.

Joseph, Peniel E., *Waiting 'til the Midnight Hour: A Narrative History of Black Power in America*.
New York: Henry Holt and Co., 2006.

Josephs, Samuel. "Whose Revolution Is This? Gender's Divisive Role in the Black Panther Party." *The Georgetown Journal of Gender and the Law* 9 (2008): 403–26.

Jowett, Garth. "Brainwashing: The Korean POW Controversy and the Origins of a
Myth." In *Readings in Propaganda and Persuasion: New and Classic Essays*, ed. Garth S.
Jowett and Victoria O'Donnell, 201–11. London: Sage, 2006.

Juguo, Zhang. "Du Bois' Quest for Solution to the American 'Negro Problem.'" *Journal
of Historical Science*, no. 4 (2000): 93–101.

———. "The Thought of William E. B. Du Bois in Comparison with Booker T. Washington: Similarities and Differences." *Nankai Journal* 3 (2000): 67–74.

———. "W. E. B. Du Bois and the Pan-African Movement." *Journal of Hebei Normal University* 24, no. 3 (2001): 69–74.

Jun, Helen Heran. *Race for Citizenship: Black Orientalism and Asian Uplift from Pre-emancipation
to Neoliberal America*. New York: New York University Press, 2011.

Kahin, George McTurnan. *The Asian-African Conference*. Ithaca, NY: Cornell University
Press, 1956.

Kahn, Jeffrey. "International Travel and the U.S. Constitution." Legal Studies Research
Paper, number 00-18, Southern Methodist University Dedman School of Law, Dallas,
2008.

Kaplan, Amy. *The Anarchy of Empire in the Making of U.S. Culture*. Cambridge, MA: Harvard
University Press, 2002.

Karl, Rebecca E. *Mao Zedong and China in the Twentieth Century: A Concise History*. Durham,
NC: Duke University Press, 2010.

Kelley, Robin D. G. *Freedom Dreams: The Black Radical Imagination*. Boston: Beacon Press,
2002.

Kelley, Robin D. G., and Betsy Esch. "Black Like Mao." *Souls* 1, no. 4 (1999): 6–41.

Kennan, George F. "Moscow Embassy Telegram #511, February 22, 1946." In *Containment: Documents on American Policy and Strategy, 1945–1950*, ed. Thomas H. Etzold and John Lewis Gaddis, 50–63. New York: Columbia University Press, 1978.

———. "The Sources of Soviet Conduct," *Foreign Affairs* 25, no. 4 (July 1947): 566–82.

Killens, John Oliver. "Black Man in the New China." *Black World* 25, no. 1 (November 1975): 28–42.

Kimche, David. *The Afro-Asian Movement: Ideology and Foreign Policy of the Third World*. Jerusalem: Israel University Press, 1973.

King, Richard H. *Civil Rights and the Idea of Freedom*. New York: Oxford University Press, 1992.

Kinkead, Eugene. "Have We Let Our Sons Down?" *McCall's* 86, no. 4 (1959): 23, 74–81.

———. *In Every War but One*. New York: W. W. Norton, 1959.

Kissinger, Henry. *On China*. New York: Penguin Press, 2011.

Klein, Christina. *Cold War Orientalism: Asia in the Middlebrow Imagination, 1945–1961*. Berkeley: University of California Press, 2003.

Knaus, John Kenneth. *Orphans of the Cold War: America and the Tibetan Struggle for Survival*. New York: Public Affairs, 1999.

Knight, Nick. *Rethinking Mao: Explorations in Mao Zedong's Thought*. Lanham, MD: Lexington Books, 2007.

Koen, Ross. *The China Lobby in American Politics*. New York: Harper and Row, 1974.

Kornfeder, Joseph Zack. *Brainwashing and Senator McCarthy*. New York: Alliance, 1954.

Kraus, Richard C. *Pianos and Politics in China: Middle-Class Ambitions and the Struggle over Western Music*. New York: Oxford University Press, 1989.

Krenn, Michael. *The African American Voice in U.S. Foreign Policy since World War II*. New York: Routledge, 1999.

———. *Black Diplomacy: African Americans and the State Department 1945–1969*. Armonk, NY: M. E. Sharpe, 1998.

Krueger, Stephen. "Passports in the Twenty-First Century." *Global Jurist* 9, no. 1 (2009): 1934–2640.

Kruse, Kevin M., and Stephen Tuck, eds. *Fog of War: The Second World War and the Civil Rights Movement*. New York: Oxford University Press, 2012.

Kuumba, M. Bahati. *Gender and Social Movements*. Walnut Creek, CA: AltaMira Press, 2001.

Kuznitz, Leonard A. *Public Opinion and Foreign Policy: America's China Policy, 1949–1976*. Westport, CT: Greenwood Press, 1984.

Kwon, Heonik. *The Other Cold War*. New York: Columbia University Press, 2010.

Kwong, Julia. *Cultural Revolution in China's School, May 1966–April 1969*. Stanford, CA: Hoover Institution Press, 1988.

Landsberger, Stefan. *Chinese Propaganda Posters: From Revolution to Modernization*. Amsterdam: Pepin Press, 1995.

Landsberger, Stefan, and Marien van der Heijden. *Chinese Posters: The IISH-Landsberger Collections*. Munich: Prestel, 2009.

Larkin, Bruce D. *China and Africa, 1949–1970: The Foreign Policy of the People's Republic of China.* Berkeley: University of California Press, 1971.

Latty, Yvonne. *We Were There: Voices of African American Veterans from World War II to the War in Iraq.* New York: Amistad, 2004.

Law, Yu Fai. *Chinese Foreign Aid: A Study of Its Nature and Goals with Particular Reference to the Foreign Policy and World View of the People's Republic of China, 1950–1982.* Fort Lauderdale, FL: Breitenbach, 1984.

Layton, Azza Salama. *International Politics and Civil Rights Policies in the United States, 1941–1960.* Cambridge, UK: Cambridge University Press, 2000.

Lech, Raymond B. *Broken Soldiers.* Urbana: University of Illinois Press, 2000.

Lee, Chin-Chuan, ed. *Voices of China: The Interplay of Politics and Journalism.* New York: Guilford Press, 1990.

Lee, Christopher, ed. *Making a World after Empire: The Bandung Moment and Its Political Afterlives.* Athens: Ohio University Press, 2010.

Lee, Erika. *At America's Gates: Chinese Immigration during the Exclusion Era, 1882–1943.* Chapel Hill: University of North Carolina Press, 2003.

Lee, Lily Xiao Hong, and A. D. Stefanowska. *Biographical Dictionary of Chinese Women: The Twentieth Century 1912–2000.* Armonk, NY: M.E. Shape, 2003.

Lee, Robert. *Orientals: Asian Americans in Popular Culture.* Philadelphia: Temple University Press, 1999.

Leese, Daniel. *Mao Cult: Rhetoric and Ritual in China's Cultural Revolution.* Cambridge, UK: Cambridge University Press, 2011.

Leites, Nathan, and Elsa Bernaut. *Ritual of Liquidation: The Case of the Moscow Trials.* Glencoe, IL: Free Press, 1954.

Le Pere, Garth, and Garth Shelton. *China, Africa and South Africa: South-South Co-operation in a Global Age.* Midrand, South Africa: Institute for Global Dialogue, 2007.

Levine, Harold. "Twenty-One GIs Who Chose Tyranny: Why They Left the US for Communism." *Commentary*, July 1954, 41–46.

Lewis, David Levering. *W.E.B. Du Bois: A Biography 1868–1963.* New York: Henry Holt and Company, 2009.

Li Huang. *War Drums on the Equator.* Translated by Gladys Yang. *Chinese Literature* 7 (1965): 3–72.

Li, Xiaobing, Allen R. Millet, and Bin Yu. *Mao's Generals Remember Korea.* Lawrence: University Press of Kansas, 2001.

Lifton, Robert Jay. *Thought Reform and the Psychology of Totalism: A Study of Brainwashing in China.* 2nd ed. Chapel Hill: University of North Carolina Press, 1989.

Lin Biao. "Long Live the Victory of the People's War," *Peking Review*, no. 36 (September 3, 1965): 9–89.

Liu Liangmo. "Paul Robeson: The People's Singer." In *Chinese American Voices: From the Gold Rush to the Present*, ed. Judy Yung, Gordon H. Chang, and H. Mark Lai, 204–8. Berkeley: University of California Press, 2006.

Liu, Peter Han-Shan. "An Analysis of the *New York Times* Editorial Attitude toward the

Representation of Communist China in the United Nations: 1949–1976." MA thesis, Southern Illinois University, 1969.

Louis, Joe, Art Rust, and Edna Rust. *Joe Louis: My Life*. New York: Harcourt Brace Jovanovich, 1978.

Lucas, Scott. *Freedom's War: The US Crusade against the Soviet Union, 1945–56*. New York: New York University Press, 1999.

Luce, Henry. "The American Century." *Life*, February 17, 1941.

Lumsden, Linda. "Good Mothers with Guns: Framing Black Womanhood in the Black Panther, 1968–1980." *Journalism and Mass Communication Quarterly* 86, no. 4 (Winter 2009): 900–922.

Lüthi, Lorenz M. *The Sino-Soviet Split*. Princeton, NJ: Princeton University Press, 2008.

MacFarquhar, Roderick. *The Hundred Flowers and the Chinese Intellectual*. New York: Praeger Publishers, 1960.

MacFarquhar, Roderick, and Michael Schoenhals. *Mao's Last Revolution*. Cambridge, MA: Harvard University Press, 2006.

Maeda, Daryl. *Chains of Babylon: The Rise of Asian America*. Minneapolis: University of Minnesota Press, 2009.

Mao Zedong. "Chairman Mao's Theory on the Differentiation of the Three Worlds Is a Major Contribution to Marxism-Leninism." *Peking Review*, November 4, 1977, 24.

———. "In Memory of Norman Bethune (December 21, 1939)." In *Selected Works of Mao Tse-tung*, vol. 2, 337–38. Beijing: Foreign Languages Press, 1965.

———. "On Contradiction (August 1937)." In *Selected Works of Mao Tse-tung*, vol. 1. London: Lawrence and Wishart, 1954.

———. "On New Democracy (January 1940)." In *Quotations from Chairman Mao*, 199. Peking: Foreign Language Press, 1966.

———. "On the Correct Handling of Contradictions among the People (February 27, 1957)." In *Selected Works of Mao Tse-tung*, vol. 5, 392–93. Peking: Foreign Languages Press, 1977.

———. "The Orientation of the Youth Movement (May 4, 1939)." In *Selected Works of Mao Tse-tung*, vol. 2, 246. Beijing: Foreign Languages Press, 1965.

———. "Problems of War and Strategy (November 6, 1938)." In *Selected Works of Mao Tse-tung*, vol. 2, 224. Beijing: Foreign Languages Press, 1967.

———. "Red and Expert (January 31, 1958)." In *Long Live Mao Zedong Thought*. Peking: Red Guard Publication, 1969.

———. "Reply to Comrade Kuo Mo-jo (Guo Moruo): To the Melody of *Man Chiang Hung*, January 9, 1963." In *Ten More Poems of Mao Tse-Tung*, 22–23. Hong Kong: Eastern Horizon Press, 1967.

———. "Serve the People (September 8, 1944)." In *Selected Works of Mao Tse-tung*, vol. 3, 227. Beijing: Foreign Languages Press, 1965.

———. *Talks at the Yan'an Forum on Literature and Art, May 1942*. Ann Arbor: Center for Chinese Studies, University of Michigan, 1980.

———. "Talks with African Friends," August 8, 1963. In *Quotations from Chairman Mao Tse-tung on Propaganda*, ed. Robert Friend, 26. Beijing: Foreign Languages Press, 1967.

———. "The Situation in the Summer of 1957 (July 1957)." In *Selected Works of Mao Tse-tung*, vol. 5, 473–82. Beijing: Foreign Languages Press, 1977.

———. *Statement in Support of the Afro-American Struggle against Violent Repression, April 16, 1968*. Peking: Foreign Languages Press, 1968.

———. *Statement Supporting the Afro-American in Their Just Struggle against Racial Discrimination by U.S. Imperialism, August 8, 1963*. Peking: Foreign Languages Press, 1963.

Marable, Manning. *Race, Reform, and Rebellion: The Second Reconstruction in Black America, 1945–1990*. 2nd ed. Jackson: University Press of Mississippi, 1991.

Markel, Seth M. "'We Are Not Tourists': The Black Power Movement and the Making of 'Socialist' Tanzania, 1960–1974." Ph.D. dissertation, New York University, 2011.

Martin, Waldo E., Jr. *No Coward Soldiers: Black Cultural Politics in Postwar America*. Cambridge, MA: Harvard University Press, 2005.

Mason, Mary G. "Travel as Metaphor and Reality in Afro-American Women's Autobiography, 1850–1972." *Black American Literature Forum* 24, no. 2 (Summer 1990): 337–55.

Matthews, Tracey A. "'No One Ever Asks What a Man's Role in the Revolution Is': Gender Politics and Leadership in the Black Panther Party, 1966–71." In *Sisters in the Struggle: African American Women in the Civil Rights–Black Power Movement*, ed. Bettye Collier-Thomas and V. P. Franklin, 230–56. New York: New York University Press, 2001.

May, Elaine Tyler. *Homeward Bound: American Families in the Cold War Era*. New York: Basic Books, 1988.

May, Lary, ed. *Recasting America: Culture and Politics in the Age of Cold War*. Chicago: University of Chicago Press, 1989.

Mayer, William E. "Why Did So Many G.I. Captives Give In?" *US News and World Report*, February 24, 1956, 56–72.

Mbembe, Achille. *On the Postcolony*. Berkeley: University of California Press, 2001.

McAlister, Melani. *Epic Encounters: Culture, Media, and U.S. Interests in the Middle East, 1945–2000*. Berkley: University of California Press, 2001.

McDuffie, Erik S. *Sojourning for Freedom: Black Women, American Communism, and the Making of Black Left Feminism*. Durham, NC: Duke University Press, 2011.

Meerloo, Joost Abraham Maurits. *The Rape of the Mind: The Psychology of Thought Control, Menticide, and Brainwashing*. Cleveland, OH: World Publishing Company, 1956.

Meisner, Maurice. *Mao Zedong: A Political and Intellectual Portrait*. Cambridge, UK: Polity Press, 2007.

Melley, Timothy. *Empire of Conspiracy: The Culture of Paranoia in Postwar America*. Ithaca, NY: Cornell University Press, 2000.

Mercer, Kobena. *Welcome to the Jungle: New Positions in Black Cultural Studies*. London: Routledge, 1994.

Mershon, Sherie, and Steven Schlossman. *Foxholes & Color Lines: Desegregating the U.S Armed Forces*. Baltimore, MD: Johns Hopkins University Press, 1998.

Milton, David, and Nancy Dall Milton. *The Wind Will Not Subside: Years in Revolutionary China*. New York: Pantheon Books, 1976.

Mina, An Xiao. "A Tale of Two Memes: The Powerful Connection between Trayvon Martin and Chen Guangcheng." *The Atlantic*, July 12, 2012.

Mittler, Barbara. *A Continuous Revolution: Making Sense of Cultural Revolution Culture*. Cambridge, MA: Harvard University Press, 2013.

Mohanty, Chandra Talpade. *Feminism without Borders: Decolonizing Theory, Practicing Solidarity*. Durham, NC: Duke University Press, 2003.

———. "Feminist Encounters: Locating the Politics of Experience." In *Destabilizing Theory: Contemporary Feminist Debates*, ed. Michèle Barrett and Anne Phillips, 74–92. Stanford, CA: Stanford University Press, 1992.

Monson, Jamie. *Africa's Freedom Railway: How a Chinese Development Project Changed Lives and Livelihoods in Tanzania*. Bloomington: Indiana University Press, 2009.

Monteiro, Anthony. *Africa and the USA: The Peoples Must Unite*. New York: National Anti-imperialist Movement in Solidarity with African Liberation, 1975.

———. *Africa Demands Freedom Now*. New York: National Anti-imperialist Movement in Solidarity with African Liberation, 1976.

———. "Angola: Key to Freedom for Southern Africa." *New World Review* 44, no. 2 (March–April 1976): 9–13.

Moore, Carlos. *Castro, the Blacks and Africa*. Los Angeles: University of California Center for Afro-American Studies, 1991.

———. *Pichón: Race and Revolution in Castro's Cuba*. Chicago: Lawrence Hill Books, 2008.

Moore, Robin. *Music and Revolution: Cultural Change in Socialist Cuba*. Berkeley: University of California Press, 2006.

Moshkin, J. Robert. *Turncoat: An American's 12 Years in Communist China—The Story of Morris R. Wills*. Englewood Cliffs, NJ: Prentice-Hall, 1966.

Mullen, Bill. *Afro-Orientalism*. Minneapolis: University of Minnesota Press, 2004.

———. "Du Bois, Dark Princess, and the Afro-Asian International." *positions* 11, no. 1 (2003): 217–39.

Mullen, Bill, and Fred Ho, eds. *Afro-Asia: Revolutionary Political and Cultural Connections between African Americans and Asian Americans*. Durham, NC: Duke University Press, 2008.

Mullen, Bill, and Cathryn Watson, eds. *W. E. B. Du Bois on Asia: Crossing the World Color Line*. Jackson: University Press of Mississippi, 2005.

Myrdal, Jan. *Report from a Chinese Village*. New York: Pantheon, 1965

Nadel, Alan. "Cold War Television and the Technology of Brainwashing." In *American Cold War Culture*, ed. Douglas Field, 146–63. Edinburgh: Edinburgh University Press, 2005.

———. *Containment Culture: American Narratives, Postmodernism, and the Atomic Age*. Durham, NC: Duke University Press, 1995.

Neils, Patricia. *China Images in the Life and Times of Henry Luce*. Savage, MD: Rowman and Littlefield, 1990.

Newton, Huey. *Revolutionary Suicide*. New York: Penguin Books, 2009.

Nixon, Richard M. "Asia after Viet Nam." *Foreign Affairs* 46, no. 1 (October 1967): 111–25.

Nudelman, Franny. "Trip to Hanoi: Antiwar Travel and International Consciousness." In *New World Coming: The Sixties and the Shaping of Global Consciousness*, ed. Karen Dubinsky, Catherine Krull, Susan Lord, Sean Mills, and Scott Rutherford, 237–46. Toronto: Between the Lines, 2009.

Ogbar, Jeffrey O. G. *Black Power: Radical Politics and African American Identity*. Baltimore, MD: John Hopkins University Press, 2004.

Okiro, Gary Y. "Toward a Black Pacific." In *AfroAsian Encounters: Culture, History, Politics*, ed. Heike Raphael-Hernandez and Shannon Steen, 313–30. New York: New York University Press, 2006.

Onishi, Yuichiro. "The New Negro of the Pacific: How African Americans Forged Cross-Racial Solidarity with Japan, 1917–1922." *The Journal of African American History* 92, no. 2 (2007): 191–213.

Oropeza, Lorena. *¡Raza Sí! ¡Guerra No!: Chicano Protest and Patriotism during the Viet Nam War Era*. Berkeley: University of California Press, 2005.

Orovio, Helio. *Cuban Music from A to Z*. Durham, NC: Duke University Press, 2004.

Palsey, Virginia. *21 Stayed: The Story of the American GIs Who Chose Communist China*. Ann Arbor: University of Michigan Press, 1994.

Passin, Herbert. *China's Cultural Diplomacy*. New York: Frederick A. Praeger, 1963.

Patnaik, Utsa. "On Famine and Measuring 'Famine Deaths.'" In *Thinking Social Science in India: Essays in Honour of Alice Thorner*, ed. Sujata Patel, Jasodhara Bagchi, and Krishna Raj, 46–68. New Delhi: Sage, 2002.

Peck, James. *Washington's China: The National Security World, the Cold War, and the Origins of Globalism*. Amherst: University of Massachusetts Press, 2006.

Perez, Emma. *The Decolonial Imaginary: Writing Chicanas into History*. Bloomington: Indiana University Press, 1999.

Perlmutter, David. *Picturing China in the American Press: The Visual Portrayal of Sino-American Relations in Time Magazine*. Lanham, MD: Lexington Books, 2007.

Phillips, Caryl. *The European Tribe*. New York: Farrar, Straus & Giroux, 1987.

Phillips, Kimberley L. "'Did the Battlefield Kill Jim Crow?' The Cold War Military, Civil Rights, and Black Freedom Struggles." In *Fog of War: The Second World War and the Civil Rights Movement*, ed. Kevin M. Kruse and Stephen Tuck, 208–29. New York: Oxford University Press, 2012.

———. *War! What Is It Good For? Black Freedom Struggles and the U.S. Military from World War II to Iraq*. Chapel Hill: University of North Carolina Press, 2012.

Plummer, Brenda Gayle. "Castro in Harlem: A Cold War Watershed." In *Rethinking the Cold War*, ed. Allen Hunter, 133–55. Philadelphia: Temple University Press, 1997.

———. *Rising Wind: Black Americans and Foreign Affairs, 1935–1960*. Chapel Hill: University of North Carolina Press, 1996.

———, ed. *Window on Freedom: Race, Civil Rights, and Foreign Affairs, 1945–1988*. Chapel Hill: University of North Carolina Press, 2007.

Porter, Eric. *The Problem of the Future World: W. E. B. Du Bois and the Race Concept at Mid-century*. Durham, NC: Duke University Press, 2010.

Prashad, Vijay. *The Darker Nations: A People's History of the Third World*. New York: New Press, 2008.

———. *Everybody Was Kung-Fu Fighting: Afro-Asian Connections and the Myth of Cultural Purity*. Boston: Beacon Press, 2001.

Pratt, Mary Louise. *Imperial Eyes: Travel Writing and Transculturation*. London: Routledge, 2008.

Pulido, Laura. *Black, Brown, Yellow, and Left: Radical Activism in Los Angeles*. Berkeley: University of California Press, 2006.

Qing, Simei. *From Allies to Enemies: Visions of Modernity, Identity, and U.S.-China Diplomacy, 1945–1960*. Cambridge, MA: Harvard University Press, 2007.

Quinn-Judge, Sophie. *Ho Chi Minh: The Missing Years, 1919–1941*. Berkeley: University of California Press, 2002.

Race, The Floating Signifier. Narr. Sut Jhally. Perf. Stuart Hall. Media Education Foundation, 1996.

Ransby, Barbara. *Ella Baker and the Black Freedom Movement: A Radical Democratic Vision*. Chapel Hill: University of North Carolina Press, 2005.

———. *Eslanda: The Large and Unconventional Life of Mrs. Paul Robeson*. New Haven, CT: Yale University Press, 2013.

Raphael-Hernandez, Heike, and Shannon Steen, eds. *AfroAsian Encounters: Culture, History, Politics*. New York: New York University Press, 2006.

Ratcliff, Anthony J. "Liberation at the End of a Pen: Writing Pan-African Politics of Cultural Struggle." Ph.D. dissertation, University of Massachusetts, Amherst, 2009, paper AAI3372273.

Reale, Egidio. "The Passport Question." *Foreign Affairs* 9, no. 3 (1931): 506–9.

Redding, Arthur. *Turncoats, Traitors, and Fellow Travelers: Culture and Politics of the Early Cold War*. Jackson: University Press of Mississippi, 2008.

Renqiu Yu. *To Save China, to Save Ourselves: The Chinese Hand Laundry Alliance of New York*. Philadelphia: Temple University Press, 1992.

Rhodes, Jane. *Framing the Black Panthers: The Spectacular Rise of a Black Power Icon*. New York: New Press, 2007.

Rishell, Lyle. *With a Black Platoon in Combat: A Year in Korea*. College Station: Texas A&M University Press, 1993.

Rittenberg, Sidney, and Amanda Bennett. *The Man Who Stayed Behind*. Durham, NC: Duke University Press, 2001.

Roa, Raul. "Speech to the Security Council, April 18, 1961." *Playa Girón* 3 (1961): 220.

Robeson, Paul, and Philip Sheldon Foner. *Paul Robeson Speaks: Writings, Speeches, Interviews, 1918–1974*. New York: Kensington Publication Company, 2002.

Robin, Ron T. *The Making of the Cold War Enemy: Culture and Politics in the Military-Intellectual Complex*. Princeton, NJ: Princeton University Press, 2001.

Robinson, Cedric. *Black Marxism: The Making of the Black Radical Tradition*. Chapel Hill: University of North Carolina Press, 2000.

Robinson, Greg. "Internationalism and Justice: Paul Robeson, Asia, and Asian Americans." In *AfroAsian Encounters: Culture, History, Politics*, ed. Heike Raphael-Hernandez and Shannon Steen, 260–76. New York: New York University Press, 2006.

Rodriguez, Besenia. "'De la Esclavitud Yanqui a la Libertad Cubana': U.S. Black Radicals, the Cuban Revolution, and the Formation of a Tricontinental Ideology." *Radical History Review* 92 (Spring 2005): 62–87.

Rotberg, Robert I. *China into Africa: Trade, Aid, and Influence*. Washington, DC: Brookings Institution Press, 2008.

Rucker, Walter. "Crusader in Exile: Robert F. Williams and the International Struggle for Black Freedom in America." *The Black Scholar* 36, no. 3 (2006): 19–34.

Said, Edward. *Orientalism*. New York: Vintage Books, 1979.

———. "Orientalism Reconsidered." *Cultural Critique* 1 (1985): 89–107.

Salter, Mark. "Passports, Mobility, and Security: How Smart Can the Border Be?" *International Studies Perspectives* 5 (2004): 71–91.

Sanders, Mark A. "Afterword: The Black Flame Then and Now." In *Worlds of Color: The Black Flame Trilogy, Book Three*. Vol. 13 of *The Oxford W. E. B. Du Bois*, ed. Henry Louis Gates Jr., 241–55. New York: Oxford University Press, 2007.

Sandoval, Chela. *Methodology of the Oppressed*. Minneapolis: University of Minnesota Press, 2000.

Saunders, Frances Stonor. *The Cultural Cold War: The CIA and the World of Arts and Letters*. New York: New Press, 1999.

———. *Who Paid the Piper? The CIA and the Cultural Cold War*. London: Granta, 1999.

Sautman, Barry. "Myths of Descent, Racial Nationalism and Ethnic Minorities in the People's Republic of China." In *The Construction of Racial Identities in China and Japan*, ed. Frank Dikötter, 75–95. Honolulu: University of Hawaii Press, 1997.

Sauvy, Alfred. "Trois mondes, une planète" [Three worlds, one planet]. *L'Observateur*, August 14, 1952.

Savage, Barbara Dianne. *Broadcasting Freedom: Radio, War, and the Politics of Race, 1938–1948*. Chapel Hill: University of North Carolina Press, 1999.

Sawyer, Mark Q. *Racial Politics in Post-revolutionary Cuba*. Cambridge, UK: Cambridge University Press, 2006.

Schafer, Edward H. *The Golden Peaches of Samarkand: A Study of T'ang Exotics*. Berkeley: University of California Press, 1963.

Schaller, Michael. "Détente and the Strategic Triangle, or, 'Drinking your Mao Tai and Having Your Vodka, Too.'" In *Re-examining the Cold War: U.S.-China Diplomacy, 1954–1973*, ed. Robert S. Ross and Jiang Changbin, 361–89. Cambridge, MA: Harvard University Press, 2002.

Schatten, Fritz. *Communism in Africa*. New York: Praeger, 1966.

Schein, Edgar H. *Coercive Persuasion: A Socio-psychological Analysis of the "Brainwashing" of American Civilian Prisoners by the Chinese Communists*. New York: W. W. Norton, 1961.

Schram, Stuart. *The Thought of Mao Tse-Tung*. Cambridge, UK: Cambridge University Press, 1989.

Scipio, L. Albert. *Last of the Black Regulars: A History of the 24th Infantry Regiment (1869–1951)*. Silver Spring, MD: Roman Publications, 1983.

Shapiro, Judith. *Mao's War against Nature: Politics and the Environment in Revolutionary China*. Cambridge: Cambridge University Press, 2001.

Sheridan, James E. *Chinese Warlord: The Career of Feng Yu-hsiang*. Stanford, CA: Stanford University Press, 1966.

Shinn, David H., and Joshua Eisenman. *China and Africa: A Century of Engagement*. Philadelphia: University of Pennsylvania Press, 2012.

Shogun, Robert, and Tom Craig. *The Detroit Race Riot: A Study in Violence*. Philadelphia: Chilton Books, 1964.

Shoup, Laurence H. "Shaping the Postwar World: The Council on Foreign Relations and United States War Aims." *Insurgent Sociologist* 5 (Spring 1975): 9–52.

Singh, Nikhil Pal. *Black Is a Country: Race and the Unfinished Struggle for Democracy*. Cambridge, MA: Harvard University Press, 2004.

———. "Culture/Wars: Recoding Empire in an Age of Democracy." *American Quarterly* 50, no. 3 (September 1998): 471–522.

Singham, A. W., and Shirley Hune. *Non-alignment in an Age of Alignments*. Westport, CT: Lawrence Hill and Co., 1986.

Slate, Nico, ed. *Black Power beyond Borders: The Global Dimensions of the Black Power Movement*. New York: Palgrave McMillan, 2012.

———. *Colored Cosmopolitanism: The Shared Struggle for Freedom in the United States and India*. Cambridge, MA: Harvard University Press, 2012.

Smethurst, James. *The Black Arts Movement: Literary Nationalism in the 1960s and 1970s*. Chapel Hill: University of North Carolina Press, 2005.

Smith, Barbara. *The Truth That Never Hurts: Writings on Race, Gender, and Freedom*. New Brunswick, NJ: Rutgers University Press, 2000.

Snow, Edgar. *Red Star over China*. New York: Random House, 1938.

Snow, Philip. *The Star Raft: China's Encounter with Africa*. New York: Weidenfeld and Nicolson, 1988.

Spiller, Harry, ed. *American POWs in Korea: Sixteen Personal Accounts*. Jefferson, NC: McFarland and Co., 1998.

Spivak, Gayatri C. *Nationalism and the Imagination*. London: Seagull Books, 2010.

Springer. Kimberly. *Living for Revolution: Black Feminist Organizations, 1968–1980*. Durham, NC: Duke University Press, 2005.

Stephens, Michelle A. *Black Empire: The Masculine Global Imaginary of Caribbean Intellectuals in the United States, 1914–1962*. Durham, NC: Duke University Press, 2005.

Stephens, Ronald J. "Narrating Acts of Resistance: Explorations of Untold Heroic and Horrific Battle Stories Surrounding Robert Franklin Williams' Residence in Lake County, Michigan." *Journal of Black Studies* 33, no. 5 (2003): 675–703.

———. "'Praise the Lord and Pass the Ammunition': Robert F. Williams's Crusade for Justice on Behalf of Twenty-two Million African Americans as a Cuban Exile." *Black Diaspora Review* 2, no. 1 (2010): 15–28.

Streeby, Shelley. *Radical Sensations: World Movements, Violence, and Visual Culture*. Durham, NC: Duke University Press, 2013.

Stringer, Kimberly. *Living for the Revolution: Black Feminist Organizations, 1968–1980*. Durham, NC: Duke University Press, 2005.

Strong, Tracy B., and Helene Keyssar. *Right in Her Soul: The Life of Anna Louise Strong*. New York: Random House, 1983.

Sukarno, Ahmed. *Dibawah Bendera Revolusi* (Under the Banner of Revolution), vol. 1. Jakarta: Panitya Penerbit, 1963.

Swarup, Ram. *Brain-washing in Red China*. New Delhi: Society for the Defense of Freedom in Asia, 1955.

Taketani, Etsuko. "The Cartography of the Black Pacific: James Weldon Johnson's *Along This Way*." *American Quarterly* 59, no. 1 (2007): 79–106.

Taylor, Ian. *China and Africa: Engagement and Compromise*. New York: Routledge, 2006.

Teufel, June. "China's Approach to Africa." *Far Eastern Economic Review* 3 (October 1963): 443–44, 469.

Thaxton, Ralph A., Jr. *Catastrophe and Contention in Rural China: Mao's Great Leap Forward Famine and the Origins of Righteous Resistance in Da Fo Village*. New York: Cambridge University Press, 2008.

Thompson, Heather A. *Whose Detroit? Politics, Labor, and Race in a Modern American City*. Ithaca, NY: Cornell University Press, 2001.

Thompson, James. *True Colors: 1004 Days as a Prisoner of War*. Port Washington, NY: Ashley Books, 1989.

Torpey, John C. *The Invention of the Passport: Surveillance, Citizenship, and the State*. Cambridge, UK: Cambridge University Press, 2000.

Truman, Harry S. "Special Message to the Congress on Greece and Turkey: The Truman Doctrine," March 12, 1947; Document 171; 80th Congress, 1st Session; Records of the United States House of Representatives; Record Group 233; National Archives.

Tsui, Shu-chin. *From Academic Freedom to Brainwashing: The Tragic Ordeal of Professors on the Chinese Mainland*. Taipei: China Culture Publishing Foundation, 1953.

Tyson, Timothy B. *Radio Free Dixie: Robert F. Williams and the Roots of Black Power*. Chapel Hill: University of North Carolina Press, 1999.

———. "Robert F. Williams, 'Black Power,' and the Roots of the African American Freedom Struggle." *The Journal of American History* 85, no. 2 (September 1998): 540–57.

U.S. Department of State. "Memorandum of Discussion of the 237th Meeting of the National Security Council." February 17, 1955, *Foreign Relations of the United States, China, 1955–57*, 2: 285.

———. "National Security Council Report 68 (NSC 68)," April 7, 1950. In *The World Transformed: 1945 to the Present*, ed. Michael H. Hunt, 36–39. New York: Bedford/St. Martin's, 2004.

Von Eschen, Penny. *Race against Empire: Black Americans and Anticolonialism, 1937–1957*. Ithaca, NY: Cornell University Press, 1997.

———. *Satchmo Blows Up the World: Jazz Ambassadors Play the Cold War*. Cambridge, MA: Harvard University Press, 2006.

———. "Who's the Real Ambassador? Exploding Cold War Racial Ideology." In *Cold War Constructions: The Political Culture of United States Imperialism, 1945–1966*, ed. Christian G. Appy, 110–31. Amherst: University of Massachusetts Press, 2000.

Wang Hui. *The End of Revolution*. London: Verso, 2009.

Ward, Stephen M. "The Third World Women's Alliance: Black Feminist Radicalism and Black Power Radicalism." In *The Black Power Movement: Rethinking the Civil Rights–Black Power Era*, ed. Peniel E. Joseph, 119–44. New York: Routledge, 2006.

Wei, Chunjuan Nancy, and Darryl E. Brock, eds. *Mr. Science and Chairman Mao's Cultural Revolution: Science and Technology in Modern China*. Lanham, MD: Lexington Books, 2013.

Weisbrot, Robert. *Freedom Bound: A History of America's Civil Rights Movement*. New York: W. W. Norton and Company, 1990.

Welch, Rebeccah E. "Gender and Power in the Black Diaspora: Radical Women of Color and the Cold War." *Souls: A Critical Journal of Black Culture, Politics and Society* 5, no. 3 (Summer 2003): 71–82.

———. "Spokesman of the Oppressed? Lorraine Hansberry at Work: The Challenge of Radical Politics in the Postwar Era." *Souls: A Critical Journal of Black Culture, Politics and Society* 9, no. 4 (October 2007): 302–19.

Wendt, Simon. *The Spirit and the Shotgun: Armed Resistance and the Struggle for Civil Rights*. Gainesville: University Press of Florida, 2007.

———. "'They Found Out That We Really Are Men': Violence, Non-violence, and Black Manhood in the Civil Rights Era." *Gender and History* 19 (November 2007): 543–64.

West, Michael O., William G. Martin, and Fanon Che Wilkins, eds. *From Toussaint to Tupac: The Black International since the Age of Revolutions*. Chapel Hill: University of North Carolina Press, 2009.

Westad, Odd Arne. *The Global Cold War: Third World Interventions and the Making of Our Times*. Cambridge, UK: Cambridge University Press, 2007.

White, W. L. *The Captives of Korea: An Unofficial White Paper on the Treatment of War Prisoners*. New York: Scribner's, 1957.

Whitfield, Stephen J. *The Culture of the Cold War*. Baltimore, MD: John Hopkins University Press, 1991.

Whiting, Allen S. *China Crosses the Yalu: The Decision to Enter the Korean War*. Palo Alto, CA: Stanford University Press, 1960.

Widener, Daniel. "Seoul City Sue and the Bugout Blues: Black Dissent and the Forgotten War." In *Afro Asia: Revolutionary Connections*, eds. Fred Ho and Bill V. Mullen, 55–87. Durham, NC: Duke University Press, 2008.

Wilensky, Julie. "The Magical Kunlun and 'Devil Slaves.'" *Sino-Platonic Papers*, no. 122 (July 2002): 1–51.

Wilkins, Fanon Che. "'In the Belly of the Beast': Black Power, Anti-imperialism, and the African Liberation Solidarity Movement, 1968–1975." Ph.D. dissertation, New York University, 2001.

Williams, Robert F. "An Afro-American In Africa." *The Call: Journal of the Afro-Asian Writers Bureau* 9, no. 1 (1969): 20–22.

———. *Listen, Brother!* New York: Worldview Publishers, 1968.

———. *Negroes with Guns.* New York: Marzani and Munsell, 1962.

———. "Testimony of Robert F. Williams." In *Hearings before the Subcommittee to Investigate the Administration of the Internal Security Act and Other Internal Security Laws, Second Session, Part 1: February 16, 1970.* Washington, DC: US Government Printing Office, 1970.

Williams, Robert F., and Mabel Williams. *Robert and Mabel Williams Resource Guide.* San Francisco: Freedom Archives, 2005.

Winance, Eleutherius. *The Communist Persuasion: A Personal Experience of Brainwashing.* New York: P. J. Kennedy, 1959.

Woodard, Komozi. *A Nation within a Nation: Amiri Baraka and Black Power Politics.* Chapel Hill: University of North Carolina Press, 1999.

Worthy, William. "Africa, Truth and the Right to Travel." *International Socialist Review* 23, no. 4 (Fall 1962): 116–18.

———. "The American Negro Is Dead." *Esquire,* November 1967, 126–37, 167–68.

———. "Our Disgrace in Indo-China," *The Crisis* 61, no. 2 (February 1954).

———. "The Red Chinese American Negro." *Esquire,* October 1964, 132, 173–79.

———. "Reporting in Communist China." *New Republic,* March 25, 1957, 9–11.

Worthy, William, Sr. "Retirement of Dr. William Augustus Hinton: An Appreciation of Dr. Hinton." *Journal of the National Medical Association* 45, no. 1 (1952): 71.

———. *The Story of the Two First Colored Nurses to Train in the Boston City Hospital.* Boston, 1942.

Wright, Robert Anthony, and Lana Wylie. *Our Place in the Sun: Canada and Cuba in the Castro Era.* Toronto: University of Toronto Press, 2009.

Wu Ch'êng-ên. *Journey to the West.* Trans. W. J. F. Jenner. Beijing: Foreign Languages Press, 2003.

———. *Monkey Nobel of China.* Trans. Arthur Waley. New York: Grove Press, 1994.

Wu, Hongda Harry. "The Labor-Reform Camps in the PRC." In *Two Societies in Opposition: The Republic of China and the People's Republic of China, after Forty Years,* ed. Ramon Hawley Myers, 75–93. Palo Alto, CA: Hoover Press, 1991.

Wu, Judy Tzu-Chun. *Radicals on the Road: Internationalism, Orientalism, and Feminism during the Vietnam Era.* Ithaca, NY: Cornell University Press, 2013.

Wyatt, Don J. *The Blacks of Premodern China.* Philadelphia: University of Pennsylvania Press, 2009.

Wylie, Raymond F. *The Emergence of Maoism: Mao Tse-tung, Ch'en Po-ta, and the Search for Chinese Theory, 1935–1945.* Stanford, CA: Stanford University Press, 1980.

Xiaoyang, Guo, and Ma Yanhong. "On W.E.B. Du Bois's 'Double-Consciousness' and Its Influence on Black American Literature." *Journal of Northeastern University* 9, no. 3 (2007): 279–82.

Xing, Jun. *Asian America through the Lens: History, Representations, and Identity.* Walnut Creek, CA: AltaMira, 1998.

Yan, Yunxiang. "McDonalds in Beijing: The Localization of Americana." In *Golden Arches*

East: *McDonald's in East Asia*, 2nd ed., ed. James L. Watson, 39–76. Stanford, CA: Stanford University Press, 2006.

Yang Jisheng. *Tombstone: The Untold Story of Mao's Great Famine*. Trans. Stacy Mosher and Guo Jian. London: Penguin Books, 2012.

Yardley, Jim. *Brave Dragons: A Chinese Basketball Team, an American Coach, and Two Cultures Clashing*. New York: Alfred A. Knopf, 2012.

Yoshihara, Mari. *Embracing the East: White Women and American Orientalism*. Ithaca, NY: Cornell University Press, 2003.

Young, Charles S. "Missing Action: POW Films, Brainwashing, and the Korean War, 1954–1968." *Historical Journal of Film, Radio, and Television* 18, no. 1 (1998): 49–74.

Young, Cynthia Ann. *Soul Power: Culture, Power, and the Making of a U.S. Third World Left*. Durham, NC: Duke University Press, 2006.

Young, Kenneth Ray, and Dan S. Green. "Harbinger to Nixon: W.E.B. Du Bois in China." *Negro History Bulletin* 35 (October 1972): 125–28.

Yu, George T. "China's Role in Africa." *Annals of the American Academy of Political and Social Science* 432 (July 1977): 96–109.

———. "Sino-African Relations: A Survey." *Asian Survey* 5, no. 7 (July 1965): 321–32.

Yu, Yang-Chou, and Daniel Riffe. "Chiang and Mao in U.S. News Magazines." *Journalism Quarterly* 66 (1989): 913–19.

Yun, Lisa. *The Coolie Speaks: Chinese Indentured Laborers and African Slaves in Cuba*. Philadelphia: Temple University Press, 2008.

Zhang Xinglang. "Gudai Zhongguo yu Feizhou zhi jiaotong" [Communication between ancient China and Africa]. In *Zhongxi jiaotong shiliao huipian* [Assembled reports of historical data on Chinese-Western relations], vol. 3. Taipei: Shijie shuju, 1962.

Žižek, Slavoj. *The Sublime Object of Ideology*. London and New York: Verso, 1989.

Zweiback, Adam J. "The 21 'Turncoat GIs'? Nonrepatriations and the Political Culture of the Korean War." *Historian* 60 no. 2 (1998): 345–62.

Index

Note: page numbers in italics refer to illustrations; those followed by "n" indicate endnotes.

black-nationalist organizations, socialist-
oriented, 201
blackness, 8, 156–57, 216
Black Student Voice, 157
Brady, Anne-Marie, 15, 57, 165
"brainwashing" discourse, 82–83, 86, 91–92,
99–100, 244n32–245n33, 246n47
Brezhnev, Leonid, 198
Brown, Elaine, 192
Brown, John, 174, 176
Burgess, G. Thomas, 16

Cabral, Amílcar, 274n36
Caetano, Marcello, 205
Canada, 144–45, 259n41
capitalism: Deng administration adoption of,
209; global, China's integration into, 215;
Luce on U.S. discourses and global capi-
talism, 5; Mao's rejection of stage of, 48,
166–67; racial, 6
Carpenter, J. Henry, 73
carrot and club analogy, 173–74, 175
cartoons, in *Crusader Weekly Newsletter*, 123, 128,
129, 137–38, 139. *See also* propaganda art and
posters, Chinese
Castro, Fidel, 105, 124, 125, 125–26
Central Cultural Revolution Group (CCRG),
114–15
Césaire, Aimé, 258n24
Chaloupka, William, 138
changqi douzheng (protracted struggle), 34
Chen Guangcheng, 216–17, 218, 219
Chen Jian, 58, 241n8
Chen Jianking, 255n11
Chen, Xiaomei, 11, 258n26
Chen Yinghuang, 248n64
Chiang Kai-Shek, 45
Chicago Committee to Defend William Wor-
thy, 104
Chile, 204
China. *See* People's Republic of China
China Peace Committee, 136–37, 185
Chinese Communist Party (CCP): African
political movements and, 202; agrarian-
centered philosophy of, 25; civil war and
victory of, 25–26; Cultural Revolution
and, 114–16, 209; foreign revolutionary
movement ties, 111; foreign visits, control
of, 51; GMD, alliance with, 24–25, 231n1;
Great Leap Forward and Hundred Flowers

Campaign, 49–51, 236n42; Korean War,
calculation on, 77–78, 241n8; Long March,
25; moderation of, after taking power, 26;
poster art and iconography, 132–35; ritu-
alized demonstrations and mobilization
of citizens, 58, 237n66; Soviet relationship
with, 24, 28–29; Tibet rebellion and, 59;
U.S. favoring of GMD over, 23–24. *See also*
People's Republic of China
Chinese Exclusion Act, 2
Chinese government. *See* Chinese Communist
Party; Mao Zedong; People's Republic of
China
Chisholm, Shirley, 200
Chow, Rey, 10
Ciendfuegos Gorriarán, Osmány, 264n93
Civil Rights Act (U.S., 1964), 175
Civil Rights Movement: China's endorse-
ment of, 131–36; Estes on masculinism
and, 236n50; Freedom Riders, 126, 258n35;
Garvin on, 175; Montgomery Bus Boycott,
95; Western expatriate statements from
China on, 260n56
Clayton, Buck, 2
Cleaver, Kathleen, 193, 201, 257n7
Clifford, James, 63
closed-door policy, 232n23
Clough, Ralph N., 96–97
Coe, Frank, 116, 259n50, 260n56
Cold War: "American Orientalism" and,
246n48; atomic bomb as symbol for,
138–39; meaning of, 4; passport regulation
and, 104, 253n119; Worthy on communism
vs. democracy narrative in media, 81
"color line," 62
color metaphor in Du Bois's *Worlds of Color*, 63
Comintern International (Soviet), 24
communism: Du Bois's shift to, 39–40; First
Indochina War and, 94; Garvin on, 159–60;
racist depictions of, 33; union purge of,
232n17; U.S. anti-communist, anti-China
discourse, 26–27, 30–34; Worthy on communism vs. democracy narrative in media,
81. *See also* Chinese Communist Party;
Marxist-Leninist philosophy
Communist Party of the Soviet Union (CPSU),
111–12
Communist Party of the United States
(CPUSA): Chinese criticism of, 111–12; David
Graham Du Bois and, 44; Du Bois and, 42;

Garvin and, 161; travel restrictions against, 72; Williamses, attempts to silence, 142

Congo, 255n11

Congress of Racial Equality, 76–77

"Consider Me" (Hughes), 36

containment culture, 31–33, 63, 74–75

Council on African Affairs, 40, 234n12

Coz, William, 87

Crowder, Richard, 119

Crusader Weekly Newsletter: cartoons in, 128, 129, 137–38, 139; on China-U.N. conflict, 130–31; counterfeit editions of, 142–43, 144, 145, 264n90; creation and purpose of, 123–24; from Cuba, 127–28; distribution from Canada, 259n41; open letter to Khrushchev in, 261n80; U.S. denunciation of, 146

Cuba: 26th of July Movement, 258n32; Afro-Cuban culture, restrictions on, 262n84; black radicalism and, 124–26; race relations in, 141–42, 262n82; Soviet Union and, 124, 141; Tricontinental Conference (Havana, 1966), 263n88; Williamses and, 125–26, 141–46, 263n86, 263n88; Williamses media from, 127–31; Worthy and, 104–6

"Cuba: A Declaration of Conscience by Afro-Americans," 106

Cuban Revolution, 124–26

cultural representation, 8, 56–61

Cultural Revolution. *See* Great Proletarian Cultural Revolution

Czechoslovakia, 198

Dalai Lama, 59

Dark Princess (Du Bois), 234n11

Davis, Angela, 212

decoloniality: African American struggle and, 6; black radicalism and, 9; Du Boises and, 40, 47, 48–49. *See also* Afro-Asian and Afro-Chinese solidarity; anticolonial movements

Deng Xiaoping, 22, 114, 115, 209, 256n17

desegregation of U.S. military, 78, 242n10, 242n12

Diem, Ngo Dinh, 147

Dikötter, Frank, 89

Ding Xilin, 57

Dirlik, Arif, 48, 258n26

Dixiecrats, 232n17

dongfang hei (the east is black), 17

"Dongfang Hong" ("The East Is Red") (opera and song), 17

Dongping Han, 172

Douglas, Aaron, 79

Douglas, William O., 252n113

Douglass, Frederick, 174, 176

Du Bois, Shirley. *See* Graham Du Bois, Shirley

Du Bois, W. E. B., 22, 39, 47, 71; 1936 trip to China, 44–45, 239n94; 1962 trip to China, 69; on anti-communism, 31; on Chinese-African friendship, 47–49, 68, 235n34; Chinese citizens' familiarity with, 212; communism, shift to, 39–40; *Dark Princess*, 234n11; death of, 70; defense of account of, 59–60; Garvin and, 163; on Japanese aggression, 240n94; on Korean War, 79; Monkey King parable and, 37–38; *Pittsburgh Courier* editorials, 239n86; political isolation of, 40–41; scholarly neglect of final years of, 38–39; *The Souls of Black Folk*, 67; as "suspect citizen," 233n10; travel, concept of, 62–63; *Worlds of Color*, 37, 61–69; "Worlds of Color" (essay), 238n80; writing style and genre blending of, 238n77; "Yellow Sea," 239n86

Du Boises' trip to China (1959), 39; Chinese-African friendship, Mao's development model, and, 47–49; Chinese economy, celebration of, 46–47; Chinese government staging tactics for foreign visitors, 56–60; cultural representation and politics of seeing, 60–61; Du Bois's masculinist account of, 52–54; Graham Du Bois's feminist account of, 54–55; Graham Du Bois's summation of, 38; Great Leap Forward, Hundred Flowers Campaign, and, 49–51; opportunity to travel and previous experience of, 43–45; return trips, 69–70; similarities in Du Bois and Graham Du Bois accounts, 51–52; U.S. political isolation and, 41–43; *Worlds of Color* and, 61–69

Dulles, John Foster, 95

Du Ping, 243n23

East Asian studies, 15

"The East," Du Bois on, 49, 239n83

"the east is black" (*dongfang hei*), 17

"The East Is Red" ("Dongfang Hong") (opera and song), 17

East-West dialectic, 11

economic development and industrialization of China, 46–47, 48 educational system and philosophy in China, 164–65, 168–73, 181, 267n17. *See also* Garvin, Vicki

Egypt, 29

Eisenhower, Dwight, 33

Elbaum, Max, 6

Ellis, Eddie, 157

Empire, Hardt and Negri's concept of, 256n11

Epton, Bill, 192, 200

Esch, Betsy, 110

Estes, Steve, 236n50

Evans, Harriet, 152

Evers, Charles, 199

expatriate community in China: antiforeign sentiment and, 186; Civil Rights Movement connections made by, 260n56; Cultural Revolution and, 181–87; members of, 116; pampering, manipulation, and surveillance by Chinese government, 185; paradoxes of, 160–61

The Facts on Angola (Horne), 207

Fairbank, John King, 28

Fair Play for Cuba Committee (FPCC), 106, 125–26, 259n41

Fanon, Frantz, 258n24

Fast, Howard, 73

Federal Bureau of Investigation (FBI), 120, 146–47, 157, 195

Fehrenbach, T. R., 249n74

Fellowship of Reconciliation, 76–77

feminism: black feminist scholarship, 14, 229n35; female revolutionary internationalism, 12; Garvin and, 177–80; in Graham Du Bois's travel account, 54–55; W. E. B. Du Bois and, 53; Williams's *Listen Brother!* and, 150–54; women of color in Chinese propaganda art, 154–56, 155, 156. *See also* gender and gender politics

Fennell, Vera, 15–16

First Indochina War, 94–95

"The Foolish Old Man Who Removed Mountains" (*Yugong yishan*), 171, 268n40

Ford, Gerald, 205–6

"foreign experts" (*waiguo zhuanjia*) status, 185

foreign policy, Chinese: Africa policies, 29–30, 202–7; Congo and, 255n11; orchestration of foreign visitors as, 57; rightward shift of, 204–5, 208–9

foreign policy, U.S.: black views of, 33; closed-door policy, 232n23; containment, 31–33, 63; isolation of China, efforts toward, 27

the four modernizations (*si ge xiandaihua*), 209

Franklin, John Hope, 212

Freedom Now Party, 106

Freedom Riders, 126, 258n35

Frente Nacional de Libertação de Angola (FNLA), 206–7

Fu Ru Tie, 137

Gallo, Rubén, 9

Gao, Yunxiang, 15–16

Garrison, William Lloyd, 174, 176

Garvin, Vicki, 162, 169, 191, 192; about, 158, 160; on China's youth, 159; course on African American history and black resistance, 172–80; Cultural Revolution and, 181–82; as editor in Beijing, 186–87; in Ghana, and invitation to China, 161–64; as labor organizer in U.S., 161; on Mao personality cult, 186–87; marriage, 188–90; return to U.S., 191–92; Shanghai Foreign Languages Institute and, 164–65; speech in New York, 159–60; speech in Shanghai on Black Power, 188; teaching on women's rights, 177–80; teaching practice linked to Mao's philosophy, 168–72, 190–91; tours of China organized by, 192

gender and gender politics: Du Bois's masculinist account of China trip, 52–54; Estes on Civil Rights Movement and, 236n50; Garvin on, 177–80; Graham Du Bois's feminist account of China trip, 54–55; internalization of cultural beliefs about revolution and, 156; mother images and maternal sacrifice narratives, 150–51; patriarchal sexual promise of Orientalism, 240n95; "soul brothers" and, 119; Williams's *Listen, Brother!* and, 150–54; women of color in Chinese propaganda art, 154–56, 155, 156. *See also* masculinism

Gerlach, Talitha, 260n56

Ghana, 161–64, 240n95

Gibson, Richard, 125, 143

Gilroy, Paul, 65, 236n40, 238n77

Gitelman, Lisa, 9

Glissant, Édouard, 65

GMD. *See* Guomindang

Gong Peng, 102

"good Asians"/"bad Asians" trope, 33–34

Graham Du Bois, David, 43, 44, 235n23
Graham Du Bois, Shirley, 22, 39, 56; 1962 trip
    to China, 69; defense of account of, 60;
    Garvin and, 162, 163; on Korean War, 79;
    on "Land of Tomorrow," 37; McCarthyism
    and, 42–43; radical leftism and, 43; ties to
    China after Du Bois's death, 69–70, 241n96.
    See also Du Boises' trip to China (1959)
Great Leap Forward (GLF; da yue jin), 49–51,
    113, 236n42
Great Proletarian Cultural Revolution (GPCR;
    wuchan jieji wenhua dageming): Deng and
    CCP distancing from, 209; "The East Is
    Red" and, 17; events of, 113–15; expatriate
    responses to, 181–87; foreigners in China
    and, 115–16, 161; Jiang Qing vs. Wu Han
    and, 255n16; Killens on, 211; personal sto-
    ries of, 213–14; Western China enthusiasts
    and, 160
Green, Regina, 233n10
Guevara, Ernesto "Che," 124
Guomindang (GMD; Nationalist Party): CCP,
    alliance with, 24–25, 231n1; civil war, de-
    feat, and exile to Taiwan, 25–26; Du Bois
    on, 45; U.S., relationship with, 23
Guo Moruo, 44, 136
Guzman, Pablo "Yoruba," 192

Hai Rui Dismissed from Office (Hai Rui ba guan),
    255n16
Hall, Stuart, 8
Hampton, Tommie, 87
Han ethnic identity, 89
Hanoi Hannah (radio), 148, 265n109
Hardt, Michael, 256n11
Harlan, John, 87, 89
Harper, Lucius, 232n23
Harrington, Philip, 96, 97, 102
Harris, Nigel, 231n1
Hatem, George, 260n56
Hayhoe, Ruth, 164
He Liliang, 162
Hennings, Thomas Carey, 252n116
Henry, Milton, 196
Hevi, Emmanuel John, 237n66, 251n101,
    251n103
Hewlett, Edward, 87
Hinton, William, 192
"The History of the Negro in the U.S." (stu-
    dent presentation), 180–81

Ho Chi Minh, 94, 148
Hollander, Paul, 65–66
Hoover, J. Edgar, 31, 195
Hopkins, Chuck, 200–201
Horne, Gerald, 43, 207
Horness, John, 116
House Un-American Activities Committee,
    31
Hoxha, Enver, 275n57
Hua Guofeng, 209
Huang Hua, 162–63, 266n6
Hughes, Langston, 36, 107
Hundred Flowers Campaign (baihua yundong),
    50–51
Hunter, Edward, 83, 85–86, 244n27

imaginary identification, 239n93
imagination and imagining: Anderson's
    "imagined community," 257n16; defined,
    7; dissonance of, 10; East–West dialectic,
    11; Kelley on, 256n16; political imagining in
    Chinese and American public spheres, 219;
    radical imagining, work of, 6–7
Immigration and Nationality Act of 1952
    (McCarran-Walter Act), 105
imperialism, Japanese, 25, 44–45, 66, 170,
    240n94
imperialism, U.S.: black radicalism and, 5;
    carrot and club metaphor and, 173–74; Chi-
    nese statements against, 34–35, 109, 138,
    156; Congo and, 255n11; in Cuba, 105–6; Du
    Bois on, 49; Garvin on, 173–74, 176; Luce
    on, 4; prison-camp propaganda on, 82;
    racial discrimination linked to, 8, 118, 128,
    132, 208; Soviets and, 111–12; Williams on
    Vietnam and, 148
imperialism, Western: China's rightward shift
    and, 207; Crusader on, 128; in documentary
    on Williamses, 141; Du Bois on, 44–45, 53,
    68, 239n80; Garvin on subjection of Afri-
    cans and Asians by, 163; Mao on capitalism
    and, 166; Worthy on, 74, 80, 98
India, 112
Inman, Cecil Mark, 249n74
"In Memory of Norman Bethune" (Mao), 170,
    268n40
intelligentsia in China, 50–51, 239n94
intermediate zones (zhongjian didai), theory
    of, 110
international decolonial collective, 40

internationalism: Chinese philosophy of, 110; Du Bois and, 40, 42, 53; Du Bois's *Worlds of Color* and, 68; essentializing images of, 10; female, 153, 154–55; Garvin on Black Freedom Movement and, 188; gender and, 14; Mao on, 23, 30; Mao's intermediate zones theory and, 110; "March of the Volunteers" and, 3; proletarian, China's shift away from, 204, 206, 208; racial, Chinese rhetoric of, 11, 116, 135, 138; racial, scholarship on, 15–17. *See also* Afro-Asian and Afro-Chinese solidarity; *specific persons and topics*
international relations, field of, 15
Iriye, Akira, 8, 257n18
Isaacs, Harold, 244n32
Isacson, Leo, 73

Jaffe, Louis, 253n119
James, C. L. R., 73
Japanese imperialism, 66, 240n94
Jiang Qing, 255n16
jiedao banshichu (street committees), 97–98
Jim Crow racism: Fu Ru Tie on, 137; "New Jim Crow," 218; White and, 100; Williamses and, 121–22, 128. *See also* white supremacy
Jin Jingyi, 140
Johnson, Alonzo S., 88, 90
Johnson, Charles, 157
Johnson, James Weldon, 211
Johnson, Lyndon B., 138, 148
Johnson, Matthew D., 16
Jones, Andrew, 230n38
Jones, Claudia, 73, 115–16
Jordan, Vernon, 199
Journey of Reconciliation, 76–77
Jowett, Garth, 243n23

Kairov, I. A., 164
Karl, Rebecca, 267n23
Kelley, Robin D. G., 110, 256n16
Kennan, George, 31
Kennedy, John F., 124
Kent, Rockwell, 73, 252n113
Kheir, Ahmed, 270n88
Khrushchev, Nikita, 28, 262n80
Killens, John Oliver, 209–12
Kim Il-sung, 77
King, Martin Luther, Jr., 187–88, 211
Kinkhead, Eugene, 83
Kissinger, Henry, 197, 198, 205, 206, 208

Klein, Christina, 246n48
Korean War: African American views on, 78–79; Chinese calculations on entry into, 77–78, 241n8; events of, 77–78; repatriation agreement, 84, 245n37; U.S. military desegregation and, 78; Worthy's reporting on, 79–81. *See also* prisoners of war
Ku Klux Klan, 89, 103, 120, 130
Kuomintang (KMT). *See* Guomindang
Kuumba, M. Bahati, 15
Kwon, Heonik, 246n48
Kwong, Julia, 181

Lamont, Corliss, 73
laodong gaizao or *laogai* (labor reform), 190
laogai dui (indoctrination and reeducation lectures), 82, 87, 91
Lavan, George, 253n118
"Learn from Comrade Lei Feng" (*Xiang Lei Feng tongzhi xuexi*), 171
Le Dequan, 54
Leese, Daniel, 171–72
Lei Feng, 171
Lenin, Vladimir, 48, 134, 167
Lewis, David Levering, 239n89
"Lift Every Voice and Sing" (Johnson), 211
Li Huang, 255n11
Li Jinhui, 2
Lim, Anne B., 128
Lin Biao, 114, 115, 140, 165, 256n17, 261n65
Li Rui-hua, 169
Listen, Brother! (Williams), 150–57, 153
"The Little Red Book" (*Quotations from Chairman Mao; Mao zhuxi yulu*), 17–18, 160, 166, 184, 202
Liu Liangmo, 2, 255n2
Liu Shaoqi, 114, 115, 137, 256n17
Long March (*changzheng*), 25
long movement, 5, 256n12
Look Up and Live (TV), 246n48
L'Ouverture, Toussaint, 174, 176
Lowry, John, 119
loyalty, paradox of, 233n10
Luce, Henry, 4–5, 256n11
Lumumba, Patrice, 204, 255n11
Lu Shaoquan, 138
Lynn, Conrad, 197–98

Mackensen, Paul J., Jr., 98, 250n95
Malcolm X, 122, 123, 136, 163

Mallory, Mae, 119, 153–54

Malveaux, Julianne, 233n10

The Manchurian Candidate (film, 1962), 245n33

Mao Dun, 47

Mao Zedong, 184; Afro-Asian solidarity and, 47–48; appeal of, among U.S. radicals, 183; Cultural Revolution and, 113–15; death of, 209; détente with U.S. and, 193–95, 198; with Du Boises, 22, 71; on Du Bois's death, 70; on education, 165, 190–91; Great Leap Forward and, 49–51; Korean War and, 77; Long March and, 25; Monkey King parable and, 37; on the past, 160, 170; personality cult around, 166, 186–87; poetry of, 70; racial internationalism and, 11; Saunders on, 200; socialist art and, 133–34; Soviet Union and, 28; statements on African American struggle, 109, 111, 131–36, 259n50; on violent revolution, 131; Williamses and, 130; Williams's "An Ocean's Roar of Peace" and, 256n1

Mao Zedong, works and speeches of: "The Foolish Old Man Who Removed Mountains," 171, 268n40; "In Memory of Norman Bethune," 170, 268n40; "On the Correct Handling of Contradictions among the People," 167, 173; *Quotations from Chairman Mao* ("the little red book"), 17–18, 160, 166, 184, 202; *Selected Military Writings*, 166; *Selected Readings from the Works of*, 166; *Selected Works*, 160, 166; "Serve the People," 171, 268n40; "The Orientation of the Youth Movement," 169–70

Mao Zedong Thought: about, 166–68, 267n23; agrarian-centered, 25, 167; foreigners' attraction to, 160, 201–2; Garvin and, 169–74, 190–91; intermediate zones theory, 110; Mao's jokes about, 208; "mass line" philosophy, 114; Monteiro on, 208; on permanent revolution and protracted struggle, 167; PLA and, 165–66; "red and expert" (*you hong you zhuan*), 165, 181; "three worlds theory," 113

"March of the Volunteers" ("Yiyongjun jinxingqu"), 1–3, 87

marriage: interracial, 101, 242n12, 251n103; New Marriage Law of 1950 (China), 178

Martin, Trayvon, 217–18, 219

Marxism: Garvin on growth in, 159–60; "Sinification of," 166, 267n23

Marxist-Leninist organizations, 201–2, 274n36

Marxist-Leninist philosophy: Cuba and, 124; Garvin on African American activists and, 176; Mao Zedong Thought and, 166–67; particular Chinese model of, 25, 28, 48–49

Marx, Karl, 48, 167

masculinism: in Du Bois's depiction of China, 52–54; Estes on Civil Rights Movement and, 236n50; in scholarship, 14; "soldier" figure, returning POWs, and hypermasculinity, 86, 246n47; Williams's *Listen, Brother!* and, 156–57. *See also* gender and gender politics

"mass line" philosophy (*qunzhong luxian*), 114

mass media. *See* media

maternal sacrifice narratives, 151

Mayer, William E., 83

May Fourth Movement, 169–70

May Seventh Cadre Schools, 190

Mbembe, Achille, 256n6

McAlister, Melanie, 246n48

McCarran-Walter Act (Immigration and Nationality Act of 1952), 105

McCarthy, Joseph, 31

media: Benjamin's materialist and noninstrumentalist approach to, 8–9; as key mode of cultural representation, 8; Korean War and, 80–81; as transnational political practice, 9; travel, political production, and, 9–10; travel restrictions on journalists, 95–97, 252n115; U.S. anti-China campaign in, 27–28; on U.S. POWs, 81; Worthy on American press, 253n118. *See also* black media; *specific persons and works*

migrant workers in China, 217–18

military desegregation order (U.S.), 78, 242n10, 242n12

Miller, Arthur, 73

missionary prisoners in China, 98, 250n95

Mobutu Sese Seko, Joseph, 204, 206

Mohanty, Chandra Talpade, 68

Monkey King (Sun Wukong), 37–38, 240n95

Monson, Jamie, 16, 275n47

Monteiro, Anthony, 208, 275n54

Montgomery Bus Boycott, 95

Moore, Carlos, 130

motherist frame, 151

Movemento Popular de Libertação de Angola (MPLA), 206–7

Mullen, Bill, 234n11

ideology and, 89–90; deaths among, 81, 93, 249n74; indoctrination lectures used on, 82, 87, 91, 243n23; nonrepatriates remaining in China, 84–86, 92–93; recreation activities, 247n56; Robeson and, 87–88; torture and treatment of, 81–82, 243n22; Worthy interviews with returnees, 86–90, 93–94

propaganda art and posters, Chinese: about, 132–35; artistic censorship, 260n54; "Bei yapo minzu lianhe qilai jianjue fandui mei diguozhuyi" (Oppressed peoples, unite to resolutely fight against U.S. imperialism), 156; "Dadao Meidi! Dadao Su xiu!" (Down with American imperialists and Russian revisionists!), 17–18, 18; "Jianjue zhichi Meiguo heirende zhengyi douzheng!" (Resolutely support the just struggle of Black Americans!), 132, 133, 134–35; "Jianjue zhichi Meiguo heiren fandui zhongzuqishi de zhengyi douzheng!" (Resolutely support the just struggle of black Americans against racism!), 108; "Jianjue zhichi Meiguo renmin . . ." (Resolutely support the American people . . .), 149; "Mei diguo zhuyi cong feizhou gun chuqu!" (Get out of Africa, American imperialists!), 155; "Mei diguo zhuyi zai quan shijie renmin de chongchong baowei zhi zhong" (U.S. imperialism is surrounded by the people of the world), 138; "Quan shijie renmin fandui Mei diguo zhuyi de douzheng bi sheng!" (The fight against U.S. imperialism by people of the whole world will succeed!), 34–35, 35; socialist realism, 134, 260n54; style influence on black radicals, 257n7; on U.S. urban rebellions, 187–88; "Wan'e de zhimin zhuyi . . ." (The evil system of colonialism and imperialism . . .), 7; women of color represented in, 154–56, 155, 156; "Zhichi Meiguo heiren kangbao douzheng de sheng ming . . ." (Statement in support of Black Americans' antiviolence struggle . . .), 188; "Zhong, Fei renmin qingyi shen" (The feelings of friendship between the peoples of China and Africa are deep), 210, 210–11

propaganda, Chinese: "brainwashing" discourse in U.S. about, 82–83, 86, 91–92, 99–100, 244n32–245n33, 246n47; indoctrination lectures used on American POWs,

82, 87, 91, 243n23; indoctrination techniques, 83; Robeson, use of, 87–88

propaganda, U.S.: anti-China campaign, 27–28; anti-communist discourse, 26–27, 30–34; "brainwashing" discourse, 82–83, 86, 91–92, 99–100, 244n32–245n33, 246n47

Prosser, Gabriel, 174

protracted struggle (changqi douzheng), 167

Provisional Government of the African-American Captive Nation (PGAACN), 263n86

Pu Shan, 97

Quotations from Chairman Mao (Mao zhuxi yulu; "the little red book"), 17–18, 160, 166, 184, 202

racial capitalism, system of, 6

racial ideology, Chinese, 89–90, 248n64

racial internationalism, 11, 116, 135, 138

racial liberalism, 32

racial uprisings in U.S., 187–88

racism and racial discrimination: against African Americans, 232n17; David Graham Du Bois on lack of, in China, 235n23; Du Bois, China, and, 44–45, 48–49; U.S. international image of progress on, 31–32, 242n10. See also Jim Crow racism; white supremacy

Radio Free Dixie, 128–30, 142, 259n41

Radio Havana, 262n82

Radio Peking, 91

Randolph, A. Philip, 76, 79

Rangel, Charles, 199

Reale, Egidio, 253n119

Reape, Harold, 119

"red and expert" (you hong you zhuan), 165, 181

Red Guards (hong weibing), 115, 182, 186

religious practices, African American, 88–89

representation: cultural, 8, 56–61; limits of, 255n9

Republic of New Afrika, 269n80

Revolutionary Action Movement, 263n86, 269n80

revolution, permanent (buduan geming), 167

Rhodes, Jane, 8

Rich, Marvin, 136

Rittenberg, Sidney, 116, 147, 208, 240n94, 259n50, 260n56

Roa, Raul, 258n34

Roberto, Holden, 206

Robeson, Eslanda Goode, 35–36, 79

Williams, Robert F. and Mabel (*continued*)
international networking, 117, 130–31; life
and background in U.S., 120–21; *Listen,
Brother!*, 150–57, 153; Mao's statement on
black liberation and, 135; media from Cuba,
127–31; NAACP and, 121–22, 126, 257n16;
in North Vietnam, 148; "An Ocean's Roar
of Peace," 117, 256n1; organization presi-
dencies (Robert), 269n80; *Radio Free Dixie*,
128–29, 142; relocation to China, 146–47;
return to U.S. and State Deptartment outreach to, 195–98; Senate subcommittee
testimony, 195–96; on "soul brother and
soul sisters," 118; on Soviet-U.S. détente,
262n80; sun metaphor and, 117–18; Sweden
and Canada considered as locations for,
143–46; on Tanzania Zambia Railway Authority, 274n45; Tso's "To Robert Williams,"
117–18, 137; on Vietnam War, 147–51; visits
to Cuba, 125–26; Worthy on, 106
Williams, Roosevelt, 88, 90
Willis, Morris, 249n71
women: Chinese policy on women's rights,
177–78; of color, in Chinese propaganda
art, 154–56, 155, 156; Du Bois on, 53; foot
binding and, 54–55; Garvin's teachings on
women's rights, 177–80; Graham Du Bois
on, 54–55; maternalist narratives in Williams's *Listen, Brother!*, 150–54; motherist
frame and maternal sacrifice narratives,
151. *See also* feminism; gender and gender
politics
world revolution (*shijie geming*), Mao's theory
of, 134
Worlds of Color (Du Bois), 37
"Worlds of Color" (Du Bois), 238n80
World War II, end of, 23–24. *See also* imperialism, Japanese
Worthy, Bathsheba, 76
Worthy, Mabel Posey, 76
Worthy, William, Jr., 73, 99; on American
press, 253n118; background and family,
76–77; "Ballad of William Worthy" (Ochs),
107; in China, 96–102; on China's outreach,
261n65; containment culture and, 74–75;
Cuba and, 104–6; defenses and criticisms
of, 103, 252n115–253n117; Du Boises' journey and, 73; emerging black radicals and,
109; Korean War coverage, 77–81; Mackensen interview, 98; on Montgomery Bus

Boycott, 95; passport problems, 73, 95–97,
102–4, 105, 251n107; POW interviews,
86–90, 92–94; on right to travel, 107; on
roots of U.S. China policy, 72; on street
committees (*jiedao banshichu*), 97–98; transnational political practice and, 75; Vietnam
and, 94–95; White interview, 98–101; on
Williams, 106; Zhou interview, 97
Worthy, William, Sr., 76
Worthy v. Herter, 103
Wu Ch'êng-ên, 37
Wu Han, 255n16
Wu, Judy Tzu-Chun, 16

xia hai (jumping into the sea) fables, 256n1
xin minzhu zhuyi geming (new democratic revolution), 48
xuanchuan hua. See propaganda art and posters,
Chinese

Yalta Conference, 23–24
Yan Shao Hua, 101–2
"Yellow Sea" (Du Bois), 239n86
yellow superiority discourses, 89–90, 248n61
"Yiyongjun jinxingqu" ("March of the Volun-
teers"), 1–3, 87
Young, Charles S., 86
Young, Cynthia, 13
Young Progressives of America, 44
Youth Organization for Black Unity, 200–201,
204

Zhenbao (Damansky) Island, 198
Zheng Fenyi, 255n11
Zhen Hui, 102
Zhen Jinti, 140
Zhen Kaizhu, 140
Zhongguotese shehuizhuyi (socialism with Chi-
nese characteristics), 209
Zhou Enlai, 22; on Africa, 193, 202; Africa
visit, 112; at Bandung, 29; Cultural Revolu-
tion and, 114; death of, 209; Du Bois and,
240n94; indoctrination lectures and, 82;
Nixon visit and, 193–94, 198; Williams and,
272n11; Worthy interview with, 97
Zhu Boshen, 57
Zhu Le, 96
Zhu Zhuyi, 255n11
Žižek, Slavoj, 69, 239n93
Zuo Zhongling, 117–18, 137